Born into a show business dy by the acting bug from a yo inspired by the art of perfom ..y in life. Her career has seen her tour extensively with theatre, play lead roles in numerous well-known television commercials, as well as documentaries and independent feature films for both cinematic and televised release, appearing alongside many named actors. She has also worked as a model, TV presenter and singer. This book is her incredible life story.

# If the Shoe Fits

## THE STORY OF A REAL LIFE CINDERELLA

# EMMA FLETCHER

### WITH PAUL BURTON
### FOREWORD BY DAVID KING
### AFTERWORD BY DENIS INGOLDSBY

**HIRST**
publishing

**If the Shoe Fits**
Emma Fletcher

First Published in the UK in December 2010 by Hirst Publishing

Hirst Publishing, Suite 285 Andover House, George Yard, Andover, Hants, SP10 1PB

ISBN 978-1-907959-16-5

Copyright © Emma Fletcher 2010

The right of Emma Fletcher to be identified as the author of this work has been asserted by her in accordance with the Copyright, Designs and Patents Act 1988.

A CIP catalogue record for this book is available from the British Library.

Cover Design by Robert Hammond

Printed and bound by Good News Digital Books

Paper stock used is natural, recyclable and made from wood grown in sustainable forests. The manufacturing processes conform to environmental regulations.

**www.hirstbooks.com**

# Contents

This book is dedicated to my wonderful grandparents who raised me as their own daughter. I thank them for all the precious years they devoted to my well-being and continue to treasure all they taught me. They will continue to live on forever in my heart and forever in my memory, as I remember them both with great affection for their endless kindness, compassion and selflessness. They were the light of my life and the sunshine for my soul.

*Shoot for the moon. Even if you miss it you will land among the stars.*

- Les Brown

# Foreword

It was a cold November night in 2007 at a charity function in London's West End, when I first met the lovely Emma Fletcher.

I was producing the evening's entertainment, for a star-studded celebrity crowd. The main attraction of the evening was the American performer Harry Connick Jr. and Emma was there as a special guest of the organisers.

To say I was captivated with her is an understatement. There was a magical aura surrounding her that I will never forget. She held her hand out to introduce herself to me and from that moment I was hooked.

Since then, I have followed Emma's career and seen her in films, television commercials, musicals, plays and so much more. Every part she plays, she excels in. Every role she performs is as if it were written especially for her.

Emma told me about the book she wanted to write. I was captivated with her story and hung on to her every word as the fascinating story of her life began to unfold. I encouraged her to put pen to paper and was thrilled when she told me she was finally going to write the book that would tell the world of her incredible and heart wrenching upbringing.

It is an honour to know this remarkable girl and it is an even bigger honour to know that Emma counts me as one of her closest friends.


**David King**

**International Theatre Producer**

# Introduction (by Paul Burton)

Best-known as the home of the original Star Wars film series, Elstree Studios in Borehamwood, Hertfordshire, also became the location for the auditions I was holding for a new short drama film. Subsequently renamed and re-written by yours truly before it finally went into production, *Amy* has at the time of writing, been broadcast on satellite television over thirty times. It was on this date that I first met the subject of this book – Emma Fletcher.

Emma greeted me warmly as she strolled over to meet me in the Whitehouse Building at the historic studio complex. We then proceeded to sit down and chat while I waited for the other actresses auditioning that day to arrive. Little did either of us know at that moment, our first-ever meeting, I was fated to co-write her life story!

Following the completion of *Amy*, in which Emma was cast in one of the lead roles, we kept in-touch and I eventually offered her one of the lead roles in a short drama film the following year, which I was making for satellite television, called Resentment. The film in question starred Vicki Michelle MBE, best-known for her role in the classic Croft & Lloyd sitcom, 'Allo 'Allo! Again, Emma and I found ourselves on set together at Elstree Studios.

By this stage, Emma had told me a great deal about her life and career. Inspired by what she told me, I asked her if she would allow me to co-write her life story with a view to it being published. Emma agreed and the rest, as they say, is history.

This book features me acting as a kind of tour guide through Emma's life, adding comment and background material where appropriate. It has been compiled as a result of a series of prolific production notes prepared by Emma. But for all my contributions towards this book, it ultimately features Emma's very personal thoughts, opinions and religious views. And while they don't always match my own, I do believe they make compelling reading.

I hope you enjoy reading the result of the huge amount of blood, sweat and tears that went into creating this book - the life story of a very unique woman.

*Paul Burton*

*Writer, Filmmaker and Film & TV Historian*

*www.paulburton.org.uk*

*October 2010*

# Introduction (by Emma Fletcher)

'Wow!' and 'Gosh!' are normally the first two words people say to me upon hearing my life-story for the very first time. This is usually followed immediately with the words: 'You could write a book!'

My journey so far has been an unusual one to say the least. Raised by my maternal grandparents and witnessing the untimely death of both my mother and father, whilst still in the prime of their lives, I was subsequently rejected by close members of my immediate family from a young age. This led me to become affectionately known amongst my friends as: 'The real Cinderella'.

They say most people do not recall memories earlier than the age of three, unless those memories evolved from traumatic experiences. Perhaps this is why I have such early memories. My life has truly been a roller-coaster of emotional events but I am grateful to God for blessing me with a happy disposition, which has more often than not helped me to get through some of the more traumatic events in my life with a smile on my face, even when my heart was heavy.

My maternal grandmother always used to say to me: 'One day someone will write a book about your life' and funnily enough, I always knew they probably would.

I have always believed that, no matter with what life confronts you, it is possible to get through it in a way which will ultimately serve you well. If you are faced with a problem, I have always felt you should change your attitude not your goal, for the outcome will be greater if your attitude is born from wisdom and positivism rather than arrogance and negativity. This is my humble view for what it is worth. Forever the optimist, I firmly believe God only gives you challenges He knows you can overcome and ultimately which will help you grow. Without rain we could not appreciate the sunshine, without the difficult times, we could not appreciate the good. When you cry out to God for what you have lost He, in response, will show you what you have found. So, do not fear that which you do not understand; instead embrace the chance of the rewards of new discovery. Yes, sometimes it is hard to remind yourself of all this when you are face down inside a bottomless black abyss but if you can climb out and pick yourself up, what you will discover will amaze you. What you will discover is a new found strength you never knew you had inside of you. Having been face down in that black abyss myself on many an occasion, I know it is possible to come out on top. Don't be afraid to fall. We learn from our misguidance. Just keep reminding yourself that without risk there can be no growth; for you must take a chance and try a new path in order to grow. My grandmother always used to say to me 'If you fell down a hole, you'd probably come out with a silver coin in your hand'. What a marvellous outlook on life and what conviction and belief she instilled in me in my ability to remain strong, even in my darkest hour. So think to yourself, if you fall, the next time you will know where to tread. If you fall, the next time you will tread more carefully!

Amidst the adversity I've experienced in my life, I always knew from a young age I wanted to follow in the footsteps of many people in my family and enter the unforgiving world of show business. Perhaps it was a quest for love or just a cry for attention but from as early as I can recall, it was always my dream to one day appear on television or stage and see my name in lights. I've always believed I grew up under the guidance of a bright shining light. Perhaps that is why I have always reached for the stars.

I had worked with Paul Burton on a couple of short films for television by the time I finally announced to my family and friends Paul had indeed won me over with his charm and I was now going to go ahead and write my story with him. Paul and I had remained in contact after I appeared in his short television drama, *Amy*. Upon getting to know me better, Paul was amazed by my life story and uttered those famous words I had heard so many times before now: 'You could write a book!' 'Yes, I could!' I believe was my response. 'Well, I'd like to write it with you,' continued Paul. This was a new response to me!

After several months of Paul trying to convince me I did indeed have something interesting enough to place in print, I eventually agreed to write my story with him.  My family and friends' reactions upon telling them I was finally going to write a book were, I am pleased to say, one of encouragement all round. The question I kept getting asked by everyone was: 'What is the premise for the book? Will it be a how to follow your dreams book, a how to get into the world of acting book, a self-help book or one of those inspirational, real-life story books?' And my answer? 'I hope, all of the above.'

My story is indeed that of the real Cinderella. My story is one of compassion and overcoming heartache, whilst maintaining a smile on my face at all costs. It is also the story of reaching for your dreams. It really is true what 'they' say: 'Smile and the world smiles with you, cry and you cry alone.'

I hope this book will make you laugh, cry a little and search your soul to help you become the person you truly are worthy of becoming.

This is my story...


*Emma Fletcher*

*www.emmafletcher.org*

*October 2010*

## Author's Note

Please note, for legal or privacy reasons, the names of certain people have been changed or not included within this book.

Legal advice has also been sought in advance with regards to the content of this book.

The content of this book depicts the language and wisdom that was solely derived from my viewpoint, as well as any events which occurred from that particular time and is not in any way meant to be used as a reprisal or an opportunity to be vengeful or vindictive in inference to any person but rather to serve a purpose as to translate what transpired in my life and the valuable lessons learned from those experiences.

*1*

## First Steps

**God, give us the grace to accept with serenity the things that cannot be changed, courage to change the things which should be changed and the wisdom to distinguish the one from the other.** - Reinhold Niebuhr

*Paul: It was yet another concert night at Wembley Stadium and Emma had booked her usual seat, not in the stadium – but by the window in her maternal grandparents' bedroom, which overlooked the iconic venue. Not for the first or last time, Fletcher stared at the bright lights for hours, wishing it was her performing on stage and holding the crowd spell-bound. In time, her dream of taking to the stage would become a reality and ultimately prove that a real-life Cinderella can go to the ball. Emma's story however, begins before she was even born.*

Emma: My mother's maiden name was Claudia Jane Rose and my father's name was Martin Roy Fletcher. However, they were never known to me as 'mum' and 'dad', as I was in actual fact raised by my maternal grandparents, Vera and Sam and it is to they whom I shall refer to as mum and dad throughout this book, whilst I will refer to my real parents as Claudia and Martin. To avoid me any confusion as a child, Claudia and Martin used to sign their respective greetings cards to me as 'Mummy Claudia' and 'Martin', with the word 'Dad' placed in brackets after.

Interestingly, for the first eight years of my life I was told I had to call my grandparents who raised me 'RoRo' and 'Pappa Sammy', the same titles my three first cousins used for them. RoRo was the name given to Vera by my first cousin, when as a child she found the name Vera too difficult to say and it came out as RoRo. I recall always saying to Vera and Sam: 'Why do I have to call you RoRo and Pappa Sammy? You are my parents. Why can't I call you mum and dad?' Their response was always the same; they did

17

not want to offend my paternal grandparents or my father Martin, as Martin and Claudia were still my mother and father, even if by name alone. So for the first eight years of my life mum and dad were indeed referred to by myself as RoRo and Papa Sammy.

My father Martin was the only child to my paternal grandparents, Rose and Bill. Meanwhile my maternal grandparents had two girls, my real mother, Claudia and her elder sibling, who I will refrain from naming in this book.

Before she was 12 years old, Claudia was, to all intent and purpose, what one could describe as a fairly 'normal' child. This was until she reached puberty and her hormones took over. As a result she started to behave a little oddly and it caused mum to worry a great deal. In those days any kind of mental illness was always brushed under the carpet due to embarrassment. Now her illness would be treated with drugs and she would be sent back into the community but at that time it was something to be ashamed of, particularly in the Jewish community. It wasn't until Claudia was older and her behaviour became more peculiar, that she was diagnosed as having some sort of personality disorder, a branch of schizophrenia and was later also diagnosed with suffering with OCD. (Suffers of schizophrenia are prone to develop Obsessive Compulsive Disorder, as there is a distinct overlap in both the brain area affected by each condition and the characteristics displayed.) I have a feeling today her illness may have been classed as a branch of Bipolar but from what I understand, it was a more severe case and sadly manifested itself in the worst possible way.

As Claudia was not the easiest of children because of her condition, her elder sibling had to take a back seat at times. For instance, if Claudia wanted a particular toy, rather than cause a row, which I believe was part of Claudia's condition (someone with Bipolar or personality disorder will often find a large emotional outburst may be triggered by any small thing), to keep the peace Claudia would admirably be handed over the toy by her sister. This wasn't mum teaching Claudia bad manners, this was appeasement. Claudia was nevertheless an extremely bright,

18

intelligent and caring individual, even although riddled by this unfortunate and challenging condition.

Claudia and Martin met in the crazy late Sixties aged 18 and 22 respectively. They met in the Jewish community and immediately fell in love. They were both Jewish hippies! Despite mum and dad's misgivings, Claudia, a beautiful aspiring model with raven hair and piercing blue eyes, later impressed everyone by winning a contract with the famous *Christian Dior* house as their 'Hat girl', which immediately boosted her career. Meanwhile Martin was an aspiring rock star and heavily into The Beatles and rock music of his generation. Alongside his cousin and best friend Henry A Winkler (not the *'Fonz'*, however now an actor of his own merit) they formed the band The Gobbledegooks. Martin became heavily involved with the band, partly as a drummer but also with the PR. The band toured and later went on to support The Rolling Stones at London's famous Albert Hall and even had a couple of hits in the top 40 British charts with their own songs. In fact, Henry was recently given a birthday present of a CD compilation and was delighted to find one of the band's hits included amidst the mix.

So all in all, Claudia and Martin were living the dream: Claudia with her modelling career and Martin with the band.

The story goes that Claudia wanted to become an actress as well as a model. I believe the closest she actually came to this was working as an extra on *The Saint*, which starred future James Bond actor, Sir Roger Moore and which was filmed at Elstree Studios in Borehamwood, Hertfordshire. This was a studio complex that I myself was later destined to work at with Paul Burton. She came home beaming and excitedly recalled: 'Roger Moore spoke to me, he spoke to me!' 'What did he say?' mum asked. 'He said: Excuse me love, can you move out the way? You're blocking the lens!'

Whilst we are on the subject of James Bond I must take this opportunity to tell you I have always fancied myself as a bit of a Bond girl and one day a few years ago I almost inadvertently became one! On my usual shopping spree to my local shopping mall, I parked up my car in the parking lot as per usual, got out then nearly jumped out of my skin as an extremely loud noise, which sounded like a bomb exploding, occurred exactly as I shut my car door. Then it happened again. I ducked for cover. Suddenly I could hear a couple of cars chasing each other and they were getting closer. As quick as a flash I ran to the doors of the entrance of the mall and bolted inside. People were starring at me as I made my hasty entrance. I must have looked a little like a deer in headlights! As I looked around, I noticed by the entrance on the inside of the door was a sign, which read 'Loud noises possible due to filming.' I had just driven straight onto the set of *Tomorrow Never Dies*, which starred Pierce Brosnan. Now completely embarrassed by my hasty entrance, I brushed myself down; straightened my hair and casually walked into the mall as if nothing were amiss. I did wonder however why the sign was not placed on the outside of the entrance rather than on the inside but it dawned on me I had somehow managed to drive into a restricted area of the parking lot that day. I think the production company must have just opened up that section of the car park for a few minutes when I drove in. I figured this might be as close as I was going to get to being a Bond girl, so I can live with the embarrassment. Warning: expect the unexpected when going on a simple shopping spree. Wear your best frock and glam jewels, in case you unexpectedly find yourself in the middle of a Bond movie! Mission accomplished: over and out.

My grandparents on my father's side owned a shop unit in Kenton, in northwest London. The shop was a lady's hairdresser at the back, which was run by my grandfather Bill, who was a hairdresser and at the front of the unit was a lady's clothes shop, run by my grandmother Rose. I used to visit the shop often as a child and loved to try on all the clothes and jewellery, walking around the shop in attire and shoes, which were far too big for my tiny frame.

I would fondly use Al Pacino's depiction of Lieutenant Colonel in the 1992 film *Scent of a Woman* as a fair description of Bill's character. Although he was difficult and liked to challenge people, he had a good heart and loved me very much. In fact, I think he would have done anything for me. My real father, Martin, in comparison, was the complete opposite of his father. He was a free spirit and very much into living a hippy lifestyle. He was a kind and happy soul with a warm heart. I recall when I was a child he often used to sit me on his knee and say 'Sing Emma, sing!' It was he who encouraged my early singing voice to blossom. Sadly however, Martin's happy disposition was overshadowed by the fact he suffered from ill health and was diagnosed with an extremely severe form of Crohn's disease from his teenage years, which often required hospital treatment and later a colostomy.

Both sets of parents decided it would not be advisable for Martin and Claudia to marry, as Martin could not handle stress with his condition and Claudia needed an emotionally stronger man. However, they were in love and as sure as young love blossoms, they decided to wed regardless. When Claudia first went to meet Martin's parents she was wearing quite a short high-fashion skirt, which was so short it was apparently more like a belt! I believe Bill informed Claudia exactly what he thought of her attire, which was obviously quite embarrassing for her. Bill wasn't a bad person though. He just liked to test people's strength. He was, however, an honest man it's true, often to the point of bluntness. With Bill one always knew where they stood but underneath the hard exterior could be found a layer of softness and kindness, belonging to a man with a heart of gold, whose superfluous generosity never ceased. It was in fact Bill's tough outlook on life which offered me the opportunity to find great strength within myself and taught me to stand-up for what I truly believe, which surely is what life is all about?

Claudia and Martin's engagement party was held at a hotel in Middlesex and their wedding took place a couple of years later at a northwest London synagogue. Claudia had two little girls as bridesmaids. Representing my mother's side of the family was Anna Mitchell, daughter of my second cousin the actor Warren Mitchell and his wife Connie and on my father's side, was Joanna Wax, daughter of my uncle Mitch and auntie Myrna.

When I was a child I used to look up to Anna as the older sister I would so love to be like. I placed her on a pedestal. I admired her for her strength of character, beauty and her words of wisdom. We have become very close over the last few years and during this time Anna has very much warmed my heart by telling me she now looks to me in the very same way. What a beautiful gift her words were to me, far more precious than any diamond or pearl. The same is also true of Joanna, whom I also hold in great esteem. How wonderful to know the very same two young girls my mother and father chose to be their bridesmaids I am now also able to hold dear to my heart in adulthood.

Whilst on one level I am pleased Claudia and Martin did marry, else I would not of course be here to tell my story, I am however sad for both of them and for my family for the heartache that ensued.

I think it is fair to say Claudia and Martin were both fun-loving, charismatic Peter Pan child-like adults and in the Sixties this mentality could remain fuelled by a generation where responsibility was not at the forefront of people's focus, especially 'wanabee' rock-stars and models. And so the story goes; all of Claudia and Martin's friends were bearing children, so Claudia and Martin decided they wanted to complete their love for one another by bearing a child too. Claudia became pregnant fairly early into marriage. Pregnancy caused her hormones to become uncontrollable and her illness started its journey into chaos. During her pregnancy, Claudia sadly started to starve herself as her behaviour unwittingly became more capricious.

*Paul: Emma's birth date is 16 October; a date she was quick to point out to me is the same date her fictional hero Superman arrived on earth! However, being a professional actress, Emma was not willing for the year of her birth to be published!*

*Four weeks premature and weighing in at only 4 pounds and 15 ounces, Fletcher's first captivated audience was at the Middlesex Hospital in Mortimer Street, London, at 6.10am. The first week of Emma's life was fated to be spent in an incubator.*

Emma: Claudia and Martin decided they wanted to call me 'Sunshine', as they felt I was their little ray of light but both sets of grandparents were dead set against this hippy notion and so Claudia and Martin decided to compromise with the name Emma Jane instead. As it happens, I've always believed I grew up under the guidance of a bright shining light - perhaps that is why I have always reached for the stars.

I am happy to say the joy of my birth was the general consensus of both sets of my loving and wonderful grandparents and most of my family, although according to some members of the family, it was arguably not the noticeable feeling of Claudia's elder sibling and her husband.

Claudia's sister married a few years before Claudia did and a few weeks after I was born she was enjoying the birth of her third child. At a time when, understandably she felt she should be receiving and enjoying the attention from her own parents, I came along and arguably took some of the attention away from her and from her three children.

Being a sensitive child, I used to be fearful of visiting Claudia's sister and her husband. More often than not I would always go home from the experience in tears. The latter had a big booming voice, which frightened me so much as a child that I used to ask mum and dad to find out if he would be home before going round there. He was an established professional musician, so often was away on tour.

Shortly after I was born Claudia's illness took a terrible turn for the worse and she announced she was not well enough to look after a child. Both she and Martin decreed I should be adopted. I do not recall this myself but according to members of my close family, whilst the legalities of my adoption occurred, for the first year of my life I was placed in day foster care and spent many an hour with different foster families. One thing I am certain of is, had Vera and Sam had any say in the matter, they never would have allowed me to have been fostered out and I would have remained in their care at all times but it was not in their jurisdiction to prevent this.

During this time two family friends stepped forward and offered to adopt me: one a kind and wonderful neighbour of many years and the other a good family friend of Claudia's. As an only child, my father did not have any siblings to step in to offer adoption services. Martin's father Wolf, who later changed his name to William but to me will always remain 'Bill' and his wife, Rose, were also unable able to step in and offer their services. I think the reason Rose did not come forward to adopt me is she knew what a difficult life Martin had growing up with Bill and probably did not want me to go through the same difficulties. Rose however never spoke a bad word about anyone and nor did anyone ever have a bad word to say about her. She was a peacemaker, always trying to smooth over other people's disagreements. She was a kind and generous woman. She had herself wanted to divorce Bill many times over the years due to his somewhat fractious and inordinate behaviour but in those days divorce was seen as an embarrassment, so she stayed with him and pretty much did everything for him. As previously mentioned, Claudia's elder sibling and her husband already had three children of their own and the possibility of taking on another child was probably not something they felt they could offer. So options for finding me a new home were limited.

Although already both in their sixties, Claudia's parents, Vera and Sam, admirably decided they wanted to adopt little Emma Jane. The adoption went though court and by the time I was one, mum and dad had gained legal guardianship over me. Now legally adopted, I was living with my maternal grandparents, whom to me were and always will be, 'mum' and 'dad'. Nevertheless, I was still under the court's jurisdiction and if mum or dad wanted to take me out of the country they had to gain the court's permission first at all times, until I reached the age of 18. By the time I reached six, Claudia and Martin divorced and mum and dad were once again forced to reapply to the court to continue to attain legal guardianship over me.

24

Vera and Sam used to tell me I kept them young and I believe this is probably true. I am aware how lucky I am, not only to have been raised by two wonderful people such as my mum and dad but also to have received unconditional love from them both. If it were not for them, then I would have undoubtedly been sent to a children's home and placed up for adoption. They were indeed a godsend.

My earliest memories are of lying on my back in my pram under the apple tree in my maternal grandparent's garden and looking up at the sky. I was a happy child and always used to greet everyone with a cheerful 'hello'. I was always fascinated by life and I can recall being upset even if someone stepped unnecessarily on an insect. In fact, I still feel this way today. The idea of death upsets me greatly and from an early age I could never understand why anyone would want to hurt one of God's creatures. Life to me was - and is - precious and is to be treasured. It is a gift from above and both humans and animals are to be respected on this planet.

Ultimately, I believe my feelings towards life and the universe were probably what led me to the notion of wanting to become a vegetarian from a very early age. I've never felt it essential for the human race to survive on meat. I recall the trauma mum had during every mealtime of trying to encourage me to eat meat or fish. I would completely smother my food in ketchup, so it no longer resembled the dish I was eating. Then I would swallow it down almost whole, chewing it as little as possible, so as not to allow the meat of the animal to touch my tongue. Mum would always say to me every mealtime: 'You inhale your food! Don't eat so quickly, slow down.' Eventually she gave up the fight and informed me when I turned 16, if I still wanted to give up meat, then she would allow me to become a vegetarian. As soon as I turned 16 I gave up all meat and fish within an instant. My body could not take the shock and I became ill for a couple of weeks. After an appointment with the doctor I was told I had to go back to eating fish and white meat again and then I could slowly wean myself off them, in order to allow my body to adjust to the change. This I did and I have continued to be a vegetarian to this day.

25

As previously mentioned, mum was already in her sixties when she adopted me and understandably decided she required a little bit of extra help on the odd occasion, so she hired an au pair to come round once a week to help out with odd jobs. The famous Irish singer now turned politician, Rosemary Brown, also known as 'Dana', lived opposite us with her family. She immediately volunteered her services. Dana became like a much-loved older sister to me. She used to come round and play games with me, read to me bedtime stories or just help to put me to bed. Over the years Dana formed her famous pop band with her brothers. I really missed her whenever she went away but was always so very excited to hear all her great stories about her growing career and increasing popularity upon her return from her tours.

It is argued most people do not recall memories earlier than the age of three, unless those memories evolved from traumatic experiences. Perhaps this is why I have such early memories. I recall teething, sitting in my parents' kitchen in Wembley Park in north London crying with pain, as my teeth felt like they would pierce through my gums at any moment. This is actually one of the good memories! I recall taking my first proper steps in my parents' dining room. I stood up and held onto the sideboard for dear life. Mum stood at the other end of the room and beckoned me forward with outstretched arms. I took the plunge and stepped forward, eventually falling into her open arms. She cried. These were my first steps. These were good tears.

I recall Claudia and my father Martin, fighting in their car. Martin was in the front driving. Claudia sat in the back with me. They got out and started to slap each other like silly children. I had a red balloon. It disappeared out the window of the car. I could not go near balloons for nearly a year after this. I didn't speak for a while after this incident either. I was upset to discover a few years ago, when reading my notes during a regular doctor's visit, I had been diagnosed as 'depressed' during the period after this event. I personally think the word depressed is a bit severe for a three year old but I guess the medics were trying to illustrate a point. The words 'shocked' or 'traumatised' would possibly have been more appropriate in my opinion.

When I was a child I had a favourite toy, which had been given to me by my father, Martin. It was a six-inch tall version of the Disney dog Pluto. It went everywhere with me. One day the girl who lived a couple of houses up the street, asked if she could borrow Pluto for a couple of days to show her mum, as she wanted her mum to buy her one just like it. I said she could borrow it. After a couple of days I asked my neighbour if she could return the toy to me but it turned out she had given Pluto to a friend of hers for a birthday present instead. I was so upset. Mum told me to value its memories. This incident made me recognise how temporary everything is in life and how everything we own is really just on loan to us for a short time. It turned out this lesson would serve as an important lesson for me to learn in life, as I experienced so much loss later on in my young life.

I recall Martin one day appearing on our doorstep with hair past his shoulders, a long-reaching beard, rings on every finger, a flower-powered suit, complete with flared trousers and holding a turkey for roasting in his hands. It was quite a feast for the eyes and I'm not talking about the turkey! If the turkey wasn't enough to give me nightmares, sadly what came next was. For some reason, Martin and dad got into a very heated row and in the heat of the moment dad told him he was not to come round to the house anymore. I cried my little heart out until my eyes were sore. As it turned out, Martin did in fact come round to the house again many times after this row occurred but the incident left me quite shaken and for a long time after this I was always so fearful that one day I may not see him again. In fact, Martin used to collect me along with Claudia every Sunday afternoon, to take me from home round to spend the day at Rose and Bill's and occasionally I would also be collected after school on a Wednesday to receive this same treat. Aside from mum and dad, whilst growing-up Rose and Bill were my other two best friends. Martin would also occasionally take me to spend time with his first cousin, my 'auntie' Myrna and her husband Mitch Wax and their three children Joanna, Lee and Steven. I loved spending time round at the Wax household. They were and always have been, so kind and loving towards me and have between them always remained concerned about my well-being, as have their extended families and my visits to their home always made such a pleasant contrast to the way Claudia's sister and her family treated me.

Going round to the Wax family was always such a special treat and provided me with a slice of normality over the years. The Wax family are a very creative and talented bunch of individuals. Spending the Jewish Passover every year at their house was nearly the only time I was ever presented to any amount of Judaism, in my otherwise fairly removed Jewish existence but it was also somewhat akin to being a participating interactive audience member of a West End musical. The Passover service is usually held every year by Mitch; who for the last two years has been the President of Edgware Reform Synagogue and also an active member of the shul for the last fifty years. In later years the service was occasionally taken by Mitch's daughter Lee, who became one of the first female reform rabbis in the UK. Mitch, Joanna and Lee all have tremendous singing voices. In fact the family of Joanna's husband, Guy Sigalov, were close to the well-known Israeli singer Ofra Haza. Joanna received the honour of singing with Ofra around the family dinner table one evening and it was here the beautiful and ethereal voiced singer returned the favour by informing Joanna it was indeed she who felt honoured to be singing with Joanna. To this end Ofra Haza also asked Joanna to help her translate some of her album into English. Joanna's children have also taken a keen interest in the performing arts one way or another over the years and Myrna's sister Penny too. Penny was once head of the LWT (London Weekend Television) whilst her daughter Tiffany is now training to be a stage set director; all continuing the legacy of the family's show business dynasty one way or another.

Joanna's husband Guy is also an extremely creative individual. Guy is the inventor of a musical laser instrument called OptiMusic, which became world famous and is currently displayed in the Science Museum. A few years back Guy asked me to record a children's CD for him, which was set to be sold around the world. I recall when he gave me my cheque in payment for my services being so tremendously excited; as it was the first substantial cheque I had ever received in payment for a performance. All my other work up until that time had either been cash in hand or had gone through my then management company but this was the first cheque I had ever been handed directly and it almost tingled in my palms!

Also on my father's side of the family is my cousin former LBC deejay and entrepreneur Richard Jacobs. Richard began his radio career as a Senior Producer at LBC and Talk Sport and then went on to launch NetFM; the UK's first independent radio company. Richard successfully moved on to become the Business Development Manager of WRN, the UK's leading broadcast and Transmission Company. So as you can see, going into the entertainment industry was for me quite a natural thing to do, although in some ways it was probably seen to be more of an acceptable ambition to follow on my father's side of the family than it was on my mother's side, even although I had family on both sides in the industry.

Interestingly, from the age of 14, Mitch was a tailor, working for his father, making clothes for the rich and famous. He later became a dancer, as part of the Jazz dance group Viar Columbe, which were based near the station, Sevres Babylon and then later became a repertoire actor. At the age of 22, upon being invited to an opening of the jazz club The Saint Germaine Du Pres, at Maxims in Juan le Pain, Mitch met and sat at the same table as the wonderful Edith Piaf, Gervaliez and one of my favourite artists, Marc Chagall. During his later years as a tailor, Mitch made outfits for certain scenes in The Who's film, *Quadrophenia*, John Reece Davies' outfit for *Showgun*, outfits for the novelist Will Self and also for Paul McCartney for *The Birth of the Beatles*. Mitch is now a fine-artiste himself and lectures on many subjects, including the works of Chagall and the Impressionists and also on Jewish values. He won the Jack Petchey award in 2010 for being a motivator and inspirer but he wins the award from me for offering me kindness and support, along with his wife Myrna and the rest of their family, through some of my most difficult years.

Back to my early years, I recall the day I was in my pram and another child in his pram went by pushed by his mother. As he passed by the child stuck his tongue out at me. I can remember feeling really upset by this and wondered what I had done to make this child stick his tongue out at me. Since I was a child, I believe it's interesting to note, I have over the years been known to look for blame in myself when people have upset me.

So as a child, it became my mission to ensure everyone around me was always smiling. 'Smile and the world smiles with you.' I couldn't bear to see people upset or crying, although sadly I was to see a lot of this during my lifetime. There was a time in my life I felt close to the youngest daughter of a family group of relatives, who shall be referred to as The Drummond family but sadly these joys of my childhood were ephemeral. The Drummond family consist in part of two girls; one my age and one a few years older and their parents, all of whom live just outside of London. Looking back, I now know most of the closeness I felt was sadly based around my ability to give into this relative's constant needs as a child. She seemed to me to be the type of child who would always cry if she did not get what she wanted. The easy solution for me was to make her laugh and give in to her every whim. I can even recall this extending to one year when mum had arranged for me to have a small birthday party at home, with all my close friends from school present, the girl, who I would argue became upset she was not the centre of attention, proceeded to take over the entire party and I allowed it for a quiet life.

Whenever certain relatives from this same family group used to upset me with their emotional outbursts or unkind words, mum would always say to me: 'Darling, you do the right thing and go round there and apologise, even if you haven't done anything wrong.' So I learnt very early on in life that even if I had not done anything wrong, if I apologised it made all the upset go away. The only problem with this theory is, it meant I took all responsibility for blame, even when I was not at fault. I would nevertheless always oblige to this request, as I so desperately wanted to be loved and appreciated, even if at the expense of my own happiness. I even started to develop a tiny stammer in my speech whenever I had to apologise to such people. I later transferred this behaviour into my adult relationships with men too, which is why

30

I believe I managed to get myself into a selection of abusive relationships later in life.

For those of you who are interested in the psychoanalysis behind this learnt behaviour, here comes the science bit: when children face trauma they often split themselves off from the emotions and thoughts connected to that trauma, as it becomes easier to deal with in this fashion. Of course this is not really 'dealing with' or resolving the issues associated with the trauma at all but in fact burying them. This process of disassociation allows the individual to continue their daily routine as if nothing were wrong, literally splitting themselves off from the pain associated with the event. However, as the distress caused by the event has not been dealt with properly, the emotions connected to the event usually eventually resurface at a later date in a different guise, such as guilt. This is referred to in psychology as 'splitting' or 'disassociation' and although upon the surface this disassociation appears to help us be able to move on with our lives, in actuality it is doing the exact opposite; as really it is preventing us from moving forward in a healthy way. In fact usually, unless the associated feelings are addressed at the time of the occurrence of the trauma or abuse, the individual can carry with them through life a feeling of shame and inward blame and with it uncertainties about themselves. The traumatic incident then becomes played out again in different ways, such as entering more abusive relationships, partly as the abuse becomes familiar but also, as this is the subconscious mind's way of trying to heal itself through the repetition. And you thought this book was going to be a light read!

It took me years to understand people are flawed, especially as I always had a tendency to see only the good in people. I had always felt if someone is upset with you, then you must have done something wrong in order to cause this upset; else why would they be upset with you? It also took me years to realise how 'Transference Effect' works and that people pass their feelings onto others in order to escape responsibility for their own shame. Can you say therapy? Thank God I eventually got there and I know this now but it has taken me a lifetime of heartache, counselling and reading many books on psychology to get to this place.

With reference to this sentiment, I recall an incident from when I was around 13. I was always a rather sensitive teenager. I was standing quietly in line to pay for items in a local supermarket, when a woman abruptly ran up to the line, pushed me quite fiercely out the way and started screaming I had no manners and should let her go first. I was naturally quite shaken by this incident and felt very intimidated, to the point of crying after I left the supermarket. I think my tears were partly from embarrassment and shock rather than from anything else; from fear other people in the store might be under the impression I had done something to trigger this woman's bizarre behaviour. I went home that evening after school still upset from the incident and searching my thoughts for an answer as to what I possibly could have done to upset this woman to trigger such behaviour. I searched my thoughts for ages, trying to find an answer but of course there was none to be found. I was so used to receiving the blame from certain people in my family, even when I had not done anything wrong, that my learnt behaviour had become: 'If someone shouts at you, then you must have done something wrong in order to make them shout; else why would they shout at you?' As a child the only time a voice was raised in the house by mum or dad was when I had misbehaved, so why should this scenario be any different? When I was younger, quite often the only times I would misbehave were when mum and dad were bickering about something. I soon discovered that if I misbehaved at this time it would stop their argument by uniting them in their reprimand of my behaviour and subsequently they would soon forget what they had been bickering about, which was usually something minor anyhow. I hadn't at this age and nor did I until years later, come to the realisation I was not always at fault or blame for others bad behaviour. In the case of members of my own family, the upset I faced became so regular, that as both a child and as a teenager, I was unable to separate the way they treated me from other daily events in my life, as the upset became too regular to distinguish between the two. Other people's bad behaviour, I later came to realise, is more often than not their own insecurities manifesting

32

themselves in the form of looking for a scapegoat in order to refract away from the real issue; which is often themselves. I only wish I had of learnt this lesson much sooner, as it may have saved me from a lot of heartache I experienced at the hands of these members of my family early on in my young life.

A few years ago I found myself in a similar position to the above but this time I had a very different reaction to the incident. A few friends and I were sitting outside a cafe around a table the owners of the cafe had placed on the pavement directly outside. A woman came up to me pushing a pram and started to scream at me at the top of her voice in the middle of the street that I had no respect and was blocking her right of passage. Whilst I again felt a little uneasy at this women's strange display of behaviour, with a wiser head on my shoulders and now more comfortable in my own skin, I realised I had in no way been the instigator of this women's behaviour and nor had I done anything wrong. This incident did not therefore result in having the same effect on me and did not want to make me burst into tears on the spot! Instead, I was able to remain very calm as I got up and moved my chair so the woman could pass. As I stood up the woman screamed 'Go on, go and call the police. What do I care? I'm due a visit by the pigs anyhow!' Now that my suspicions of her disturbed disposition were confirmed, I politely replied 'Actually, I was just moving my chair so you could pass' and guess what? She walked past calmly and carried on about her way without another single amplification!

As I have gotten older, I have gained a sense of resolution and containment about myself, which I did not have when I was younger. It was impossible for me to be able to attain this resolution when I was younger, as I was too much directly in the firing line of the heartache and could not see the woods for the trees, so to speak. Although I knew deep in my heart the way certain members of my family were treating me was wrong and often I found myself being misrepresented by them - which incidentally is one of the most frustrating things in life, especially if you are like me an honest-Jo and not looking for trouble - yet I could not see just how abnormal their behaviour was until I was completely removed from the situation. That life was all I knew and I had nothing else to compare it to. It wasn't until I completely removed myself from the situation many years later in my life, that I was able to look at it through objective eyes. As a teenager and even as a young adult, I was however far from resolved, as I was still struggling to understand the world I was living in.

One thing age has taught me with complete certainty is, you cannot attain a rational answer from someone who is not rational and you will drive yourself crazy in the process of trying. Sometimes you have to let things go and recognise you are not responsible for everything that happens around you. You are not that powerful. You are not God.

Today if someone upsets me, rather than over-analyse to death to the point of making myself ill - as I have so many times in the past - as to why someone should choose to behave unkindly towards me when I am showing them nothing but kindness, I now try and let things go. Whilst I try not to judge other people' actions or behaviour - as you can never truly understand the reason behind another person's choices unless you have walked in their shoes - I have learnt that whilst I can't change other people's behaviour or work out what makes them tick, what I can do is take a look at why I allow myself to become so affected by their behaviour and try and change how it effects me by changing my reaction to it. Not an easy thing to do it's true but if you can't change someone else's behaviour towards you, then change your attitude towards their behaviour.

Attitude is just perception. In fact every feeling we have is just perception. For example; think of that special memento you own. The object itself is just a bunch of molecules clumped together in a certain shape but it is the perception you place upon that object which gives it its immediate value. Think of a place you have frequented with a loved one. Suddenly that place has a warm, fuzzy feeling attached to it. Now imagine the very same place as being a place you had a terrific row with someone (if you're gonna have a row, let's at least make it terrific!) Now that place holds a different set of emotions for you but now imagine once more if

34

you will, a nice event which occurred in that room and the feelings are turned back again into positive ones. Let me illustrate with the following example; you find yourself back in the same room where you had broken up with your long term love, when out of the blue your eyes meet the man or woman of your dreams. If you're a lady you suddenly become a damsel in distress, accidentally dropping your most prized possession, a lipstick pen from your purse, all the while looking in his direction. You bend down, surreptitiously following the curves of your leg, holding his stare all the while. He takes the bate; immediately leaping to your rescue, finishing his mission in an heroic stance, pen pointing upwards in your direction. Your eyes meet again in this darkened, mist-filled room. Its love at first sight! Sound like a Jackie Collins novel? Maybe - but even you have to admit now that room doesn't feel quite so awful does it? Suddenly your perception of it has completely changed, as you have now created new memories around it, which feel good. It is the same with problems you face in your daily life. Every problem reveals who you are, by how you deal it. What you are going to do about the problem reveals your personality and how you deal with it makes you impressive or not. You control your own happiness. Your happiness is not defined by your circumstances but your attitude towards your circumstances.

One of the first words I used to say as a child was 'Why'. 'Why' was my favourite word and I just couldn't stop saying it! I had a burning desire to know how things worked and why the world is the way it is. In fact I wanted to know everything. Questioning is after all, the way one learns. As Nietzche writes *He who has a why to live can bear with almost anyhow*. I was indeed always driving my mum mad with a paradigm of questions such as 'Why is the sky blue?' and 'Why is the grass green?' My mum's standard reply to these questions was usually: 'Because!' I am still as inquisitive now, although I have as an adult also learnt to let things go with the realisation some things are not ours to know.

Like a lot of children, I used to love playing dress up when I was growing up. Mum had a lovely big airing cupboard and there was a dressing-up box filled high with old clothes and bits and bobs which she had accumulated over the years. It was a kid's paradise! There used to be an old, large army blanket inside this box and my cousin Sam (short for Samantha) and I would hang it over a clothes-drying rack and make a tent out of it. Along with Kate, Sam's immediate next-door neighbour and our third partner in crime, once a week all our poor parents and grandparents were forced, by the three of us, to sit through a Sunday ritual of an all new singing, dancing performance we had all made up each week, in costumes retrieved from mum's famous fancy dress box. This weekly ritual must have driven them mad but they never complained and always sat dutifully with a smile on their faces. I thrived in the fact everyone was watching me. In fact mum always used to tell me she thought I could sing before I could talk and dance before I could walk. These shows were an early taste of performance for me – and I loved it!

Around the age of five, mum and dad sent me to Sunday school to study Hebrew. This was my only nod to Judaism at this age. Mum and dad had both come from traditional religious backgrounds but their conceived war years had knocked the interest for religion out of them both. Although they still had an affinity with being Jewish, it was not displayed in the house as I grew up and being that a number of the men in the family had also married out - a number of the cousins I felt close to whilst growing up were not affiliated with Judaism either - my Hebrew classes really were the only connection I had to my Jewish roots. I used to find the language quite difficult to get to grips with, so had a tendency to switch off occasionally during class. I can clearly recall once hiding in the closet and springing out in the middle of the lesson exclaiming at the top of my voice 'Shalom!' I gave the poor teacher such a fright!

As a young child my second cousin, Warren Mitchell, who was always more like an uncle to me due to the age difference, was always very kind to me. Warren was also always very fond of his first cousin, my real mother Claudia. He used to invite mum and dad and myself to stay during the summer at his second home in Sand Banks, which for the first few years of my life is exactly where we spent our summer holidays and often my lovely auntie

Sybil, Vera's sister and a second mum of sorts to me, would come away on holiday with us too.

When I was younger Warren had a very large Old English Sheep dog named, Barnaby. Barnaby was larger than me and so Warren used to place me on Barnaby's back and walk me around the garden. I would always exclaim my utter joy at this garden bush track adventure with the words: 'More, more!'

Over the years Warren's family gatherings were always a feast for the eye. From a young age, being invited to his parties I always felt as if I were stepping directly into a television set. Always present were the glorious Una Stubbs and wonderful Dandy Nichols, the grand Arthur English and Arnold Diamond and the deliciously eccentric Ken Campbell, who I was very fond of. (Ken took me out around London on a couple of occasions when I was younger.) Also present were the rest of the cast of *In Sickness & In Health* and the delightful Felicity Kendal, all of whom I saw so often growing up, they started to feel on some level like distant relations and I am certain they must have felt like immediate family to Warren.

One day whilst on holiday in Warren's Sandbanks' apartment, we met a man who told my parents he used to work with Brian Epstein, the manager of The Beatles. This man, whose name escapes me, took a fondness to little Emma Jane and used to sit me on his knee, like my father Martin had before him and sing me Beatles' songs and spoil me rotten with ice-cream! He always used to tell mum and dad he thought one day I would be a star.

There was another adult who also took a shining to little Emma Jane and wanted to spoil me with ice-cream too. I recall very clearly, even although I was only two and a half years of age, sitting at the dining table in a hotel in Bournemouth we were visiting and a woman coming up to our table and saying: 'What a beautiful young girl and what beautiful golden locks, may I buy her an ice-cream?' Mum and dad agreed the woman could buy me an ice cream and thanked her kindly. My hair was indeed golden and curled and people would often refer to me as 'little Goldie Locks', as did mum and dad.

Later that day by the pool, the very same lady came up to me and asked if I would like to go up to her room with her for some sweets. Now, although even by the age of two and a half, I had been told so often not to talk to strangers, to a two and a half year-old child this woman was no longer a stranger, as my parents had already spoken to her once at the dinner table and in any case, what she was offering sounded like heaven! I think even at this age I was attracted to adventure, so I walked hand in hand with the lady to her hotel room. We travelled many flights up in the lift then walked into a room with brightly coloured patterned wallpaper, where we were confronted by lots of sweets in a glass dish. I stayed with this woman, chatting and playing merrily in her room for around twenty minutes. By the time the lady took me back down to the poolside, the hotel manager was just about to call the police and mum was in floods of tears. This was the first time I can recall I had seen mum cry and this really upset me. When my parents saw me they hugged me as if they would never let go.

Both sets of my grandparents and my wonderful auntie Sybil were always the only real joy I had in my life. My auntie Sybil always told me what joy I brought her too, as she had not had children of her own; losing her husband early in life and never remarrying. She told me she viewed me as the child she never had and I too viewed her as an additional mother figure. I think I spoke to my auntie Sybil nearly every day of my life until she died. It is sad to say but I personally feel I did not receive this type of joy from everyone in my family during my childhood. I really wish I could say differently.

*If you can't change other people's behaviour towards you, then change your attitude towards their behaviour.*
- Emma Fletcher

# 2

# *Loss and Found*

**Nothing in life is to be feared. It is only to be understood.** - Marie Curie

*Paul: Moving to a new school is always hard. However, it can feel even harder if the child, for whatever reason, feels they don't fit in. And as popular as she was with the other children, a feeling of being different now presented itself to Emma as she climbed onto the next rung of the education ladder and found herself at junior school.*

Emma: When it came time for me to attend a junior school, I found myself attending a place called Buxlow in Wembley. It wasn't actually a Jewish school but as it so happened most of the children in my year were Jewish. There were about 15 children in my class and there was only one class per year. Indeed, I think there were only about 100 children in the whole school. So you really got to know everybody and everybody got to know you and your personal business!

Buxlow took me into their kindergarten at the age of nearly four, a year earlier than the other children, as the headmistress was keen to help along mum and dad's decision to start my education at this time. Subsequently, the headmistress decided to hold me back after the first year because she wanted me to be the right age for the rest of my schooling. I remember this really upsetting me at the time. The fact I had been informed I would have to repeat the year again made me think I wasn't very bright. This of course was not the reality. The headmistress simply felt I was not the right age to ascend to the next year - but it also upset me for another reason too, as it meant a number of the young people I had now become friendly with would no longer be in my class.

Whilst always popular at junior school, possibly due to my continually happy disposition, which incidentally I firmly believe God granted me to cope with the upset in my life; it was nevertheless always apparent I was different to the other children at school. Every day at school close, when the young parents used to collect their children, my wonderful grandfather and dad to me, always stood alone. While the other children's parents discussed their hair, nails and weekend, my dad had a look in his eye of a man who had braved the Second World War. Samuel Rose was a dignified and remarkable man. He was the quintessential gentleman; always upright both in posture and honour and extremely regimented in his method of raising children; even if at times this meant raising a strong arm. (As a child I was often sent to my room with a firm smack to my backside but this never did me any real harm. As a teenager I was also only allowed young men to visit me at home if they had undergone a strict moral interview by dad first. I always knew however, he was vetting these men only because he had my very best interests at heart. In fact, perhaps if I had taken more heed of his advice, it would have saved me a lot of heartache and perhaps even have stopped me from getting into abusive relationships later on in my life.) What could these young parents possibly have in common with my parents, who were from a very different generation? Then the teasing started. It was initially started by a young boy named Floyd (not his real name), who started to tease me about why my parents were so old. 'They are not old,' I would retaliate, 'they are 21!' Well at least this is what they had told me and for a number of years I had innocently believed them. 'But they look so different,' were the response from all the children, 'they look so - old'. This hurt. But in some ways I was the lucky one. I got to have two sets of parents - something the other kids could only dream of! I had my mum and dad that I lived with and I also got to visit my real parents twice a week. I also had the love of my other grandparents and my wonderful auntie Sybil too. There was no doubt in my mind I was loved.

As the other children's parents started to befriend one another and consequently started to ask their respective children back to their houses to play after school, this privilege was not extended to me and the only way I ever really got to see friends outside of school was if mum allowed me to invite the children round to play at our house instead. Eventually I started to befriend a young girl named Sara, who was seen as a bit of an outcast to the other children due to her parents' native tongue being Italian. Sara and I became the best of friends during junior school, pushed together by the measure of us both being unwilling outcasts. Sara lived near the school and as we got older I often used to walk back to her house after school with her and play with the numerous animals her parents kept; a dog, cat, hamster, guinea pig, rabbit, fish and even an injured blackbird they were nursing back to health - it was like a zoo! Sara and I were however, always in great competition with one another. It was due to this friendship I discovered very early on in my life I have an exceedingly competitive nature; where winning became the only option, to the point I could not bare to lose in any area of my life. In fact by the time I reached the final year at junior school I was the fastest runner in the entire school and was winning many trophies to salute this. This winning streak continued through high school and soon earned me the nickname 'The Legs'. It was this winning streak, which also caused me to excel in popularity at school. I have, however, always remained fully aware, popularity based on such shallow ideals usually is and in fact was very hollow.

When I reached the age of seven I attained my first taste of fame. I attended Buxlow School's usual Spring Term evening fête, which was held in the large grounds of one of the local neighbouring schools. Buxlow had organised for a BBC1 Radio deejay to host his normal daytime show live from the site that day. The deejay asked if anyone would like to volunteer to announce live on air the next record he was about to play. I rushed forward as fast as my little award winning legs would carry me. First to the finish line, I was awarded the job. I announced to Britain the next song and was then presented live on air with the record as a keepsake. The song was called *Street Fever* and performed by Tasha Thomas. The B-side did not go down very well with my parents however, as it was called *Drinking Again*. Need I say more? Although I did not manage to hear myself on the radio, all my young friends in the neighbourhood were soon knocking on my door that week to tell me they had heard me live on air. It was fun to be famous, even if for only five minutes of Andy Warhol's fifteen minutes of fame!

The experts say ask a boy of seven what he wants to become and you shall find the man. When I was seven I knew with complete certainty I wanted to become an actress and wasn't shy in coming forward to tell people. I'm sure people thought it was just a phase I would grow out of but of course I never did. During junior school I got myself involved in all the school plays and although I was never given the lead part, I thoroughly enjoyed being involved in all the various school productions over the years.

There was one other young girl in the year above me at school, who also shared my interest in performance. We soon became very good friends. She too felt like an outsider at school but I thought she was brilliant! Her name was Debbie Chazen. Debbie had a dream of becoming an actress. Even as a child she was an outstanding performer. (I remember in the final year of Buxlow Debbie gave a magnificent BAFTA award winning performance of the children's song *Puff the Magic Dragon*, although shamefully she says she doesn't remember this moment of glory now!) Debbie's parents were wonderful, caring people and they very quickly became friendly with mine. We lived fairly close to one another and often used to go round to our respective houses to play. Sadly though, Debbie and I lost contact after junior school, with no transport or cell phone to keep us connected, we simply went our separate ways. Debbie of course went on to become a much-loved and well-known actress. We both thought of each other over the years and I am pleased to say that, after many years of not being in contact, out of the blue we both contacted each other during the very same month and immediately became the best of friends again.

Even although we were Jewish, we still found cause to celebrate on Christmas Day at home. I used to get so excited about unwrapping my Christmas presents. Mum and dad had a pillowcase they'd fill to the brim with presents and it was almost bigger than me! When I became old enough I would later return the favour every year, showering them both with gifts. This was my way of showing them how much they meant to me. As a young child I never used to be able to sleep the night before Christmas. I remember one Christmas Eve thinking I had spotted Father Christmas! I hadn't, it was in actual fact dad I had seen. He was wearing red pyjamas with white stripes around the collar, sleeves and ankles and it was this set of nightwear he was wearing when I saw him coming into the room to drop off my Christmas sack. I was very innocent in this way as a child.

Sadly, Christmas was not always a time of joy for me. Every Christmas, from as early on as I can remember, mum and dad would take me to family gatherings at the Drummond household. I would often find myself confronted with upset and you could place money on it, I would end up walking part of the way home on my own in the deep snow before mum and dad chased after me because something unkind had been said to upset me by one or more of the members of the household.

By the age of seven it was announced to me my real father, Martin, had Leukaemia, which at that time was an almost untreatable cancer. It was also around this time the news came that Claudia and Martin were getting divorced; although they still claimed to love each other dearly. I can clearly recall sitting on the stairs in mum and dad's house and crying my eyes out. Mum came and answered the barrage of questions I put to her and they, as usual, all started with the premise 'Why?' Mum carefully explained to me my parents still cared about each other but felt they could no longer live together. She of course had no explanation to offer with regards to Martin's Leukaemia but continued to explain Claudia and Martin had met other people and were going to get re-married. And that's exactly what they did. Both Claudia and Martin remarried shortly after divorcing, to their parents' dismay, non-Jewish spouses - and suddenly being Jewish mattered! Martin remarried a Finnish woman (whom the family strongly believed married him on his death bed for his money but Martin enjoyed her company at this difficult time; so that was perhaps the main thing). Claudia meanwhile sadly remarried an extremely troubled alcoholic named, who for the sake of this book I shall call Trevor.

Trevor was actually a very kind man and I was very fond of him. Sadly however, he was always drunk. I remember in his often-dazed state he would laugh and tell me how I probably had many stepbrothers and stepsisters all around the world, as he would recount how he had encountered many ladies upon his travels. This news probably should have bothered me but I used to like hearing him say this, as I had always secretly longed to have siblings and the thought of having even a step brother or sister somewhere in the world used to bring a smile to my face.

By the time I was nearly eight the unthinkable happened. Mum had a small heart attack and ended up in hospital for two weeks. This was the first time dad had had to look after me without mum around. The house felt so empty and we both missed her terribly. We visited her every day at the hospital. I hated the smell of the hospital corridors, all I could smell was death. One day as I visited her in hospital, she asked the nurse to pull the curtains round her bed, as she said she needed to tell me something. As I sat next to her on her bed she proceeded to say the words which felt like a knife was being plunged slowly through my heart. She announced my father Martin had passed on to the next world. I couldn't really understand what it all meant but I knew it meant I was never going to see him again. My fear of one day never being able to see my dear father again had now come to fruition. I cried uncontrollably.

After my real father died it shook my entire world and it did, without notice, even at my young age make me aware of my own mortality. His death seemed so final – I wasn't going to see him again. After Martin died I very rapidly became unafraid of death. By the time I was nine I thought I knew everything, as Martin's death had succeeded in making me grow-up very fast.

Upon mum's return to our family home in Wembley Park in north London, she gently announced to me, that after discussion with Martin's parents, it had been agreed if I now felt I still wanted to call them mum and dad, then I would be allowed to do so. This time I cried happy tears but they were also tinged with sadness, for the reason I was now allowed to finally call someone mum and dad meant I had also lost my real father in the process.

After Martin died once again mum and dad both found themselves in the position of having to reapply to the High Court to continue retention of legal guardianship over me, rather than it being allowed to return to Claudia; whom it was decided was unsuitable to attain this role due to her condition. It was also deemed I would continue to be under the court's jurisdiction until the age of 18, should anything ever have happened to mum or dad during this time. It must have been a very difficult thing for Vera and Sam to have to request legal guardianship over their own daughter's child but they knew she was not well enough to look after me. Whilst under Vera and Sam's care, dad was expected to keep extensive notes on every major purchase he made in my name and this order, which was under an Affidavit of the High Court, continued with the condition I was not allowed to leave England or Wales without the court's jurisdiction first, until I attained the legal age of 18. In this regard, Dad was forced to send to the High Court on a regular basis, right up until this time, extensive proof of the above. I recall one year a school trip being organised to the Lake District and dad being required to send out a letter to the court in advance, with both leave and return dates of the trip. The court then had to agree to grant application before access was given for me to go on the trip. In fact, letter's even had to be written to the court with contact details of where I was going to stay, even when we went on summer holidays in regions of England. The court would then grant the application for my trip as long as an undertaking for my return, as dictated by them, occurred each time exactly on the date stated in advance. This entire process must have been quite a strain on a man of dad's age.

Money for my schooling was eventually awarded to mum and dad by the court as part of my father Martin's legacy and also partly from tax benefits awarded towards my upkeep, due to their age. I recall how certain members of the Drummond family would comment over the years as to why mum and dad were spending money on placing me in a private school. It would never cease to amaze me how these family members chose to dwell on the financial element of the situation rather than to recognize what mum and dad had sacrificed in their lives in order to so obviously try and protect me from receiving any more heartache and give me the best chance in life they could. Never once was a single comment made to me over the years by these same family members in relation to how sorry they were to hear of the loss of my father or show any understanding as to how or why this decision was born from that consequence.

When I went back to school after the loss of my dad a small group of children, initiated by the same particular little boy who had caused me upset about living with my grandparents, made it their mission to try and cause me upset about my real father's death. For a while they succeeded but it was short lived. There was another boy who was a year older and much bigger, who started to join in the torment. This boy was a real bully and used to chase the smaller children around the playground and knock them down. I very quickly learnt to become good at ducking and diving and this was much aided by the fact that, not only was I swift on my feet but I have always had extremely fast reflexes. It was actually these reflexes and good balance that later would find me becoming good at martial arts. One day, this particular boy started on me. He chased me around the playground and tried to push me down. I ducked and dived for cover and he went crashing to the ground and broke his arm. After that incident the boys learnt very quickly to leave me alone!

Our head teacher had a beautiful little Charles Spaniel named Jofer, which died that same year. My fascination with the after life had by this point well and truly kicked in to over-time and I started to become convinced I had seen the ghost of Jofer walking around the school. I even went as far as painting a few paw prints around the school walls to prove my theory! I was of course suspended for a couple of weeks. Following this I set the fire alarm off. I think after Martin died the world stopped making sense to me for a while.

After Martin died I also discovered I had found the ability to see people's auras. The sceptics among us will say this was just the vivid imagination of an upset child kicking in to play. I too can be a sceptic at times and am more than willing to accept any rational explanation for this. However, I am still able to see auras today and have in my adult life visited extremely respected Rabbis and Kabbalists in Israel to discuss this ability, whom have assured me in their opinion, my gift is real. It is actually not impossible to imagine this ability may really be occurring, when you consider all any living object is really made up of just a mass of energy. Perhaps for some people it is indeed possible to focus on that energy, just as Kirlian photography is able to pick up the residue of an object's electric charge. I also developed the ability from a young age to feel what people and animals are feeling and to see events into the future before they happen. I have had many visions over the years related to both myself and to other people and they usually come to fruition. Vera also held this same gift; often having dreams or visions about people that later came true. My visions have never really for the most part extended into my dream state, although I have strangely in my life had the same dream as four different friends on exactly the same night and one of my dreams, completely out of my control, did actually happen to me the next day.

My feelings on this gift that I have been given are; just as a blind person's hearing will become stronger, or a deaf person's ability to see will become clearer, I feel because of the loss of my father it made me more sensitive or intuitive if you like and heightened my senses and perception. I found after his passing I was given a heightened spiritual awareness. This surmounts to seeing things from a *heightened perspective*. When they occur I feel almost light headed, as if I were entering another dimension so to speak. Imagine for example, you are standing at the top of a tall high-rise sliver building in New York, overlooking the traffic and pedestrians below. You can see two pedestrians about to turn a corner and cross each other's path from opposite directions. As they turn the corner they bump into one another, as they didn't see each other coming but from your *heightened perspective* you saw their paths would ultimately cross and perhaps you even predicted

47

they would bump into one another from the angle they were both walking from where you were looking. Okay, allegory over but this is, in essence, the same for my visions, which occur from viewing things in a different way, or from a heightened plane if you like.

I also feel perhaps God has given me this gift, not only to help other people but also to help me get through the tests I have been faced with in my own life. I strongly feel, although we may not be able to choose our fate, we can choose how we deal with what life confronts us with; making our own choices along the way. Sometimes these visions aid me in doing just this, as well of course as using my intuition and knowledge about the issues which confront me. My problem has always been I do not always trust my gut enough to listen to these visions and it is this mistrust, which has in the past led me to making unwise choices. I usually find my visions are always very accurate and kick myself afterwards for not listening to them. I am now learning to listen to them more and take heed of the message, which may unfold from them. I call these visions a *gift* rather than an *ability*, as I do not have control over when they will occur. They just happen. I do not see myself as a psychic, female prophet or visionary or even some type of guru and certainly I'm no Joan of Arc! I just see myself as someone who has been given the gift of insight. Human beings only use nine per cent of their brain. Perhaps I am just using an additional per cent of my brain, which would normally lie dormant when I have this foresight. I truly believe everyone will one day possess the ability to have these insights just as I do and the sceptics amongst us will not only stop their scepticism but will also have access to this same gift.

An example of a vision - or arguably a premonition - I had when I was a child, took place one day as I was looking out at the road from the school playground in Buxlow. I spotted a man driving a white van along the road. Suddenly and in what felt like slow motion in my mind's eye, I could see him losing control of the van as he came towards us near to the gates we were standing at, crashing into a lamppost and dying as a result of the crash. Then I became aware of coming out of this vision - or premonition - and

48

seeing the driver really losing control and crashing the van. He did sadly die and right in front of my eyes. The shock of this tragic event meant I couldn't stop crying nor sleep for a week. It was an horrendous accident and my premonition obviously really shook me.

I started to have premonitions more regularly from this time onwards. At first, most were not as serious as the first one. For instance; I had a dream one night when I was around 12, in which my close school friend at the time, who for the sake of this book I shall call Sky and I were on holiday with my parents and playing in a field. There was this large, tall obelisk positioned in the middle of the field, which Sky and I both decided to run around. As the obelisk was so big, I became aware I couldn't see Sky when she was on the other side of it. Then I heard mum calling us in for tea. Not being able to see Sky, I called out to her but she didn't appear. Unable to find her, I went back to my mum and explained what had happened. I had lost Sky. It was such a weird and vivid dream I decided I would tell Sky about it at school the very next day. In the event, Sky informed me she'd had the very same dream the previous night too, the only difference being, in her dream she couldn't find me. As I got older, my premonitions did in fact become more serious and on a regular basis and shortly after this time I envisaged the passing on of a great uncle of mine named Ellis, exactly one week before his passing.

Going back to my Buxlow days, it was during this time mum gave me the option of ballet or horse-riding. I chose horse-riding and actually became very good at it; winning various rosettes to place alongside my running medals. I must say however, it took my leg muscles a long while to get used to riding and even when I got off the horse for the first few months I still looked somewhat like I had the horse still between my legs! I started to develop *The Lone Ranger* swagger. I loved the sport however and would gallop off into the fields at every possible opportunity. I loved the feel of the wind blowing in my face, as the horse and I became at one in the gallop. I think this was one of the few times in my young life I could feel completely free.

It's amazing however how one event can change the way someone views things but that is exactly what happened during one riding class, when an event occurred, which would teach me to face my fears front on. We were given permission by the riding instructor to be allowed to ride bare back (the horse - not me!). I immediately galloped off across the open fields on my beautiful palomino Troy, in fast pursuit of the other riders. Troy was a beautiful thoroughbred, with perfectly balanced conformation and of gentle nature. All of a sudden a thunderstorm hit. The horse immediately in front of Troy got spooked and bolted before taking off very rapidly. Troy followed suit. I lost the reins and started to tumble over Troy's head. He tried to break my fall by lifting his head but alas I flew right over the top of him and landed on my back directly in his path. Luckily for me, Troy was a horse I had ridden many times before and had formed a strong bond with. He reared up high into the air to break his fall and landed with a thud on the ground beside me. As the ground was moist from the rain it cushioned my fall. The impact on my neck may have been a lot worse had the ground been dry. I was lucky I had not broken any bones. I froze in complete shock and did not move a muscle. Troy bent his neck towards me and licked my face. I remained motionless.

The riding instructor soon galloped towards me, with the rest of the group now in close pursuit. She demanded I get back on Troy immediately. 'I'm cool where I am!' I said, still completely shaken. 'Well, we are all going back to the stables now' she continued. 'See ya!' I said 'And we are not leaving without you' she continued. 'Then I guess we are all staying here' I finalised. There was just no way I was ever getting back on that horse. 'If you don't get back on that horse right now, you will be forever afraid of horses' she said. She was of course right. If you fall off a horse you are indeed meant to get back on it straight away, to sever the onset of any fears developing. I had to face my fear right there and then. I told myself if I could get back on a semi-spooked animal in the pouring rain, whilst still completely terrified myself, I could confront anything in life.

I jumped back on that horse, at first in trepidation and put myself in the hands of both God and the horse and rode back towards the stables in the continued downpour of torrential rain. Since this day, whenever I am fearful of carrying out an action, I remind myself how afraid I was of getting back on that horse and how I managed to overcome my fear. Face your fear and do it anyway. That is my motto for life.

As an accomplished rider, one of the horses I used to ride at riding school was a beautiful black thoroughbred stallion named Viscount, who was the star of the Lloyds TSB television commercials. Funnily enough, one of the riders at the stables had a gorgeous little Labrador puppy, which he would bring on regular visits to the stables. This was the cutest little puppy you have ever laid eyes on and it would always receive a lot of attention from onlookers, who could not resist stroking this cuddly cutie. This puppy was at this time one of the stars of the Andrex toilet paper commercials. So you see, I really was surrounded by celebrities from a young age!

When I was nine I became very ill with the flu and had a 108 temperature. The doctor came round and examined me, then whispered something in mum's ear and she immediately began to cry. I think they thought I was going to die. She stayed by my bedside for the next two weeks, nursing me back to health, continually wetting my face with cold, wet flannels to keep my temperature down. Upon reflection, I don't think I realised at the time just how ill I actually was. Indeed, whenever I was ill mum would stay up all night checking I was okay. She could not ever sleep in the knowledge I was not well. Quite often when I was ill she would sing me to sleep. Mum was always such a caring individual and will always be the only 'mum' I have ever known, as will dad always be the only 'dad' I have ever known.

It was also around this time I went to see my first proper play at the theatre, starring my cousin Warren, in *Death of a Salesman* at the National's Lyttelton Theatre in London. Before this time the only staged productions I had seen and thoroughly enjoyed, were the *Holiday on Ice* ice-skating shows that were put on at Wembley once a year, which auntie Sybil would take me to without fail as a special treat. This was the highlight of every year for me but *Death of a Salesman* would be my first proper attendance at a theatrical production. Warren played Willy Loman, a 60 year-old frail sales man, who dies at the end of the play. Mum did not really want me to see the play as she felt it would be too harrowing for me, as the subject of the play is not really fitting for a young girl but as Warren was starring in it, after much persuasion, she eventually decided to back down and allow me to see it. I think they could hear me sobbing my little heart out all the way down the corridors of the theatre and into the street when Willy died. After the finish of the play we went backstage to visit Warren. This was the first time I had ever been backstage in a theatre before. I loved the smell of the make-up and the feel of the bright lights around the mirrors.

By this stage my love of all things theatrical was well and truly starting to kick in. Incidentally, it was also around this time Claudia wanted to start putting me forward for various films and musicals. One particular job she was interested in placing me forward for was for the role of Pippy Longstockings, in a production of the same name. Mum however, was dead-set against the idea of me performing at such a young age and even although at the time I was upset she would not allow me to audition for the part, upon reflection it was probably a good thing she didn't allow it, as she may have saved me from walking into more rejection and upset at this young age.

Whilst visiting Warren backstage after *Death of a Salesman*, I was introduced to his then dresser, a certain Albert Hillier. Albert and I became firm friends and from that day on he became my 'adopted' grandfather. My nickname for him soon became 'Daddy Longlegs!' Albert's nickname for himself, however, is 'The OAP' (short for Old Age Pensioner!). Since that day, Albert has taken me to many a red carpet event and introduced me to nearly everyone there is to know in the world of show business. He is my 'Daddy Warbucks'. Albert is the head honcho, the man all the stars from both sides of the Atlantic call to get a seat in the audience of a sold-out show. He is a complete enigma in the industry, a bit of a legend. Starting life on the stage himself at the age of nine, Albert knows every star there is to know either side of the Atlantic. He has in his time been a dresser to Warren, an agent, producer and ticket agent to the stars. He has worked for Barbara Streisand and also used to work closely for both Frank Sinatra and the Royal family. He has helped Goldie Hawn, Kevin Klein, Michelle Pfeiffer and Al Pacino, to name but a few, attain tickets for shows in London and escorted them around the city as a tour guide when they have been in town. Albert also helped Sam Wannamaker set-up the now famous Globe Theatre in London. He was very close to Sam Wannamaker and worked on a lot of projects with him. When I became old enough, Albert would soon ask me to accompany him over the years to various movie and theatre opening nights, the latter of which were often hosted by Albert's close friend, producer, Bill Kenwright - but for now, being too young to attend the after-show parties, I could only dream of what it may be like and regular visits to the theatre would have to quench my growing appetite for the world of show businesss instead.

Around this time I did however receive the privilege of meeting backstage, after a charity performance being hosted for the Variety Club of Great Britain at London's Bloomsbury theatre, three of whom I consider to be the nicest people in the world of showbuisness. I had been taken to see the show by members of my close family, who had subsequently invited me to a 'meet and greet' in the green room afterwards. The three hosts in question were: the loveable, huggable Frank Bruno, the wonderful Bernie Winters and of course his glorious St Bernard's dog Schnorbitz, all of whom greeted me with a warm hello. In fact, I fondly recall even having a friendly, fisty-cuffs with Mr Bruno. The highlight of the evening was of course meeting the glorious old boy Schnorbitz, whom greeted me with a slobbery, wet lick on my hand. I didn't return the favour!

More theatrical excitement came into my life around this time in the shape of a VIP visitor to my school. When it was announced to the children a special visitor would be dropping in, all the children were anxiously expecting royalty. We were informed however, the person visiting us was actually not a person at all but a new state of the art robot called Quadracon. The children were told we would be given the chance to shake its hand, walk around with it and even talk to it! I was so excited. The local press were also coming to take a picture of the day's events. The thought of meeting a real live robot excited me greatly, as did the idea of getting my picture in the local paper, which did indeed follow.

Also around this same time a very different type of excitement entered my life and with it too was born my fear of fire. A neighbour asked if I would like to accompany her and her daughter to a book signing in London for Roald Dahl's latest book launch. Always a fan of Dahl's books, I jumped for joy at the opportunity to meet with the legend. We arrived at a very run down building in the centre of London, where we faced a very long line of people waiting to get their books signed. We must have waited at least an hour to get to the front desk, where Mr Dahl was signing his books. We were finally next in line to get our books signed when unexpectedly someone shouted 'Fire!' Panic ceased hold of everyone and we were immediately ushered out of the room by a security guard and through a long corridor to a fire exit. When we arrived at the fire exit we found both sets of fire doors had been barricaded by a pile of cardboard boxes, which stretched right up to the ceiling. There was no exit. We were then hurried back along through the long corridor and out to another exit the other side of the building. The building had already started to get hot and the smell of smoke was starting to fill the rooms. When we finally all safely evacuated the building, the entire structure crumbled almost immediately to the ground. In Judaism, as well as representing destruction, fire also represents the soul and new beginnings. When I think of fire, I am also reminded of God's presence in the world.

The same is true of whenever I see a rainbow or feel the wind blowing on my skin and once again I am reminded of God's presence. Equally so, of course of the rain and the sun or the miracle of life; watching a flower grow or a baby being born. When I was 11, I witnessed what I personally consider to have been one of God's miracles. I was in the kitchen with mum, when

54

suddenly the whole room turned dark. Mum and I thought a thunderstorm was on its way. We looked out of the window to view what appeared to be the start of a heavy rainstorm. Upon closer inspection we realised what we had at first thought was rain was actually a committee of bees. The queen bee had chosen our apple tree, the very same tree I used to sit under in my pram as a baby, as a pit stop for her business meeting with her colony. Her worker bees followed in quick pursuit, with the male drones (probably droning on behind) quickly forming their nest in the tree. A man who lived a short distance up the road was, as luck would have it, a beekeeper. We called him and he immediately came round to carefully remove the bees from the tree. All the children in the neighbourhood came to watch. It was such an amazing spectacle. The whole incident reminded me how amazing life is, even right down to the birds and the bees in the trees. Whenever I feel down all I have to do is think of how wonderful life can 'bee'! So whenever those naughty blues start to creep in remember, life is also filled with greens, yellows, pinks and many other magnificent colours too.

Meanwhile, back at home excitement reared its head again in a completely different form. *The Brownie* was a national magazine for all Brownies to purchase, for the grand sum of 15 pence throughout the UK. I was so excited when at the tender age of 10 my little joke was printed in the February edition. My writing career began with the following joke: *'Why are you taking a pencil to bed with you, dear?'... 'To draw the curtains, mum.'*

**Without rain we could not appreciate the sunshine.**
**Without the difficult times, we could not appreciate the good.** - Emma Fletcher

3

# Looking for Answers

***Fall seven times, stand up eight.*** - Japanese proverb

*Paul: Childhood holiday memories are those we should cherish. For Emma however, certain holiday breaks during her childhood were, as you will read in this chapter, to sadly leave her with painful memories.*

Emma: From around the age of four to the age of nearly six', every year my parents used to take me away for our summer holidays, often with my lovely auntie Sybil in tow, as one big happy family. We would often stay with Warren in either his Woolacombe Sands home, whenever he was performing in the town's theatre, or in his holiday home in Sandbanks. I have happy memories of these holidays, riding donkeys on the sand, walking along cobbled stones and of Warren placing me on his shoulders and running along the beach with me as fast as the wind would carry us. We would stay in Sandbanks at Whitsun and sometimes in September. Warren's house was a beautiful modern building, which was so close to the beach it was almost standing on the sands. It had a large balcony facing the sea and often we all used to sit on the balcony and watch the sailing and racing boats, which went from Poole harbour and the liners from Southampton. The Isle of Wight could also be viewed from his balcony. Other years we all went to Bournemouth, Cornwall, Bude, Clovelty and Westgate. These holidays provided happy times and were usually the only escape from the rest of the difficulties I faced in my normal every day young life. But then everything changed.

When I was about 6, mum and dad decided from now on we would go every year for our summer holidays to Birchington in Kent, as we had family there. Both my great auntie Thistle, Sam's sister, who was once a well-respected and very successful opera singer and his first cousins Eva, Paulette and Jack, the latter who had married the late icon Josephine Baker, all now lived in Birchington. As they were now all getting too old to make the journey to London and Sam was that much younger, it was his duty to make the journey to them instead.

One day, whilst walking fairly far out to sea with mum, we started to encounter a little bit of quick sand. A little farther out there was a young girl crying her eyes out and screaming, as she had sunk into the sand up to her tiny waist. Her friend was desperately trying to pull her out. Not seeing the danger and always such a fearless child, even quite a tomboy (especially after Martin died - death became my friend and not something to be feared), I rushed up to the little girl, with mum now in close pursuit and we both helped pull her out of the sand. The older girl, who for the sake of this book I shall call Sally, informed us the little girl was her cousin, who for the sake of this book I shall called Jenny. They both thanked me greatly. A bond formed between us all. Incidentally, on the walk back to the beach huts we discovered an old bomb buried beneath the sand, which had landed there during the Second World War. Dad informed the police and later that day a specialist bomb squad came to carefully remove the bomb. An uncanny start, to what was about to become an explosive friendship.

As we walked back to the beach huts both Sally and Jenny said they would like to introduce me to the rest of their family and their grandmother, who they stayed with in Birchington every year. Sally and I became firm friends after this incident and continued to write to each other for many of our junior school years. Sally however, was on the last day of her holiday but Jenny's holiday had only just begun. She soon introduced me to her elder sister, who I will call Lileth and from there on every summer holiday, from the age of six to the age of 11 my parents would siphon me off to play with Jenny, Lileth and a group of her 'friends'.

What my parents were unawares of and what I was unable to find the courage to tell them until I was 11 was, every year Lileth and her group of 'friends' were emotionally bullying me and on a few occasions even went as far as physically beating me. I believe the bullying originally may have started due to the fact I was introduced to the group of friends as a heroine whom had saved Lileth's little sister. I immediately became very popular within the group because of this title. This very much appeared to put Lileth's back out who, being that she was at least three years older than I, considered herself the leader of the group and eventually the bad feeling turned into something sinister, as the bullying started to take on a different focus and became based around the fact I was Jewish. First there was the name calling and then came the violence.

Birchington is a seaside resort, which often attracts religious Jewish families. The first racist comment I recall Lileth saying was when a group of Hasidic Jews walked along the peer and a Volkswagen Beatle happened to follow. Lileth immediately turned towards me and jeered 'Is that a Jew car?' I also vividly recall her grandmother smiling at this comment. As a child I could never understand why her grandmother did not tell her off.

In the years that followed many traumatic incidents occurred between Lileth and her group of friends and myself. It was the same set of friends and their families with whom I was greeted at the start of my summer holidays upon my return to Birchington every year. At a time of year when most children are looking forward to the end of the school year and going away on holiday with their family, I used to completely dread the summer holiday season. I recall when I was around eight, Lileth and another girl encouraged me to go out to sea with them, under the guise they would teach me to swim. I was a late learner and did not learn to swim until I was nine. There were times Lileth was nice to me and being that I was a trusting soul, who always chose to see the light in people, I chose to believe the best in what she was saying. I followed both Lileth and the other girl out to sea, until the level of the water reached just above my shoulder blades. I recall Lileth suddenly shouting at the top of her voice: 'Now swim!' I started to try and paddle furiously, when without any prior warning both Lileth and the other girl jumped on top of me and held my head under the water. I struggled for what felt like an eternity. Panic reached every bone in my body but I managed to come up for air for a split second before I was being pushed under the water again by the crown of my head. My eyes now wide open, I managed to kick both girls in the gut and got free from their grip. I ran to shore in a frozen panic, too scared to tell anyone what had just happened; but to this day I have always been fearful of putting my head under water.

Another year on a girl in the group of friends, urged on again by Lileth, jumped on me from behind as I was playing behind the beach huts and pulled a skipping rope around my neck so tightly, I thought every inch of air left in my lungs would leave me for good. I managed to break free from the rope and once I regained the use of my vocal chords, screamed for help like I have never screamed before in my life. That year I did tell my mum what had happened but still did not tell her of how Lileth treated me. My mum said she had heard the screams but thought I was playing - why would anyone imagine a small child doing this to another? Mum said I was never to play with this little girl again and told me I was to continue playing with Lileth and her other friends - if only she knew. It is amazing what a child will keep to itself.

Then came the time we were all sitting in a circle playing a board game, when in an unanticipated fashion the only boy in the group pulled out a knife and very gently started to press it into the side of my leg. I got up and moved to the other side of the circle. The knife was passed round to his sister who tried the same until I got up and left the 'game' altogether. This same year also saw me being covered in talcum powder, as one of the girls sneaked up on me from behind and threw the powder in my face. It got into my hair, mouth, eyes and even up my nose. It gave me such a shock and upset me terribly.

One of my few means of escaping the upset I was continually facing every year in Birchington was to join the local Gospel choir. I first came into contact with The Minnis Bay choir one year when they were performing to an audience on the beach. I went up to the head of the choir and asked if I could join in. 'Can you sing?' she asked. 'I think so' I said. 'Well, let's here you then?' the kind and warm lady replied. I started to sing. 'You have a lovely voice' she continued. 'Come and join us back at the church after the performance.' So I did just that. This was probably the first time I had ever stepped inside a church before. After this time I sang with the choir on a regular basis every year. It was this early interaction, which formed my style of singing voice; which has always been very soulful with an injection of Rhythm and Blues.

In my childlike innocence, I still managed to give Lileth and her group of 'friends' one more chance. After an apology from them all and an invite to come and play hide and seek in the car park with them, I decided to accept their apology and join in the game. When it was my turn to hide I watched with curiosity from my hiding spot behind a parked car when I saw a young girl, whom I did not know, approach Lileth and then witnessed anxious raised arms in the air. I came out of my hiding place only to be told by the group of friends not to worry and to go and hide again. This I did. Once again the same girl appeared out of nowhere. This time a man joined her and then they both started to shout before walking off. I came out from my hiding place again and demanded Lileth tell me what was going on. The response I was given was a resounding 'Nothing!' Choosing not to believe this, I started to run back towards the beach huts when Lileth and two of her friends grabbed me and tried to hold me down. I managed to break free from their grip and started to run back towards the beach huts. As I approached the beach huts Lileth's grandmother screamed at me 'You should be ashamed of yourself!' I ran up to find mum in tears, being comforted by the very same young girl and man who had raised their arms in despair earlier. Mum hugged me as soon as she saw me and told me Lileth had told this girl and her dad she had seen me get into a car with a strange man and drive off about half an hour earlier and had said no one had seen me since. I never spoke to Lileth again after that day.

One of my favourite past-times in Birchington was to walk along this very slippery, very high wave-breaker along part of the length of the beach, which lead up to where the crab pool was. I used to love fishing for crabs, picking them up and studying them but I would always make certain I placed them gently back into the fishing pool unharmed after I had finished. I was completely fascinated by the way they moved and not at all scared they might pinch me with their sharp pincers. In fact quite the opposite, on one occasion I recall jumping into the crab pool completely barefoot to pull out a little girl who was crying, as she had accidentally fallen in.

If my parents had of known I was walking along the length of the wave-breaker to reach the crab pool, I think they would have had a fit! It really was a dangerous sport, especially for a child. If I had of slipped and fallen off the ridge, it could have resulted in an extremely serious accident. I think I was thrill seeking; looking for an escape route from the trauma I was facing in Birchington each day of my stay there. I recall one day, probably when I was around nine, loosing my balance and slipping onto a broken piece of glass whilst walking the length of the seaweed-ridden wave-breaker. The glass went right inside the soul of my foot. I regained composure and pulled the glass out of my foot but the open gash would not stop bleeding. The blood was literally pouring out from beneath. The most stunning young boy I had ever laid eyes on spotted me from beneath the ridge. He saw I was in trouble and instantly shouted up to me: 'Wait, I'm coming up to get you!' The boy raced round to the edge of the ridge, climbed up and walked carefully along to where I was now sitting. He literally scooped me up in his arms and carried me all the way back to the chalet, where mum and dad were sitting. I thought I must have died and gone to heaven! Of course mum had a fit when she saw the blood rushing out of my foot but I have to say, being carried up to the door of the chalet by this handsome young man was worth the gash on my foot and it also succeed in making Lileth and her group of girlfriends very green-eyed with envy in the process!

By the age of 11 my body shape had started to change and I felt less like a child and more like a woman. I had also suffered bereavement four times in my life now: my Uncle Ellis and my great aunt Paulette, both of whom I was very fond of had now passed on, not to mention of course my father Martin. I had also

61

lost my great grandmother Sarah, Bill's mother, who I was extremely close to. (Growing up with my grandparent's I had become very close to the elder members of the family and was bound to see a number of this generation pass away but it never got any easier each time it happened.) I had also suffered bullying; what does not kill you will make you stronger. I decided I wanted to play less with Lileth and her friends and play more on my own.

One early evening after my family had walked back to the flat we always stayed in, which was a five-minute walk along the main road, I decided to have a swim in the sea by myself. That year I was doing all my playing alone. As my parents had locked up the beach hut, I had left my clothes in between the gap of the two huts to retrieve after I had finished my swim. To my upset, when I returned to the beach hut to retrieve my clothes I found they were no longer there. Distressed at the idea of having to walk back to the flat along the main roads in a wet bikini, especially as I no longer felt like a child, I started the walk along the grass verge behind the beach huts to try and stay off the main road for as long as possible. As I reached the top of the grass verge, I found Lileth and four of her friends waiting at the top of the hill for me. They immediately jumped me and pinned me down to the ground. They then proceeded to hit me and smear my body and face with dog waste and call me a 'Jewish bitch'. I ran home in my wet bikini and covered in muck, crying my eyes out. Once I got to the door of the flat I found they had left my clothes on the doorstep. I went in and ran to the shower and cried my heart out. After showering and dressing I sat in silence in front of the television with my parents in the front room, when all of a sudden Lileth and her friends appeared at the window of our flat calling out names, which thankfully were barely audible through the glass. My parents closed the curtains. It had started to dawn on them, even in my silence, what their child was dealing with. We sat in the darkened room watching the television for the next hour, no one saying much of anything at all. The next day I told my parents everything. My parents informed me I would never have to return to Birchington again if I did not want to. We explained our reasons to our family who lived there and they informed us they had already held their suspicions about Lileth's family and grandmother over the years. Whilst my parents visited Birchington again, it took me a number of years to find the courage to return.

The only good memories I hold of Birchington are of spending time with my two lovely aunts who lived there; great auntie Thistle and great auntie Eva and also of my auntie Paulette and uncle Jack. Now that auntie Paulette and uncle Jack had passed on, Eva and Thistle became my only reason for eventually returning to Birchington. I was completely heartbroken when Paulette and Jack passed away when I was still young and also when both auntie Thistle and auntie Eva eventually passed on during my teenage years.

My great auntie Eva was a very upright member of society and a strict lady, who was not at all used to children. All the same I loved to visit her whenever we were in Birchington and enjoyed the nights I was allowed to stay in her pretty home 'Mallory Cottage.' Even today I can still picture the flowered Laura Ashley-styled wallpaper that ran through the entire length of the bungalow. I would often write to auntie Eva during the course of the year. After Eva passed on I went with mum and dad to Mallory Cottage, as dad was the Executor of her Will. As we opened the door, lying on the doorstep was the last letter I had sent her; unopened. Mum told me to keep it. I felt so sad retrieving the letter unopened but I have still kept this letter today amongst my most treasured possessions.

Other fond memories I have of Birchington are the year I met the actor Roy Kinnear and his children. They were such a kind and loving family and so kind to me. I was so sad when I heard of Roy's untimely death in 1988. Also, there was the year I met Michael Bond - the author of Paddington Bear - and his daughter. I remember informing Mr Bond, even at such a very young age, how I planned to be famous one day and he said 'Go for your dreams kid!' To this day I still treasure the signed book he gave to me of his book *Paddington's New Room*, which I believe was newly released at the time.

One particular year the flat we normally stayed in next door to auntie Thistle's flat was already booked, so we stayed in a Bed and Breakfast instead. I befriended a gorgeous grey mongrel pooch named Sammy. It did become a little confusing however every time I called him and dad turned around as well! (Mum's nickname for dad was Sammy). Every year we would visit the owner of Sammy, who would allow me to take him out for walks along the beach. One year we had not as yet had the chance to go and visit Sammy and would you believe, a few days into our stay in Birchington, he managed to run out the front door of his owner's home and ended up on the doorstep of our chalet all by himself. He had come to say hello to me! The bond I formed with Sammy the pooch helped me to cope emotionally with some of the difficult times I faced in Birchington.

I recall so vividly one year, whilst holidaying in Birchington, seeing the film *Annie* when it first premiered in the UK. I couldn't take my eyes off the screen. I felt a complete emotional affinity with little orphaned Annie.

Towards the last couple of years of my time at junior school I befriended a young girl named Alison Morland. Alison's parents were also slightly older than the other parents, due to both being on their second marriage and so Alison and I quickly became good friends, as did our parents. I was soon asked away with Alison and her parents on a week's trip to Lime Regis, to go hunting for dinosaur bones. This was the first time I had ever been away without mum and dad and it was the most fabulous holiday I had ever experienced; partly as it was a happy release from the upset I faced going to Birchington every year but also the idea of hunting for dinosaur bones was just so uber cool!

A short time after my visit to Lime Regis, I went away again with Alison and two mutual school friends from the year above. I was completely fascinated by one of the friends' routine of keeping milk and meat separate and by the time I got home from the holiday I informed my parents, who were not kosher, that from now on I was going to keep separate plates to eat my food from -

and I did! Being that at this time I was an aspiring vegetarian, this made a lot of sense to me anyhow.

After Buxlow I unfortunately lost touch with Alison. It was not until many years later we were reunited, when during my university years a close male friend announced he was having a party to celebrate his 21st birthday. The party was fantastic. It was held in a place where they had designed a playground for adults and who should be there? Sitting on the swing right beside me was Alison. It tickled us both that here we were once again sitting on swings beside one another. We immediately bonded again and Alison told me she was going on holiday that week for a week but as soon as she got back she would call me to meet up. I was so pleased to have Alison back in my life again and told mum of my joy. The week came and went and I received no call. I felt sad, as I was so sure Alison had meant what she had said. Another week went by and then there was a call. The call was not from Alison however but from the mother of one of our old mutual friends. Alison had been knocked down by a reckless driver on her holiday and killed instantly. I was devastated. Selfish thoughts entered my mind. Why did I have to see her again? I went to the funeral and her mother fell into floods of tears when she saw me, hugging me uncontrollably. I think seeing me after all these years must have raised a lot of emotions in her but she touched my heart by telling me Alison was also so pleased to have become reacquainted with me over the last few weeks of her life. Alison's parents were writers and versed well in literature. After her untimely passing, they set up 'The Alison Morland Poetry Prize' at Leeds University; where Alison had been studying. The award is still running there today in her memory.

My first summer holiday outside of the UK with mum and dad was not until around the age of 14, when we visited Italy. We travelled to the beautiful scenery of Venice. I recall for the first time in my life feeling so free during this holiday and running through the lawn of the hotel where we were staying with a guy I had befriended, shouting at the top of my lungs with free abandonment 'I feel free, I feel free!' and for that moment I honestly did.

65

We drove all the way from England in dad's new pride and joy, his metallic green Nissan Stanza, then through France and Switzerland and on into Italy. I sat in the front with the map on my lap, acting as dad's GPS navigator and mum sitting in the back enjoying the scenery. The car's number plate was ALL 7 JOY. We considered this car to be our lucky mascot but unfortunately, luck was not on our side.

After our very long and adventurous journey, we managed to drive safely to our final destination in Italy, all the way from our doorstep in Wembley. We checked into reception at around 8 o'clock in the evening starving hungry, only to be told the restaurant was now closed and they wouldn't be serving food again until the next morning. We were advised to get back in the car and drive in a straight line a few hundred yards up the road to the neighbouring hotel, who we were assured would be happy to accommodate us.

We hopped back into the car and started up the flat straight street, through to the next block. We passed a T-junction and continued along the road. There were no other cars on the road and then, as fate would have it, suddenly as if out of nowhere a car sped out from the right and crashed into our car. What occurred next felt as if it were happening in slow motion, when due to the force of the hit our car spun round and back into the tail of the car that had just hit us with tremendous speed. It caused the driver of the other car to shoot straight through the bonnet of his car and be tossed on to the ground in front of it, which thankfully had now stopped due to hitting a wall. I thought we had killed him.

Immediately police arrived on the scene and all the locals came out of their houses; touching us and our car with avid interest. Thank God my family and I were not hurt, although extremely shaken. It turned out a 'Give way' sign, which should have been facing our direction, had been turned inwards and was now facing the houses instead of the road.

The policeman started speaking to my dad in Italian. None of us spoke Italian. We started to panic. A man came up to me and asked if I spoke Italian. I said I did not. I asked him if he spoke English. He said he did not. I asked him if he spoke French. He said he did. We started to converse in basic school French. The man informed me the policeman was saying to my dad, unless he could produce his driver's licence and passport on the spot, he would be arrested and forced to spend the night in jail. My poor father was a 74 year-old man and would have been terrified had he of known what the policeman was saying to him. The policeman told us no one was allowed to leave the scene, yet my dad's papers were back at the hotel. What were we to do?

Now I would not advise anyone to try this at home, as what I did next was a very huge risk. I asked this complete stranger if he would drive me back to my hotel to collect the papers and back to the scene again before the police would even notice. He agreed. My gut told me I could trust this man, so I winked at mum and ran off as fast as my award-winning legs would carry me; jumped into this man's car and drove off. We returned less than 10 minutes later with the correct documents. My parents were immediately released from the scene of the crash. We never heard anymore from the police after this time, so they must have felt we were not at fault and it turned out the other passenger thankfully survived the ordeal. Our car however, was a complete write-off.

When we returned home to the UK dad's insurance company replaced his car with another metallic green Nissan Stanza. Dad continued to drive and thoroughly enjoy this car for many years after this time, until his first stroke at the grand age of 91, which sadly rendered him unable to drive. After this time dad asked me to take his car from him. At the time I didn't want to give up my trusty little blue metro but dad insisted I have his car. I eventually graciously agreed to accept the gift of his car, promising I would take care of it. Dad and I decided I should officially 'buy' the car from him for the grand sum of one pound, so there would be no dispute from any other members of the family at a later stage, claiming the car was rightfully theirs.

After dad passed away I continued to drive his car for a number of years, priding myself on how happy it would have made him to know I was still driving his pride and joy around and looking after it so well. I kept that car in such a good condition and I can't begin to tell you the number of compliments the car received over the years I was driving it; even although many members of my family were insisting I get rid of it, as it was by now getting so old.

It was indeed an old car, with windows that had to be wound down with some serious amount of elbow grease. It had a radio and tape player that no longer worked and it certainly didn't like going over 60 miles an hour without displaying more shake, rattle and roll than Elvis had ever experienced in his entire career! It was an old age pensioner; there was no escaping that fact. There was no showing-off in this car anymore or racing at the lights! This car was going nowhere fast but that didn't bother me, just as long as it got me to my destination eventually and safely. I have always found driving a pleasurable experience and quite often over the years I have jumped into my car and taken a long, lonely drive to nowhere in particular, just to clear my head. Many times during these moments I would be reminded of the lyrics of Talking Head's song *Road to Nowhere*:

*Well we know where we're going/But we don't know where we've been/And we know what we're knowing/But we can't say what we've seen.*

With the dignity of old age and its gracious lack of speed, that car reminded me every day at the lights, when someone sped past in their brand new, shiny open-top sports convertible, to have patience and as David Byrne sings *'give myself time to work it out'*.

I was, up until recently, still driving dad's car but sadly at the start of this year had to let it be put to rest as I knew, even although the car was sound mechanically, the bodywork was starting to fail. I cried my eyes out when the men came to collect it for scrap. That car had become more than just a car to me. It represented for the family nearly a whole quarter of a century of memories. We had laughed, cried and loved one another in that car over the years. It was embedded with all our energies. That car had taken us on holidays, family celebrations, to weddings, hospital and sadly even to funerals. It held a lifetime of memories and virtues in its walls and yet it was still just a car; metal, glass and rubber and I had to let it go. The biggest lesson I had to learn letting go of that car was the car was merely a symbol of those memories and not the essence of them. The essence of them will remain in my heart forever. It was not the car after all that was important but the experiences themselves.

Over the years all my cars have been given names. A car becomes like a second home when you drive as much as I do; so you have to give them each a name! My first car, a little electric blue Metro, was called Mad Max the Metro. It later became Mad Max Scarface the Metro, when it attained a little scratch down its side. When my dad gave me his old fashioned car I christened it Stanley the Stanza, or 'Stan' for short, as some of my friends renamed it. Now I have the little silver cutie, Alma the Almera.

Meanwhile back to Italy; the journey home from our holiday was also eventful. When we reached the arrivals collection point for our luggage, something went wrong with the mechanics of the conveyor belt, which meant we had to wait a while for our luggage to reappear. After quite a fashion I viewed my luggage zip past me at speed, as did the gentleman to my right view his luggage travel past in a similar manner. Having waited so long to be re-acquainted with my luggage and clearly very pleased to see it, I jumped at it wholeheartedly and made touch down, just as the gentleman to my right made the same, almost unique claim to his luggage. The result? We both fell on top of one another in a good old-fashioned rugby tackle. After a few giggles from both teams, the charming gentleman helped me to my feet and apologised.

My mum then noticed the gentleman was now holding a very large bag, so in her usual jovial fashion asked him if he had just stolen the crown jewels. The gentleman laughed heartily and told us he was in fact a musician and had just arrived home from a long tour. My mum continued 'Ah, how nice! We live next to Wembley Stadium. We often get a lot of loud music being played there. I hope you're not one of those loud rock-stars?' The gentleman smiled and responded 'Actually, we are heading to Wembley ourselves.' He then introduced us to his fellow band members and we continued our friendly banter.

We exited the airport still chatting when out of nowhere a hoard of photographers started snapping away. 'How rude!' mum exclaimed. The gentleman winked at me but I didn't really understand why. We reached the exit of the airport and then the kind gentleman offered us all a ride to Wembley with his band. Dad thanked him but declined the offer explaining we had already booked a taxi (now that we no longer had a car). 'No problem' continued the gentleman 'Let me at least walk you to your taxi.' He lifted my bag for me and walked us to the taxi door, then we all shook hands and both the kindly gentleman and his band departed. The taxi driver looked at us in sheer amazement, 'Do you know who he was?' he asked. 'Yes!' I responded, 'we just met him in the airport. What a nice gentleman. He was on his way to Wembley too.' 'Yes. He was!' said the taxi driver 'On his way to Wembley Stadium. That was Status Quo!' Wow, I thought to myself, just another eventful day in the life of Emma Fletcher!

The next year after our Italian holiday, we went to the beautiful Rhodesian island Ixias. During this holiday I was proposed to by a cute waiter, made my first stage appearance outside of the school arena, got drunk for the first time in my life and nearly drowned but not necessarily in that order!

On the very first day of the holiday I sat around the pool with mum and dad; as I was far too shy to talk to anyone my own age, preferring after all my Birchington encounters, to spend time with my parents and the older generation they had become acquainted with by the poolside. Very soon the couple my parents were talking to introduced me to their family and I quickly found myself in the company of a very friendly group of teenagers, all of whom were a few years older than me.

I recall one day, whilst mum was asleep by the large pool at the back of the hotel, I became happily involved in a game of tag with a couple of the guys from the group, who I will call Sean and Harry. I tagged them both, then ran as fast as my legs would carry me to the opposite side of the hotel, near the smaller pool. The boys eventually caught up with me and unexpectedly playfully picked me up with the intention of throwing me into the pool. One of the boys grabbed my arms and the other my legs and started to swing me in the air with the idea of dropping me into the pool on the count of three. Unfortunately their plan went horribly astray. As they counted up from one, just before they reached three, I pulled my legs in towards my chest into a foetal position, then with full-throttle force, pushed my legs out again in order to foil their plan. This I did but to my own detriment. The boys could not manage to contain their grip and dropped me, sending me flying and smashing into the pool. My head hit the wall of the pool and I was immediately knocked unconscious and was now sinking rapidly to the bottom.

The next thing I recalled was being pulled out of the water by both Sean and Harry, who had both dived in after me and mum standing at the side of the pool crying: 'I thought you'd drowned!' Now the interesting part of the story is this; the pool mum had been sunbathing at was at the other side of the hotel and was quite a distance to where we now were. There was no way she could have heard or seen what had happened. It turned out, while she was sleeping she had a dream I was drowning, which had disturbed her so much it had woken her up. Not seeing me near the pool she was resting by, she had immediately jumped up and run around to the other pool to find me actually drowning. My poor mum had more of a shock than I did, as I was blissfully unawares of what had just occurred when the boys finally pulled me out of the water and onto dry land.

Later during that week it was announced the hotel was holding a talent show one evening and all a sundry were welcome to enter. One of the girls in the group who had heard me warble some of my best notes and seen me strut my funky Gene Kelly's on the dance floor earlier in the week, very kindly encouraged me to share my talent in the show. I checked in with mum this would be okay, as I was still only 15 and the other members of the group were all of drinking age. Mum spoke to a couple of the girls in the group and made them promise to look after me, which they said

71

they would. The group of friends bought me a number of drinks at the bar, to loosen me up for the kill - sorry, I of course mean talent show! I chose ouzo as my poison; it tasted like liquorice, so that was good enough for me. Now bearing in mind, up until this point I was tea-total (actually coffee total!) and for sure could not hold my drink, of course the ouzo went straight to my head. What followed next on stage was a very interesting performance of *I'm Gonna Live Forever* from *Fame*, ending in a slightly obliterated form of high-splits, to a cacophony of tumultuous cheers from the group of friends. As soon as I came off the stage I decided I was ready for bed. The rest of the group felt differently and decided it would be a good idea for me to regain my sobriety first before mum saw the state they had allowed me to get into. So they made me sit down and wait for half an hour before allowing me to return to the hotel room.

Mum would always wait up for me when I was a kid whenever I came home from friend's houses, or from school. She would without fail sit awake and worry until I was safely tucked into my bed and tonight would be no different. When I reached my hotel room, which was a parallel en suite running alongside the length of my parent's room, I struggled to place the key in the door. Mum opened the door and I fell through. 'Drunk are we?' she quizzed. Quickly jumping to my feet and brushing myself down I announced 'Of course not!' in the clearest voice I could muster. Mum asked if I was hot and enquired if I would like a drink of water, informing me she had left a bottle of cold water in the sink for me, placed in cold water, to keep it cool. You get the idea - it was cold! It was a very hot evening and I was of course feeling very thirsty. Mum said 'Drink it all up now dear!' Now unbeknownst to me, when ouzo mixes with water it immediately makes one loose their sobriety and mum of course knew this. She was testing me. I drank the entire bottle in one clean swipe, walked out of the bathroom, straight into the wall, then collapsed onto the floor into a drunken heap. I think mum left me there till the morning but to be honest, I can't really remember! All I know is, I woke up in the morning with my first ever and rather severe hangover. Mum had made her point and to tell you the truth, I have never allowed myself to get that drunk again since. Apart from the occasional cocktail, I've never been particularly partial to being out of control of my bodily senses or even much to sleeping on the floor!

As we move through life our experiences undoubtedly shape us and help us to grow, turning us into the people we become. Whilst our experiences make us wiser, the more I learn the more I become aware of how little I really know and how much more there is still to learn. Recognising this is good. It is from this recognition we allow ourselves to refrain from arrogance and remain humble. Arrogance is really self-betrayal; as it severs our desire to learn in the belief we know it all already. I try to remain humble but on the flip-side of the coin I still manage to give myself a pat on the back when I have done well or achieved an all-important goal. As important as it is to refrain from arrogance, it is also important to recognise what your talents are and when you are doing well in life. Life's tests can be hard enough, without creating the added dimension of an internal battle with yourself on top of everything else. Remember to praise yourself for your good deeds.

So why do bad things happen to good people? If God made the world so only good things happened to the good and bad to the bad at all times, His existence would be unquestionable. This would result in taking free will away; as people would of course only ever do good deeds if they felt there was a benefit at the end. But is that really what should govern a good deed? Of course not, which is why I would argue bad things happen to good people too. I believe when you carry out a good deed you get good back from it anyhow; as it makes you feel better and results in you becoming a better person. It also affects how people view you, as true beauty comes from within. The exact opposite is also true of when someone carries out a bad act. I guess this is ultimately the essence of karma.

This notion is something I wholeheartedly believe. If you think about it, it actually makes perfect sense. For example, if you are kind to people, then normally people will want to respond to you with kindness in return. So good comes back to you as a response to your behaviour. Of course the opposing is also true if you behave in an unkind fashion to those around you. This is Karma working at its most base level. The perfect ideal to aim for of course is true altruism; where you are not carrying out a deed to win a return but this does make me question whether there is such a thing as real altruism however, as even doing something good to attain the good feeling you get from it is reaping some reward. I guess that is not so bad but ultimately the goal should be to aim to do the good deed anyhow; aside from the good feeling you might get from doing it.

Whilst it remains true that real altruism is to give without wanting anything back, I am not suggesting it is such a terrible thing to enjoy the good feeling one derives from giving. Not wanting to appear a martyr here but I do try and give to charity even when I'm on my last dime of the week and yes, it does make me feel good. I feel it is so important to remain aware there are always others less fortunate than us and, not that I wish to diminish any one person's own battles; as everyone's problems are relative to their own circumstances and just as real to them as the next person but it is nevertheless also important to remind ourselves even if we don't have as much as we would like to have in our lives, we still have so much more than the homeless man on the street or the child living in a third world country. If I can help even a little to change these people's situation for the better, then why shouldn't it make me feel good knowing I am doing something in the world to help others. The thought of people who are less fortunate than me never fails but to place things directly into perspective in my own life and immediately ceases me from embarking upon any complaining mission I may be about to commence. I try and remind myself continually we all have all we need from God. I can't begin to pretend to understand why the next man should be homeless instead of me; perhaps that is in man's hands to change rather than the hands of God but I do try and remind myself every day how fortunate and privileged I am to have a roof over my head, my good health, wonderful family and good friends.

74

So think back to when bad things have happened to you in your life. You've managed to get through them somehow haven't you? Else you wouldn't still be here reading this book. I truly believe God only puts us through the things we need to go through to get us to where we need to be in life. Yes, sometimes the things we go through hurt and are a struggle we feel we could do without but you know something? God only gives us what He knows we can handle and let's face it, the results are always sweeter when you have had to earn them the hard way.

When I talk about myself, you'll notice I don't call myself a 'survivor'. For me that would signify defeat and is a negative outlook. Although I have at times indeed felt like I was the only survivor of a sinking ship; barely keeping my head above water, I prefer to not overly use the word 'survivor'. I feel the word can hold negative connotations and I prefer to use words in life which help me achieve a positive outlook. I try and hold onto the idea the tests I have been faced with are indeed sent to me straight from God, then truly there is no such thing as a survivor, as these tests were always meant for me to work through anyhow.

I often ask myself; what would I do if I saw Lileth or any of the other Birchington bullies now? Would I go back into that child-like mode of feeling victimised once more or perhaps show-off some of my newly found fancy martial arts moves? I wouldn't do either. I would probably shake Lileth firmly by the hand and thank her for turning me into the tower of strength I have become. I would tell her how my new found strength has over the years allowed me to aid many victims of bullying in the schools I have taught in and how my new inner-strength has helped me to help them get through the trauma they have faced at the hands of people like her.

*One thought can change your destiny.* - Emma Fletcher

# 4

# Enter Supergirl

**If there is no struggle, there is no progress.**
- Frederick Douglas

*Paul: The next stage of Emma's childhood was to see her joining an all girls' school. Here, valuable, sometimes painful lessons would be learnt in a high-pressured environment and puberty would be experienced. As a result, as one will soon discover, those around Fletcher were to discover she was developing both a high degree of competitiveness and rebellion. And, never far away, we are reminded of her strong desire to understand the world around her by expressing herself creatively through the means of music and art.*

Emma: At the age of 12 I started attending South Hampstead High School for girls. I recall the eldest daughter of the Drummond family once again taunting me a lot about why I was going to a private school and calling me a snob on a regular basis. Her favourite thing to say whenever I visited her family home was: 'New shoes again?' The irony was, I was usually wearing the same shoes upon every visit, whilst she indeed looked as if she were wearing new shoes every time! Mum and dad had decided once again to place me in a private Public Day School, as they felt I had been through enough heartache and bullying in my life and felt this school would perhaps provide a safer environment for me. It probably did. I recall another member of the Drummond family also saying to me: 'If the local state school is good enough for my children, then why doesn't Vera think it is good enough for you? I never went to a private school!' (Ironically, another member of the Drummond household had made similar jibes to my paternal grandparents when I started taking horse-riding lessons; one of my few joys in life at this time was also to become criticised.) I don't think this relative ever really made any attempt to consider the anxiety I had experienced in my life. I had nevertheless sat an entrance exam to South Hampstead and, as I had come in the top five of the highest results, I had been awarded a semi-scholarship for my achievement. In this regard, my parents received a reduced fees award, which helped them greatly.

South Hampstead was the top of the league tables throughout the entire time I was there. (But I can't take all the credit!) It was a tough school both emotionally and educationally speaking. Being a South Hampstead girl was hard work! If your top button was undone you could be sent home. If you didn't maintain straight 'A's all throughout the year you were at risk of being expelled. The teachers even used to give the girls underwear checks during the start of games lessons once a week; to ensure we were wearing the correct blue school uniform knickers! I am sure this practice would be highly illegal now. I recall there was one rather naughty girl, whom upon being asked in the 'knicker line-up' to raise her skirt, raised it high above her shoulders to reveal she was in fact wearing no knickers at all! How all the girls laughed!

Once again I found myself feeling a bit of a loner at school. Whilst I was extremely popular and made friends easily, I did not really feel there were many people at this school who really understood me. They had all come from highly privileged backgrounds and were in a completely different head-space emotionally to me. In the first year of high school I was starting to go through emotional changes. I started to hate the way I looked. Added to this, mum had always been ultra concerned with my appearance to the point of becoming somewhat obsessive about it. Whenever she saw me she would say 'Tuck your ears in; they are sticking out! Bite your bottom lip in; it's too big! I want to see more curls around your face' and as I used to feel my neck was too long, I used to hunch my head forward to disguise its length, (this was completely knocked out of me at acting school!) so mum's favourite line was: 'Stop slouching and sit up straight!' I was also very skinny as a young girl and into my teenage years, to the point some people believed I was anorexic. (I never was anorexic but many of the upsetting events I faced during my childhood often left me with no appetite and I often found I lost interest in my food altogether whenever I became upset, preferring instead to focus on my spiritual needs rather than physical comforts such as food.) As a child and indeed all the way into my teenage years I was convinced I looked like a cross between a giraffe and a platypus! I knew mum's intentions were nevertheless always good and really she loved me unconditionally and would have done absolutely anything for me. This was, however, just an old fashioned way of her expressing her love towards me. Despite this, mum would also always end her comments with 'You will be the belle of the ball' whenever I walked out the door.

I have, however, from a young age never been able to look at myself in the mirror without seeing someone ugly staring back. I suffer with a mild form of Body Dysmorphia, which also surmounts to not being able to take a compliment or believe people when they tell me I look nice and I have certainly found it very hard over the years to love myself in this way. I have never really liked the reflection starring back at me in the mirror. I still see that unhappy teenager who was once skin and bone and hated the way she looked. I am not that child anymore and yet I still find it very hard to look in the mirror without focusing on the parts of my body I wish I could change. The only parts of my body I have ever really been happy with are my feet. I've always thought they were my best 'feeture'!

I do not, however, blame mum's over concern about my appearance for this condition in fact, au contraire; the experts would argue it is because I was rejected by my maternal mother as a baby and not held in her arms or given constant praise by her that this condition developed. Some might even argue it is possible these feelings manifested due to the way certain members of my family made me feel over the years. Correction. No one can make you feel anything you don't want to feel but perhaps these feelings I hold about myself are a reaction to the words certain members of my family have said to me over the course of time and are an external reflection of how these words make me feel about myself internally. Although I am not certain as to the reasons why this state of mind has occurred, only as to how it has affected me over the years, I am nevertheless prepared to take ownership over my own feelings and once I was able to accept this was a problem, I was able to try and start to rectify it.

It has indeed taken me many years to accept I suffer from Body Dysmorphia but now that I have admitted it to myself I am starting to deal with it. I admit I still find it difficult even today to look in the mirror without criticising myself; I see the ears, the lip and other areas of my body, which appear distorted to me. It has taken me a long time to get to the point where I am able to receive a compliment or attention for the way I look and even today it still feels a bit uncomfortable to me when someone pays me a compliment. I usually think perhaps they need glasses! Adversly, the opposing is also true however, as if someone critices the way I look it can often have the tendancy to send me straight into a state of paranoia and concern over the part of my body they are criticing and has even resulted in making me doubt my self-worth over the years.

As beauty is really born from within, perhaps this sentiment about myself really stems from a part of me, which has over the years, been made to feel ugly on the inside; as if we don't feel attractive within, then how can we expect to feel attractive on the outside? This sentiment may have formed as a reaction to the way some of my family members treated me over the years and consequently this feeling about the way I look may really be just a reflection as to how their behaviour has made me feel about myself as a person. However, whatever the cause, acceptance and recognition is the first port of change, so I am well on my way to recovery.

Going back to mum briefly, what I want to add here is that despite expressing herself in an old fashioned way, she was nevertheless an inspirational woman, with an amazing sense of humour and we always had a lot of fun together. In fact, mum always told me she was the best friend I would ever have and she was right; alongside dad, she was my best friend. In fact, they were both two of the most amazing people I have ever had the privilege to know. Not one single day passes when I don't think of them or hold their memory dear to my heart. To know them was to love them. Mum was always my bright shinning light and my strength when I was weak but if I needed a hug it was usually dad I went to, as he was usually the more demonstrative of the two. It was however, this very same sense of humour which quickly made mum friends with all who met her and this great love for life which helped her to get though the many tragedies she faced in life as a tower of strength and equally, always providing strength for the rest of the family too during these difficult times.

Mum would often emphatically relate a humorous story to any situation in an energetic and inspiring manner to brighten the mood. This sense of humour is illustrated in the following story, when as a child I was walking home from Wembley Park tube station with mum. It was a nice sunny day and she transiently stopped in the street and said: 'Emma, let me show you something my mum used to do.' I was intrigued. 'What?' I asked. 'Look up towards the sky and keep looking.' 'Well, what are we looking at?' I asked. 'Nothing,' mum replied 'Just keep looking,' she continued. Then she started pointing and saying: 'Oh, look at that! What is it?' Gradually a crowd of people started to gather round us, wondering what we were looking at and all started to stare up at the sky towards where we were looking with great interest. Then, when mum was content with the amount of attention we were receiving she said: 'Come along Emma,' took my hand and we walked off. When we had been walking a short distance, she stopped, turned around, laughed and said: 'Look, they are all still there, starring at nothing!' She was a real character and had such a terrific personality. You really couldn't fail to love her.

In fact mum had such a terrific personality and powerful presence that over the years many of my friends would often ring up the house in Wembley not to speak to me but to share long conversations with mum instead. They loved to talk to her and she loved talking! She particularly loved telling all her fascinating anecdotes; collected from her experiences over the war years. Mum would also enjoy telling me her little anecdotes of all the various famous people she had dated or had been friendly with. Amongst the list was one of the Hilton brothers, Isaac Leslie Hore-Belisha; the man who invented the Belisha beacon and a famous boxer who lived in Wembley, all of whom mum had dated. She was also friendly with Arnold Diamond and had met Max Bygraves and had numerous interesting stories to relate about all her encounters with each.

Mum would tell me about the Thomas family we were related to, who were in her day well-known theatre producers. She would fondly relate all her little theatre anecdotes and how she used to visit the actors back-stage in their glorious make-up and costumes. Mum also informed me we were at one stage related to Steven Spielberg via his first wife, Amy Irving. She always used to say when I started to show a keen interest in acting, 'One day I must ring up that side of the family in America and try and get you an introduction to Steven.' Amy and Steven got divorced and this never happened - but not to worry, I'm still working on that one myself!

Dad also had a great sense of humour and he and I always used to create cheerful banter around the house together. One day a small fluffy toy, which was basically a cotton bud with moving eyes, arrived in the post with some junk mail. We thought this was the funniest thing we had ever seen. From that day on, dad and I would take turns in hiding this object around the house in the most ridiculous places for the other person to find. I think that ball of fluff turned up in socks, wallets, jacket pockets, video cases, you name it we hid it there! I still have this two-eyed character today. It's funny the things we turn into sentimental value.

Around the age of 12 and during my first year at South Hampstead, I started to feel a strong desire to want to change my appearance, as it reminded me too much of my past. I started to straighten my hair to loose my childlike curls. I looked in the mirror and started to hate the Jewish identity that was starring back at me. To date all my Jewish identity had managed to achieve in my life was acute heartache and upset, not to mention physical abuse. Then it suddenly occurred to me; I didn't look particularly Jewish, with my golden locks passed on to me from my father (Martin was very blonde as a child) and fine features like my mother, plus I didn't act in a particularly Jewish manner and my

81

parents did not have much affiliation with Judaism; any affiliation they had previously held had been clearly knocked out of them by the war – so I denounced my Jewish heritage on the spot.

It was the primetime of Madonna's music and the crucifix had become a fashion item and so, to my parents' dismay, I started to wear a crucifix around my neck. This was however, fairly short lived, as one day standing in line for school dinner, a girl standing beside me called; well actually this girl had changed her name so many times, no one was really sure what to call her any more, abruptly turned to me and pointing said: 'See that girl over there, I don't like her. She is Jewish.' All at once the memory of Lileth and her group of friends came flooding back as I turned swiftly to this girl and said: 'Do you like me?' to which she replied: 'Of course,' I continued: 'Well, I am Jewish.' I will never forget her response: 'You can't be Jewish, you're too nice!' I informed her this was not a compliment but I never wore the crucifix again and I started to realise that to wear a crucifix you have to earn that right. I didn't believe I had earned that right in any way and I certainly did not want to disrespect any other religion because of my confusion with my own identity. From then on I stopped believing in God and decided I hated God, so therefore there was no God. I failed to see my logic was flawed and that in order to hate something, there must be something there to hate.

Also during my first year at high school, I had another one of my peculiar spiritual experiences. Waiting by the front door of a friend's house to be collected by dad after a birthday party, one of the other girls in a playful frame of mind, thought it would be funny to squash me between the door and the wall behind it, which I was leaning on. Unbeknownst to both this girl and myself, the wall I was leaning on was in fact an open door to a cellar beneath the house. On this occasion the door was unlocked. I fell backwards down a very steep flight of stairs. Everything that occurred next felt to me as if it were happening once again in slow motion. Thud. Thud. Thud. What was that noise? It soon became apparent it was the sound of my head hitting every stone step on the way down in my fall.

The entire story of *Alice in Wonderland* popped into my head! I reached the rabbit hole in the story and saw a light at the end of the tunnel. I climbed up through the tunnel and came to a grass field with beautiful flowers and luminous colours like I had never seen before. The field stretched as far as the eye could see. My father, Martin, was standing in the distance. He walked toward me and beckoned me over. I ran up to him shouting with joy 'Martin, Martin, I thought you were dead!' With no words he placed his hand on my shoulder and turned me round. Suddenly, it was just as if I were standing in front of myself; only I was looking at myself as a young child. I watched myself grow up through the ages. Then Martin turned me round to face him and said 'You have to go back.' I remember saying 'I don't want to go back, I want to stay here with you.' Out of nowhere, something pulled me backwards and fast; back down the rabbit hole and then rapidly I was bolting awake with my head jerking upwards and gasping for air. Dad was standing over me with tears in his eyes. Everyone was crying. The young girl whose birthday party it was exclaimed 'We thought you were dead.' Dad informed me I had been unconscious for half an hour and the paramedics were on their way. He had not been able to feel a pulse for the last ten minutes of me being unconscious. For a couple of seconds I could not move my body, which scared everyone but not me. A complete calm came over my entire being and I felt no fear. I knew everything would be okay. I leapt up from the ground like a wild animal, feeling no pain anywhere, hugged my dad and said 'I want to go home now please'. So we did.

I later discovered this episode was akin to that experienced by many people, who have been the receivers of NDEs (Near Death Experiences). After this experience, I found myself to be completely unafraid of death; feeling I had been privy to experiencing something on a different plane and perhaps had even taken a glimpse into something far removed from this existence.

By the commence of the second year of high school I had started a heavy fascination with Marilyn Monroe. I felt complete affinity with what she had been through in her young life. Whilst all the other students were listening to the latest music trends, I was busily focusing all my energies on Monroe's films or reading books about her life. I also started to listen to Elvis Presley's music and reading and also closely studying the contents of books on Einstein's analysis of theoretical physics and Sigmund Freud's studies of schizophrenia; the latter in my attempt to try and understand Claudia's condition better.

Claudia's condition had sadly taken a turn for the worse again and by my first year of my new high school, I had not seen Claudia for nearly a year. Unbeknownst to me, as mum so desperately wanted to keep me sheltered from the reality of the situation, in the belief this would be for my best, I was unaware Claudia was sadly during this time spending many of her days in clinics to aid her back to health. I was allowed to visit Claudia on one occasion only during this time, with mum and dad present, probably during a period she was not at her worst. I was however too young to really understand what the nature of the place I was visiting was. During that year I missed Claudia terribly and felt very rejected by her lack of contact, even believing perhaps I had done something wrong to cause this. As an adult I am now able to reflect back on this with the realisation Claudia did not abandon me, she was at the time battling a terrible illness but as a child I did not understand this or how severe it had become. Claudia's deteriorating health had a strong impact on mum and caused her to become very over-protective of me and overly cautious of everything I did; as she would often comment she was worried I would become ill like Claudia. Sometimes her concern even caused me to worry about this too.

So now into the second year of high school, I started to spend a lot of time by myself; writing poems or painting. I found these two activities to be a perfect way to release my internal frustrations and turmoil about life and as such they started to serve as a direct emotional response to these difficulties. In fact, during my first year at South Hampstead, I had entered myself into a poetry competition as part of the Guildhall Speech and Drama award and found myself winning my first ever drama-related award. By my second year of school I had soon picked up pen and paper and started writing a series of heartfelt lyrics with accompanying melody lines to my own songs. My writing pen soon became my trusty companion and attached firmly to my hip.

So music, along with my joy for poetry and painting, became my only other outlet for releasing my emotions and expressing my internal conflicts. I wrote a number of different songs, ranging in a variety of styles. I was still influenced by Soul, Rhythm and Blues but now Funk and Jazz had finally found there way into my large rostra of records too, although eventually I found the style that suited my voice best was guitar based pop.

So whilst all the other kids of my age were busy getting their heads together to discuss the latest news and headlines on the current heart-throb, I was busily shutting myself away in my bedroom for hours on end, completely immersing myself in dissecting and studying the framework of the music of these very same stars; working out all the different ways to structure and break-up a song and write a melody line. Both sets of my grandparents realised my developing interest in music and clubbed together to buy me a piano. This became my treasured and prized item. I started to carry out piano lessons at school but found piano was not really my 'forte!' Although I still used my pianoforte to help me write a melody line and find the correct pitch, my voice was my best instrument and it was this I relied upon the most to help me create my songs. I soon discovered I had perfect pitch and this asset greatly helped me to move forward in this quest. Around this time I also formed a keen interest in the BBC television series *Rock School* and used to sit avidly hanging on every word the resident guitarist Henry Thomas would say. Henry Thomas would guide the viewer through a 'how to write music' lesson every week, which proved extremely useful for my growing interest in writing my own songs.

As my love for music developed I recall so did my interest in dancing. I used to dance around my parent's front living room or my bedroom on many an occasion, to the weekly hits on the radio. I would dance around like a little firefly and literally go wild! Dancing is an expression of life. The acting coach and Hollywood producer and director Bernard Hiller recently said to me, how someone dances is an expression of how they live; in other words are they really alive or just existing? On the opposite end of the spectrum, dad used to play his chamber music all the time when I was growing-up. It used to echo around the house continually. When I used to lock myself away in my room or dance around the living room listening to pop music, I think this was also partly a rebellion to this, although I have since formed a love affair with classical music.

Always with an outwardly happy disposition, I would usually walk around the school humming or singing to myself. People started to refer to me as 'the little songbird'. They could not have held any idea of the torment I was hiding inside and how I would spend most nights feeling alone and crying myself to sleep. I was searching for answers; I was looking for excitement, anything to help me forget my young troubles.

It was around this time I befriended Sky. I first met Sky when we were in the playground at South Hampstead High. She came over to me and playfully pushed me off a climbing frame I was happily sitting on. 'Bet you can't catch me!' she said. Well this was like a red rag to a bull and little fast legs here proceeded to chase her across the length of the school grounds and do just that! Sky was impressed and at that very moment a close bond was formed. Sky was however, the ultimate rebel without a cause. She caused havoc around the school on a daily basis and eventually started to get heavily into drugs. To me she was nevertheless, exciting although I never followed her down the drug route.

Sky, three other girls and I decided to form a band whilst at school. There was a pianist, violinist, base player, Sky as the guitarist and myself as the vocalist and songwriter. The band was however, short-lived and eventually Sky and I decided to form a duo. We became known around the school by our friends as the 'dynamic duo' and called our band the even less original name of Flaire; a combination of both my fellow band member's surname mixed with mine.

One of my great uncles; Ivor Troostwyk, who is sadly no longer with us, used to run a very famous recording studio in Camden in London, where all the top stars, including George Michael and the band Duran Duran, would record their music. Just like mum, Ivor had a terrific sense of humour. (Ivor and his wife Hilda and mum and dad were the best of friends). Ivor would walk into a room and say things like: 'Is it me, or is that picture tipsy?' Then he would go over to a perfectly straight painting and move it into a lopsided position, just for the fun of it! Uncle Ivor suggested if we were to lay down a track on tape, he would kindly pass it on to a top producer named Dennis Weinreich, with the idea of getting both Sky and myself into the studio to record our song professionally with him at a later stage.

After controlling a serious fit of giggles, Sky and I recorded the only song I had written at that point in time and I then passed it on to uncle Ivor the next time I saw him. Dennis had apparently by this point been asking if we were ready yet to let him have any material, expressing in good nature how he was looking forward to hearing our sound. The week we waited for feedback from Dennis felt like a decade, as we sat by the telephone patiently waiting for it to ring. Finally there it was. The telephone rang. Mum called out to me it was uncle Ivor with news from the studio. I rushed to the telephone and excitedly grabbed it out of mum's hand and spoke hurriedly down the receiver. 'Well, what did he say?' Uncle Ivor continued in a very serious tone, 'Dennis said, thank you very much for the tape but the next time you send him something, would you mind awfully checking first to see the tape is not blank!' I was so embarrassed. We had sent Dennis a completely blank tape. After this, although both uncle Ivor and Dennis did indeed ask us to resend the song, I never quite got round to it and, if the truth be told I didn't really see myself as a rock star anyhow. I had always had my heart set on being an actress - playing out someone else's life had always seemed much more appealing to me than living my own chaos. Reflecting back, it is probably just as well the tape was blank as the song *My Boy* was my first attempt at writing anything and, whilst it was aimed at sounding like Chuck Berry's *Riding Along in my Automobile*; to be

87

fair it probably sounded more like something fit for a children's daytime show!

Around this time I befriended a lovely girl at school named Tina Loucaides, who was in the parallel class in my year. Tina was always such a kind and friendly soul and took a great interest in my music. She was the first person I played my song *My Boy* to. Being the song was a very unsuccessful attempt at being cool, Tina did extremely well not to laugh and kept a perfectly straight face when she heard it played back. Her straight face was to be commended even more in the knowledge she was used to hearing demos of new songs; Tina's first cousin is the highly successful songwriter George Michael.

Another of my close friends at school was the harpist, Rivka Gottleib. Even from a young age, Rivka was becoming very well known for her extremely gifted talent at playing the harp and would carry weekly recitals to acclaimed audiences. She was so dedicated to her craft and would spend many hours during lunch and in between classes fine-tuning her skill. Her dedication was incredible to watch and it made me realise; if one is to succeed at their dream then a great deal of hard work is required.

Also during my junior years at South Hampstead both Helena Bonham Carter and Sarah Patterson were entering their senior years at the school. They had been discovered there by talent scouts, who had previously come to visit the school. I remember how both girls would be taken out of school for film work and would later come back to school again after shooting was complete to a lot of deserved attention. It was an exciting time for both the girls and the school. I so wanted to be like them. South Hampstead is known for a number of notable alumnae to have studied on the premises including; English painter Flora Twort, classical and contemporary pianist Joanna MacGregor, crime-writer ECR Lorac, singer and songwriter Lynsey de Paul, authors Fay Weldon, Antonia Forest and Naomi Alderman, model Daisy Lowe, actress Angela Lansbury and politicians Lynne Featherstone and Baroness Birk to name but a mere few.

Michael Jackson was another of my childhood heroes. Growing up in a show business family, I have never once really become star-struck in my life but I think had I of been given the chance to meet Michael Jackson, he is the one person that would probably have succeeded in bawling me over and would have sent tingles down my spine. I can honestly say I was really heartbroken when I learnt of his death. The only other time I have felt this saddened by the untimely passing of a well-known figure was the day I learnt of Princess Diana's death. The day Michael Jackson's death was announced on the news, Mark Summers, who was working closely with Michael Jackson on casting *This is It* and also Rabbi Shumuley Boteach, a close friend of Jackson, both sent out individual emails in response to their grief. I was one of the recipients of these emails. This was enough to start the tears rolling. Receiving such personal heartfelt communication from two people who knew Michael Jackson on a personal level sent me into floods of tears and I don't think I stopped crying for at least a week.

During my second year of high school, with high ambitions now kicking in, I entered a dance competition. I learnt the entire routine for Michael Jackson's *Thriller* and won the competition. This put the noses out of joint of a couple of girls who had also entered the competition and for an entire year after, they made life very difficult for me whenever they saw me around or outside the school, even starting fights in the playground between my circle of friends and myself. I could not believe I was being bullied once again. One day, when I was about 13, one of the girls grabbed my shoulder from behind my back, as I was about to step down the stairs and deliberately tried to push me down the flight of stairs. I had over the years trained myself to become quite alert and aware of my surroundings and I immediately and instinctively swung round, grabbed the girl's arm and hoisted her high up into the air. These two girls never bothered me again after this time.

Incidentally, I recently auditioned for a spot on the *MTV Awards*, for what was to be a tribute to Michael Jackson's life. I found myself auditioning alongside some of Michael Jackson's dancers from his previous tours and once again found I was being asked to carry out a dance routine to *Thriller*. Even to be standing alongside these guys who had worked with Michael Jackson still managed to give me a little bit of a tingle.

In the latter part of my second year at high school, the headteacher announced the school was hiring a drama teacher and that students may apply to take drama lessons as an extra-curricular activity. Mum and dad agreed I could enrol in these classes. This was not so much an attempt to encourage my burning desire to become a budding actress but Miss Hart, the drama teacher at the school, was also giving speech lessons. My parents felt this would be a perfect opportunity to help me get rid of my weak 'r' and the slight nervous falter in my speech I had developed. They also felt the classes might serve to bring little shy Emma out of her shell.

As you can imagine, I immediately jumped on the bandwagon of joining a drama group and soon found myself excelling in class. I applied to be one of the lucky few to attend a short drama course at London's famous Central School of Speech and Drama and was accepted onto the course. Once a week, over the course of the next term, I found myself learning a variety of different drama skills; such as the all-important pretending to be a tree blowing in the wind routine. I must admit to being guilty as charged as to finding these type of exercises a tad bizarre; although acting like a tree became part and parcel in my endeavour to become a fine actor in my training at acting school some years later! These drama lessons during high school did, however, start to help build my confidence and enable me to find the ability to stand up in front of my year group and deliver prose with confidence and clarity and for once not eat my words in the process. They also reawakened my childhood passion for acting.

Now 13 and enjoying the summer holidays at home and with the local neighbours' children, I distinctly recall one day playing in the garden of my next-door neighbours home, when suddenly there was a knock on the door. Dad had come over to collect me, informing me Claudia had arrived unannounced at the house with Trevor and was very keen to see me. I had at this point in time not seen Claudia for two years and cried with sheer delight when the news reached my ears. I ran back home as fast as my legs would carry me and straight into Claudia's arms. She looked different from how I remembered her. Gone were her dark locks, now replaced with dyed blonde hair and she was wearing a ring on every finger.

Claudia had bought me a gift of a dress, which she immediately tried to squeeze me into. The dress she had purchased was however, suitable for an 11 year old, the age I had been when she had last seen me. My body shape had changed and there was no way I was getting into that dress but Claudia persisted and kept trying to squeeze the small neck opening over my head. With the eventual realisation there was to be no success with her mission, Claudia took one of the rings off from her finger and gave this to me instead. The ring had a silver motif in the shape of an apple, to represent the apple of life. I placed it on my finger and wore it continually. I of course still cherish this ring to this day. The experience of Claudia trying to squeeze me into a clearly undersized dress was the first time I had ever seen a slightly manic side of Claudia but sadly was not to be the last, as I bore witness to her illness manifest itself in a similar manner again a number of times over the years.

In my 14th year uncle Ivor took both my cousin Louise, who was his granddaughter and myself to his hometown in Holland for a couple of weeks vacation. We were to travel to Holland via Ferry. I recall sitting in the bunk with Louise for an entire hour and the two of us complaining how seasick we felt. Uncle Ivor kept knocking on our cabin door to say 'We'll be there soon!' After a number of appearances, uncle Ivor finally knocked on our cabin door one last time to a synchronized reception of 'Are we there yet?' Unexpectedly uncle Ivor gave out one of his tremendous laughs. 'There yet?' he repeated. 'We haven't even left the dock!' and it was true, we hadn't. As it happens the rest of the journey wasn't too bad and the seas were fairly calm, which was lucky, as I have always suffered from motion sickness. Indeed, I used to be terrified of travelling as a passenger in Mr Drummond's car as, in my opinion, he would drive like a lunatic and swerve round corners and I used to get terribly scared.

During the couple of weeks we stayed in Holland, uncle Ivor took Louise and me to a little café in the centre of Amsterdam. As he left the table to pay a visit to the little gentlemen's room he said: 'Whatever you do, watch out. They lace your drinks here!' He was of course joking but to two teenage girls, this meant business. Here we were in the centre of Amsterdam, notorious for all its drugs and uncle Ivor had just said the two magic words: 'Watch out!' The waitress came over to take our order. 'Two hot chocolates please' we said. 'Certainly girls,' she responded. The waitress soon brought over our piping hot drinks, which were bubbling over the top with froth. 'Can we have some sugar please?' we asked. The waitress brought over a little silver container, complete with white powder inside. We poured the sugar into our mugs and started to drink. Then as teenage girls do, we started to get very excited, as we began to wonder if the substance she had given us was in fact sugar at all. We poured some of the contents of the little silver container into our hands. It wasn't granulated sugar. What was it? Was it baking sugar? Or was it some sort of drug? The waitress came over to check everything was okay. We asked her to bring the packaging of the sugar to us immediately. A strange request, she clearly must have thought but nevertheless obliged. On the side of the packaging read the words 'Droog bewaaren'. 'Droog bewaaren! Droog bewaaren!' We repeated aloud. That was it. 'Drugs beware!' We started to shriek in shrill high-pitched voices. 'We've been drugged, we've been drugged!' At that very same moment uncle Ivor made his return to the table. 'You've been what?' he said in his strong Dutch accent. 'Our drinks have been spiked! Nicki Finned! Doped!' we continued. 'Look!' we said now pointing ferociously at the packaging: 'Droog bewaaren!' Uncle Ivor gave out another of his loud raucous laughs and said 'Droog bewaaren' means... to be kept in a cool, dry place!

Another year on and once more it was time for another summer holiday. I recall this time going on an adventure holiday with the school to the Lake District. During this holiday I won my second dance award for coming first in a dance competition. Being the competitive creature I was, I was always first to volunteer my services; abseiling, paragliding, windsurfing - you name it; I was always first in line! We were given rowboats, two or three to a boat and shown how to use the paddles. Finally we were set free on the Lake. Sky and I, the dynamic duo, rowed out as far as we could in an almost feral manner. Half an hour away from shore, we looked round and realised no one else from our group was in sight. Unbeknownst to us, a Gale Force 9 wind was on the horizon and all the other boats, which had stayed nearer to shore, had already been beckoned out of the waters. The winds arrived and tipped our boat upside down and immediately we went under the water. From a young age I have always coped well in crisis situations, today would be no different. The winds, now fierce, continued as I felt myself sinking slowly into the extremely cold and choppy lake. Although shocked at unexpectedly being turned over and now starring up at the underside of the boat, I managed to keep a lid on my fear of being under the water and regained my calm in my endeavour to make my way back to the surface.

I swam out from under the boat. Sky was no longer visible, she had frozen from fear under the water. I dove back under the boat and in auto-pilot mode, grabbed her and pulled her out - quite a feat for someone who is afraid to put their head under water. I clambered on top of the now upside down boat and pulled Sky up with me. Suddenly in the distance I heard someone crying for help. Another boat with three of our friends had also turned over and they were paddling ferociously in the water. I jumped back into the water and told Sky to stay where she was. I swam up to the girls and dragged them back to our boat one by one through the water. I told everyone to hold onto the edge of our boat for dear life and paddle back to shore as fast as we could. Sky slid back into the water and grabbed the side of the boat; we all paddled as fast as humanly possible back to shore. We were picked up half way by a rescue boat and when we finally reached land everyone praised me for my bravery but all of a sudden my body went into shock and I could not move or speak for the next few hours. Being out of control of my body but with my mind still active was one of the strangest experiences I have ever felt and I did not like it. Not one little bit.

A year later and I was already proving myself to be the fastest runner in my year once again and a number of years down the line, the fastest runner in the school. I was now also the captain of both the netball and rounder's teams and good at gymnastics, due to having slight hypermobility, which basically means rather flexible; all of which increased my popularity amongst the other girls in my year. Although I was popular at school, I still felt like an outsider, as I was different due to my personal circumstances. As I have mentioned before, popularity can and usually is built upon a set of very transient and superficial ideologies. My popularity was no different. In my case I was popular with the boys because they thought I was cute, which also strangely increased my popularity with the girls too. Being the captain of the sport's teams, the games teacher would give me the unenviable task of choosing my own team members. This was a job I did not enjoy carrying out. One by one myself and whoever else was chosen to head the opposing team, were all forced to make the choice of who would be on our team. As hard as this is for the people being picked, believe me, it was equally as hard to be the one doing the picking. I didn't like the thought there would be one person left at the end who had not been picked by either team leader and would be made to feel like a complete failure. So when it got down to the last few people I used to refuse to pick any further; forcing the teacher to pick the rest of the team for me instead. Reflecting back now, I'm not sure which was the worse of the two evils for the poor victims left.

Every week we would all take the long fifteen-minute walk to the school's sports ground during our lunch break. The sports teacher used to promise each week that different girls could take a ride with her in the little 10-seater mini-bus the school had provided. So many times she promised Sky and myself a ride but never carried out her promise. One day Sky said to me, 'You're a fast runner Emma. Run back to the school and I bet you will still get there before the bus does!' That day I ran as fast as my legs would carry me. It felt like I was riding the wind. I did indeed get back to the school before the bus arrived. When the bus finally pulled in to the school drive I was standing at the entrance with a cheeky grin on my face and my arms folded in a signature pose of triumph. Both the sports teacher and my classmates were amazed and could not understand how this had happened, especially as the roads had been clear of traffic. From this day on some of the girls at the school started to fondly give me the nickname 'Supergirl,' which always embarrassed me; especially as if the truth be known, I've always seen myself as more of a Clark Kent-type of character; bumbling and fumbling but always getting the job done! (As it happens, I had always been a fan of the *Superman* character created by Jerry Siegel and Joe Shuster, not for his heroism but had always felt an affinity with the character for the fact he grew up with older parents and felt different to other people around him; alien and alone).

This nickname however, stuck with me throughout my school years due to a number of other strange occurrences which happened around me. There was the time I managed to open a window in the school that had not been opened for literally years, as it had been stuck solid and no one had been able to open it - this freaked me out; even if only a little. Then there was the time I could smell gas during the start of the Science class and no one else could smell it. No one believed me, not even the Science teacher. She asked two of the 'more sensible girls' to move around the class and see if there was a gas tap which had been left on. They could not see any tap on. She then asked the class if anyone could smell gas - no one could. I could not understand this; as to me the smell was so strong. As she held a match in her hand to continue the demonstration of her experiment I begged her to hold it away from her face. Thankfully she listened, as the flame, which followed was large. The shocked teacher immediately instructed me to find the gas leak. Like a sniffer dog I went straight to the leaking tap.

There were also around three separate occasions I was able to hear with accuracy conversations people were having in other rooms which were far a field, even whilst the radio was playing loudly in the room I was in - again this also freaked me out - a lot!

Mum was also present during one of these occasions and the experience shocked her too, especially when on each occasion the actual conversation was related back to me by the third party, with complete accuracy to the manner in which I said I had heard it. I also have a rare type of eye-sight called 'hyper latent vision', which means although my vision appears to be 20/20, in fact I am exceedingly long sighted in one eye and should really require glasses to correct this, as my other eye could have the tendency to become lazy. However, me being me, this means I can see very far away and very close up too, without too many real problems. (Having said this, I expect the day will come when I will probably require glasses for this condition). So hence the nickname 'Supergirl' stuck. I firmly believe however, these 'heightened-senses' are mainly a result of my heightened spiritual awareness, a skill I feel we possibly all have lying dormant, just waiting to be reawakened.

The nickname 'Supergirl' did not however, cease to stop me from becoming scared by the event, which occurred next. When I was around 14, I was followed home from school by a stranger. He had followed me to the train station, all the way from school and was watching me throughout the duration of my journey and now he was following me up the street to my house. I started to run. He followed in close pursuit. I approached a bus stop and frantically told the people standing there I was being followed. I begged someone, anyone, to help. No one responded. I ran all the way home with this man in close tow and eventually I lost him. When I finally arrived home and told my parents what had happened they immediately drove me down the road to the local police station. We were then asked to accompany a police officer to the train station to see if we could spot the man. He was now standing outside the entrance to the train station. The police picked him up and drove him away. Later that same day the police informed us they had recently had other complaints about this man and that, although in their opinion he was drunk and pretty harmless, they had been observing him for a while now. The incident of course left me shaken but what left me the most shaken was how no one had stepped forward to offer to help me. I promised myself after this incident if I ever saw someone in trouble I would not be the type of person to just standby and watch. Over the years since this time, call me crazy but I have stepped in and helped people on a number of occasions when I thought they may be in trouble, running to their rescue even, if necessary.

*Paul: Yet another 'Supergirl' moment was fated to come into the life of Emma when she was coming back home after New Year celebrations with a group of around five friends. Emma takes up the story.*

Emma: A fight started out on the bus we were on. We all jumped off except for one girl who was too scared to jump, as the bus had now started to gain momentum. She called out 'Don't leave me', as the bus started to disappear out of sight. Suddenly adrenalin kicked in and I turned to my other three friends and announced I was going to run after the bus. 'Are you mad?' they said. As if this idea was not crazy enough, it had also been snowing and I was wearing heels! But I knew I couldn't leave this girl on the bus on her own. I had chased thieves down the street before now (four times in total to be precise!) surely I could handle a bus with a few idiots on? So, I ran in the deep snow, in my high heels and gave chase from the centre of town all the way to the Finchley Road tube station (which is around four miles). Old sprightly sprint caught up with the bus and stayed with it most of the way! No one on the bus could believe their eyes. The fighting stopped and cheering started. Everyone on the entire bus willed me to keep running. When the bus finally stopped at the tube station everyone started to cheer loudly as I stepped onto the bus and told me I was a real 'Supergirl'!

I am not sure if my actions above surmounted to bravery as so much to recklessness - and God knows, since my father died I became more reckless - but it occurs to me, if more people looked out for one another, then perhaps there might be less victims of crime.

By the time I reached the ninth grade, I started to become more insular, choosing to spend more time alone. I recall just wanting to escape. I felt trapped in that school. It felt oppressive to me. I

97

started to get to know the headmistresses' office like the back of my hand. I wasn't essentially a naughty girl and I was never rude to the teachers; I was just getting in with the wrong crowd and focussing my attentions on the wrong things. I guess my hormones had well and truly started to kick in and were doing overtime! I started to bunk off classes, which reflected in my grades that year. I found myself getting into trouble on a regular basis at school and Wednesday detention at 4:00pm placed itself firmly on my timetable as a regular occurrence, much to mum and dad's despair. My poor parents soon received a letter home about my absences and disassociation. They were so worried. Thankfully I soon started to come out of this phase but it was not until the next year, when my all important GCSE's started, that I completely got myself back on track.

The girls at South Hampstead were informed one day our school was to be entered into a competition about saving energy. The event was set to be hosted by the popular TV presenter Keith Chegwin and the girls were to compete with girls from other schools in the independent GPDST (Girls Public Day School Trust) sector for the title and trophy. Girls were to be selected via an initial test between each year group. Having never been top of my year in high school, although I always worked hard and attained good grades, I decided now was my chance to shine. This was also my chance at trying my hand at working as part of a team and becoming less insular. I spent the next two weeks studying everything there was to know about heat and insulation. Dad had once upon a time practiced as a Chartered Surveyor for Her Majesty's service and knew everything there was to know about land, property and construction, including also being a very talented craftsman himself (Dad had built a number of the pieces of furniture in our home and carried out all the insulation and electric works too), so I also wracked his surveyor brain for any additional information he could impart over and above the information I had already researched for myself. I came top of the class in the race to be entered into the finals and soon found myself on the winning team. My studying for hours over the previous two weeks had paid off and I found I was the fastest on the buzzer with the questions; correctly answering all the questions, no matter how obscure they may be - and they were! I won the title for the school. I recall the rest of the year were so proud of me, they hoisted me up in the air above their shoulders, like a footballer who has just scored that all-important goal in the world cup. It was a great feeling and I didn't want my feet to ever touch the ground again.

I continued to write songs throughout the duration of my school and college career, honing and toning my skill. It was the only past time that succeeded in keeping my spirits high. During college Sky introduced me to a producer at the well-known rock school academy in Holloway she was now attending. Her college made claim to fame as housing one of the biggest and high tech studios of its time. I went into the studio and laid down my first ever professionally recorded track, which was a very high and squeaky version of *Ring My Bell*. Some of the notes were indeed so high, that to an Alto Mezzo voice such as mine, they felt somewhat akin to a catcall!

When I was 16, mum and I were called into a meeting with the headmistress of South Hampstead High. The headmistress didn't mess around and told us that Sky had been expelled, as they believed she was stealing money for her habit and if I didn't pull my socks up I would be out too. Then in a complete 180 oscillation, I was asked what subjects I wanted to study when I entered the Sixth Form of the school. I replied I was considering Art, Drama and English. This didn't go down too well and appeared to aggravate the headmistress, who then told us South Hampstead High was a school, which expected its students to study English, History and a Science. I informed the headmistress I didn't want to study those subjects. I wanted to study Art, Drama and English. By now the headmistress was becoming quite irritated and said: 'If you do not listen to me and take the subjects I have advised you to take, then you will disappear from South Hampstead and vanish into a puff of thin air, like dust - and go puff!' For years afterwards mum and I used to joke about this phrase. Although obviously that is not what happened, else you would not be reading this book right now!

I remember walking out of South Hampstead High that day with mum and her taking me by the hand and asking me if I had made my decision. Did I want to go into the Sixth Form or leave South Hampstead High? I told her I wanted to leave. To my surprise mum replied: 'I now understand why you found this school so oppressive. I think you are making the right decision'. At last she finally understood. However, she only allowed me to leave the school on the condition I carried out a business course at a local college. Once again I received a full-scholarship placement upon entry to the college. It was here I studied accounts and business and learnt to type and carry out shorthand. The course lasted the duration of a year. I completed it with a first class diploma.

Looking back on my South Hampstead days, I can see it was an emotionally charged time for me, although I now realise it was a relatively easy time compared to some of the days that were to follow. As you will shortly discover, I was soon to reach a crossroads in my young life, which was destined to change my life - forever.

*The past is what happened but the present is what counts.* - Emma Fletcher

# 5

# Mind Over Matter

**_Life shrinks or expands in proportion to one's courage._**
- Ariais Nin

*Paul: Popularized decades ago, the well-known phrase 'Mind over Matter' was reportedly originally used in reference to paranormal phenomena. In the case of Emma, one could argue the phrase was surely something she would have subconsciously used in her own life, in order to get through the pain and anguish she was to experience in the coming years. If the early years had presented Fletcher with a series of heartaches that no child should ever experience, then as you will discover, her early adult life was set to bring her the worse yet.*

Emma: At the top of the road near the house I was raised in, is an area known as Barn Hill. This is one of my favourite places on earth, a small pocket of green on the London horizon. If you've ever visited Barn Hill you would understand why. Barn Hill is made up of acres of fields as far as the eye can see, which are thankfully Green Belt government protected land. There is a small pond and a hiking path, which stretches though the woodlands into open fields of green a couple of miles up the road and towards horse-riding stables. The grounds of the stables back onto the land, which was where my father's parents lived. I often used to take this hike from my parents' house to my grandparents and absorb the surrounding beauty.

Growing up in the suburbs I would call myself a country bumpkin at heart but equally, I also like to be near the edge of the city; although I could never live directly in the hub of it. I like to come home at the end of an evening to quiet surroundings and breathe in fresh air.

*Paul: In order to fully understand why this area means such a great deal to Emma, I persuaded her to take us on a car journey to the aforementioned location. Here, I was able to see and take in for myself the full beauty of the area. It was a strange experience for me. Here I was seeing something for the very first time, which I was aware Emma had seen a million times previously, especially during her formative years.*

*Noticeably, Emma was visibly moved as we motored by the house she had lived in, the areas she had played in and the flat her paternal grandparents had lived in. A walk around the pond mentioned above and the land nearby, reminded me that it is more than possible to find relaxing areas of beauty so close to central London.*

*Turning round to look back at the route we have walked towards the pond areas revealed a stunningly impressive view of Wembley Stadium. The legendary towers may have gone as part of the multi-million pound re-build of the iconic stadium, which has been home to British football since 1923, but the new stadium, complete with the large 123 metre-tall arch that dominates the complex, is breathtakingly impressive.*

*I turned to look at Emma and suddenly I could sense a kind of sadness and loss in her. Maybe it was just me imagining it, or maybe it was literally me causing it, but I felt something about the trip down memory lane had produced a host of bitter-sweet memories. I know I appreciated the chance to see this part of Emma's past but I felt hugely-guilty that maybe it had stirred up memories inside her of people and times she missed or wished to forget. I decided not to ask for fear it would upset her any further.*

Emma: The kind neighbours who lived opposite our house in Barn Way as I was growing up were a lovely couple named Irene and Julius Simpson. I spent a lot of time over the years playing in their garden. They became like adopted family to me and were also extremely close to mum and dad. When they finally packed up and moved to Israel I was heartbroken and missed them greatly but mum and dad kept in continued contact with them over the years via a series of letters. They were a glorious older couple. Julius was a somewhat eccentric man with a wonderful story to tell. He always used to spend many fruitful hours entertaining us with his stories about his life. We always thought he should write a book and share his stories with others and eventually he did just that, calling his book *Memoirs of an Old Mancunian: A Jewish odyssey*. Irene and Julius were also partly responsible for being one of my only connections to a proper understanding of Judaism whilst I was growing up.

Because Barn Hill is so picturesque, film and television crews such as the famous Fountain Studios (originally Lee Studios) which was a short walk from our house, would often use it to shoot exterior footage and we would often see them filming at the top of our road. Because of this, I would often ride my bike up there with my cousin Sam to watch them filming. Sam and I both thoroughly enjoyed spying on the filming process and eventually Sam went on to carry out some extra work on the ever-popular television series *Grange Hill*. I too started to take an avid interest in the process of filming and it always fascinated me greatly glimpsing actors at their craft.

Sam lived in the same street as me when we were growing up, almost a stone's throw in distance. We would play together without fail every day after school, once homework had been completed. The day was never complete unless Sam and I had linked up for our usual dose of playtime in the street. In fact, at this time the street was lined with kids our age and we could all often be found riding our bikes free-fall down the steep pavement, which ran along the length of the road leading from my parent's house and up towards Barn Hill.

Indeed my cousin Sam and I used to go and sit by the pond whenever we needed to relax or work through life's numerous pressing issues over the years. Sam is the one person in my life who probably knows me better than anyone. We have always had an extremely strong bond; a connection if you will. In fact, Sam and I have the tendency to think so much alike, it is almost as if we were separated at birth! Sam and I have remained close since we were kids and are more like sisters than distant cousins (we are related through marriage. I am also very close to Sam's beautiful daughter Chloe.) Growing-up Sam and I often had sleepovers at one another's houses. We would creep down into our parents' kitchen in the early hours of the night to make ourselves a midnight snack of crisp filled sandwiches. Today whenever we get together, we have still quite often been known to regress and become like children again and usually you can guarantee mayhem and madness will ensue and we both still like our crisp-filled sandwiches!

Unfortunately Sam has also had her fair share of problems to deal with over the years but we have always been there for one another, serving each other as a shoulder to cry on or the offer of a warm smile. I can honestly say, Sam and I have never once had a cross word between us. How many people in life can one boast that claim about?

One sunny afternoon, whilst playing in my parent's back garden there came a knock on the door. It was from a director of a large production company, who informed mum and dad his company were planning to film a new high-profile television commercial in the area for British Telecom. This was set to be the start of what was soon to become the hugely popular series of commercials that starred Maureen Lipman as Beattie (BT - geddit?). The director asked us if they could use the front of our house to film some establishing shots of Maureen coming out of the house for the advert. This prompted great excitement and we readily agreed. A filming date was subsequently arranged for the following week. Maureen even sent us a personal message to say she was looking forward to meeting us.

Finally the day of filming arrived and all our excitement suddenly turned to disappointment, as the crew discovered they couldn't manage to get all of their equipment down our part of the road as it was too narrow. In the end they had to use one of the houses at the top of the road instead. I was devastated. I didn't even get to meet Maureen! There is a coda to this story however. Some years later I was introduced to Ms Lipman at the premiere of the movie *The Truth about Cats and Dogs*, via my old pal Albert and was able to relate this story to her. After listening to my story with a smile, Maureen then asked 'Emma, I don't suppose you happen to know where the ladies' toilets are do you?' 'I do,' I replied pointing her in the direction. A little while later, whilst still standing talking with Albert, Maureen approached us both and said 'Albert, my dear friend, your friend Emma here has just directed me to the toilets.' Albert replied in his usual jovial manner 'That's very kind of her,' to which Maureen then replied 'To the men's toilets!' Oh dear! After this, whenever Maureen Lipman saw me at any function she would always come up to me and affectionately say: 'Emma, can you tell me where the ladies is?'

By the age of 14 I had met an enigmatic young man, who for the sake of this book I will refer to as Seb. He was a very handsome and unthreatening sort from a trendy area, in an exciting part of London and was neighbours and friends to the stars. Seb loved the high-life. Over the years he introduced me to many up and coming bright young things and also to well-established stars, such as one of my all time favourite funny men, the inimitable John Cleese. Seb was an exciting young man to be around and this was the first time I had ever had such a huge crush on a boy. I could not get him out of my mind. Seb was in a band, which had successfully attained a great deal of interest from the highly sought out record label EMI Records. He often used to play me a sample of his latest recordings and talk to me in great detail about the music industry. In fact it was Seb who helped heightened my awareness of the 'who's who?' side of the industry.

Seb and I stayed friends over the years but he never once made a move on me and would often say: 'What would you say if I told you I was gay?' My response always remained the same: 'Tell me and let's see what happens,' but he never did tell me. I recall the day Seb informed me he was going to live in America. I was devastated but the truth is he probably did me a huge favour. By the age of 14 my hormones had well and truly kicked in and I found the idea of boys was now becoming the constant attention of my focus. I started to attend many parties with my young friends in my attempt to meet a nice young man.

Whilst at one particular party I went to around this time with my cousin Sam, dancing hormones must have been on the mind of one drunken guy who decided to follow me into the bathroom. I'd only met him briefly but he appeared interested. He closed the door and locked it behind him. By now I was a little worried but on this occasion fate was on my side. Trying to be Mr Cool, he attempted to impress me with some fancy chat and made it clear what he was hoping would happen. I made it completely clear I wasn't interested and wanted him to let me out. He playfully refused but I said if he didn't change his mind I would scream, loudly! He seemed confused as to why I didn't want him. Men! Still trying to act like some kind of stud, the guy brushed one of his hands through his hair and went to lean on the wall beside him but as luck would have it, it wasn't a wall at all - in fact it was the door to the shower and what's more it was open! There was a great crash as he fell through the open space and straight down into the shower tray, landing in a drunken heap on the ground. I then proceeded to walk casually over to where he now lay, turned on the shower and told him a cold shower was exactly what he needed! With that I unlocked the door, left the bathroom and rejoined the party.

By the age of 16 and now at college, I had also decided to study for an A-Level in sociology as part of an evening class, at a different local college. It was during this class I befriended a young lady who informed me her brother was in a band and then proceeded to play me some of the band's tracks. It started to feel that every which way I turned I became friendly with someone in the entertainment industry. Was it following me, or was I somehow subconsciously seeking it out? The young lady told me all about how her brother's band got into the music industry, giving me yet more tips of the trade. This band was later to become one of many of my all time favourites. They went under the nice Jewish name of Jesus Jones and went on to become huge stars in their own right.

During my first term at college a girl in my class named Abi, told me she was leaving her Saturday job in a local chocolate shop, as she said her boss was completely nutty. Good reason I thought, then asked her if she would mind if I applied for the job! 'I'll introduce you' she said, 'but be warned, she is completely off her rocker but at least she will allow you to eat as much chocolate as you can handle!' The thought of being surrounded by all that chocolate sold me the idea, that and the fact I had another type of addiction to feed - my love of music! I was buying a lot of records around this time and needed to be able to keep funding my habit. Later that day Abi and I walked into the shop hand in hand. Abi announced to her boss she was leaving but had brought a replacement - me! The lady, who was also the owner of the small chocolate patisserie, hired me on the spot. Just as Abi had said, the lady informed me on my first day I could eat as much chocolate as I liked. This was an excellent plan, as her saying this had the reverse effect on me and I didn't eat any! The lady was, however, completely nutty and I only lasted one day in the job but soon after got a job in a local chemist, to keep feeding my addiction. I stayed in this Saturday job for nearly a year but only after getting over my complete embarrassment every time a guy asked to buy condoms. I could not even look a guy in the face when he asked!

Just before the Easter holidays I made my goodbyes to everyone at college prior to the break. It was during this break I went from being a reasonable, outwardly positive young woman, returning a completely different person. I also went from dressing like, to quote one of my friends at that time, 'a complete prude' to coming back dressed, well let's just say, not so innocently. I wasn't able to bring myself to speak to anyone and went into a complete shell. This was all due to two events, which were to take place during the holiday break.

By the time I was nearly 17 I hadn't seen Claudia for nearly four years. This was the second time she had disappeared from my life. If you recall, she had also disappeared previously to this for two years when I was between the ages of around 11 to 13. My family had kept from me during the times I had not seen her the knowledge Claudia had been in and out of health clinics, as her condition had worsened and I did not discover until much later exactly how bad Claudia's mental health had become. Claudia was now living in a dangerous part of London with her alcoholic husband and occasionally would call to speak to me, to ask me to go and visit her. Vera and Sam would not allow me to visit her, as they felt it was not a safe environment for me. I was now finishing up the first term at college and learning to drive. I was ready to go and find Claudia myself if she could not come to me. I had always placed Claudia on a pedestal in my mind and now I wanted to go and find her.

I remember it was an early morning and I was in my parents' bathroom washing when Claudia's sister knocked on the door and entered the bathroom. She started with the words 'I have something to tell you.' I knew what was coming. I could sense it in every bone of my body. I didn't want to hear the words I knew she was going to say, so stopped her with an abrupt 'What?' She continued 'It's Claudia.' 'What about Claudia?' I quipped 'She's had an accident… she was run over by a car… and killed.'

The words did not sink in. I told her she was lying and continued 'Claudia is too careful for that.' I didn't want her words to be true and thought by shouting them down it would make them go away. She continued: 'I meant she was driving' I retorted 'She doesn't drive!' 'She was a passenger.' 'No she wasn't! Stop lying, she's alive, she's not dead, she's not dead, she's not dead, she's not dead, she's not dead!' I cried for days on end solidly and would not talk to a single soul during this time. I went back to college at the end of the week a complete wreck. I also took my driving test that week and passed - how ironic. I later learnt from a friend, whose parents had overheard the news, that Claudia had in fact taken her own life, whilst in hospital. Her illness had finally won. She had become another statistic. This is what my family had been trying so desperately to keep from me.

Sadly, what eventually tipped Claudia over the edge, was when she came home one day after a long stay in a clinic to find her partner, who you will recall I am referring to as Trevor, had sold all her furniture and most-prized possessions. The only thing left in the flat was the carpet and wallpaper. All her memories and the treasured items, which mum and dad had bought her over the years, had apparently been sold for Trevor to buy more drink. This was too much for Claudia to handle, so she submitted herself as a patient into The Central Middlesex hospital. Upon arrival she was greeted with rudeness by the main nurse on site who retorted 'We are not a marriage guidance service'. Claudia explained she was ill and required professional help. She called mum later that day to tell her what the nurse had said and to tell mum where she was. The nurse had also reportedly said: 'Well you can stay here one night only but you're out in the morning!' Claudia had responded with the words: 'I'm not leaving, you'll see.'

After Claudia's death I was inconsolable. My world had changed and nothing would ever be the same again. I felt I would never be the same again. I felt a mixture of emotions. I was angry with her, I was angry with God, I was angry at life and mostly I felt angry with myself that I hadn't somehow prevented this from happening.

After Claudia passed on, Trevor came round to the house to give me the only two treasured items of Claudia's he had not sold. A heart locket she wore around her neck, with a lock of my hair inside; which was taken from my head when I was a child and also a lock of her hair too. Trevor also presented me with the Dior hat Claudia had worn when she was crowned 'Miss Dior'. Poor Trevor could not stop apologising to me for Claudia's death but I told him it was not his fault. She had made her own decision. What Trevor could not have realised was how much I was actually blaming myself for Claudia's death at this time. Claudia had called mum during the week she passed away and asked to see me but mum forbade it. Claudia was very ill at the time and mum did not want me to see her in this state. I recall speaking to Claudia and she was begging to see me but mum put her foot down and said I was not allowed to see her at this point in time. She was trying to protect me but I had so wanted to see her. No one could have known what was to have occurred next but still I blamed myself, believing I should not have listened to mum or to dad and instead visited her anyway. Perhaps I should have snuck out the house and gone and visited her without their knowledge? I believed I could somehow have helped her. I believed I could have saved her. For a very long time after Claudia's passing I still believed I could have done something to prevent it. I didn't realise myself until many years later Claudia's decision to end her life was probably born long before that day and sadly was a part of her condition. Between five and ten per cent of people suffering with schizophrenia, or personality disorder, as was the label placed upon her, end their lives to stop their mental torture.

After Claudia passed away my cousin Joanna came round to see me and took a bracelet off her wrist to give to me. It was the bracelet she had worn since the day Claudia and Martin had presented it to her on their wedding day, as a thank you for being their bridesmaid. The bracelet was engraved with the words 'Love Claudia & Martin.' I was of course filled with mixed emotions upon receiving this thoughtful gift.

After Claudia died I was in a really bad place emotionally, in fact probably the worst place I have been in during my entire life. During the funeral I recall thinking I just wanted to jump into the grave with her. I recall feeling my legs turn to jelly and my body convulse forward towards the grave. Two of my friends grabbed my arms from both sides and literally held me back. I wrote a song shortly after Claudia died, with the rather strange title of *Memories of What is to Come*. It was written about a girl, myself in fact, who with adult eyes was looking at the child within; the girl she once was and trying to warn her of what lay ahead. If only I had of known. I was now facing my deepest, darkest hour. I was now face down at the bottom of that black abyss. I was in so much emotional turmoil and pain. I felt dead inside. In fact, the pain was the only thing, which reminded me I was still alive.

I had a really rough time going back to college after Claudia died. If it wasn't bad enough that a small group of girls had taken it upon themselves to be unkind to me about Claudia's death, there was also a teacher who was unkind to me too. During the business studies class I found myself bursting into tears. The teacher in question shouted; 'Emma Fletcher, stop your nonsense and focus!' I started to say 'You don't understand I...' when she shouted 'Your mother died, I get it! Don't bring your problems into my class. Get out!' And with that she sent me, now in floods of tears, out of the room. My good friend Beverley (not her real name) who was my lifesaver at college during this difficult time and in the days which followed, pursued my route out of the classroom, as did a girl named Daisy (also not her real name) and we formed a group hug outside. I don't think I would of been able to have completed the course without both their friendships. Incidentally, the head teacher at the college happened to walk past the door at this moment and saw me crying. She was very concerned I had been sent out the room in this fashion, knowing my mother had died that previous week and eventually decided to permanently dismiss the teacher in question. I sadly lost contact with the lovely Daisy over the years but I'm pleased to report we recently re-found each other again. When Daisy heard I was writing this book she exclaimed how pleased she was for me and commented how she never forgot how this teacher and 'those' girls had behaved towards me. It had really impacted upon her too; as I guess it would on any person with any real feeling of goodwill.

Claudia's death had a profound and lasting impression on dad and indeed on his health. Two years after Claudia passed away dad contracted cancer of the larynx. It started off as a dry cough. It was an ongoing cough that didn't seem to go. Eventually he went to see a doctor who referred him for tests. The tests revealed the cancer and as a result dad had to have his voice box; the larynx, completely removed. Doctors believed dad's cancer was brought on firstly because he smoked for a number of years during the army but also due to the untimely death of his daughter, which had shocked both he and mum to the core. They were forever torn. I felt so terribly sorry for the pain I knew they were both experiencing and yet there was nothing I could do about it, as I was going through the very same pain myself. All we could do was to be there for one another at this terrible time in our lives. Mum always used to cry 'A mother is not meant to outlive her child.'

When dad was in hospital, I was informed he might not survive the Laryngectomy and so, as one would imagine, that was a rough time. When I visited him in hospital after his operation, my heart sank when he revealed to me he had given up hope and lost the will to live. I can vividly recall taking him by the hand and saying: 'You are not leaving this earth. I am not letting you leave this

111

earth. I need you and you are staying here because I'm not done with you yet!' I remember Dad smiled and said 'Okay'.

Whether it was because of what I had said I don't know but against all odds he did survive. Despite this, he was so weak and thin and lived on a drip for a number of months. In fact, once dad eventually returned home, he lived in our spare room for the best part of a year. During this time he wouldn't take any visitors.

If this wasn't bad enough, when dad came out of hospital and retuned home we experienced a bad case of subsidence in our house. It never rains, it pours! This was to lead us to living in complete chaos with the house upside down for around nine months. What had led to this situation was the roots from the large tree in our front garden had decided to spread. I first became aware of the 'root' of the problem the day I went into our beautiful dining room, which was at the front of the house and discovered a large crack in one of the walls. During the following week the crack became larger. I decided to inform mum and dad who, as it turned out with everything else going on, hadn't noticed the crack. Being that dad had been a surveyor, he instantly knew the problem was subsidence. What a marvellous welcome home present! Subsequently, the builders who worked on correcting the problem, had to cut out the whole of the front of the dining room and rebuild this area, which as previously mentioned, took nine months. It also meant we didn't even have a front door. The builders had to cut away the bricks right down to the base of the house and rebuild the foundations. Security was a nightmare and for the full nine months we lived in fear of people getting into the house. During this time we lived completely upstairs. Fortunately no one went to the hassle of attempting to get into the house. I guess the 'gods' were on our side after all.

After roughly a year had past, dad gained the conviction to come out for short car trips with me and I drove him around in my little Metro. Then he started to learn to speak again using his diaphragm. It was truly incredible. Before my very eyes, I started to see him regain his willl to live. By now dad was willing to see people again and those who visited the house were really amazed

112

at how well he was speaking. However, it was a very different story when we went out of the house on our shopping trips. Dad refused to speak to anyone such as shop assistants. One day he wanted to get some things from a nearby chemist. We made our way in the car to the shop and I parked outside. As usual, dad asked me to pop inside and purchase the items he needed. Suddenly the thought came to me that I needed to persuade him to retake control of his life again and be a little more independent. This way, I thought he would regain some of his old confidence and dignity. I then found myself telling dad out loud he was more than capable of going into the chemist and speaking for himself. Dad looked taken-a-back and immediately refused. He was afraid the assistant behind the counter would laugh at him. Because of this, dad wanted me to accompany him into the shop. I stood - or rather sat - my ground and refused. I was being cruel to be kind. I persuaded him he could do this. My persistence paid off. Dad went into the shop looking like a frail and nervous elderly man and came back with a huge smile on his face and his head held high; his dignity now back in tact. I know dad realised my actions had been born from love.

*Paul: As Emma previously mentioned there was a second event that happened during that same Easter holiday from college that was to result in a sudden and dramatic change in her character. It should be noted these are strictly Emma's personal take on the events that took place one night when she was 17.*

Emma: It was because of Sky that by the age of nearly 17, like Claudia before me, I decided to enter the crazy world of modelling. Sky, a tall model type herself, had already started to create a buzz in the modelling industry and had acquired some of the top agencies' interest. She had however, been carrying out modelling assignments for a small independent modelling agency to gain experience and told me she had spoken to one of the photographers at the company, who was keen to meet with me. So via Sky, I met up with her photographer, a young man, who for the sake of this book I will call Gustav. Gustav took a strong liking to me and told me he wanted to date me. I was not interested. Sky tried to encourage me and said: 'Go out with him on one date, he likes you' but I told her I was simply not interested. My world was taking on a variety of new shapes and forms. This was a time of certain new discovery, a time to decide what I wanted from life and it was actually all a little scary. One thing I was sure about was I was ready for a boyfriend but I certainly did not want to go out with someone I was not interested in. I did, however, agree to meet up with Gustav as a friend. He seemed a nice guy, so we met up occasionally a few more times over the coming months and a friendship started to unfold between us.

A few months into our friendship and just weeks after Claudia's passing and still a complete emotional wreck, I agreed to another meeting with Gustav. By now all the girls at college had already lost their virginity and I was curious to find out what it was like. I would argue Gustavo decided to take advantage of this and my emotional state at the time. He blatantly asked if I wanted to lose my virginity. To my surprise, I found myself saying to him I did, adding I had always wondered what it was like. So, Gustav invited me to come to his studio. When the day arrived on which we had arranged to meet, Gustav took me up to his studio attic. I remember stripping down to my underwear and then immediately changing my mind. I recall saying: 'Sorry, this is wrong. I'm sorry, this is a mistake'. I grabbed my clothes and went to change so I could leave but Gustav wouldn't let me. He jumped on top of me and attacked me. It was a solid half an hour of scratching his chest and producing blood, screaming and begging him to stop. With each time he entered my body, it felt as if a knife were being forced inside me. It was a horrendous experience and I felt completely violated.

As soon as I got home I stood in the shower for over an hour and scrubbed every part of my body over and over. Even today the memory of this attack stays with me and I still relieve it in my head at times. I think part of the reason I managed to find myself in various abusive relationships after this time was partly due to the fact I didn't value myself after this experience and also because I started to equate sex with emotional pain. I've always been very strong with regards to my career but until fairly recently I was a doormat in my personal life.

On the day of the attack, I found myself having to put a smile on my face and carry out a photo shoot for the popular television series *The Clothes Show*. One picture was taken in a mini-wedding dress and for the second Gustav draped me from the waist up in only a transparent veil - something I would never have agreed to, had I of been thinking with a clear head. I was still very much in a state of shock.

*Paul: As one would have expected, I was incredibly upset when Emma related these events to me. I was surprised, however, when she revealed she has never reported the incident to the Police.*

Emma: So why didn't I go to the police? Well, firstly I didn't tell anyone about the incident for two years afterwards. I tried so desperately to forget what had happened. What it also led to was my becoming very confused sexually and I became frightened of being around men. I also wasn't sure at the time if I had been raped. I couldn't even bring myself to say the word. I was very, very confused. I also feared I wouldn't be believed if the case went to court. I was fearful the jury might say I had led Gustav on, even although I had screamed and scratched his chest to the point of drawing blood for the full thirty minutes the attack took place. I certainly did not end up consenting to sex.

What my attack did was give me the impetus to eventually take-up self defence classes. I wanted to learn the skills that would give me the ability and confidence to defend myself. It is all about defence when you learn or practice martial arts, not about the attack. The skills I learnt did eventually unfortunately come into use, when a guy attempted to attack me when I was waiting on a railway station one night. The guy who attempted to attack me certainly got a shock, as he obviously didn't think I would be able to defend myself.

Going back to the time I was originally attacked, I went back to college after the Easter break having lost both my mother and my virginity in the most horrendous way imaginable. I was not the same girl anymore. I started to wear short skirts but was at the same time very confused about how I felt about the attention I was receiving from men towards me but continued to wear these short skirts nonetheless. I was a mess and unsure as to what message I was trying to convey.

As previously mentioned, there were a couple of girls who began bullying me when I returned to college. I was, as I said, going in wearing short skirts and looking less like a nun. Given this, I guess I was giving them plenty of ammunition for their firing squad. But what hurt the most was they continued to bully me after word reached them my mother had passed away and they even went as far as making awful comments about her death.

My parents were becoming increasingly worried about my erratic behaviour and emotional outbursts, which occurred over the coming months and gave me a greeting card with the following words by M Joye (they had changed the 'my' and 'I' to 'our' and 'we':

*To our Teenager*

*It's hard sometimes, when people are changing their lives, to understand each other, or even to talk. You are struggling right now for independence and the right to live your own way... and we sometimes struggle for the strength to let you do it. We wish now and then for the days when a kiss or a hug could make your world bright again, but your world is more difficult now, and you want to make your own way in it - which is as it should be. We only want you to know... that when you get hurt, we will hurt for you, and that deep down, we always have confidence in your ability to find your place in your world. If you ever need a caring heart, or someone to listen to your deepest dreams or concerns, we will be there for you, and remember, above all else... that we love and care for you.*

They had added on the end: 'Mum and Dad. With love xxx'

For the next two years I could not even look at a guy. I didn't know who I was or what planet I was from and what's more, I

116

could even feel my stutter starting to come back again and with a vengeance. During this time I went through a lot of teenage angst and to my regret my poor mum faced a lot of slammed doors and raised voices, which was really just my anger at Claudia's death manifesting itself in a different guise. I loved mum so much but it did not help that her response to my emotional outbursts was to try and hold an even tighter reign over me. She continued to be so fearful I would go down the same route as Claudia. Whilst mum and dad gave me the greatest love I could have ever have asked for, their parenting was becoming over-protective to the point of at times almost feeling a bit neurotic, especially for a teenager in angst who was so desperately searching for her freedom. But who could really blame them? I knew in my heart both mum and dad were really just trying to protect me from following in Claudia's footsteps but what they seemed to be forgetting was I was a different person to Claudia and my characteristics were very different to hers.

Mum's reaction to Claudia's death was therefore to restrict everything I did to a minimum, as she continually repeated how fearful she was of me becoming ill like Claudia. She had raised Claudia in the same restrictive manner and this was a very difficult way to be brought up at times. Sometimes I did indeed feel like I would go stir-crazy, if I could not be allowed to just live. I looked around me and to the mind of a strong-willed teenager it did at times feel as if I were the only normal one, surrounded by people with many varying levels of neurosis, psychosis and just plain old Jewish anxiousness! Death did on a couple of occasions seem like an option. The tighter my mum started to try and wrap me in cotton wool, the more I started to wear revealing clothes. Perhaps I was trying to regain ownership over my own body, although with adult eyes I now realise identity and power over oneself is born from within and does not necessarily have to be defined by the clothes we wear. (This is actually one of the reasons why religious people wear plain and simple clothing as, apart from retaining their modesty, they are aware the way to regain complete ownership over oneself is to not feel the necessity to meet a certain trend or look of the time.) I recall how Mr Drummond rather unhelpfully continually used to tell me I looked like a tart -

and I probably did but I was a teenager in trouble screaming out for help. Why could no one hear my screams? Incidentally, Mr Drummond had on occasions, particularly when I was younger, mistakenly called me 'Claudia Jane' instead of Emma Jane. As it was felt by other members of the family he was not one of Claudia's greatest fans, to a child and even to a teenager, whenever he accidentally referred to me as 'Claudia Jane' I believed he did not like me either, which as one can imagine also always managed to cause me a great deal of heartache.

So still facing the bottom of that dark pit once referred to as my heart, I knew if I wanted to survive there really was only one way forward; and that was up. To quote Meister Eckhart; *Truly, it is in the darkness that one finds the light, so when we are in sorrow, then this light is the nearest of all to us.'* I knew now, more than ever, it was time to seek out that light again, at whatever cost and the greatest cost of course being myself.

I finished up my year at college and by the age of 17 I was already modelling for a full year of my life. I hated the industry. It was filled with an array of bitchy 'wanabees'. I also found myself starting to get asked out by women. I never did go out with any women and I was never even remotely attracted to a woman. I had however, as previously mentioned, put an intentional block on my memory about what had happened to me with Gustav. I found this disassociation made it easier to deal with what had happened. I could not bring myself to even look at a man, as whilst I still found men physically attractive, on an emotional level this attraction still scared me. As a confused teenager I could not understand what was wrong with me so I started to question if I was gay. I remember one night at around 3am lying in bed sobbing my little heart out. It woke mum up. She came into my bedroom and sat on the side of my bed and stroked my hair. 'What's wrong darling?' she asked. 'I - am - a - lesbian!' I wailed! My mum's reaction is probably one of the best reactions she could have given me at that point in time: She laughed! 'What's so funny?' I asked. 'You're not gay!' she responded. 'I'm not?' I questioned 'Well then why can't I manage to keep a boyfriend?' Mum proceeded to ask me why I thought I was gay and eventually, after a series of sensitive questions, I opened up to her that I had been raped. It was such a release to say these words, although at the same time it broke mum's heart. We hugged each other and cried - yet more tears.

During my time as a commercial model I worked for the highly respected *Cosmopolitan* photographer Angelo Valentino and a variety of other commercial photographers. I also carried out various catwalk shows in nightclubs and department stores. One recollection I have of one particular modelling assignment was when I was being photographed for a fashion shoot in an outside location near to Hyde Park. As the photographer was busily snapping my picture, on the road immediately behind him a lady pulled over in a brand new fashion red Lamborghini and jumped out just in time for the car to burst into flames. The fire brigade rushed to the scene and so did the lady's partner in crime. I recall the man crying 'My beautiful car, my beautiful car' and the lady simply saying 'Don't worry darling, we'll just buy another!' The photographer, who was also a photographic journalist, suddenly ceased taking photographs of me, turned around and started to take quick firing snapshots of the burning vehicle instead. I was left standing in the middle of the street, dressed in a freakishly bizarre high-fashion outfit, with a bunch of tourists taking snap shots back and forth of both the car and me. I'm not sure which sight was more freakish, the burning Lamborghini or my outfit, which was also on fire with its garish colour alone!

I also started a course in make-up and theatre make-up around this time and became good enough to become one of those girls who moves from department store to department store making people up in order to help sell the products. I must admit I didn't really enjoy the job. To the active person I am, the job itself at the level I was carrying it out was too static. The only real highlight I can recall was serving the wonderful Barbara Windsor and Boy George with make-up. I think the latter purchased more make-up than the first! As well as selling make-up, I also started modelling somc of the clothes for each of the department stores I worked in.

A good friend of mine used to be a seamstress and at one point worked closely with the fashion mogul Vivienne Westwood. The friend in-question kindly invited me to a couple of Westwood's fashion house parties. They were quite a spectacle with room upon room filled with uber models such as Naomi Campbell and Kelly Brook. One could not turn their head without bumping into another magazine cut-out. And so this became my lifestyle at this time.

I eventually decided it was time to leave the department store and the world of modelling and get what I considered was a proper job. I found the industry to be fairly incestuous and seedy and the job itself quite vacuous. I remember one photographer saying to me: 'Darling, remember you are just a glorified clothes-horse!' and to be honest most days that is exactly how I felt.

The deciding point for me to eventually abandon my career in both modelling and make-up altogether was when the mother of a girl I had gone to both junior and high school with, walked into Selfridges department store for a make-over and found me standing in front of the counter. 'Emma!' she said: 'Fancy meeting you here! What are you buying?' 'I work here' I replied: 'Really? What a waste of a good education! You were meant to go to Oxbridge.' she continued. For some reason this comment resonated deeply within me and made me reflect on my life a great deal. This comment became my deciding factor for realising it was the right time for me to get out of modelling and make-up and to find myself a sensible nine to five.

Talking about make-up, by now I had also started 'making up' for lost time with guys! I was starting to re-find my femininity and started to date as many boys as I could and, if the truth be told, became a bit of a heartbreaker. I dated boys, kissed them, then told them I didn't want to see them again and then dated some more. I was not ready to allow myself to get emotionally involved or too attached. In fact my time in the modelling industry had found me being chatted up by three different guys; one who turned out to be young blood working for the Italian Mafia, one who had just asked out a male friend of mine immediately before asking me out and one who was secretly also dating someone else but of course I don't find a guy that is just two-timing me, no siree, I have to find the one guy who just had to push the boat out that little bit further and was in fact three-timing me. I declined all three offers! Nope, the dating game has never been easy for me.

Speaking of which, then there are those dates, which make you wonder why you bothered even stepping out the front door. Come on ladies, we've all been there! We've all had that date which makes you walk away wondering why you bothered waxing or setting the table with your finest cellar red, haven't we? You haven't lived until you've experienced the art of the bad date. Okay, so let's bring it on with my three classic gems straight from Beelzebub's diary, oh and back up off the gas because we're in for a bumpy ride.

Perching at a healthy number three in the chart is the rather sweet but somewhat hygienically challenged northwest London date. Sitting in a rather plush hotel cafeteria, exchanging a throw of polite conversation across a glass table, this poor date sneezed right across the table. Now desperately in need of a tissue, as his nose is running the London Marathon all on its own, I politely pass the poor guy a tissue, then discreetly look in the other direction to give him the chance to play catch-up with this game of tag he is ensuing with the contents of his nose. Finally, when I am sure he has finished the procedure of clearing his nasal passage, I casually look back in his direction ready to start up conversation again, when suddenly he notices the spray he has created over the once clean glass table. Without hesitation he reaches for the now somewhat soaked tissue and rapidly wipes the table. It's a goal! He has successfully managed to give the glass a new frosted look. Words such as 'meh' and 'bleh' and 'is it really as late as that?' rapidly spring to mind and start to spurn my lips into action towards the words 'leaving' and 'now!'

Challenging the number one slot but still sitting safely at number two is my date from across the Atlantic with his sexy American droll, offering to take me out for a slap up meal. 'Don't eat a thing all day' he said. 'This will be my treat.' How nice I thought. It's not often I get taken out for a meal. Now, I have never been of a materialistic nature and whilst checking a guys' bank balance has never been my first priority, it was still very nice to be invited out to dinner. In fact I have usually always been a bit overcautious when I guy asks me out with the offer of a slap-up meal or the offer of a slap-up anything for that matter, as I'm always concerned if I allow the wrong type of guy to buy me a drink or a meal they may expect a different type of slap-up in return. So usually I go Dutch!

I don't define my interest in a guy according to how much cash he carries in his back pocket anyhow and my interest in a guy's material worth has never stretched to the make and model of his car, watch or cell phone. The only drive I am usually interested in is their spiritual drive. On this occasion however, Mr American's drive would be a very different type of full-throttle ahead! He picked me up and drove us straight to the rather swanky restaurant Smolensky's on the Strand, gaining Brownie points for opening the car door in both the departure and arrival lounge. Another Brownie point for opening the door on the way into the restaurant and three strikes for pulling out my chair once inside. Ker-ching! The menu comes and in a gentlemanly fashion, he orders for us both. 'Starters only please,' he tells the waitress. 'Any drinks?' she replies. 'Tap water and we will be sharing the cheesy potato skins for starters'. 'Any main courses sir?' she continues. 'We'll decide that later.' Later arrives and the waitress makes her return to our table. 'Any main courses sir?' 'Just the check please,' he replies in his broad Yankee accent. I must have been showing the disappointment on my face that we were not staying for the main dishes, as he turned to me and said 'I've got the mains covered. I'm taking you somewhere else for that.' I'm intrigued, I thought. He checks the check but doesn't pay by cheque! '£3.50!' he exclaims 'For potato skins? Can we split the check?' 'Sure!' I reply, somewhat taken aback. Now, although I'm not materialistic but when a guy offers to take you out for a slap up meal 'his treat', well you kinda don't expect him to ask to split a £3:50 dish! Okay, I thought. He's short of change. He probably only has dollars left. No problem. He reaches inside his trouser pocket and starts counting out his pennies on the table. 'Don't worry! I've got it!' I announce. 'You can shout for it next time!' Little did I know my date still expected VAT!

We drove to a Marriott Hotel in Swiss Cottage and went into one of their small private bars. Jeffrey Archer was sitting at one of the small tables. My date knew him and went over to say hello. Should this have spelt out trouble? We sat down at one of the little round tables and I started to wonder when this terrific slap up meal was about to materialise, having eaten only one and a half potato skins the entire day! My American pal then slid his hand across the little table and lifted it slightly to reveal a sealed condom underneath his palm! 'What's that?' I exclaimed in complete shock! 'I think you know what it is,' he said. 'But why are you showing it to me?' 'Darn really?' he replied. 'I shouldn't have listened to my secretary. She told me to ask you after the meal. I knew I should have asked you beforehand!' My first thought was: 'Meal, what meal?' My response was of course slightly different 'Before, after, during, it's all the same to me. The answer is still not then, not now, not ever, never!' Of course I got a taxi home!

Interestingly, as mentioned, I have always had a hard time allowing a date to pay for me, wondering what I would be expected to 'owe' them in return, until fairly recently when one of my aunts said to me 'Emma, do you think you are not worthy of being treated to a meal and spent money on?' and for a moment I really had to consider if this was part of my reason for not accepting a meal ticket. It is true, I have always believed people who are generous with their money are usually generous with their love; that is as long as their intention for spending money on you is good. So why is it that once I have got to know a guy and ascertain he does not want to buy me a meal just to jump into the sack with me, I still have a problem with receiving the offer of a meal or a gift from a guy? I have to admit I love to shower those I love with gifts as a sign of my affection for them, so why was I not allowing myself to be showered in this way in return? I recently made a new pact with myself that from now on I will allow the right type of guy to spend his money on me if he so desires, as my aunt is right; I am worth it! This seems like a perfectly good new rule to me.

And just when you thought it was safe to go back into the dating waters again, along comes the top date from hell and most definitely one to 'never try this at home.' I bring you my first ever blind date. A girlfriend of mine insisted I meet a friend of her husband's. 'Okay,' I said after much persuasion. We spoke over the telephone and arranged a date, time and place to meet. He told me he would pick me up outside a local Starbucks at 2:00pm on a Sunday afternoon, in his silver Yaris and that we would drive up the road to a little local restaurant he knew for a coffee and chocolate cake. Did someone say chocolate cake? I was sold. At 2:00pm on the dot, true to his word he pulled up in his little silver Yaris, got out, walked over to me and shook me by the hand. 'You must be Simon. Nice to meet you, I'm Emma.' 'Good to meet you too' he said. 'Hop in and I'll drive us up the road to that neat little restaurant.' After some deliberation I did indeed hop into the car and after only a few moments realised this guy had an accent, which my guy certainly didn't have over the telephone. You guessed it, wrong guy!

Now, what were the chances of meeting a guy with a silver Yaris outside my meeting point at 2:00pm, claiming to be my date? But somehow I'd succeeded to do the impossible. I demanded he pull over else my three options were; 'I'll jump you and we both die, I'll jump you and pull the key from the ignition and we might crash and both die, I jump out and die and you are had up for murder!' See a pattern emerging here? The odds were not really in my favour! Eventually he pulled up and yes he tried to jump me and yes I took the incident to the police and yes we found out who he was and no, unfortunately nothing was ever done about it, as unfortunately it was a whole year later by the time I discovered who this nut job was, by which time the initial incident number and records related to the case had gone missing. Oh and if by the way you're wondering how I managed to find out who this guy was a year later, it was when he approached me once again when I was stuck one evening at traffic lights near the same Starbucks where we had first met. Noticing me, he had walked over and knocked repeatedly on my car window. I wound the window down a tad (by this point I was trained in martial arts and feeling fairly fearless) he placed a business card in my hand and asked me out on a date! Oh and if you're still wondering, I did end up eventually meeting the real blind date and he was a lovely guy - close but no cigar!

Then I met the most gorgeous young man I had ever laid eyes. For the sake of this book I will call him Daniel. He was the sweetest and kindest guy I had ever met. Daniel and I became physically intimate very quickly, when suddenly out of nowhere I pushed him off me screaming at the top of my lungs 'NO!' Daniel sat me down softly and we spoke for a long while. He managed to gently get out of me what had happened with Gustav and suddenly a floodgate of emotions, which I had long since buried rather than really dealt with, opened up. For once the tears I cried served as a cleansing experience for me. As the Jewish proverb says *'What soap is for the body, tears are for the soul.'* This was the first guy that had ever bothered to care about my well-being in this way and I fell for him immediately. We dated for a short while but no sooner had I met Daniel, he told me not to get too attached as he planned to go and live in America in three months time to fulfil his ambition of becoming a film director. This he did but for the years that followed Daniel and I remained in close contact by telephone and even met up on occasion both sides of the waters. This was the second time however a guy I had become close to had left to cross the Atlantic.

Shortly after the time Daniel left for the States, I started to feel I could once more begin to open up my heart to men again and I soon became very friendly with another young man. However an incident happened which, although I would rather not go into detail about, let's just say this man 'stole some cookies from the cookie jar' which, suffice to say, sadly set me back again for a while.

I started to make many trips to New York to visit both my American family and on one occasion Daniel. In fact, the first time I went to New York, I actually went to visit a friend I knew out there, whom I was invited to stay with. When I got out there however, her mother had arrived unannounced and I was informed there was now nowhere for me to sleep in her tiny

125

apartment. I soon found myself walking through the unfamiliar streets of New York, wandering through this concrete jungle into the early hours of the evening and wondering what on earth I was to do. As Daniel was also in New York at the time, I stayed with him at his friend's apartment for one night and then for the rest of the vacation was invited to stay with old family friends of mum, Sue and Morris Nachtomi, in their fabulous Trump Tower Penthouse Suite. I recall standing on a street corner in the pitch black of night, too scared to know which way to move after my friend had said there was now no bed for me. I hailed a taxi and asked the driver to take me to Daniel's address. The taxi driver looked at me as if I were crazy then said 'Hop in.' He drove me round the block and then back to exactly the spot I had initially been standing, give or take a couple of feet and said 'You're here!' Graciously he didn't charge me for this little scenic route excursion!

Falling completely head over heels in love with NYC, one particular year my good friend Beverly and I decided to take a couple of week's vacation and take a rather large bite out of the Big Apple. Beverly was working for the BBC at the time and we both ended up carrying out work for the first week of our vacation for the fabulous Freddie Hancock. We became very friendly with Freddie and spent many an afternoon chatting to her in her beautiful New York apartment, which overlooked Central Park and she told us many stories about her life and her turbulent marriage to the much-missed comedian, Tony Hancock.

Employment-wise, after I left the modelling industry, fate was to lead me to work for a company called Ratner's, as a personnel assistant. I stayed there for about nine months but once again had managed to find a job I hated. I only stayed because mum advised I did so, in order that I should not appear to be a job hopper. I started to let my creative streak slide somewhat during my time spent working at Ratner's. Feeling, however, I still very much needed to channel my energies into some form of creative outlet, I eventually started to write comedy scripts. I wrote a number of episodic ideas around a few successful comedy shows, which were already being aired. Once I had completed the scripts I shelved

126

them and forgot about them for a good couple of years until one day my cousin and much-loved comedy writer Ronnie Woolfe offered to read one of them and give me an honest opinion on my work. Ronnie said he thought they were excellent and that I should approach one of the production companies with my ideas. Roger Limb, who I met after my time at Ratner's, who is the brother of the very successful comedy script writer Sue Limb, gave me a clear run down on how to approach production companies and also gave me advise on how to approach record companies with my work. To this day I must confess to not having done anything with my scripts as yet but more recently I gave a couple of my scripts to my good friend Debbie Chazen to read, who after reading them said to me 'Get them out there and put me in them!' so I will indeed get round to hopefully doing just that one day soon; but I must get round to finishing writing this book first! But thanks go out to Debbie for the kick up the old proverbial!

The head office of Ratner's was somewhat akin to a prison cell. Workers had to report where they were going, even if they vacated the room just to go to the toilet. The only good thing about working at Ratner's was the office was located very near to where my dear paternal grandparents lived, so I would pop in to have lunch with them nearly every day. I really wasn't enjoying the job at all but not wanting to appear a job-hopper and determined to stay in a normal nine to five, I stayed at Ratner's for nearly nine months before deciding it was time to make a change; a change in order to grow.

***You must take a chance and try a new path in order to grow.*** - Emma Fletcher

# 6

## Aunty Beeb

**Sometimes when I consider what tremendous consequences come from little things... I am tempted to think... there are no little things.** - Bruce Barton

*Paul: One could seriously argue that the BBC is as famous around the world as the British Royal Family. With a long and rich history of radio and television production, the uniquely funded corporation was fated to be Emma's place of employment - even if, at the time, it was just behind the scenes. And, as you will read, Fletcher's employer at the BBC would eventually inspire her to take a route back into education.*

Emma: Whilst at college a representative from the BBC, affectionately known in the industry as 'Aunty Beeb', had come to talk to us about the company and search for new talent. My close friend Beverly had been head hunted by this same representative and gone straight into working for the BBC directly from college. Beverly stayed at the BBC for many years, working her way up the ladder to the position of producer. The same lady, Catherine, who had headhunted Beverly, had also approached me at the time, asking me to go and work for the BBC. In the weeks that immediately followed me leaving college, I found myself continuing to be hunted down by Catherine to go and work at the BBC as a floating P.A. I turned down the offer at the time, as I thought the notion of a 'floating' anything sounded too precarious and I had only just cropped my wings and left one flighty job already to pursue something more grounded. The BBC had at that time just set up a new system called 'The Reserve', which happened directly around the time of Producer's Choice. This term came about at the BBC after they made a large number of people redundant and then reassigned them on temporary contracts. There was a bank of employees, whose names were placed in a database held by the BBC and people were then called upon to cover any absent members of staff. It was basically in-

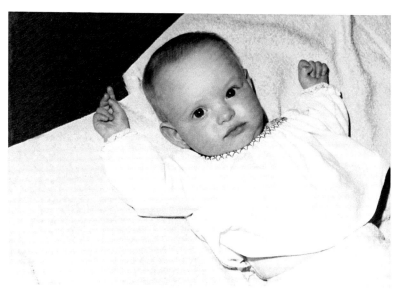

Me at 7 months old. I was always such a happy baby.

Aged 3 years and 11 months. Playing on the beach
outside Warren's Sandbanks' home.

My first piano, bought for me by my father Martin.
At the tender age of 4 here.

On the beach in Westgate, Kent. I could be quite a tomboy at times and
was always very adventurous. I was probably around
the age of 5 and a half here.

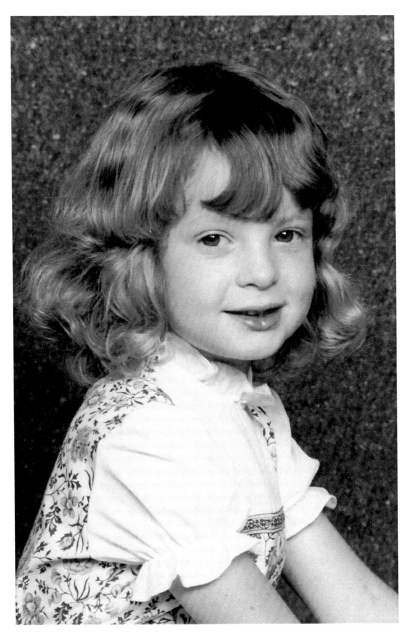

You can see just how golden my hair really was in this photograph. This led to mum and dad giving me the nickname 'Goldielocks'.
I'm aged 4 years and 8 months in this photograph.

Aged 6 and a half. From a young age I have always loved to be surrounded by nature and animals.

On the beach in Birchington, Kent with my wonderful grandparents Bill and Rose (my father's parents). Aged 7.

Cheesy grin! Playing on my bike was one of the few times in my life I felt completely free. I was nearly 8 here.

Aged 8 with my cousin Sam. How we loved to dress-up and put on a weekly show for the family.

Pictured here in my Brownie uniform aged 10, visiting my great-grandmother
Sarah (my father Martin's grandmother).
She was such a dear soul.

At home with my dear dad and mum, Sam and Vera.
To know them was to love them.

My first graduation day was a very proud moment for both myself
and both sets of grandparents.

A special birthday with my cousins. Taken out as a treat to London's famous
Nip N Tuck restaurant. From left to right: my cousin Rachel, me and my
cousins Louise and David.

Bill and Tom Kenwright's restaurant 'Azzuro'. At the piano is harmonicst Larry Adler. Tom Kenwright and Albert Hillier, my 'Daddy Longlegs', stand to my left (right of picture). Evenings out with Albert always proved to be so much fun.

Bernard Hiller's London Masterclass, June 2010. What a life-changing experience. I am at the front, bottom left of picture.

house cover, which meant I could be moving between offices all the time, in the roles of either: production assistant, runner or secretary. It occurred to me there might even be days when I would not be required for cover at all. All the job titles seemed fantastic but as I had just left one precarious career, I continued to decline the BBC rep's continued quest for me to work for her.

Catherine was not however prepared to give up the ghost. She had continued to call me many times during the time I was working as a model and make-up artist, then there had been a hiatus and I hadn't heard from her for a while but now her chase was about to recommence. Five months into working at Ratner's, my mother received a telephone call from Catherine when I was out, once again ringing to register my interest in the BBC and checking to see if I was now keen to work for them. Catherine was a lady on a mission! I started to wonder if there would ever be an end to this woman's continued pursuit of her goal. On this particular occasion mum had let on to Catherine I was not happy in my current job. If the truth be known I think mum secretly wanted me to leave Ratner's and go and work for the BBC anyhow, as they were such a good company to work for and also she could see how unhappy I was working at Ratner's and this concerned her.

Catherine called me directly on my personal line at Ratner's. So either she had found out my extension via her own detective handiwork or mum had given it to her. I never did find out, which probably indicates mum had indeed passed on my details. Catherine asked me outright to leave Ratner's and go and work for her at the BBC. Whilst her continued pursuit was extremely flattering, I still felt the position they were offering seemed too precarious, so continued to decline her request. Catherine continued to call me sporadically over the next few weeks at Ratner's, with her intermittent calls becoming more closely spaced apart, until one day I said to her 'You really have to stop calling me at work. You will get me the sack!' to which she replied 'Well, that is the idea. Then you can come and work for me!' We both laughed. I did give my notice in to my boss shortly after this conversation and immediately accepted the vacancy at the BBC and not a moment too soon it turned out, as just after this conversation Gerald Ratner, the CEO of the company, announced to the world in his infamous speech that his jewellery was 'crap';

*We also do cut-glass sherry decanters complete with six glasses on a silver-plated tray that your butler can serve you drinks on, all for £4.95. People say, "How can you sell this for such a low price?" I say because it's total crap.'*

Realising I was probably now sailing on a sinking ship I knew it was time to move on and shortly after I left Ratner's to join the BBC, Ratner's ship did indeed go under rather rapidly. As it turned out, after all the fuss surrounding the BBC, as it is such a large organisation over the course of the next year I worked for them there was not one single day I was ever out of work; as there was always the requirement for cover.

During the first six months of my year at the BBC I worked in radio or anything connected with music. This included working on the television programme *Top of the Pops*. I was fortunate enough to hear live recordings at the famous studios by David Bowie and Cyndi Lauper. I recall the day Bowie was leaving the studios there were a handful of press photographers waiting outside for him to make his exit. Instead I walked out. Cameras started to flash in my face until one photographer shouted 'Hold fire. She's a no-one!' to which I shouted back: 'At least, not yet!'

Whilst working in Radio I met my life-long friend Roger Limb, one of the BBC Radiophonic Workshop composers. I had the privilege of working at the famous Radiophonic Workshop for a couple of months with all the composers. These guys were responsible for all the incidental music, which occurred as background music in television shows and also for the famous sound effects on Doctor Who. As soon as the guys in the workshop got wind of my interest in composing my own music, they immediately and very generously, opened up their doors to showing me around the studios. Oddly enough, whilst I was at the Radiophonic workshop, the head of the workshop, Brian, asked me if I would kindly help him draw up some blueprints, as the workshop was being refurbished. I had never drawn a blueprint before in my life and although I thought this a rather unusual request, I also knew working at the BBC meant anything goes, so agreed to help. Little did I know in just under a year I would be studying for a degree in interior architecture; living, eating and breathing blueprints!

Roger and I became firm friends very rapidly and he kindly helped me record some of my own music at the studios at the end of each working day. Once again, this started to formulate a desire in wanting to get back in touch with my creative side again, which I had allowed to slide somewhat during my time spent at Ratner's. Upon request, I agreed to help be Roger's 'page turner' during a live performance he was giving and found myself completely enjoying the buzz of being a part of a live performance; even if only as a page turner! It dawned on me it was time to turn a page in my own life once again too. I immediately got back to writing my own songs. Around this time, I recall Roger helping me put the dots on the page for one of my songs, entitled *Bass Line. Bass Line* was a mixture of jazz and a musical styled number. Later that night, whilst photocopying the sheet music at the local newsagents in Wembley Park, an elderly gentleman peered over my shoulder at the photocopier and informed me he was a musician for, funnily enough, the BBC Philharmonic Orchestra. He started to sight read my music. 'Marvellous!' he declared. 'Is it Sondheim?' 'No' I replied 'It's all mine!' This was a very proud moment for me.

Perhaps it was partly due to Claudia's death that I was propelled into action and started to seek out a path for my dream or maybe it was the search to fill a void that was now inside of me since her passing and with it a renewed desire to feel loved; but I decided it was now time to embark upon my quest to turn my long over-due dream into a reality. So around this time I made it known to Albert I had decided I wanted to learn more about the entertainment industry; with a view to one day pursuing a career in performance. Albert immediately offered me an invite to an all glittering, all singing, all dancing, extremely lavish, red carpet event.

I can actually very vividly recall the very first red carpet event I attended with Albert. I stepped foot into the room of the party after the show feeling as if I had just stepped foot into a fairy tale. I felt like Cinderella being invited to the ball for the very first time. The chandlers sparkled, the candles on the tables glowed over the beautiful display of flowers on each table and a jazz band was playing Gershwin's *Rhapsody in Blue*; one of my all time favourite musical numbers. As everyone entered the room, they immediately found themselves with a camera being pointed in their face and their photograph taken. Albert grabbed me to have my photograph taken with a plethora of different stars, one after the other and each name as big as the next.

In my private life and outside of the realms of this book, I have never been one to name-drop; as having grown-up around so many celebrities I have never been star-struck but for the sake of this book and to set the scene, I will have to make an exception to this rule on this occasion, as the list of famous faces was endless and deserves a mention in this story. The stars were literally coming out of the woodwork. Everywhere I turned there was yet another famous face starring back at me. In fact, the only person I didn't recognise was me! I started to feel less like Cinderella and more like 'Charity Hope Valentine' in my all-time favourite movie, *Sweet Charity*. I was definitely a fish out of water. It was as if all eyes were on me questioning 'Who's she?' and 'Should we know?' What was a girl to do? Should I break out into an all singing, all dancing Fosse routine? I soon found myself being introduced by Albert to a number of the faces starring back at me. First in line were the royals and politicians; greeting the likes of Sarah Ferguson, John Major and William Hague. Then I found myself discussing politics with Mo Mowlam. Next in line were the actors, presenters and musicians, all at the top of their field. I was introduced to Emma Thompson; who if the truth be told I was a little in awe of, Bob Hoskins, Richard E Grant and Jennifer Ellison, then soon found myself exchanging polite dialogue with the delightful June Brown and Kate O'Mara, before meeting funny guys Bradley Walsh and Freddie Starr and the extremely handsome Sir Cliff Richard to name but a mere few, all of whom continued to spend time talking to Albert, whilst I starred contently into Cliff's gorgeous brown eyes. Next to walk in the room were the dynamic presenters Ant and Deck, both looking very dapper in their black ties and penguin suits, followed by the wonderfully eccentric Paul O'Grady, the daytime presenter Gloria Hunniford and the lovely Emma Forbes. Of course, I was finally introduced to the hosts of the evening; Tom and Bill Kenwright and Bill's date, Jenny Seagrove.

Soon we were shown to our tables. At our table were more famous faces. I started to feel completely out of my depth and a little nervous, when a young lady around my age came and sat down beside me looking completely bored. 'What do you think?' she questioned in a rather monotone fashion. Now feeling completely at a loss for words, what I said came out completely differently as to what I meant to say. 'I think I feel a little sick!' I said. 'I've never been to such a spectacle before! Who thinks up an event such as this?' I questioned. 'My dad!' she announced. Lucy Kenwright and I couldn't stop giggling after this and a bond was immediately formed between us. Over the years, whenever I saw Lucy at these parties, we would always have a giggle about this moment.

As soon as all the guests were seated, we were presented to a fabulous buffet of choice upon choice of delicacies. Seated at our table were a host of footballers and their managers and four very dear acquaintances of Albert's: the delightful Cherie Lunghi and her daughter Nathalie, the bubbly Miriam Margolyes, the wonderful Frankie Vaughan and the lovely Bob Holness and his wife Mary. During the meal I required the little ladies facilities and needed to squeeze past Bob's chair to get out. As you can imagine in my cheeky Fletcher manner I couldn't resist saying to the very amiable Bob, 'Excuse me, can I have a 'P' please Bob!' Bob laughed politely at my poor attempt at a joke, although I am certain he must have heard his catch-phrase said back to him in this manner at least a hundred times before. Bob and his adorable wife Mary and Frankie were so kind to me that evening. They really all looked after me; dancing with me on the dance floor and making me feel one of the team. They all made the evening so special for me and Bob and Frankie, the perfect gentlemen they both were, refused to leave the party until they had re-found both Albert and myself on the dance floor, to wish us farewell for the evening. By the time they found us, both Albert and I were throwing our very best shapes on the tiles, boogying the night away with Albert egging me on shouting: 'Go the Snake!' (This is Albert's nickname for me on the dance floor, as he thinks I look like a snake when I dance!) When we finally left the party, we were all very kindly given a going away gift at the exit: perfume for the ladies and after-shave for the men.

This evening was the first in line of many similar evenings to come and soon after this, Albert invited me along to a string of high-profile celebrity events. One of the next events he asked me to was the opening night of Adam Kenwright's first production. I soon found myself becoming friendly with Adam and he too would often ask Albert to bring me along to his numerous events over the following years. Adam's first opening night, held in London's Café Royal, was once again a grand spectacle and very much a feast for the eyes. As soon as I stepped foot into the room I felt like a thorn between two roses; immediately finding myself standing between the two striking presenters Zoë Ball and Dani Behr. As if this weren't bad enough, to add insult to injury, the Baywatch cast were also present amongst Adam's guests.

Albert suddenly took my arm and pulled me along the length of the dance floor with the words: 'There's someone I want you to meet.' I then found myself being turned round to end up face to face with one of my childhood heroes; David Hasselhoff. As a child I loved Knight Rider and never missed an episode. Albert introduced me to David as 'an actress', which was odd actually, as at that time I was still actively pursuing my singing career rather than my acting but I think Albert was reacting to the dream he knew I really held inside me. 'So you're an actress?' David questioned. 'Hardly,' I replied 'but I would like to become one, one day'. David very generously spent time offering me a great deal of career guidance that evening and also introduced me to

Cameron Mackintosh who offered me yet more. Albert then left me for a while in the care of the wonderfully jolly and enigmatic Christopher Biggins, whilst he disappeared into the celebrity ether to network with a number of people he needed to catch-up with. Christopher was great fun to talk to and made certain I didn't feel lonely whilst Albert continued his celebrity recce. This was the evening I was also introduced to actor David Soul, harmonicist Larry Adler and Albert's close friend and actress Fleur Bennett. Over the years Larry, David and Fleur would often accompany both Albert and myself to many of Bill's parties. I so wanted to be like Fleur. She was in my eyes a beautiful, talented working actress. She used to relate to me all the work she was carrying out and I always used to think to myself, one day I would like to be walking in similar shoes to hers and treading the acting career path for myself.

I can also recall the first film premiere Albert took me to. The sheer excitement and terror I felt both at once was incredible, as Albert escorted me down the red carpet upon entrance to the famous Empire movie theatre in the heart of London's Leicester Square. I had never walked the length of the red before, so felt very nervous as my feet made touchdown, especially as so many people were starring at me wondering who on earth I was! I walked beside Albert in my little red number and the crowds generously started to cheer 'You go girl', even although I am certain they had not a clue between them who I was! How could they? After the film we were shown back onto old red one by one. Cameras started to flash wildly as I exited. 'Great!' I thought. 'My little red frock must be a hit. Maybe I'll be this week's 'It' girl in the gossip column of *Hello!* magazine. Just then I turned slightly to see the model Caprice standing directly behind me and realised the camera flashes were of course for her little blue and not for my little red!

So many of the stars Albert introduced me to over the years were always so generous with their advice. I found myself during the course of time being offered career advice by so many actors at the top of their game, including the lovely Anne Hathaway, whom I had the pleasure of meeting over a glass of bubbly in the green

135

room for her film *Ella Enchanted*. I recall Anne saying to me 'always follow your dream'.

Quite often Albert would take me to the famous Cheeky's Restaurant in London, or to its sister restaurant The Ivy, after outings to opening nights of new theatre productions or film premieres in the West End. These restaurants are usually booked six months in advance but Albert, being Mr Theatre Mafioso himself, has always been able to ring either of these two restaurants on the very same day and get the best table in the house. Both Cheeky's and The Ivy are the restaurants which are popular places for the stars to gather after the opening night of any new production and both restaurants prove to be excellent networking ground; especially if your name is Albert Hillier! I recall having gone with Albert to meet up with Vanessa Feltz and her husband at that time Michael Kurer, for the after party of Val Kilmer's film, *The Saint*. A year later, Albert and I happened to be sitting beside Val Kilmer and his table of guests in Cheeky's restaurant. As Mr Kilmer was leaving he came over to our table to re-introduce himself to Albert, offering me a gentlemanly handshake too, recalling Albert from having met him at the party of *The Saint* the previous year. As I said, good meeting grounds!

Over the years I found myself accompanying Albert to a large selection of elite film premieres and being introduced to so many movers and shakers, that I lost count of the number of stars I met. As the years passed, some of the big names I found myself being introduced to were stars I could only ever dream of meeting, let alone sitting in front of them at the premieres of their own movies and then greeting them afterwards. The stars included: Arnold Schwarzenegger at the premiere of his film *Jingle All the Way*, Madonna at *Evita* and Olivia Newton-John for the re-release of *Grease*. Albert showed me a taste of the high-life, a taste of Hollywood and what it was like to mix with the A-listers and what's more, I liked it!

One of the best shows Albert ever took me to see was to feature one of my favourite singers Ruthie Henshall, at the Albert Hall. We met up with John Gordon Sinclair before the show that day, who was supplying Albert with some tickets for the show. As Mr Sinclair was at that time dating Ms Henshall, Albert and I were of course given the best seats in the house. The next year another fabulous treat was also in store when Albert got me a front row seat at The Café Royal to see and later meet and greet both the amazing Cleo Laine and George Martin.

I must say it was always such a gas hanging out with Albert. Albert's cheeky and fun nature, alongside mine, always meant we would become like mischievous little kids again in one another's company and over the years both Albert and myself always enjoyed playing pranks on one another. In fact, Albert often refers to himself as 'The Joker of the pack' and in true form to this statement, his business card has a picture of a joker from a pack of cards emblazoned in full technicolor on the back of it.

As mentioned, Albert always placed me in one of the front two rows of every show he got me tickets for. On one occasion I was five minutes late - good old London underground - so the usher told me I had to sit at the back until half time. The show was starring my old friend Roy Kinnear. Albert had also given his good friend Cheri Lunghi tickets to see the show and had chosen exactly where we were both to sit. During the first half of the performance Roy was meant to chuck a bit of water out of a bucket and towards the audience. Albert however had another plan in mind. He called up Roy in advance and arranged for him to fill the bucket a bit higher than usual with rather cold water and chuck it over me instead. Thanks Albert! Albert had told Roy exactly where I would be seated in the audience. As I was late, Cheri had been placed in my seat instead. Roy could not see the faces of the members of the audience from the stage, so he just followed Albert's instructions and threw the water in the direction of stage right, second row, fifth seat in from the right. Needless to say, Cheri got soaked! I immediately realised what had happened and did not know what to do with myself! Whenever I saw Cheri after this time she would joke 'Thanks for the soaking Emma!' Personally I blame London underground. So whenever I go out with Albert I have Maureen Lipman calling out 'Ah, there's my little toilet friend!' and Cheri Lunghi saying 'Thanks for the soaking Emma!' What must people think? But not to worry, I got Albert back.

Before Albert gave up smoking, one evening just before we went into a movie premiere, Albert decided to quickly have one last cigarette before entering the auditorium. He asked if I had a lighter as he could not find his, as it had rather mysteriously gone missing. I was ready for this moment and had bought him a new lighter. As Albert released the lighter fuel, what he found instead of a flame was a long trail of water, which squirted out rather rapidly and soaked his nice newly pressed shirt just before we walked into the theatre. What can I tell you? I was just returning the favour!

The *piece de resistance* however, came from Albert. I fondly recall how on one particular occasion Albert called me up to ask me what I thought of the actor Jon Cryer. 'Very cute!' was my response 'I wouldn't mind dating him!' Unbeknownst to me Jon was actually standing beside Albert and listening in to the conversation the entire time. By the time I had finished my sentence he had taken the telephone from Albert's hand and was now on the phone answering instead. 'So let's meet up!' he said. Actually we did meet up after this time, with Albert in tow and we all had a bit of a giggle about the whole conversation.

I knew how lucky I was to be able to attend so many premieres at the flick of a switch, however, in the late 1990s there was one particular premiere I desperately wanted to attend that even the inimitable Albert was unable to get me a ticket for; so I decided I would just have to gate-crash it instead! The movie in question was the premiere of Arnold Schwarzenegger's new flick *Eraser* and I was determined to be at the premiere. A couple of friends and myself decided to make it our mission to attend. My good friend Beverly was working at the BBC at the time and had managed to attain an official invite to the party. She kindly informed me who was co-ordinating the event and where the secret location for the party would be held. The after party was being held at Alexander Palace in London. We knew the time the film was set to show in Leicester Square and we knew the duration of the film. All we

138

had to work out now was how long it would take the coach to get to Alexander Palace after it had picked everyone up from Leicester Square.

By the time the coach load arrived at Ally Pally, my two friends and I were already waiting in the back parking lot dressed to the nines in our evening gowns. As soon as we saw the coach arrive and the celebrities start to poor out, we quickly and rather skilfully may I add, hoisted ourselves over the back railings in our heels and gowns and gracefully walked in with all the other stars. We were of course stopped at the front desk and told our names were not on the list so we could not go in. Our response? Obviously we announced the name of the organiser in a rather haughty fashion, then demanded to be told the name of the person on the door, informing them we would have to report them for their complete incompetence and for not carrying out their job properly, as our names had clearly been left off the list! Before you could say 'Schwarzenegger', we were all escorted personally into the main event. There were stars literally oozing out of the woodworks. Everyone who was anyone was there. Mr Schwarzenegger was extremely friendly and went round to everyone, including ourselves and greeted us with a firm handshake and an hello. The set up was magnificent. There was a large dinosaur in the centre of the foyer and the main room had been turned into a funfair. When everyone took to the dance floor I immediately started to go crazy, throwing some of my best funky shapes in my most unenviable manner, alongside Martine McCutcheon, Julia Sawalha, Richard E Grant and a large handful of other celebs. Then the funniest thing occurred. Singer Mick Hucknell walked onto the dance floor and as he did, all eyes turned to him. All the celebrities present started to copy his moves. However, what all the other stars were completely unawares of was, Mr Hucknell's eyes had met mine as his feet made touch down and caressed the dance floor and for the fun of it, he was actually copying my every dance move. No one else realised he was copying my every move and continued to copy him, as I continued to lead the way on the dance floor. He winked at me and we carried on with our game, with the rest of the crowd completely oblivious they were actually copying me not him. What fun!

During the second half of my year working at the BBC I worked in television. I worked on a variety of top shows during this time including; working in the Science and Features Department on the show *Tomorrow's World*, the newsroom and also with the children's presenters. In the newsroom I worked alongside Peter Sissons, Moira Stuart, Anna Ford, Kate Adie, Andrew Harvey and Martyn Lewis and I also had brief work-related interactions with Kilroy Silk. My job was to assist the presenters in their preparation and development of scripts, which were to be read on the news and also I was a runner when required. On budget day I was one of the main runners and was up and down the stairs all day. These were the days I felt fit enough and not yet of slight superannuation to run up and down the stairs all day without complaining I'd twisted something in the process! Anna Ford was the news presenter who was the most taken with me. In fact, so much so, that when I eventually informed her I was planning to leave the BBC to go and study for a degree, she asked me to forget my degree and stay on and work solely for her. I told Anna that, whilst very flattered by her offer, I needed to get my degree.

Working with the children's presenters was great fun too. I worked alongside Philippa Forrester, Andi Peters and Toby Anstis and also had brief interactions with Simon Courtes. There was actually a bit of a class war going on at the Beeb between the newsreaders and the children's' presenters, which used to make me smile being bang in the middle of it. During my time spent working with the children's' presenters Toby Anstis and myself became firm friends and started to go everywhere together. We were almost attached at the hips during this time. A rumour started that we were dating but this was not true. Rather oddly someone sent a box of bubble wrap to our office, marked for the attention of the two of us. It turned out to be from a young lady who was a tad obsessed with Toby. We were only ever just good friends but; apart from the bubble-wrap incident, which we both found a bit bizarre, a little disturbing and also sort of amusing at the very same time, we did find the rumour quite hilarious nevertheless and often used to play up to it!

My fondest memories of working at the BBC are probably of working both with the Radiophonic composers and also with the children's' presenters. We had such a crazy time in the children's' office in particular. Andi, Toby and I used to play music very loudly in the room and dance on the tables! The head of the BBC, Alan Yentob, held office immediately down the corridor to ours. One day his PA knocked on the door and said 'Mr Yentob has asked if you would kindly keep the noise level down and get off the tables!'

Then there was the day I was asked by the head of the children's presenter team Paul Smith, if I could help him out and collect the comedy duo Trevor Williams and Simon Hickson, from *Going Live!* and *Live and Kicking,* from reception and take them down to make-up, as the lady who usually collected them was away. Paul gave me a brief description of how to get to make-up. Soon after collecting Trevor and Simon and walking round the BBC for a while, I realised I had not one clue where we were going, so turned to the duo and apologised. 'Not to worry', said Simon, 'the BBC's round, so if we keep walking, we'll get there eventually!' and that we did!  The fact the BBC was built in a circular formation was actually a standing joke with everyone who worked there, as people would always comment 'Watch your back!'

Andi asked me one day if I would like to help him out in the famous 'broom cupboard'. This was the name given to the small studio he presented the continuity links from. 'Would I ever!' I replied. I was given the task that day of operating his sidekick, the puppet Edd the Duck. I joked for a long time after how my one claim to fame was having my hand up Edd the Duck's butt! My boss, Paul Smith, joked that seeing as how close Edd and I had become and that we had formed such an affinity for one another, perhaps I would be happy to carry out a day of sending out signed autographs on postcards on behalf of Edd, to his many numerous fans. I was of course to act as Edd's scribe. 'Sure!' I said. I dutifully spent an entire afternoon signing my hand to Edd's autograph and placed them into the BBC post box to be sent out to all his fans. Later that day Paul came to check my handiwork and discovered I had signed all the autographs with only one 'd'!

So they all had to be redone. Well, how was I supposed to know Edd was precious?

I often got invited to rehearsals for various BBC and non-BBC shows taped at BBC Television Centre. One of the rehearsals I vividly recall being invited to was for the show *This is Your Life*. The information about who the person was who was to be surprised that evening was strictly confidential and during the rehearsal Michael Aspel was extremely careful to deliver his lines, in a manner which would not let on to the few audience members present, which star was to receive the famous red book treatment. Unexpectedly Michael introduced through his famous sliding doors Philippa Forrester. Spotting me in the audience, as there were only around five of us sitting there, Philippa excitedly beckoned me onto the stage. Eventually and with a little bit of added persuasion from Michael Aspel, who wanted someone to run his lines with, he asked if I would help him out and I agreed. Michael started asking me a series of questions about the undisclosed star and I answered completely made up on the spot sentences, utterly unawares of whom I was talking about. It was actually quite comical.

Also, while I was working at the BBC, I was given the chance to watch Adrian 'Ade' Edmondson filming his latest production. The first thing I recall thinking was how much waiting around the actors had to deal with. I have been quite fortunate in my career as an actress and have not as yet had to endure too much waiting around but I always take a good book with me just in case.

I was also invited by my friend Beverly to accompany her to see *Joseph and the Amazing Technicolor Dreamcoat* at the London Palladium, at that time starring Phillip Schofield. Beverly had managed to secure two free tickets from the BBC and an invite to the party afterwards in the Green Room. Funnily enough, shortly before the time Phillip Schofield took over the role from Jason Donovan, I had been invited out to one of Bill Kenwright's famous parties with Albert and been introduced to Jason Donovan. After speaking with both myself and Albert about the play and having spoken to him about the content of the show, I had really wanted to see it for a long time now; so double jumped at the ticket being offered to me by Beverly.

The week Beverly and I went to see the show was the opening night of Phillip Schofield's run of the show, which was why there was a party being thrown in one of the Beeb's Green Rooms afterwards. Beverly and I had managed to get to the theatre slightly behind schedule and were told we were not allowed to take our front row seats in the auditorium until the second half of the show. We were shown to two seats right at the back of the auditorium; far removed from the rest of the audience. We felt somewhat like two naughty schoolgirls, sat right at the back of the class. During the first half of the show, Phillip had a planned routine where he was to come off stage and wonder into the audience to give someone a 'golden ticket'. He wandered towards the back of the auditorium and then spotted the two lonely figures of both Beverly and myself in the back row. With microphone in hand, he announced to the auditorium, 'I've found my lucky golden ticket winner.' He walked up to us and said 'Oh dear, my poor friend's at the back of the auditorium, all by yourselves' then handed me the golden ticket. During the interval Beverly and I were kindly shown to our correct seats, which were in the front row, stage left. At the start of the second act Phillip broke the third wall but still remaining in character spoke to the audience with words akin to: 'Well, I gave my golden ticket out to someone right at the back of the auditorium, now I will shake the hand of someone at the front of the crowd.' He started to walk down stage left and moved towards where I was sitting, holding out his hand for me to shake. With the bright lights on Phillip, he probably could not really see the face of the hand of the person he was about to shake until I moved forward to take his hand. As he shook my hand and spotted my face, he nearly fell back on stage in surprise and declared 'My golden ticket lady again!' The audience laughed, as did Phillip, as did I.

After the show Beverly and I found our way up to the Green Room and were greeted by the one and only Nigel Havers, who, the charming and suave gentleman he is, immediately fetched me a glass of red wine. Then he said 'Can I introduce you to Phillip?'

The next thing you knew, before you could even say 'Technicolour Dreamcoat', he gently turned poor Phillip round from his standing point to introduce him to both Beverly and myself. Phillip nearly jumped out of his own skin! 'Hi', I said. 'I think you may have dropped this!' and handed him back his golden ticket. After explaining to Phillip who I was, we all had a good laugh about the entire situation.

It was during my time working as a PA in the Science and Features department that my boss expressed the view he felt I was an intelligent woman (well, what can I tell you, the salary was low!) and he strongly felt I should leave the BBC and go and study for a degree (then again, perhaps this was just his way of getting rid of me!). I had been expressing a desire to go back and study for a degree in the arts for a while now. I had been particularly interested to study for a degree in drama, as I had once before, upon leaving college. However mum was, just as she was back then, dead set against the idea of me studying for a degree in drama and both her and dad would not even allow me to bring a prospectus for a drama course into the house. They were just trying to protect their asset - me. They were fearful of me not succeeding in a career in acting, so encouraged me to go down the normal education route first but the bug was well and truly inside me, eating away like a nasty disease and every time I thought it was in remission it would over the years rear its nasty little head and say 'I'm back!' But for now, the bug would have to be kept under strict lock and key. Mum and dad informed me I would be allowed to study for an arts degree, after which time if I still took an interest in studying a drama course at a later stage in life, they might consider it. It was, however, this particular boss in the Science and Features department, who kindly sat with me over the period of a few lunch breaks and not only helped me look through all the different prospectuses for art courses but also helped me fill out my application to UCAS (Universities and Colleges Admission Services) for my degree. I eventually left the BBC to go back and study for my long overdue 'What a waste of a good education' undergraduate degree.

With my mind now firmly made-up to study for a degree in art, having had to place the idea of studying for a degree in drama to the back of my mind, I attended a few open days at different art schools in London, including Goldsmiths and The London Institute - which were and still are two of the best art schools in London. Prospective students were asked to bring along a portfolio of their work. I quickly gathered together some of my artwork from my school days and some of my drawings made in my spare time, framed each piece of work neatly and placed them in a small portfolio ready to take with me. During the open day at The London Institute I was advised by one of the course tutors, upon looking at my work, that my style of art was more design orientated than fine art based. He recommended I apply for their new course, which was a Bachelor of Arts in interior architecture. After being invited to attend interview at The London Institute for this course and also to interview for a similar course at Goldsmiths, I started to prepare myself for the day of the interviews. Sadly, what came next led to one of my relatives and myself not speaking the following year.

The younger daughter of the Drummond family came round to visit the house in Wembley one day, to visit both Vera and Sam and me and expressed her interest in viewing my portfolio. She clearly wasn't impressed with my work and at a time, when I would have very much appreciated family support, she sadly seemed unable to show any encouragement in my desire to apply for a degree. In fact, her words were, in my opinion, so unkind with regards to the lack of talent she described she felt I had, I felt unable to visit the Drummond family household due to these hurtful words for an entire year after.

I am pleased to write however, I did get offered a place at The London Institute, which was my first choice, to study for a Bachelor of Arts degree with Honours, with a major in interior architecture and retail and exhibition design and a minor in the history of art and design. The course was extremely tough; incorporating both retail and exhibition design, technical studies, visual studies, graphic and 3-D design, photography, business studies, retail management, marketing, and CAD (Computer

Aided Design). There, now you have half of my resumé! During the course I was auspicious enough to attain a work placement at *The Economist* newspaper in their Graphic Design department and even get some of my work published on the front page of the newspaper, as well as creating logos for some of the main articles too. Seeing my artwork in print like this was a real buzz and to be honest, a bit of a boost for the old ego too.

Just before I started my course at my new university, I decided it was time to leave home. This was much to mum's upset. I had grown up in a household where every night mum would say to me: 'Don't leave me; I might not be here in the morning. I'm old. I might die in the night'. This had always made it very hard for me to make the decision to leave home but I now felt I was at an age where I needed my independence. I moved in with a friend and another man I had not met before who, for the sake of this book, I shall call Jerry. Unfortunately, no sooner had I moved out did I need to move back home again to mum's complete joy, as during the first week of being in my new flat Jerry pointed a gun at me and what's more fired it! It turned out to be a replica but the whole experience made it far too uncomfortable for me to want to remain at the premises.

Upon my first day at university I arrived early to make sure I had plenty of time to settle myself in and to find a good seat in the class. I was shown the room by the secretary, who informed me I was not early but in fact late and that the class had already commenced. I sheepishly knocked on the door and received a huge verbal telling-off from the tutor for being late and was informed the next time this happened I would not be allowed into the room once the class had started. I sunk into my chair. The tutor then pointed at me and asked me a question about an architectural type of structure. Being it was my first day I really didn't have a clue what he was talking about so responded: 'I'm sorry, I don't know.' 'Haven't you been listening and taking notes in previous classes?' Previous classes? I informed him this was my first day. The tutor then completely softened his tone and said: 'Ah, you're not late, you're early! You want my next class.' Of course it turned out when my class did actually commence it was indeed the same tutor who was taking the previous class but he had a good sense of humour and we joked about this incident for a long time after. Oh and by the way, I was never late to any of his lessons after that!

My poor parents didn't get to see much of me during the first year of my degree, as I literally spent most of my time at home with my head in my books, working right the way though into the early hours of the night on more than one occasion. Having said that, being that dad had once been a chartered surveyor and as it happens also a great seamstress - perhaps this is even where I got my flair for art, (incidentally Claudia was also a great artist as was my dad Martin and his parents before him), dad took a very keen interest in my work and it gave him much continued pleasure watching me conceptualise and design both the internal structure of buildings and exhibition layouts from scratch to completion. It was partly due to this course and the process of seeing a product materialise from a vision to completion, even if only to model scale, that I realised it is possible to make any vision a reality. I soon came to realise humans are the architects of our own dreams.

Whilst at the London Institute I became friendly with a small group of girls. We would often spend time together working through design ideas and of course chatting about which guys we thought were cute on the course, which believe me, offered plenty of light relief from the often stressful nature of the course. One girl in the group named Claire lived near me, so we always travelled home together and started to form a close friendship. These friendships were very important for the survival of this course and this light-hearted banter also served to keep ones spirits high through the long hours of work endured. I was devastated to learn after completing my course at The London Institute that a long over-due telephone call from Claire was, as with Alison before her, due to a car accident. Claire had fallen asleep at the wheel of her car, just weeks after graduation and died instantly. I could not believe this was the second close friend I had lost in this way. On a personal level I started to become paranoid that everyone I got close to would either die or leave me somehow.

Just before my final year at The London Institute my fears came to fruition once again, as a group of friends and myself went to stay at a friend's house in Oxford. I woke up in the middle of the night and screamed out my grandmother Rose's name. The next day I found out my beloved grandmother had passed away that night at exactly the moment I had called out her name. I was left feeling devastated and heartbroken once more. This was now the second time in my life I had foreseen when someone close to me was going to die, the first similar experience happening to me with regards to my uncle Ellis.

Towards the second half of the year, the school announced the course was having funding issues. We were advised if we left after the second year we could still attain an HND (Higher National Diploma) and then use the two years towards completing our BA (Bachelor of Arts) with Honours degree elsewhere. Not wanting to hang around and then later discover I was too late to apply to finish my degree elsewhere, I quickly placed on my 'go-getter' hat and started to apply to other universities to transfer my degree. I asked the course tutor at The London Institute which degree course in London he could recommend would be similar to ours and would be the best for me to apply to at another university. He suggested the Middlesex University had the best course at the time. I immediately sent off an application to the university directly, hence avoiding all the officiality of UCAS, now that I was already in the system. I soon found out the name of the head of the course and called her personal line at the university. She explained to me the course already had a full register and there was no way they could allow me to join the course. The government only allocated 'x' amount of seats to each course and she explained all seats had already been taken. 'I'll bring my own chair!' I jested. She laughed but continued to inform me there was just no way of placing me on the course. I was informed I would be placed on a waiting list but was also told the list was long and there were a good number of people already in front of me waiting for someone to drop off the course ready to take their place. Now placing on my somewhat demonstrative and possibly slightly annoying hat, I called the head of the course every other day for around three weeks; leaving jovial messages on her answer phone to remind her who I was - as if by this stage she could ever forget, even is she wanted to! One day I found my luck was in and she picked up the telephone and said: 'Okay, your persistence has paid off. I can see how much you want this and how determined you are. You're on the course and we're even giving you a seat!'

I had got to the point in my career as a student of architecture, where I was completely exhausted from so many late nights of drawing blueprints. On one such occasion, when one of the course leaders commented the next day one of my drawings was a few millimetres out, which in ratio to reality he said meant 'The building could fall down!' I replied through sheer tiredness 'So, let the building fall!' This was when it dawned on me I didn't care to become an architect! When I started the course at The Middlesex University I decided therefore, to change my minor to my major. This was once again another very tough course, where long hours of study were part and parcel. The course incorporated learning about: art and design, the history of art, community art, human resource management, philosophy, psychology, colonial, political and social discourse as well of course as continuing three-dimensional design for my minor studies. And now you have the rest of my resumé - well almost!

I thoroughly enjoyed my degree years, even although things on the domestic front, in relation to the Drummond family, were not always going well and in fact often felt as if they were going from bad to worse. I continued to sense a deep routed feeling of enmity towards me and I could never understand what I had done to cause this ill will, which as a child and well into my teenage years continued to upset me greatly. As an adult and now removed from the situation, I am able to see with a sense of clarity it was not necessarily anything I had done to cause these feelings of animosity. I only wish I could have discovered this knowledge as a child, as it may have saved a lot of pain and tears. I had at least for now finally found a constant outlook for my creativity and threw myself completely into my work at school. The tutors on my

149

degree course were of exceptional standard and one of my main tutors had been enviably taught directly by my favourite artist, Salvador Dali.

I recall one particular day, when I was unusually late for class, having to walk into the pitch black of the lecture theatre. Everyone else, who had been in the theatre for a while, had of course found their eyes had got used to the dark. They could see around the room but coming into the room straight from a lit hallway, I could see nothing in front of me at all. Suddenly I spotted the hand of a guy beckoning me towards where he was sitting and indicating there was a free seat next to him. The lecturer stopped talking to allow me enough time to clamber, in my embarrassment with everyone watching, through the numerous bodies to get to where the gap was, where no one was sitting. Bearing in mind everyone else could see around the room, they of course knew what was coming. I on the other hand had not a clue! What was coming was this guy had decided to lead me straight into sitting in a gap. There was no seat, just a gap where a seat had once lived and I innocently walked straight into his trap! I sat down with a thud and landed on my posterior on the floor. The entire room cheered. I guess it served me right for being late!

It was during this very same course that, as well as attaining a sore backside, I also managed to knock myself out and attain concussion in the very last term of my course. This resulted in having to extend my deadline in order to complete my degree. At high school, whenever I was bored in class, instead of passing notes around the room, I used to look up new words in the dictionary and learn their meaning to improve my lexicon and impress my peers. I have thankfully always been gifted in English and have always been a competent writer and speller. This resulted in me often being referred to by some of my peers as 'the walking dictionary' and later by some of my students too when I became a teacher. During my final term at university however, whilst on a weekend trip with my boyfriend at that time, I managed to successfully knock myself out on a shelf and my good spelling days were about to take a tumble, at least into the immediate future. Just like a bad film, the incident rushed back to me in a succession of short flash backs over the course of the following two weeks. I well and truly had concussion. In fact, it was so bad that over the course of the next few months I forgot how to spell simple words such as 'and' and 'but'! Strangely enough, the more complicated words did not cause me too many problems. Because of this, I received an extension on my final coursework at university under extenuating circumstances, bought myself a large dictionary and finished the entire course a number of weeks after everyone else had already left the premises. I was so worried I wouldn't graduate the same time as everyone else but thankfully I did and attained both an HND and a 2:1 BA degree with Honours, both in interior architecture and the study of the history of art and design, including art practice in the community, respectively. So much for my 'what a waste of an education' now huh?

My university years unfortunately completely saw me loose touch with my Jewish identity and heritage, as I was the only Jewish person on both my courses. What it did bring me however, was an appreciation of architecture and art and even modern art became more accessible to me. Do you have any idea how hard it is to create a piece of art that spells out the word 'love', using only colour, shape, line and no words? No, really! If you think this might be difficult, try differentiating between the concept of love and passion or even anger and aggression! A single circle in the centre of a canvass, with nothing else around it hanging on the wall of The Tate Gallery, suddenly began to have more meaning to me after art school.

My parents were friendly with Sir Rhodes Boyson. He had watched me grow up over the years and seen me progress through my school years. As it happens, when I was at university I met him again at the opening of a friend's estate agent, after not having seen him for a number of years. I recall Sir Rhodes, as he has since become known, asking me what I was doing with my life at that point in time and I informed him I was studying for a degree in art. Sir Rhodes commented: 'A fine girl such as yourself studying for a degree in the arts?' and then the final *piece de resistance*; 'What a waste of an education! You were in line to study

151

law or medicine or something of the ilke at Oxbridge.' Once again I was being gently nudged for my choice in career paths. I knew Sir Rhodes meant well, as he had always been very fond of me but I distinctly recall responding: 'Sir Rhodes, may I ask you a question? Do you and your wife own your house.' 'Of course', he replied. I continued: 'Do you also own a car?' 'Indeed' was the response. I continued further: 'And did you and your wife choose the style, make and model of your car and the furniture to adorn your home?' 'We did' he replied. 'Then aren't you lucky there are people in the world like me studying for degrees which will enable you to make those choices, else we would all be living in homes and driving cars which looked like cardboard boxes - the same and indistinguishable from the next man's - and what a boring world that would be - would it not?' 'Clever girl' I believe was his final response!

Whilst I was at university I met one of my boyfriends, who for the sake of this book, I will call Joseph. Joseph was a professional magician by trade. How we met was of course by magic! We met at a small gathering of friends, after a New Year's Eve party. One of the friends in the group had asked Joseph to perform a magic trick when she had discovered his chosen career path. As she handed me a pack of cards to hand to him, I happened to notice one of the cards had a blank face, so I pulled it out and surreptitiously handed it to Joseph. Boy did we both have fun with that one with the group of friends! But yes, sadly Joseph did a disappearing act on me in the end. Sorry, I had to get that one in there but not before inviting me out to Vegas to meet the magnificent Siegfried and Roy and their stunning white tigers. Their show was one of the most amazing performances I have ever seen and I was literally mesmerised, which more than made up for Mr Magic going AWOL upon our return and not that I'm knocking the magician but the tigers were magnificent!

Incidentally, the first time I got invited round to 'meet the folks' I was secretly wondering why everything in the house was positioned at such a low level. Was this some kind of magic trick or perhaps even a house fit for a magician? The light switches were almost waist high and the work surfaces in the kitchen also appeared low but I was too embarrassed to ask why. I then found out the exciting news the house did have some very special magic about it, as it had previously been owned by *Star Wars* legend R2-D2, Kenny Baker. We soon sat down to a wonderful Friday night roast, and a very nice veggie roast for me, both served by his mother. Then my favourite item on any dinner plate arrived on the table; roast potatoes. I was advised to tuck in. I placed my fork into one of the potatoes to discover this particular potato was rock hard. What was I to do? Should I risk seeing if all the potatoes were of this same consistency, possibly embarrassing both his mother and myself in my plight? Perhaps I could dismiss this particular spud by refraining from my favourite item on the menu altogether and feign my dislike of the vegetable, questioning how they ever got onto my plate? 'Opps, I thought they were turnips!' Nope, this wouldn't' work. I knew I probably couldn't afford to refuse to eat it, as this was the first time I had been invited back to meet his parents and in a Jewish household refusing the lady of the house's food is actually akin to starting World War 3! No food equals a feud! I was just going to have to find a way to break open that sucker of a spud whilst Ma Joseph wasn't looking. His mum walked back into the R2-D2 kitchen. Here was my chance! I dove in, knife and fork a blast. The potato bounced off the plate, catapulted off the window, back onto the table, off the table and then landed on the floor with a thud to be gobbled up immediately by the cat! Joseph's father laughed uncontrollably. Mrs J walked back into the room and exclaimed 'Did I hear a noise?' 'You did!' announced her husband 'It was the cat!' And you wonder why that relationship didn't last the distance!

I often went with Joseph to The Magic Circle on a Monday night. I'd always been fascinated with the art of magic and slight of hand and was always determined to discover how the tricks were done. Once a year when I was young, we all would visit a good friend of dad's who lived by the river, a few miles up from Henley and I would get the chance to meet his neighbour, Uri Geller. I recall as a child meeting and being completely fascinated by his spoon bending tricks, which had partly been the start of my interest in magic and the art of illusion. I was later to meet Uri Geller again at the magic circle one evening with Joseph and was always amazed at how his spoon bending illusions appeared so real - or were they?

Through Joseph I became good friends with the magician Marc Paul. Marc later asked me to appear in a magic video he was making with co-star magician Anthony Owen and magician and stand-up comics Daniel Butler and John Lenahan. A fun-packed day was had by all! The day ended with us all going out for a meal to celebrate the wrap. John Lenahan's good friend and comedienne exquisite Jo Brand came along for the ride; offering some of her straight-laced humour to sugar-coat the day's events. This shoot was the first time I had ever had the spotlight of a professional camera turned on me and whilst I loved the attention, I was thoroughly nervous about the whole experience. The guys, however, made me feel very relaxed and at ease and it turned out to be an 'ace' day. This was my first taste of making friends with the camera and I was keen to get re-acquainted again shortly. This I did when Marc asked me to film with him again the following year; this time for a television pilot he and fellow magicians Paul Andrews and Anthony Owen were putting together, with help also from fellow magicians Nick Reade and John Danbury. The show was called '*Could it be Magic?*'

Just before making the first video with the guys from Dynamic FX, many magicians in The Magic Circle had started to recognise me as 'Joseph's girlfriend'. Joseph invited me to accompany him to be a member of the audience of *The Paul Daniels Magic Show*. We got stuck in traffic and arrived a bit late. As soon as we walked into the studio the entire crew turned their attention to the latecomers trying to discreetly sit down. The lighting crew decided to shine their large gels on us to emphasize the point. Paul Daniels recognised Joseph as a fellow magician and made reference as such. Before I could sit down he pointed a finger in my direction and said I wasn't to sit down but was to come and join him on the stage. I smiled sweetly and continued my mission to place my posterior neatly on the chair beneath but he was onto me! I was the girlfriend of a fellow magician and was going to have to pay for the pleasure! Paul continued to persuade me to come onto the stage and I continued to shake my head in polite refusal. Eventually however and with the encouragement of applause from the audience, generated I must add by Paul, I agreed. I was then given a release form to sign and asked if I would mind assisting Richard Turner, a well-known magician who had come over from Texas to be on the show. I said I would be glad to help. I remember in make-up the director saying to me: 'Don't worry darling, the camera loves you, you've got absolutely nothing to worry about. It's easy; just go out there and have fun!' I remember thinking to myself, 'he may not have anything to worry about as he knows what he is doing but me, on the other hand, now that is a whole different story!'

Richard Turner blew me away. He was amazing and it turned out he was also registered as blind, yet this had in no way affected his slight of hand. A funny moment occurred when Richard showed the audience all the different styles of shuffling; ending each time with the cards suited and in the right order, showing a variety of shuffling techniques right down to the most basic shuffle he could muster. Richard expressed the idea it couldn't get more basic than that. 'Oh yes it can!' I thought to myself. 'Lucky you've never seen my DIY shuffle.' Richard must have overheard my inner dialogue, which clearly spoke to soon, as he said 'Would you do me a favour and give the deck a shuffle?' I lay the cards on the table and spread the suckers around like butter! The audience nearly wet themselves they were laughing so hard. I'm certain that kind of shuffle is probably illegal in Texas!

The next part of my journey through life was to see me break up with my first long term boyfriend, experience more upset at home and seek out the comfort of God as a response. This began my internal battle between my upwardly moving career in the entertainment world and leading a religious lifestyle.

*It is possible to make any vision a reality.*
- Emma Fletcher

## 7

## *Music to My Ears*

**One learns by doing a thing, for though you think you know it, you have no certainty until you try.** - Sophocles

*Paul: Emma's journey through the music industry would alone justify the subject of a book! In this chapter, however, one is really able to learn and appreciate just how much music means to Fletcher. It is also an opportunity to discover how and why both fate and religion came together and inspired Emma to take a slightly different path in her life as well as in the world of show business.*

Emma: Now in the final year of my degree at The Middlesex University, mum fell down the stairs and cut her head open. Both her eyesight and hearing had deteriorated. She was suffering with glaucoma and was by this stage registered as blind. She had misjudged the stairs. On discovering her lying at the foot of the stairs, I instantly saw her head was bleeding very badly. I managed to get her into the bath and wrapped a towel around her head in an attempt to stem the bleeding. Despite the shock, which this experience obviously gave her, mum could seemingly do nothing but demand where her beloved handbag was! She was rushed to hospital in an ambulance and was still demanding her handbag up until the moment the ambulance doors were closed. On being examined at the hospital, doctors informed me mum had split open one of her legs during the fall and were worried this could cause a thrombosis. Because of this possibility, I was given the worrying news mum might not even make it through the night. Fortunately however, mum was a fighter and not only made it through the night, but came home as well - still enquiring where her handbag was! This entire incident managed to greatly shock and upset me and reminded me just how fragile mum had become.

Almost immediately after this time I broke up with a guy I had been dating seriously for a year and a half and became quite ill. When this relationship ended, even although I knew it was not the right relationship for me, it left me shattered. I could not think clearly for a very long time after. I think really this was more to do with the fact I was experiencing a loss again; rather than it was to do with the breakdown of the relationship itself.

It was the break-up of this relationship however, which caused the on-set of my short-lived eating disorder to develop and caused mum to contact the local doctor's surgery to make an appointment for me to see a counsellor. Very soon after this relationship ended I stopped eating and became stick thin. Eventually I found I was unable to hold my food down inside me anymore; as my stomach had shrunk and the food I ate came right back up. This was when mum started to become very concerned and made the appointment for me to go and see a counsellor at the local surgery. I refused to go but she told me if I wasn't going then I would have to cancel the appointment myself, as she was not going to do it for me. Clever! I was always brought up to have manners, so I rang the doctor's surgery to cancel the appointment and of course somehow they encouraged me to go in for the session. This session helped but I did not really talk about the main issues at hand, as the counsellor was male and I did not feel comfortable talking to him about what had happened to me in the past, so surfed around the real troubling issues.

Having spent so many years studying again and then becoming ill, I started to feel it was time for a bit of light relief in my life and decided perhaps it was the right time to rekindle my love affair with writing music; once again to serve me as a form of emotional release. I started to realise however much I tried to ignore the desire to be on stage, it just kept following me through life and people I met kept encouraging me to pursue my dream. I soon found myself befriending a girl at The Middlesex University who, you guessed it, was managing a band that had a record contract with a large label and once again I found myself being privy to finding out more about how the industry worked. I soon found

157

myself picking up pen and paper once again and starting to write lyrics and melodies to my own songs once more.

During the very same month I rekindled my love affair with music, a good friend asked me to go with her to a spiritual lecture on Judaism. Knowing I had become ill of late, she felt the lecture would be of benefit to me and might also be able to bring me some inner-peace. I did indeed find many comforting words in the lecture and decided to continue going to more. Not one to be taken in on comfort alone, I decided to research my new discoveries and found a lot of what I discovered made a great deal of sense to me; as well of course as continuing to offer me comfort at this time.

As my interest in my own faith started to increase and my knowledge of Judaism too, I started to realise this God I had hated for so many years perhaps did exist after all. It began to dawn on me that my anger towards God was in fact really just anger towards myself. Just as humans have the ability to become the architects of their own dreams, they are also the best architects of their own downfall. In fact, whenever we get angry with God, we are really just angry with ourselves. This realisation was ever more evident when it occurred to me we are all a part of God. My re-awakening of God's existence was not, however, born from blind faith but from information and the attainment of knowledge. Whilst I will not deny my gut in my decision-making, I feel we also have to allow our mind and soul to meet in order to make rational decisions. These days whilst I try hard to base my decisions on intellect, rather than purely upon emotion, all the while I still allow myself to remain faithful to my spiritual needs too; for when we neglect our spirituality we also neglect our intellectual and emotional health in the process. To live a life of purpose and balance we need to integrate all three areas into our life and allow them to work together, as one harmonious unit. A friend said to me recently 'The world is so large now, I'm certain God has forgotten some of us!' God has not forgotten us. He is the source of everything. Everything that ever was or will exist in this world is a manifestation of the Creator. It is not possible for God to forget us. It is us who have forgotten He.

The realisation of God's existence was in fact my 'eureka moment'. With this new realisation also came hope. I had up until now been lost for so long. For indeed, without hope all is lost but suddenly now I felt found. I had been devoid of allowing myself to believe in a higher presence for so long, feeling perhaps a higher presence might exist but allowing my internal anger and frustrations at my circumstances to have short-sighted my vision in this area. After Claudia passed on I had a short love affair with Buddhism, introduced to me by my cousin Anna. I had found Buddhism to be a beautiful and worthy religion and at the time it brought me a great sense of inner peace and calm over the many days I sat and chanted *Renge*. I was most inspired by the Buddhist ideology of how one gets out of life what they put into it; which is basically the essence of Karma - but my romance with Buddhism was short-lived as, in my most humble opinion, I did not feel that for me it was able to answer all my burning questions - but now I had started a discovery into my own religion and found it did indeed answer those very same questions. Could it be the very essence of myself I had been trying to escape for so long - being Jewish - was perhaps now the one thing that was about to save me? The only problem was, I was not certain a religious lifestyle was for me; as surely it was not conducive to run alongside a life choice in the entertainment industry? And so my internal battle had begun.

By the final year of my degree I took up singing lessons with the singing teacher Janet Edwards, as a hobby really. The class, which was over a two month period every weekend, consisted of a small group of around five people. My trip up to town to attend this class became the highlight of my week. I distinctly recall one of the first things Janet telling us was her husband was an architect and she felt anyone who was good with numbers or art would be a good musician and an even better singer. Perhaps I was in with a chance, I thought. She explained she felt singing was akin to architecture, as she said the creation of harmony is similar to the rule of the 'Golden Section' in architecture; which surmounts to balance.

One of the very first things we concentrated on, as any good-singing teacher will, was breathing techniques and control. Over the years I had always had problems making my voice heard, as so often I felt bullied into submission by certain members of the Drummond family; which was partly the reason for the onset of my slight stammer. I would open up my mouth to speak and end up almost eating my words. Because of this, from quite an early age I believed I didn't have anything to say that was worth listening to or have anything to say that would be of interest to anyone else. In my anxious state, I started to form a habit of speaking very quickly and rushing and mumbling my words, to get whatever I had to say out of the way as quickly as possible. Interestingly, whenever I have been stressed in my life, my voice is always the first thing to suffer. I once read stress related illness often manifests itself where the host is most stressed. This causes emotional problems to transfer to body symptoms; which makes sense why over the years the first thing to suffer was always my voice, as it was symbolic of a residue of a past life - of not being listened to. I found Janet's classes helped me to re-find my voice and when I started to sing I found I had the confidence to allow myself to sing with a powerful voice that, for the very first time, could finally be heard. Around this time I also started some jamming sessions in a friend's studio, to attain some practice at studio work again. My friend, Paul Rose, an extremely talented vocalist and now voice over artist too, helped my voice become stronger still.

I soon found myself auditioning for and later joining a new tribute band, which was being put together by a local singer and musician. There were five singers in the group and one pianist. The idea was to form a harmony group and sing old classic songs, with the intention of going round retirement homes to put a little love into the resident's days. Our days of gigging didn't really get off the ground but being a part of the group was in itself a great experience and I made some wonderful friends in the process, as well as honing my skills in harmonisation.

Holding onto my realisation of refuelling my music aspirations, I was then recommended by a friend in the industry to contact the singing teacher to the stars, Tona de Brett. Tona has a large resumé to her name, teaching a plethora of stars to sing over the years and has also helped Johnny Rotten to shout in tune; no mean feat! I recall one day towards the end of one of my lessons, Tona asked me as per usual to carry out my scales. The doorbell and telephone rang at exactly the same time. Tona quickly opened the front door to let her next client in and then rushed to take the call. I turned round to find the singer Paul Young standing next to me. He was a very tall and handsome man. I froze. Paul turned to me and said: 'Very good, don't stop!' Paul started to sing my scales for me, so I joined in and we carried on with our scales. Up and down the vocal ladder we went, until Tona returned to the room. All in a day's work for the one and only marvel that is Tona de Brett!

Tona's son, John, was at the time running his own recording studios and offered to help me lay down some of my own tracks and also helped me create a backing track for them too. Over the course of the next couple of years I made a number of visits to John's studio and I also found myself working with a variety of other top producers; experimenting working with different ideas and sounds to create a demo of my own music. My song-writing skills had vastly improved since the days of *My Boy* and by the end of the year I started to feel confident enough to actively start approaching management companies with my demo, which incorporated three self-penned numbers; *Move Your Body* and *The Bare Truth*, both of which were pure dance/pop tracks and my jazz/show number *Bass Line*. I generated interest for this demo but eventually started to move away from dance, feeling I preferred guitar based pop, which I also felt was better suited to my voice. I created a second demo of three more songs; *Let's Talk*, *Picture of You* and *Anything You Want* in this new style. *Let's Talk* became my flagship track and would later generate a lot of interest for me from some of the biggest names in the industry.

Eventually I felt ready to approach my first management company, with a view to gaining a deal. I put on a sweet, frilly little mini-skirt and teased my hair into its soft natural curl. A close friend offered to drive me directly to the door of the management company of a very well known international artist. I knocked on the door, demo in hand and a woman answered the door. 'Yeah?' she said. 'Hi, my name's Emma. I rang earlier in the week to ask if I could deliver my demo and well, here I am and here it is!' Her gracious response was: 'You look like a complete tart!' then slammed the door in my face!

And that, my friends, was my first experience of trying to get my demo heard by a professional manager.

Around this time I was given some contact names by a deejay friend, Daniel Barres and also by Ricky Simmonds, one of the regular original cast members of the TV series *Grange Hill*. I was later also helped by Ricky's father Phil, who was working in the music industry at the time, both of whom I had met over the years, as they had lived at the bottom of my street in Wembley. I was later reacquainted with Phil again via Cyril Myers, the father of a good friend who lived in Manchester. (Cyril Myers was responsible for casting look-a-like talent for the ever popular television series *Star's in Their Eyes*). What a small world the world of showbiz is, as Paul Burton says; 'It's a small world but I wouldn't want to pay the electricity bill!'

Over the course of the next year I generated interest from some of the biggest names in the industry, including Mick Hucknall's manager Andy Dodd, who wrote to me expressing great interest in my voice but said unfortunately he could not consider representing me as So What Arts, his management company, worked solely for Simply Red. I also received the same positive response about my voice from Sue Harris at Blitz, who was at that time concentrating solely on the career of Peter Andre and great interest from Jeff Wayne at Wow! Records, who worked alongside my friend Adam Lamb on launching the music career of Catherine Zeta-Jones. I continued to receive more interest from managers Stephen James of The Dick James Organisation, part of Djamus Ltd., who at the time had a massive hit in the charts with a remix of an old classic *Do a Little Dance, Make a Little Love, Get Down Tonight*. More interest soon arrived again in the shape of Chris Hamill and Guy Phetham at Jupiter Red Spot Studios, who were responsible for producing Peter Andre's hit *Mysterious Girl* amongst many other chart successes at that time and continued interest from Chirstian Jepp and Steve Marshall at Big Life Management. Big Life was headed by Jazz Summers, the man responsible for masterminding the international success of bands such as Wham!, Soul II Soul, Soup Dragons, Coldcut, The Orb, Yazz, Lisa Stansfield and more recently The Verve, Badly Drawn Boy, Richard Ashcroft and one of my all time favourites, Snow Patrol. More great response to my sound came from Sevi at Stephen Budd Management, Graham Carpenter at Pachuco Management, who expressed interest in producing *Let's Talk*, Ian Carlile, Just Another Management Co, Ian McAndrew at Wild Entertainment, and also Ginga Records and Steve Gilmour at Backlash Music Management, all of whom expressed how much they absolutely loved what I was doing. With each encouraging word came the eventuality of getting a step closer to realising my dream. For those of you reading this book, who are perhaps not well-versed on some of the above folk in the British music industry, these guys were the people to generate interest from at that time and were all very big names behind the scenes.

Upon hearing my music, the guys at Stephen Budd Management kindly forwarded it to three other management companies, as did Justine Kavanah at Innocent, which was part of Virgin Records, Moose at Multiply Records, Tony Wadsworth at Parlophone Records and Peter Evans from Native Management. In fact, Peter Evans forwarded my demo to a relatively unheard of A & R (Artists and Repertoire) guy at the time named Simon Cowell. Although Simon Cowell was producing a number of successful acts at this time, he was still a relatively unknown in the public domain. Also around this time I sent a letter off to a 'Miss' Louis Walsh of Carol and Associates, mistaking Louis' name for Lois - opps! I only got standard letters back from both Simon and Louis' record companies but all the interest I was receiving elsewhere and the fact my demo was getting passed around the industry was encouraging enough and was the deciding factor for me to stay on my path of pursuing my singing career and of hopefully hitting the big time.

All the time I was actively pursing a career in music, both my interest in my religion and my faith were also fast growing; not to mention my visions had also kicked into overdrive.

A close friend asked if I would like to go with her and another friend to Eilat for a short break. I decided I would go. I had not been to Israel for years. The day before I was due to fly, my ex-boyfriend, Daniel, happened to call me. I hadn't spoken to him for many months at this point. He announced he had started to become religious and was currently studying at a Yeshiva (a male seminary) in Jerusalem, learning from the scriptures. He encouraged me to take a day out of my Eilat trip and meet up with him in Jerusalem. My friends did not mind. Daniel recommended I buy James Redfield's book the Celestine Prophecy and read it en route the long coach journey from Eilat to Jerusalem. This I did and found the book fascinating. Then something peculiar happened. I started to feel as if there were two outer-worldly eyes piercing the back of my neck. I looked round but there was no one there. Perhaps it was just the nature of the book I was reading? I continued to read on. The character in the book was taking a trip through the desert in search of a manuscript. How funny I thought, so was I. The hills turned into high ridges and distant baron valleys. The vegetation was now coarser. I looked up. Correct. The hills had now turned into high ridges and distant valleys. The vegetation was now coarser. The character in the book noticed a narrow crossroads ahead as they rounded a bend, then a small oddly shaped plant to his right and a small puddle of water to his left. I looked up. Sure enough there was the crossroads and an oddly shaped plant to my right and the small puddle of water to my left. Then a baron valley appeared, as if mirroring the book. Weird! I read on. The jeep in the story came to a halt, as a vehicle a hundred yards ahead blocked the way. The characters in the book then became stuck in a ditch and waited for 50 minutes before driving off safely. Suddenly, as I read the words, just as if they had flown off the page, another coach around a hundred yards ahead became visible. It was stuck in a ditch. It blocked our passage. Our coach screeched to a halt and we too became stuck in a ditch.

We waited for exactly 50 minutes for another coach coming the other way to pass by and help us back on our journey. By the time I reached Daniel I was an excitable bundle of nerves and convinced someone wanted me to be in Jerusalem.

The day's trip started with a visit to the Western Wall. As I approached the wall I suddenly fell into floods of tears and could not stop crying. It was as if someone had turned on a tap! I immediately understood why the term used to describe the wall is 'the Wailing Wall'. As I drew closer and touched one of the large stones on the wall's surface, I felt as if everyone I had ever lost was standing there with me. It was a very emotional moment and something in me shifted forever after this.

Upon my return from my trip I announced to my family I had decided I wanted to go and spend a few months at a women's seminary in Jerusalem. They were horrified. 'You will be brainwashed!' mum exclaimed. I assured her I wouldn't and explained this was something I felt strongly I needed to do. As clichéd as it sounded; all my hate for God had now started to turn into great love.

My grandfather Bill had diabetes and after his wife Rose passed away, in his grief he had stopped taking care of his health. He spent the next year of his life in hospital after contracting gangrene in his toe and eventually had to have his leg amputated to the knee. I visited Bill everyday in the hospital for the entire year. On one occasion upon my arrival to the hospital, I discovered Bill had been granted release for the day. He had made his way home with the intention of purposefully overdosing on insulin. I found him. The thought of Claudia and not being able to save her rushed through my mind. I managed to resuscitate Bill but he was not best pleased. This was once again another upsetting experience in my young life. I continued to visit Bill in the hospital everyday throughout the duration of his stay there, checking-up on his well-being. Bill was not permitted any more day releases due to his emotional state of mind but I knew he was in the care of good hands in the hospital and being looked after well. The last time I saw Bill I went to tell him I would be going to

Israel for a short while but would see him immediately upon my return. He looked at me and said: 'I don't want you to go.' A cold chill ran down my spine. I knew this was the last time I would see him. I wondered if I should cancel my trip but didn't want to add fuel to my thoughts. After discussion with Bill we both decided I should still go on my short trip. During my time at seminary Bill did indeed pass on and once again I woke up in the middle of the night calling out his name at the very moment he passed away. I decided to spend the next three months of my life at seminary in Israel, coming home only to attend Bill's funeral.

Daniel had given me a list of ten names of girls he said I should look out for whilst at the seminary. In a very weird and wonderful set of strange coincidences that commenced on the plane and continued throughout my entire stay in Israel, I met each of those girls in exactly the order he had written their names down on the list, without even hunting them down but through sheer chance. I felt strongly as if something or someone were watching over me during my time in Israel. Something weird was definitely happening to me and all those girls became a very significant part of the three months I spent at the seminary. I started to realise how our lives are not just a series of coincidences or chance meetings but in fact how every single moment is fine tuned from above and how our lives our being guided accordingly. To quote the novelist and poet Anatole France; *'Chance is the pseudonym God uses when he does not want to sign his name.'*

I truly believe we are each given a certain amount of time on this earth and then, when your number is called, well then that's your lot! Both my NDE experience and the time I was 'lost out at sea', showed me this; as what could have both times proved to have been fatal incidents, resulted in nothing more than a scare. Fate or luck? I hear the sceptics among you cry.

Well let me push the proverbial boat out a little farther. When I was studying at the seminary in Israel, every Tuesday morning a few girls I had become friendly with and myself would meet in the foyer of the school. We would then proceed to take a bus ride into the centre of Jerusalem, to carry out our big weekly shop on the

166

eastside of the main market. 'The centre of Jerusalem? Well, that's just asking for trouble!' I hear the sceptics amongst you cry once more... but wait for it!

One particular Tuesday, we all met in the foyer as per usual ready to set off, when a girl none of us had ever met before came up to us and had a *'Final Destination'* freak-out. She started to beg us not to go to the market, saying she had a vision it was going to be bombed that day and explained if we went we would all die. At first we all laughed, nervously it's true, believing her to be a bit of a nut job but when someone repeats themselves a number of times in this fashion, eventually believe you me, you listen! This girl panicked us all enough into making an executive group decision not to go to the market. An hour later it was revealed on the news a suicide bomber had taken out the eastside of the market at exactly the time we would have been there. This girl had saved our lives. Clearly our numbers had not been called that day. Perhaps she had been sent to us with a life saving message from above? My poor mum had seen the footage on the news in the UK and thought I was dead. By the time I managed to get through to the UK, as the telephone lines were continually blocked, my poor mum was having a nervous breakdown. There were lots of tears when we finally got to speak. This experience and other times I have been in what could have turned out to be fatal incidents, give me solace in the knowledge there is a bigger force watching over us and perhaps we are not alone or completely in control of our own destiny.

An even stranger event was to take place just under a year later when I visited Tsfat, an ancient city in northern Israel, with a group of friends. Tsfat is one of the four holy cities of Israel and has a mystical history. While we were there we learnt of the holy Ari Mikvah, which is located close to where some very holy rabbi's are buried. A mikvah (a pool of fresh running water) is normally provided for the benefit of Jewish women. This is where they can go to cleanse themselves after their monthly cycle. There are, however, also men's mikvah's; as in the one I am about to describe. The main function of a mikvah is more about the

167

enhancement of the spiritual side of a person; as opposed to the enhancement of their personal hygiene.

The mikvah we had heard about was indeed one just for men. One of the girls at Ascent, a youth hostel we were staying at, said she would act as a tour guide and take us to the mikvah. We agreed and dutifully followed this girl to the mikvah, taking in the musty air of our surroundings as we passed through the nearby cemetery where the rabbi's were buried. It was dark and very creepy as we made our way there and a bit like something out of a scary movie. When we finally got to the building where the mikvah was located our guide announced she would stand outside and keep guard. Well, it was a men's mikvah after all! The main idea of a mikvah is that you get undressed, duck yourself under the water in the small pool and spell out God's name in Hebrew. This process is meant to cleanse you spiritually. There is a myth that carrying out this procedure in this particular mikvah would help you to find your soul mate. 'Great, let's jump straight in!' I thought. The six other girls I was with started to get undressed, when suddenly I felt it was the wrong thing for me to do; as it was a man's Mikvah after all. So despite their encouragement, I decided not to join them. One by one each of the girls ducked down into the pool and spelt out God's name in Hebrew.

As they did this I started to hear a mantra of four notes, men and women's voices singing loudly. The strange thing is it didn't sound like Jewish music. In fact it didn't' sound like anything I had ever heard before. Forgetting where I was, I started to wonder if there was perhaps a church nearby. The girl keeping guard outside popped her head round the door to make sure we were all okay. I mentioned the music and asked her what it was and where it was coming from. With this, the girl in question began to freak. She started to shout 'You can hear the angels, you can hear the angels!' I asked her what she meant and she informed me I was apparently hearing angels, which it is written fly over the area. I was starting to get slightly freaked myself now and mentioned it wasn't angels I could hear but merely a chorus of people singing. The girl continued to explain there is a myth that surrounds Tsfat that angels fly over the city keeping guard and that only highly spiritual

168

people are believed to be able to hear them. The girl believed the myth but said she herself had never actually heard the voices. She seemed over the moon she had finally met someone who she felt could hear them.

Despite her joy at her new discovery, her elation suddenly turned to complete fear and she ran off leaving us all in the building alone and unsure of the route back to the hostel. I could still hear the singing at this point. I went outside the Mikvah and walked around the outside edge of the building but not a sound was coming from outside. As soon as I went back inside I could hear the voices loud and clear again. The stranger thing was, at first none of the other girls could hear what I was hearing. I explained to them what I was hearing and what our now departed guide had told me. All of sudden and one-by-one, each of the other girls started to hear the singing too. We did all finally manage to find our way back to the youth hostel with the notes we had heard still fresh in our heads. We continued to sing the notes repeatedly as we walked back along the darkened path to the hostel; all seven of us singing all the way back and possibly looking somewhat like Snow White's seven dwarves!

As soon as we arrived back at the hostel, I suggested we go over to a piano to try and play the notes. I had a crazy notion the notes might spell out God's name in Hebrew somehow, which incidentally is made up of four letters. The strange thing was, as soon as we reached the piano, which was located just inside the entrance to the hostel, not one of us could remember any of the notes. And to this day I still can't recall them!

A second and equally chilling event was to occur during this same trip to Israel. Now back in Jerusalem and after having attended a close friend's wedding, I decided to reside back in my room. I suddenly and inexplicably became overwhelmed by emotion and started to cry, a lot. My tears became uncontrollable. Then a strange feeling came over me. It almost felt as if my dear mother Claudia's presence were in the room with me. I had never felt this sensation before. I would have completely overlooked this feeling, were it not for what occurred next. Suddenly, in my head, I could hear her voice. She was asking me to repeat aloud a sentence she was telling me. I repeated the sentence out loud but it was not in English. It was in Ivrit. I do not speak Ivrit, so there was no possible way I could have ever had a clue if what I was saying were in fact making any sense at all or was merely complete gibberish. No sooner had I repeated the sentence aloud I felt a strange sensation of cold run through me and noticed what appeared to be a whitish light disappear through the wall. Immediately after this the two girls I was sharing the dorm with entered the room declaring 'You look like you've just seen a ghost!' I explained to them what had just occurred. They both spoke Ivrit, so asked me to repeat the sentence to them. I spoke the words aloud until they too looked as if they had just seen a ghost. They then both continued to explain to me my sentence did indeed make sense and more to the point was grammatically correct too. 'So what did I say?' I asked, still completely ashen. I had apparently said in perfect Ivrit 'Don't cry. Everything will be alright. I am here for you.'

During my second and third returns to Israel I studied again at the woman's seminary in Jerusalem and received the privilege of being taught by some of the world's top spiritual leaders in Judaism. I soon discovered Judaism, unlike many other world religions, considers and allows room for science and spirituality to work together in its explanation of the universe. Judaism is a way of life, rather than a religion and works closely around a set of ideals, which are manifested in the real world. It was this ideology which drew me towards wanting to learn more. In fact, during my stay in Israel one of the rabbis I was learning with placed two books in my hands, which he informed me were of great value to him. Both books had been passed down to him over the generations through his family and both had been signed by the authors; Sigmund Freud and Albert Einstein.

When I finally came back to the UK I was a different person. I had become very religious and dressed and acted accordingly. I decided to keep the holy Sabbath for four weeks, as a sign of respect to Bill's passing but soon found I gained so much from it myself, that I continued to keep it for many years after this time.

As it happened, my parents found a lot of contentment and solace through my religious values too. Mum and dad received a lot of joy from the Friday nights we sat around the table and sang beautiful, spiritual songs together, as did I. Certain relatives from the Drummond family, however, found as many possibly ways to mock my new found happiness and I even found myself once again being mocked for way I was dressing. I recall being informed I must be mad and insane to become religious and it was inferred 'Only an unstable person becomes religious.' Once again it left me questioning why members of this family group were so unable to share in my happiness at having found a new outlook, which brought me peace. Surely seeing me now finally on my way to happiness and inner-peace was a good thing?

During the entire time I was actively pursuing my religious beliefs I was, nevertheless, still in a constant inner battle with my desire to want to continue to perform on stage and the desire was killing me. Around this time I also started to carry out some work as a classroom assistant in a local school; to earn some of those all-important paper notes with the Queen's head on and to help towards paying some of mum and dad's bills. It was actually this career move, which would later be partly responsible in ultimately helping me make my decision between a career in acting or leading a religious lifestyle. But for now I was still stuck in no-mans land.

The next set of circumstances I found myself dealing with upon my return to the UK was the property Bill and Rose had left me. I was advised by dad to hold on to the property and rent it out but made a choice to sell it instead. This choice was based purely on emotions rather than any logical input and was born form the feeling I would be unable to go into the flat again, as there were too many memories there for me to confront.

After discussion with mum, certain members of the Drummond family asked if they could keep various items of furniture from the flat suggesting, as I was still living at home they would be of no use to me. I decided I would give these family members various items of furniture, which included a nest of tables and chairs but the only piece I wanted to hold onto was a cherry mahogany table for memory's sake; as it had been one of Rose and Bill's favourite items of furniture. The rest of the pieces of unwanted furniture were set to be donated to charity prior to the sale of the flat.

What came next was unfortunately more unkind words and upset. A few weeks after this time I bumped into the elder daughter of the Drummond household in synagogue, both of us accompanied by a friend. She came and sat down beside me, which completely surprised me, as usually she would completely ignore me whenever I spoke to her. During the service she turned to me and said 'I want that table!' I explained to her it was of sentimental value and then she snarled some very acidulous words in my direction before moving to another seat. This was probably one of the last conversations we ever had.

Incidentally, this had not been the first time this member of The Drummond family had upset me but I hoped it would be the last. During the wedding of one of my cousins, this family member had snuck up from behind me, whilst I was on the dance floor and suddenly grabbed the bottom edge of my dress. She had then proceeded to pull it up to my shoulders, exposing my under-wear to everyone in the middle of the dance floor. I screamed as I had such a shock. As you can imagine all eyes turned to look at me. The guy I was dancing with covered me quickly. Even today you can still hear me scream on the videotape of the wedding. Thankfully the camera was not on me at this point. The only good thing that came out of the entire incident is that I got a date with the gorgeous guy I was dancing with! So you see, there really is a silver lining to every dark cloud!

In the contract with the buyer I sold Bill and Rose's flat too there was a clause which dictated I had to completely empty the flat of all my belongings before they moved in, else they could charge me a penalty for any individual items left in the flat. The buyer had previously agreed to take on some of the remaining items of Bill's furniture; but the day before the final exchange, the buyer called me late afternoon to inform me she no longer wanted any of the furniture we had agreed upon. She said I was now to remove it that same day, else she would start to charge me for its upkeep from the following morning. As fortune would have it, the garage was not included in the same contract, so all I had to do was move the furniture into the garage. The only problem was the garage was not located directly next to the house but a few hundred yards around the block.

My good friend Enid (not her real name) offered to go with me to the flat later that evening, to help me remove all the remaining pieces of furniture. With a fair amount of ease we managed to move the bedside tables, a small table lamp, dinning chairs and a set of nesting tables into the garage. A short while later we smacked our hands together in triumph ready to leave, believing our job was done. 'That was not so bad after all' I said. We got to the front door and suddenly I let out a short, shrill scream 'The bed!' I had completely forgotten we still had a bed to move! It was an old fashioned heavy styled construction and the frame alone weighed a tonne. How on earth were we ever going to shift this giant?

We turned the mattress on its side and somehow managed to manoeuvre it between the doorframes and out onto the front lawn. Now we had to move the frame. Believe me when I tell you, this was going to be no easy task. I grabbed one end of the bed, pulled it onto its side and with great effort started to push it out of the flat inch by inch. Half an hour later and voila! It was now on the lawn. We turned it back on its base and threw the mattress back on top. Enid and I then proceeded to wheel it into the road. By the time we reached the road from the front lawn, poor Enid was completely overcome by fatigue. She jumped on top of the bed and literally collapsed with exhaustion.

The only thing left for me to do was to keep pushing that bed down the road, with Enid still lying on top of it! Goodness only knows what we must have looked like. We laughed till our sides ached; wondering how we would be perceived if anyone saw us. A number of cars drove past and after a fair few double-takes in our direction, the drivers started to hoot us on with encouragement. A police car then drove past and the police officer kindly decided to help escort us safely to our destination. Now that's what you call 'bedlam!'

Becoming more religious I had not performed on a stage for a while but was once again getting itchy feet to do just that. I soon found myself selected to perform on stage at The Ministry of Sound, in association with Flame Models and Scene magazine, as one of the finalists in a modelling competition. The competition was being sponsored by *Sky* television and the magazines; *Scene* and *OK!* The winner of the competition was to receive a modelling contract with a top agency. I really just entered for the fun of it, via the suggestion of a friend and partly due really to my desire to get back onto a stage. Out of the hundreds of girls that entered the competition, to my sheer surprise I was picked as one of the eight semi-finalists to appear in the live show, hosted by television personality Melanie Sykes. The show was being judged by an array of celebrity judges. Amongst the line-up were: Brandon Block, Beverley Bloom, Mark Bloom, Tania Bryer, Rio Ferdinand, Frank Lampard, Mark Rodol, Mandy Smith, Claudia Winkleman and Ronit Zilkha. I did not win the competition, the title went to Lucy Becker, who is now a glamour model for *FHM* but the experience gave me a renewed taste of fame. I recall at the time having a conversation backstage with both Melanie Sykes and Mandy Smith about the fame-game and sharing with them my desire to perform. They were both so very kind with their words, which in summary, surmounted to me believing in myself and going for my dreams. I very recently had the pleasure of meeting Melanie Sykes again and was able to recount to her how I had indeed listened to her words and was now following my dream.

My friend Adam Lamb, who was at the time working for Jeff Gilbert at JG Management (which later became Chymical Management), was in the audience during the competition. JG Management had a plethora of big artists attached to their rostra including: Lisa Stansfield, Alison Limerick and Catherine Zeta Jones. Adam approached me after the show to congratulate my performance. He was not the only person to single me out and congratulate me after the show that night. In the Green Room during the after show party, a young man came over to tell me how much he had enjoyed my dancing in the show. The man in question was my childhood hero Henry Thomas. I told him I was more interested in singing than modelling and he immediately asked me when he could hear me sing. 'Right now!' I said and confidently started to sing on the spot (this would not be the only time I would sing on the spot to industry folk). I sang a snippet of Aretha Franklin's *Mocking Bird* and Henry, rather flatteringly, went wild for my voice. We exchanged telephone numbers there and then and stayed in contact for many years after this time.

Adam, who was also standing in the vicinity of me singing aloud to Henry, informed me he had got wind of my singing and writing ability and asked if I had any songs he could listen to. After hearing a few of my songs Adam invited me into the office to meet with both him and Jeff, with the intention of signing me up to their management company as one of their new artists. Adam was at this time just in the process of forming his own leg of the management company under the name Dreamscape Artists and Management and was actively looking for his first artist to place on the books. He asked if I would be interested to be his first signed act and I of course agreed. A contract was immediately drawn up and a business plan put into action by Adam to start the launch of my new music career. Between both Adam and myself, we had over the past few years managed to build a database of contacts, so we combined efforts, giving ourselves ample ammunition to move our plan off the page and into action.

The first part of the plan was to get me into the studio over the coming months, to record some of my own material and also to attain a catalogue of other songwriters work for me to record. I had by this point in time written well over thirty songs myself and was still trying to get some of them recorded in the studio. In the interim, Adam started to send out to various songwriters three of the songs I had already recorded in different studios over previous years, to generate interest in my voice. Very quickly Adam started receiving an eclectic variety of songs sent to him by many different songwriters, all of whom upon hearing me sing, expressed their interest in the quality of my voice and were keen for me to record some of their work. As ears started to prick up, people started to compare my voice to Karen Carpenter, which was a huge compliment.

We were sent a number of tracks to listen to by both Sony/ATV Music Publishing and Warner Music Publishing and also gained interest from manager Nick East, who was introduced to me by Tona de Brett. We were soon also approached by a company called Z Management, who offered us their services of producers and engineers and later we worked on some ideas with the well-known producer Chris Bandy. This was a very exciting time for both Adam and myself. The next part of the plan was to create an image, complete with stage name, get some publicity shots and of course the simple job of attaining a record contract and not necessarily in that order!

Stage two of the plan for the next year was to get me to record a quality demo of around three to five good solid tracks, gig with these songs and then set up meetings with some of the major labels to play them my demo and talk them through our business and launch plan. During this time I also continued to carry out some singing practice with a couple of pianist friends Albert had put me in touch with, one of whom was a writer of his own musicals; Alexander Bermange. Funnily enough, I found myself being accompanied on piano by Alexander many moons later in an audition for a West End musical - like I said, it's a small world.

I had up until now been calling myself the very lame name of Emerald, as this was one of the many nick-names given to me at school; as my chameleon-like hazel eyes turn a bright shade of green in direct sunlight. The amount of nick-names I have collected over the years are worthy of a book all to themselves! When Adam asked me to think up a new stage name for myself, I asked mum what name she thought might work. As I was at the time still slap-bang in the middle of a continued battle with my singing career and leading a religious lifestyle, mum joked: 'How about the name Emma Holy?' The name struck a poignant chord (b flat major I believe it was!) and after a play on the pronunciation of the word holy, I became Emma Holli.

One of the first songs Adam arranged for me to record was an American guitar based pop track called *I Know Where You Are* by songwriter Kris Holland. As soon as I heard the song I was sold on it. I immediately fell in love with the melody line and lyrics of the song. Adam and I travelled to Kris' management company's personal recording studio in Oxfordshire and spent the day laying down the track, only stopping intermittently for chocolate-chip cookie breaks to keep our energy high.

Over the course of the year I found myself being approached by the singer and songwriter Stephen Tin Tin, Duffy, the writer of one of my all time favourite songs *Kiss Me*, via our contact at Warner Publishing. Stephen Duffy had been passed a copy of my song *Let's Talk* by someone in the industry and had apparently fallen in love with my voice straight away. He approached Adam to ask me to sing vocals on his next song. I jumped at the chance but unfortunately the project did not materialise, as Stephen became busy on another project and in the end our diaries never seemed to match up. Warner also put Adam and me directly in touch with Andy Goldmark, who had a huge hit at the time with Jennifer Paige and *Crush* and also with the team of writers and producers behind the band Six Pence None the Richer.

I was also soon approached by Mark Winters at Active Music Management. Mark Winters was, alongside Simon Fuller, one of the original creators of The Spice Girls. He was forming a new band called 21st Century Girls and was keen for me to be a part of it. Mark gave me what was to be the band's debut single to listen to and whilst it was a good fun song, after discussion, both Adam and I felt at the time this was not the route we wanted to take, so declined the offer to continue the pursuit of our own plan. After successfully recording some more songs it was time to start approaching record companies for a deal. (Mark Winters later released the song *I Love My Radio* by Taffy, which was an instant hit the year of its release)

At the start of July that same year, I was approached by my friend's father, Cyril Myers. He wanted me to appear as an Olivia Newton-John look-a-like in the popular television show *Stars in*

*Their Eyes.* He also presented me with the gift of a song to sing as an entry for the *Eurovision Song Contest.* Whilst I was extremely grateful for his help and did later on meet the show's host, Matthew Kelly, through Albert to discuss the idea, I felt going down the path of a look-a-like contest or the Eurovision route was not for me, so did not pursue either option further.

Around this time, Adam decided it was the right time for us to start attending some industry events, to start getting my face recognised amongst my peers. As Albert had done before him, Adam started to take me to a succession of parties. On one occasion, he took me to a prestigious evening of music awards. Once again, I walked into a room crawling with stars; this time pop-stars, rather than thespians. The lovely television presenter Jill Dando asked if she could sit beside me at our table. We clicked immediately. Jill was actually a very easy person to click with. We chatted all night about politics, music, religion and our planet in general. She was a very inspiring woman to talk to. We discovered we had a lot of similar views and a bond immediately formed. Jill and I agreed to keep in touch and exchanged details. Sadly, Jill never got the opportunity to use my number, as shortly after this time her life was tragically cut short when she was murdered. This deeply affected me, as she was such a young, vibrant and beautiful soul, taken so viciously from this world all too soon.

Adam soon started to set up meetings for me to meet the A & R folk at various record companies. We were immediately given the chance to visit both Sony Music and Polygram to talk through our ideas. During the coming months we worked with and continued to generate interest from, top producer Chris Bandy and songwriter Andy Goldmark and also both manager Nick East and Dean Stratten at Mushroom Records, who also expressed an interest to work alongside Adam on my career as well as Peer Music, who showed a keen interest in publishing my written word.

We also sent some of my music to Brandon Baskhi at BMI music publishers, in our search to secure a publishing deal for my song writing skills. Brandon immediately wrote back to me and set up a meeting at one of his offices in the stunning surroundings of

178

London's Regent's Park. As soon as I got there, Brandon placed a verbal deal on the table and informed me, whilst also handing me a large pile of paperwork to read for homework, that as soon as I acquired a record deal he would automatically give me a publishing deal. This news was literally music to my ears.

A number of months later, Adam placed me in touch with the solicitor Mel Goldberg, a very successful solicitor who represents a number of sport and music personalities in the entertainment industry. The plan was to ask him to help me sort out any legal documents I now had to deal with, including a new contract Adam and I were now putting together - as Adam was in the process of branching out on his own. Mel Goldberg was extremely helpful to me and carried out a lot of work on my behalf. Never once did I hear him say '*Show Me the Money!*' In fact Mel carried out most of the work for Adam and me entirely for free. He invited us into his office for an initial meeting and I gave him a live rendition of one of my songs. He immediately wrote to me after this time and said:

*Dear Emma,*

*I was glad to have the opportunity of meeting you last Thursday and I confirm that I shall be happy to act on your behalf with regard to the completion of any recording contracts and to give general advice, as and when required, in connection with your career. I look forward to receiving a copy tape, as I do believe that you are talented and given the lucky breaks, which we all need, you have the opportunity of having a flourishing music career.*

*With kind regards,*

*Mel Goldberg*

After hearing my demo Mel wrote to me again saying:

*Dear Emma,*

*This is just a note to let you know that I have now had another opportunity of playing the demonstration tape, which I liked very much indeed. There is no doubt that you have enormous talent and all you need now is a few lucky breaks and to think positive. If you are performing anywhere in the London area please let me know and I shall be glad to come and listen to you. Separately I have got a client who is putting together a pop show/opera and I shall give him your details with a photograph plus a copy of your tape.*

*Warmest regards,*

*Mel Goldberg.*

Mel Goldberg continued to take a keen interest in my career for many months and came to view his potential investment, by watching me perform on stage in my first ever big stage performance - at the world famous London Palladium.

The next chapter in my life can only be described as bitter sweet. With my music career flourishing and now finally starting to live the dream, my personal life was in contrast filled with more sadness.

***I started to realise this God I had hated for so many years perhaps did exist after all. This realisation was my 'eureka moment'.*** - Emma Fletcher

## 8

# The Bitter Sweet Taste of Success

**What lies behind us and what lies before us are tiny
matters compared to what lies within us.**
- Ralph Waldo Emerson

*Paul: As we have seen, Emma had by now endured years of hard work in her
attempts to 'make it' in the industry. One chance was all she really needed to
make her dream of recognition a reality. And, as we will see in this chapter, a
certain prestigious London West End theatre was to be the venue where
Fletcher would take another dramatic step up the entertainment ladder to
deserved success.*

Emma: My manager decided it was time to get me out of the
studio and for me to start performing some live gigs. He got me
to start singing initially at a small local karaoke bar to gain some
confidence and find my mojo. The venue was appropriately called
The G Spot and was owned by a mutual friend. I would go there
to sing once a week on a regular basis. The venue attracted a lot of
up and coming singers and I soon found myself singing alongside
a couple of young men; who later went on to form half of the
popular boy band, Blue.

Around this time Albert took both a friend and myself to view the
premiere of Drew Barrymore's movie *Never Been Kissed*. A small
section of Regents Park had been cordoned off for the after party
and the popular deejay Omar was on the deejay stand. The band
West Life were also there promoting their first ever single and
who else should be there too but my old friend Toby Anstis. At
this point in time I hadn't seen Toby in quite a while and he
approached me with a huge hug and asked what I was doing now.
I told him I was writing my own songs and chasing the dream of
becoming a singer. Within an instant Toby asked his friend Omar
to allow me to sing one of my songs a cappella to the guests. 'No

way!' I replied in my nervous state but before you knew it Omar had already announced over the microphone he had a surprise guest who would be singing one of her songs. Yes, a complete surprise, I thought to myself - both to me and everyone else, as not one person will have a clue who I am! Nerves got the better of me and I made a dash to the little ladies' portable cubicles with my friend now in tow. (It's just a fact of life; girls always go to the toilets in twos!) Suddenly, whilst in the cubicle I heard Omar announce my name onto the stage. Quickly I went about finishing up my business and rushed to open the door of the cubicle. The door handle of the cubicle was stuck. I couldn't get out! Omar continued to announce my name onto the stage. My friend called out from her cubicle 'We're coming!' All eyes must have moved to the direction of the toilets for sure. In my haste to get out, I opened the toilet door with such vigour I slipped on the floor outside by the sinks and, as it would just so happen, there was a stray toilet seat also on the floor, so I made my grand entrance out of the toilet cubicles in a complete slide formation with toilet seat in tow and of course looking a bit 'flushed!' Everyone cheered and clapped. Although now completely embarrassed I could nevertheless see the funny side. I performed my song to the crowd to rapturous applause. Presenter Ben Shepherd approached me after and was very kind with his words saying he felt I had a lot of talent and really hoped I went far with my dream. Thankfully he didn't add any toilet humour to this compliment!

In the same year I also successfully auditioned for another group that was being set-up by a local charity organisation. The group, which called themselves J-Mex, was aimed at a jazz orientated audience. Again, this group never really got off the ground but the regular rehearsals and jamming sessions we had were very useful practice and freed me up vocally as a singer. I was however starting to get itchy feet and dying for a larger audience to perform to.

News soon reached me of a talent show being held at the world famous London Palladium. They were looking for singer songwriters with original work. The idea of treading the stage of the London Palladium excited me greatly and so I decided I just had to apply to audition for the show. After a call-back for a second audition, I soon received the exciting news over the telephone I had been accepted into the show. When the production assistant rang to tell me the good news I had actually been expecting another call, so when she gave me the news it did not sink in at first. 'You're in!' she repeated. I think upon second awakening I may have actually deafened the poor girl with a scream so high-pitched, it should normally only be audible to dogs. Mum was as equally excited about the prospect I was to perform on the London Palladium stage and immediately rang all her friends to let them know. She was so proud of me and over the course of the rehearsal period, continually required to be kept in the loop about the progress of the show. She expressed how she couldn't wait to see the show and see her 'baby' up on stage. Although concerned with me following a career in performance, mum's belief and support towards my ventures over the years had, nevertheless, always been one of encouragement. Mum had always let me know she believed I was capable of achieving anything in life and instilled me with the very same belief.

Performing on the London Palladium stage was finally the first step towards my dream. After all these years of hard work, this was finally the beginning of my dream becoming a reality. This was the chance I had always been waiting for and it was now just one step away.

The production team of the show informed us there would be a break coming up between rehearsals, during which time a friend asked me if I would like to go with her and her family for a short vacation to America. I told mum I was considering going and she was delighted. That next day I had one of the strangest experiences of my life. When I awoke in the morning I recall feeling a strange vibration come over the entirety of my body and a humming noise in my ears. Suddenly I felt as if I was floating above my bed. I looked up to the corner of my room and in an instant I felt as if I were in the corner of my room. I looked down beneath me and could immediately see my music centre underneath. Was this still a dream? Too scared to turn and look to see if I could see myself lying on my bed, I closed my eyes and willed myself back into my body.

I landed on my bed with what felt like a thud. Assuming I must be dreaming, I reached out a hand and picked up my clock. The time read as exactly 6:00am and not a second over. It was a Sunday and much too early to be awake. I was of course freaked out by the fact I felt as if I had been hovering above my bed. I had heard of people having out of body experiences but didn't believe they were real. I opened my eyes wide in complete panic and then looked towards the window. I remember saying/thinking: 'Please God don't let me go flying out the window like I've heard can happen!' I looked at the window and before you knew it, my face was touching the window pain and my nose was starting to push itself slowly through the pane of glass. I screamed out loud/in my head and zoomed with terrific speed back onto my bed and 'crash landed'. Now I was fully awake. I grabbed my clock and read the time. It read as exactly 6:00am and still not a second past. What had just happened? I jumped out of bed; all the blood left my head. I felt dizzy and ran out of my room screaming at the top of my voice 'mum!'

Mum was in the bathroom and beckoned me in. My shouting had given her a shock. I told her what had just happened. Mum, being a very highly spiritual person herself, was quite shaken by the incident too and believed it to have been a real experience, which incidentally so did my rabbi in Israel when I later rang to tell him. Mum took my hand and looked me in the eye and said: 'I don't want you to go to America.' I knew she was trying to tell me she felt this experience was a warning. 'I won't be here when you get home', she said. Not wanting fatalistic words to once again be true in my life, I replied with a defiant but gentle: 'Don't be silly, I'm going.' Suddenly I thought of Bill and how I had known in my heart he wouldn't still be here upon my return and that I knew I should have stayed. I also thought of Uncle Ellis and how I knew he was going to pass on the week he died and my grandmother Rose too. I turned to mum and said: 'You're right, I'm not going.' Mum's face turned a paler shad of white. My response told her I was having the same feeling about her life coming to an end as she

184

was. She said: 'You must go, I want you to go.' I said I wouldn't go but after a long calm chat we both agreed the best thing to do in order to fight this feeling we were both experiencing was indeed for me to go. I recall mum saying to me: 'What do you think this experience means?' I told her I felt it was a message for her; to let her know everything would be okay and that there is a safe place to go after this life. We left it there.

Around a week later my friend and her family came to pick me up from my home on what turned out to be a beautiful sunny afternoon. I did the strangest thing. I picked up my suitcase and walked out the house without saying goodbye to mum. I had never done this before in my life. She called me back with tears in her eyes. I hadn't even realised I had carried out this action. Perhaps saying goodbye was just too painful? I ran back inside and hugged her and immediately started to cry. She stroked my hair and said: 'Everything will be okay, you will see.' As we left the house I said aloud to God: 'Don't you dare take her from me'.

Our holiday started at the family of my friend in middle America. We stayed there for only a couple of nights before moving on to New York. The morning we left for New York I walked down the very large centre staircase of the house we were staying in and in a trance like state said out loud: 'What will I do without you?' When I reached the bottom of the staircase my friend turned to me and said: 'What will you do without who?' 'What?' I replied. My friend continued: 'You just said 'what will I do without you!'' A cold shudder went down my spine as the thought of mum entered my mind. I remember exclaiming: 'Oh no, mum!' In that instant I knew something had happened to her. We arrived in New York hours later. As soon as we checked in at reception the concierge informed me there was a message waiting for me on the telephone service in my room. It was the voice of Mr Drummond. His deep voice, for the first time gentle. He said mum had had a severe stroke of the brain stem and the doctors said she only had hours to live. Suddenly I found myself picking up a large heavy armchair Hercules' style, lifting it up high over my head and throwing it across the room in rage at God. I must stress I am not a violent person and I must add nothing was damaged but to this day I am still amazed at how my adrenalin allowed me to pick up this very heavy chair in the manner I did. This was once again, another incident of paranormal strength. My friend and I ran downstairs and checked out of the hotel, fighting our way through both a convention of rabbis and Islamic priests! I asked them both to make a prayer for my mum.

The entire journey home on the plane was the worst experience of my life. I had no idea if we would make it to the hospital in time for me to see mum again. When we finally arrived at the hospital a nurse told me to speak to mum, suggesting doctors believe the last thing to go is a patient's hearing and that she may somehow be able to still recognise my voice. Believing this myself anyhow, I spent a good few hours by mum's bedside talking through some of our happier memories. On a couple of occasions, whilst I was talking and holding her hand, mum's breathing pattern changed in what appeared to be in co-ordination to what I was saying. Two family members of the Drummond family, who were also present, also expressed how they believed mum was trying to let us know she could hear me. Mrs Drummond requested I stay in the hospital with mum on my own after she and her daughter had left but the truth is I did not feel strong enough to stay with mum to watch her take her last breath. That would have broken me.

That night I asked dad if I could put up a sleeping bag on the floor in his room. I didn't want to be alone. He said I could. We fell asleep. At around 3:30am, only a few hours after I had left the hospital, a loud thud woke us both up. We grabbed the clock and looked at the time and then at each other. Panic froze us both. The telephone rang instantly. It was the hospital. My wonderful mum had passed away in that exact instant. To this day I firmly believe, as do my family, she had waited for me to come home from America before leaving this world. We later discovered the thud was mum's favourite painting falling to the floor from the wall. I later spoke to a rabbi about the picture falling. He informed me, in Judaism we believe when someone passes on and their soul leaves their body it is at first confused and darts around the room, often knocking down something of value to them; often to let the living know they are there. That was enough for me. During the week of shiva (the Jewish week of mourning) that picture fell down everyday and I kept putting it back up on the wall again. Oddly, as soon as the week of shiva was over the picture never fell of the wall again and remained there until it was taken down when the house was sold a number of years later.

When mum passed away I lost my voice completely for the entire day. My old trouble with my voice had returned. My larynx and vocal chords shut down completely from the shock. I recall a member of the Drummond family thinking I was pretending but I wasn't. My entire larynx and vocal chords just ceased to operate, tightening through the shock of losing mum.

Mourners at a house of shiva usually sit on low chairs and do not do anything. Friends rally round and do things for them during this time. On the first day of the shiva the youngest daughter from The Drummond family came up to me and said: 'Get up out of that chair and stop being lazy. Do something!' Then two other relatives from the same family group approached me with similar jibes and continued with comments, which suggested they felt I was not mourning any more than they were; as they commented that mum and dad were not in fact actually my real mother and father. Eventually the Rabbi present took one of the relatives aside and told them to allow me to mourn in my own way, as according to Jewish law, I was Vera's daughter and not her granddaughter, as I had been adopted by her and raised as such. After this comment was made I decided to go and sit in the garden with some other family members to get some air. In my upset I accidentally spilt some water on the grass, hardly the biggest crime but sadly this small accident found me becoming the receiver of more abuse at the hands of the elder daughter of the Drummond family. I could not understand why they could not just leave me alone to mourn in peace.

Later that week dad announced to me that the mother of the Drummond family had asked him to tell me they now wanted me to refrain from calling him dad anymore and go back to calling him Papa Sammy, now that mum was not alive. I told him I was not going to 'go back' to calling him Pappy Sammy, as I had not called him that since I was 8 and in any case, he was the only dad I had ever known. I told him if he didn't want to answer me when I called him dad then that was his choice and if so we would never speak again. He saw the funny side of what I was saying and we both laughed but in truth what I had been told had been requested hurt a great deal. I did not blame dad for asking me this. Dad may have been an upright and intelligent member of society but he was never a strong-minded man. Mum had always ruled the roost, she was the matriarch of the family and he had always been guided by her wisdom. When my lovely auntie Sybil heard of what had been asked of me she too was very shocked and upset, as any normal person would be, so arranged for both my relative and myself to meet at her house to try and resolve our issues. Sadly, no resolution could be found.

That same week I announced to dad I had decided I wanted to place a heart shaped stone at mum's graveside, which read: 'Loved by granddaughter Emma, who was raised as a daughter.' When the Drummond family got wind of my intention I was told by Mrs Drummond I was not to carry out my intention but thankfully, after discussion with other family members, vindication of my good intention was provided and I was advised it would be a perfectly lovely thing to do. As I valued the opinions of these other members of my family as being the opinions of caring and rational minded people, I decided to go ahead and carry out my intentions as planned. During this time I was also asked by Mr Drummond to leave home and get my own place. How could I leave my dad at this time? He was mourning and needed me and in fact I needed him too. Why couldn't they see that?

Just under a couple of months after mum passed away my performance at the London Palladium was to take place. This was such a hard performance to carry out just weeks after mum had passed away, especially knowing how much she would have loved to of been present. She was so looking forward to being a part of the audience. It made it a little easier for me knowing I would have family and good friends there to support me but that still didn't take the tinge off knowing mum could not be there too, to share in my moment of glory.

What came next did indeed bring a cheer to my face. My old friend Albert approached my cousin Warren and asked him if he would agree to appear in the show as a special guest and Warren agreed to do so for charity, as well as for me. So as well as having family in the audience, I ended up having family on stage with me too - all be it in the guise of Alf Garnett! As well as Mel Goldberg coming along especially to see me perform my number in the show, Albert had brought with him theatre producer Cameron Mackintosh, who was apparently also keen to hear me sing and meet with me again, having heard so many kind words about my performance abilities from Albert.

Somehow fate had led me to appear in a show that was being hosted by some of the biggest names from the world of show business. The judges included: lyricist Don Black, Michael Grade, Trevor Horn, choreographer Arlene Phillips, The Lord Levy, David Altschuler, Malcom Dagul, Deborah Yamin Joseph and impresario Harvey Goldsmith CBE. As it happens, I had become friendly with Harvey Goldsmith's niece whilst at college. She had offered to give her uncle a tape of me singing but at that time I had not felt ready to have my voice heard by such an important person in the industry. Now things were different.

The show was hosted by the much-missed television presenter, Jeremy Beadle. I was the first act to go on stage to perform. Waiting behind the curtains I was suddenly overcome by complete fear. Jeremy was so kind. He took me aside and helped calm my nerves. He told me to count to 10 slowly, take a deep breath and watch my footing on the steps. He took my hand and guided me onto my starting position on the stage, which was just behind the curtains and said: 'Go kid, knock 'em dead!' I remained completely frozen to the spot, as Jeremy walked onto the famous Palladium stage to announce me on. My heart was beating so fast it felt as if it might take off. The audience loudly applauded Jeremy's entrance and then there was a moment of silence before he gave a short introductory speech, then announced me onto stage with the following words:

*Ladies and gentleman, let's get on with the show. We've got our first performer. It's the toughest job in the world to open it and I know that you're going to give a very warm welcome. If any of you have been to Tom Kenwright's restaurant Azzuro, you may have heard this young lady… Emma Jane has balanced her career with her true passion, which is singing, writing and dancing… She was a finalist in last year's Face of the Year. All her songs are based on her own experiences and the title she is going to sing, Rain, is no exception. Ladies and gentlemen will you please give a really warm welcome to Emma Fletcher.*

The show's house music then started as I walked down the stairs and onto the stage. When I got to centre stage there was complete silence. The musicians did not start to play. More silence. I thought I was going to be sick on the spot on which I stood. Someone in the audience sniggered. I was in complete darkness. The only thing I could focus on was the 'Exit' sign. A little voice inside my head started to scream: 'Get me out of here,' then finally and not a second too soon, the music started. Don't ask me how but somehow I managed to successfully sing my way through the entire length of the song without any hiccups but all the while that little voice inside my head was still screaming at me to get out and all I could manage to focus on through the entire length of the song was the exit sign!

On an aesthetic level I had wanted my performance to somewhat resemble that of James Brown's acrobatic dance moves on stage and so during my self-penned number, as I was belting out my top notes at the top of my larynx, I started to 'get down with my bad self' on the dance floor and inadvertently assumed a somewhat squat position whilst singing. The audience appeared to enjoy my performance. Warren came up to me afterwards and gave me a huge hug and said: 'Well done darling. I never realised you could sing so well but next time, would you mind awfully remaining in the upright position? Only you looked as if you were trying to go to the toilet!' He was of course right and since then I have always maintained an upright stance, unless indeed I'm on the toilet!

My first performance at the London Palladium was admittedly one of the most terrifying and exciting experiences of my life but also one of the saddest moments too, knowing my dear mum could not be there to share my joy with me. My performance was itself tinged with sadness, as I missed mum so much. This pain gave new meaning to my song *Rain*. I felt so much pain in my heart, it actually hurt. After mum died I felt as if my heart had literally been torn out and put back inside me again in the wrong order but I had nevertheless managed to somehow make it through my performance. In my mind, I was performing my song for my mum.

Mum always had this feeling about robins. She once said she would send a robin to watch over and look after me after she passed on. As it happens, in Judaism we believe birds are very spiritual creatures and many people believe robins to be spiritual messengers. During the week of my performance, I called the daughter of an old friend of mum's, as her mother, mum's friend, had sadly just passed away too. I was ringing to offer my condolences. I mentioned to this friend what mum had promised to me with regards to the robin and she informed me, strangely enough, her mum had promised the same. Oddly enough, whilst we were talking on the telephone, two robins came and sat in the garden and watched me throughout the duration of our conversation.

Another robin-related story occurred during mum's stone setting, a year after her death. As I was walking through the cemetery ahead of other relatives in order to be alone, I entered an almost trance-like state, with my eyes closed. Suddenly I had a strong feeling I should open my eyes and look down. I did and in that moment I noticed I was just about to place my right foot down onto a robin. Rather than moving or flying away in fear, this little fella just sat there and starred back at me with its little eyes wide open and its head titled to one side. I just smiled at the robin feeling its presence was hopefully a message being sent to me from my mum. I wondered if it was her reminding me she was there for me. One of the most unusual things about this story is it is said you rarely see birds in a Jewish cemetery. This recollection also reminds me of when I visited Claudia's gravestone for the first time in a while. I was with a friend and had forgotten to bring with me the number of her stone and was thus having trouble locating her grave. A robin suddenly appeared and flew beside us. I decided to follow the robin's flight path through the cemetery, as we attempted to find Claudia's grave. The robin appeared to be leading us directly to the stone. To both my friend's and my own amazement it finished it's flight course by landing directly on her stone.

Over the next year my flight course was mapped out for me too. My manager Adam arranged for me to gig in a number of pubs and small venues, including a place called The Spot in Islington. This was a small venue with a tiny stage and a house band appearing once a week. Audience members were invited to go up on stage and sing impromptu; braving the possibility of a host of boos, in the hope of instead wining the audience over and receiving gusto of cheers.

When I had gained enough confidence, I started to sing at larger industry venues. Adam arranged for me to start signing at a well-known industry venue called The Kashmir Klub. The venue, which was run by Tony More and Marie Claire D'ubaldo (the songwriter of Celine Dion's *Falling into You* and *One and One*) was where many stars sung to an elite audience. The Kashmir Klub was held every Tuesday and Thursday night at a pub called The Baker and Oven near Baker Street tube station. Singing at the club was by invite only. The venue attracted stars such as Belinda Carlisle, Simon Climie; the famous Nashville writer and singer of the song *I Knew You Were Waiting for Me* and originally half of the band Climie Fisher, Lawrence Gowan and Eric Clapton's guitarist Alan Darby. New artists started on the Thursday night and graduated to a Tuesday review night if they were good enough. After successful audition I performed on a Thursday at the start of the month and soon found myself graduating to a Tuesday review night later that same month.

The first Tuesday night I was to sing there a group of friends had come along to support me. We ate dinner in the audience until it was my turn to go up onto the stage. That was the custom at the venue, all very laid back and relaxed. The waitress kept coming over with baskets of bread. Each time she placed the bread on the table my heart missed a beat, as the paper napkins the bread was placed on in the basket kept getting dangerously close to the many lit tea light candles on the table and my fear of fire took a hold over me. Eventually my heart could take it no longer and I asked the waitress to 'Please be careful!' 'It's fine' she announced, as she placed the basket, with over hanging napkin directly into the flame of one of the candles. The entire napkin lit up like a ball of light. The entire audience gasped. The young lady on stage continued to sing. Always fearless in the face of adversity, my instincts kicked in. I quickly picked up everyone's glasses, sniffed the contents to see which contents were non alcoholic, then poured them over the flames. Eventually the fire went out and to my embarrassment the entire room applauded. A minute later the young lady on stage finished her number and I was then called up on to the stage. Completely embarrassed about what had just happened and concerned I had ruined the glory for the other young singer, the only words I could muster up were 'Well, you thought you'd seen me set the place alight already but now you're really going to see me set the place alight!' A loud cheer arose and then I sang. The reviews I received were terrific. I was complimented on my ability to create extremely well structured, catchy, songs, relevant to the time. The Kashmir Klub's magazine, 'Annabel's Diary' printed a guest review on my set, which read as follows: *'More contrast was provided by Emma Holli, purveying impeccably written songs about ex-lovers and other familiar topics in her own distinctive style.'* After this encouraging review I decided to continue to pursue my singing career and for a while longer, or at least for the next year, I forgot about my dream to act.

Over the course of the next year I attended a number of other band's gigs to check out my competition and continued to gig myself. After one particular gig I participated in as an audience member only, as I was singing merrily to myself, the popular radio deejay Neil Fox came up to me and said: 'You've got a great voice there. You should do something with that talent!' On another occasion I went to a gig at a pub with a few friends as an audience member but when the singer had finished her set a number of my friends dared me to go up onto the stage and start singing. After a lot of persuasion I asked the saxophonist if he would care to do a round of *Let It Be* with me. We brought the house down and ended up jamming impromptu to a few other numbers. Unbeknownst to me, the singer was meant to be coming back on stage later that night but didn't return, as I had apparently unawares stolen her set in a style which had made James Brown famous!

Tony Moore had set me up with the fabulous session guitarist David 'Dzal' Martin. Dzal has over the years worked as a session player for many accomplished artists and bands including: Terry Reid, Rick Wakeman, Alvin Stardust, Cheetah, Whitney Houston, Meatloaf, Roxette, Nazareth, Nick Kershaw, Tom Robinson, Phil Spalding, Edwina Hayes, Ben Elton, Alan Bleasdale, Right Said Fred, Adrian Snell, The Box Frogs and the Equals, to name but a few. I felt so privileged to work with Dzal. I continued to gig with Dzal for a short while after this time and I have to say, not only is Dzal a phenomenal guitarist but he was an absolute pleasure to work with and so supportive to our cause.

By this time, Adam and I had already long since started our hunt for a record deal, with the idea of launching my career the following year. Adam was however, going through the process of leaving the management company he had been working for and making Dreamscape an independent venture. Whilst this was occurring, a bit of an hiatus occurred in our continued search for a deal so I approached Adam to ask if he would mind if I continued the search by myself for a while, at least whilst he was sorting out the legalities of his company. Adam encouraged my search and informed me I should approach Denis Ingoldsby at First Avenue Management, as he said he felt Denis would really like my style and sound and also informed me Denis was the best manager in the business. At the time Denis was managing, writing and producing records for the girl band Eternal, Michelle Gayle, Dinah Carol, George Michael, a number of *The X Factor* winners, All Saints, to name a mere few and is still managing bands today such as the Ndubz and the band Tatoo. Adam told me he had previously that week seen Denis at a music awards event and said I should use that knowledge to my advantage. I did. I found out who the Head of Sony Music was and rang up First Avenue Music that week claiming to be 'Sonia', PA to the Head of Sony Music Entertainment. My ridiculous Sloane accent was fantastic! I asked Denis' receptionist if she could tell me when Denis would be in the office that week, so I may place a time in the diary for my boss and Denis to meet. Denis' PA dutifully gave me the information I required and I thanked her kindly and told her I would ring back to confirm a date once I had spoken with my boss.

I now had in my hands the dates of when Denis would be in his office. This was like gold dust! I drove up to First Avenue Management dressed in a short skirt and ridiculous outfit and yet another equally ridiculous accent. This charade was for the secretary's benefit rather than for Denis', as I wanted the receptionist to remember me, in order to pass my demo onto Denis! I approached the receptionist and informed her I had met Denis at the Music Awards ceremony on such and such a particular date and that he had told me to drop by with my demo when I was in the area. She then asked if I would like to go up and say 'hello' to him. This was an incredibly tempting offer but far too risqué for my plan, plus I really did not want to meet him dressed in this attire - I had tried that once before if you recall and for sure fire didn't want the same funky reception! I informed the receptionist I would not like to meet with Denis that day as I was in a hurry to get to another meeting but would be grateful if she would just let Denis know Emma Fletcher had popped by to say hello and that this was the demo he had asked me to drop in for him. The receptionist promised to give Denis my demo and indeed she did.

The next day I rang up to speak to Denis again and now with a completely different accent, I claimed to be Emma Fletcher from Sound Music calling to speak to Denis. As fate would have it, Denis was actually waiting for a telephone call from someone named Emma Fletcher from a company with a similar name, so his PA put me directly through to him! I did not know what to say, so told him the truth about my plan. He laughed and laughed and told me he would listen to my music that night and said I should call him the next day around 6:00pm so he could tell me his thoughts on my voice. Stunned I put down the phone and counted the seconds until 6 o'clock the next day arrived. I called him on the dot at 6:00pm. Denis came to the phone with an apology he had not had the time to listen to my music as yet. My response was a playful 'Typical! Men! Say they will do one thing and then what do they do? Quite the opposite! Well heed my warning, you have one last chance to listen to my demo, or else!' Denis asked what the or else was and to be honest I had not really thought my plan through well enough to know the answer to that question, so said: 'I will just have to sing down the phone to you!' 'Great, sing!' exclaimed Denis. 'Pardon?' I replied, not expecting this as a response to my greeting, as I was of course only joking. 'Sing, right now!' And so I did. I sang my little heart out down the phone. I finished. There was silence. My heart sank as I started to think about how much Denis must have disliked my voice to remain so quiet. All of a sudden he gave a loud shriek: 'I love you! That was fantastic darling! I wasn't expecting that! I want to meet you right now!' And so we did. I got in my car and drove to meet up with Denis that evening. He took me out to dinner at a little Italian restaurant near Ealing Studios and an instant friendship formed, which by the way still strongly exists to this day.

Shortly after this Denis took me into his studio to lay down some tracks with his top producer Nigel Butler. Denis was particularly enamoured with my song *Let's Talk* and felt it would be an instant hit. With stage name complete Denis felt it was now time to create an image for myself and suggested I cut my long hair short to accentuate my neck, the very same part of my body I had been hiding all these years. He also wanted me to get some publicity shots taken with this new style. I was not sure I was comfortable cutting off my long locks, so told him I would think about it. It was shortly after this time that my dear mum sadly passed away and so finally, as a reaction to her passing I went and cut all my long hair short and thus found my new look. In fact I loved my short hair so much that I ended up keeping it this way for a very long time after. Denis was so kind to me during the days and weeks, which followed mum's passing. He was such a caring friend. Many nights were spent with Denis and me speaking over the telephone for hours on end about life, the universe, the planet

196

and stars. Denis had been very fond of my dear mum, whom he had got the chance to know before she passed on and had often had long chats with her over the telephone, as had many of my friends before him over the years, including Albert, Henry Thomas and Roger Limb. Mum had always affectionately called Denis 'Dennis the Menace' as a term of endearment, whenever he called to speak to me. She trusted Denis to look after me and she was right, he always has been a kind and caring friend to me over the years.

Sadly, the song *Let's Talk* was never recorded in it's entirety with Denis as he became very busy with a number of his top stars and time for newcomers in his busy schedule started to become fewer and more far-between. I was already in line behind another new singer named Nathalie Jordan, who had just finished vocals on a remake of *Private Number* with the band 911. After mum passed on however, my battle between music and religion started to become more prevalent, with religion now starting to take the lead between the sparring sides. The wait to get into the studio to record my song started to interest me less and less, until eventually I chose to give up my singing ambitions completely in favour of a more religious lifestyle. I did not feel I was the loser by giving up on my singing ambitions however; as for me the taking part had been the all-important winning streak and now I had found a new path, which had started to inspire me more.

Although I have always been of a highly competitive nature, I believe the important part is not in the winning but in the taking part. These words are not just a cheap attempt at becoming a poor metaphor for loosing but from the realisation of how we can learn so much about ourselves from the taking part. For if you don't try, then you are only cheating yourself but it is actually the times we loose we learn more about ourselves than the times we win. For these are the times true discoveries are made; as we discover who we really are from what we are and are not prepared to do - but nevertheless I always aim to win!

***If you are not willing to loose, then you are not prepared to win.*** - Emma Fletcher

# 9

# Education, Education, Education

***I like a teacher who gives you something to take home
to think about besides homework. -** Edith Ann*

*Paul: Eventually choosing to combine her skills in the arts with a career in the
world of teaching, Emma describes in the following chapter the various events
that led her into the classroom. And, as with her employer at the BBC, an
employer in the world of education was to inspire Fletcher to take vital steps in
her career - in this case towards finally going to drama school.*

Emma: The story of my first teaching post takes us back a year in
time, as it actually starts from the year before I trained for my Post
Graduate degree course to become a teacher of art and design.
After graduating from art school and starting to realise I didn't
want to be an architect and perhaps my music career was not
going to keep a roof over my head alone, I sat down and made a
list of all my qualities. I'm a good listener, I told myself. I'm also a
good talker and I enjoy working with children. I thought about
training in art therapy or even training as a counsellor but decided
against both deciding I would train as a teacher. Teaching requires
you to be a mother, counsellor, policewoman and punch bag all at
once - who wouldn't want to teach?

Whilst looking into teaching courses to apply for, I went to the
local 'one-stop' shop for careers advice. 'Train as a junior school
teacher', I was told. 'There is not enough call for art teachers.'
'Am I once again choosing a precarious career path?' I asked
myself. 'Is everything in the arts just flighty and precarious?' As it
happens the advice I was given was inaccurate and there is just as
much call for art teachers as there is for any subject teachers, but I
wrongly listened to this advice and applied for a course to train as
a junior schoolteacher instead. I was offered an interview and
immediately offered a place on a teaching course at The Middlesex

University. Four weeks into the course and upon attending a lecture about which individual elements make up salt, I suddenly had a complete knee-jerk reaction to what I was learning and to my complete embarrassment burst into tears bang in the middle of the lecture hall! I knew I had chosen the wrong course and I think I was just overcome by emotions, as well as being completely over-tired, as even by the end of the first month of the course we had been worked solidly into the ground. One of the tutors quickly took me aside and asked me what was wrong. I wailed: 'I don't care that sodium and chloride make salt. I just want to draw!' 'Okay', he said 'I think you need to see the head of art!'

I was taken down the hallway to see the head of art, still sobbing. When I had calmed down I was given an immediate interview for the parallel course in teaching art. I was asked to bring in some examples of my art work the next day and informed if I was good enough, I could start the art course - the next year. 'Next year?' I began to wail again! 'But I want to start it now!' I was informed I had already missed so much work that even in missing just the first four weeks it would be impossible for me to catch-up properly. I said I thought I could but the head of art insisted I defer for the year. Upon reflection I am very pleased I did defer, as when I did finally start the course I found by the end of the first four weeks I had already completed four full, brimming at the sides, no prisoners held, it's your money or your life, folders of work; averaging at one of these per week!

During my year out before commencing my post grad degree, which was also around the same time I was still actively chasing my singing dream, I joined a teaching agency and asked to be placed in a school as a teaching assistant. 'At least I will be earning money and gaining experience', I told myself. I informed the agency the only real experience I had working with children at that point in time was voluntary work. I used to take under privileged children out on day trips. 'Can you sign?' I was asked. Well I had learnt the alphabet in sign language as a Brownie and apart from the one finger salute, which my mum had always told me never to use, I told the agency that was pretty much the extent of my signing. 'Great' they said. 'We will get you into a school covering for a teacher who is away for three days. You will be working in their profoundly hard of hearing unit'. 'Okay, how hard can this be?' I thought to myself. 'I can go from singing to signing - no problem!'

Working in a school with profoundly hard of hearing children could not have been more opposing to my singing career; which was based completely on the quality of sound. Walking into the classroom was like entering a foreign country. Everyone was speaking in a language I did not understand and what's more, they were not using sound. The classroom was almost completely devoid of sound, apart from the occasional noise of furniture moving or feet touching the ground. These children were communicating via expression and feeling alone and what's more they didn't miss a beat. There was no way of ever lying to these kids or disguising how you were feeling, they could see right through the façade.

I soon learnt that little Amrit's favourite group was The Spice Girls. 'Really?' I exclaimed. 'But how do you know?' 'Easy', she answered, 'I like the beat.' She was of course referring to the vibration and sound waves that resonated to her ears. It is very unusual for someone to be completely deaf and most people who are hearing impaired are able to detect or perceive at least some sound frequencies. By the end of the three days I was asked if I would like to stay until the end of the week, as the lady I was covering for was still off sick. 'Sure,' I said, 'I would love to.' By the end of the week I found I had already managed to acquire a minimal amount of language for myself and was signing some basic words fairly proficiently. 'You've picked this up very well,' the head of the department commented. 'Yes' I declared, 'That's because I'm Jewish and an artist, so I talk with my hands anyway!' I was then asked to stay on another week; the week became a month and eventually turned into the entire school year. By the end of my contract with the school I had become fairly proficient at using basic BSL (British Sign Language).

An amusing little aside I must share with you was when a young lady from Australia, who was also profoundly hard of hearing from birth, was working at the school with me. Every time I would sign at the students to stop talking she would let out a loud gasp. One day I just couldn't resist any longer and had to ask her why she was gasping every time I asked the children to stop talking. As it turned out, what means 'stop talking' in BSL is a very similar sign for something extremely rude in Australia - well they have to do everything upside down to us, don't they?

During the school summer holidays, I was in Spain with a few friends when a poor homeless man came up to us gesturing with his hands for some spare change. It occurred to me he might be deaf, so upon handing him some change I started to talk to him in sign language and he was completely taken aback. Sign language is almost international. I had a good few minutes 'chat' with this man. I think it made his day. It certainly made mine. Not only was it a great feeling to know I had put a smile on this man's face, as he probably didn't get many people who could or would bother taking the time to talk to him but it was an amazing feeling to realise here was I in Spain, unable to speak a word of Spanish, bar perhaps 'Ola' and 'Adios amigos' - but this was not going to get me very far - and yet here I was able to converse with this man. One thing this incident reminded me of once again is 'smile and the world smiles with you'. It can never hurt to offer someone a smile or a friendly word. Make it your *modus operandi* to smile at five people each day. You never know, not only may you be brightening someone's world a little; you might just even make their day. Every person you meet in life is important; so thank them for being a part of your day and remember; there are no ordinary moments as every moment is extraordinary.

I loved teaching in the hearing impaired unit and found it so rewarding. I did however become very upset when one teacher in Amrit's music lesson refused to wear the monitor, which helped Amrit hear a little of what was being said. 'She can't hear anything, so what's the point?' this woman retorted. 'Her favourite group is The Spice Girls I replied, 'and she loves to listen to the high frequencies!'

I worked with one child named Omar whilst at the school, whom no one else would work with anymore, as he was extremely violent. After six months of being at the school, the head of the department informed me the school did not have enough money to keep me on as well as now bring in a supply teacher to look after Omar, so asked if I would be prepared to be next in the firing line to look after him. Not wanting to leave the school, I decided to give working with little Omar a chance. Omar had become so violent that sadly he was no longer allowed to work in a room with other children, so I had to work with him in a separate classroom.

After week one, Omar had successfully managed to punch me in the nose and knock me to the ground. I was admitted to hospital straight away but fortunately no serious damage had occurred. Mum pleaded with me to leave the school after this incident but I decided to give Omar another chance. It took me a good couple of months to calm the animal inside of him, including chairs being thrown at me on a daily basis, regularly being stabbed with sharpened pencils and literally going home black and blue from bruises. I somehow managed to always respond to Omar in a calm fashion, which was a new experience for him and quite different to the usual 'lock-down' situation he had previously been used to.

Over the course of the next two months, Omar stopped his violent behaviour towards me altogether. He started to give me eye contact and even started to learn some sign language skills, which up until this point he had not attempted to do and had literally locked himself away in a world of no communication and darkness. Thankfully I learnt that by the time Omar reached high school age he had turned into a fine young man. My experiences at this unit were very rewarding but I promised both myself and my mum and in fact my rabbi too, I would never put myself in a dangerous situation like this again with my work. Over the years I have worked with children with various conditions from Down's, Lowe and Aspergers Syndrome, severe Autism, ADHD and ADD, Vision impairment, selective mutism and profound emotional, physical or behavioural conditions but I have never once put myself in a position again where I would suffer physical aggression at the hands of a student. Working with these children has reminded me continually how lucky I am to have my good health and I also feel privileged to have been given the honour to work with such special children; which for me is what the word 'special' in 'special needs' stands for. Over the last few years during my career as an actress I have often asked my agent to allow me to take a few weeks out of my busy acting schedule to go and carry out days of supply teaching with these special children. This not only keeps me grounded but also allows me to feel I am giving something back to society. Perhaps this defies the meaning of true altruism; as I am also getting something special back from working with these wonderful children but if that is the case then perhaps that is okay anyhow.

My Post Graduate degree was enjoyable but I soon found myself once again enduring many hours of lengthy study into the late hours of the night. I immediately found I was excelling to a high standard on the course and found myself selected by my university to represent teaching practice standards for the government officer's viewing during an HMI (Her Majesty's Inspector) of the university. No teachers like an OFSTED (Office for Standards in Education) inspection and especially not a student teacher. I am certainly no exception to this rule. Although I was aware it was really the university being inspected and not me, it still meant the pressure was on me. To add insult to existing injury, during my two school placements as a trainee teacher I found myself being placed in two schools which were both undergoing an OFSTED inspection and then again, when I carried out my NQT (Newly Qualified Teacher) preliminary year, I once again found myself working in a school which was being inspected. These guys were well and truly on to me! Thankfully, I have always been the type of person who keeps organised files - in fact I am the type of person who keeps files on files; which helped me a great deal during this time. All this filing however, left very little time for anything else in my life and my dream of appearing on the stage started to slowly take a back seat again and almost disappeared into the ether - or so it would appear - until it successfully managed to catch-up with me once again in its continual game of tag and bite me directly on the backside!

Immediately after graduating from my teaching degree I became friendly with a vibrant young lady named Melanie (not her real name), who I was introduced to amongst my circle of friends. Melanie and I formed an immediate friendship, which was partly born from the fact we had both grown-up with our grandparents. Melanie's mother had also suffered from mental illness and sadly had also been too unwell to look after her. Melanie, like myself, had trained for a degree in art and design and then later a Post Graduate degree in teaching art. We were both art teachers at the time of meeting and found the coincidences did not end there. Shortly after acquiring the starting grounds of a firm friendship with Melanie, she informed me she was getting married and would contact me upon her return from her honeymoon for a coffee and catch-up. Sadly whilst on her honeymoon, Melanie was struck down by a freak-lightening storm and died instantly in her fiancés arms. I was very shaken and saddened by this event and once again it brought the sad reality of the loss of a friend into my life.

Around this same time and when dad had reached the grand age of 90, I had a phone call from a local shopkeeper who informed me dad was near to his shop, wandering around at the bottom of the street. Without hesitation I rushed down the road and true enough there was dad looking dishevelled and just wandering around. I asked dad what he was doing and he replied he didn't know. Worse than this, he admitted he didn't know where he was. I then asked him where he had parked the car. Again, he didn't know. I soon discovered where he had parked the car - in the middle of the street. By now it was holding up other drivers and nearly causing a serious accident. I left dad in the safe and caring hands of the shopkeeper for a couple of minutes, whilst I quickly went to move the car to a safer place by the side of the road, after which time I rushed back to retrieve dad. Instantly I realised he must have suffered a stroke. I took dad by the hand and led him back to the car. I quickly drove him to the doctors who, after a series of tests, confirmed my theory. Dad had indeed suffered a small stroke.

Shortly after this time dad had a series of small strokes and was sadly never fully the same again. During the next year of his life I washed, bathed and even helped feed and toilet him. It was so upsetting to see this wonderful, intelligent and independent man, whom had been such an upright and kind member of society and had even been driving right up to when his first stroke occurred, go down hill like this and loose his independence. Throughout this very upsetting time I experienced yet more problems with certain relatives of The Drummond family, continually suggesting I leave dad and find my own place to live.

Sadly, dad's physical state of health started to deteriorate rapidly and his state of mind became increasingly worse. It was now more than I knew how to cope with. Dad now required the help and attention of professionals and unfortunately, whilst not my first choice of preference, he needed to be placed in a care home. I recall once again a relative from the Drummond family originally not wanting dad to be placed in a care home as she said it would be so expensive. My response was merely: 'Well, I would rather dad's money go towards looking after him in his lifetime than to us when he is no longer here.' Unfortunately this was not the only time I bore witness to talk of money by the Drummond family during the time of dad's poor health. Previously to this, upon purchasing a plank of wood to help support the underneath of dad's mattress in his bed, both myself and the local neighbours were privy to the loud booming voice of Mr Drummond resonating down the street, requesting money be paid to him before he brought the plank of wood into the house. Whilst I am certain this family member's intentions were probably of good merit, having never been of a particularly monetary nature myself and always believing money is not what brings one true happiness, I could never understand why these family members, in my opinion, seemed to rate the value of money so highly over what to me was surely really the important issues at hand here and that was dad's comfort and happiness.

I visited dad every day at the home. It was a hard time. With each stroke his memory deteriorated further, until he no longer knew who I was. I remember one day dad taking my hand in his and saying 'I don't know who you are but I know I love you.' I guess it is true what they say; feelings really do stay with you forever.

After dad became ill my entire world was rapidly changing. I now found myself living all by myself in the large house I was raised. It was a lonely time. I no longer felt like chasing a precarious career in the world of the arts and was very much looking for some sort of stability in my ever-changing circumstances. I decided to leave my aspirations of appearing on stage and for the time being at least, to once again place them on the back burner. I started to feel perhaps I should move into using my skills in the arts to teach, instead of applying them on a stage. The idea of me changing career paths once again should have worried the close remaining members of my family at this time but it didn't, as they probably felt this was a more sensible career choice anyhow.

During the time dad had become ill, I had unfortunately managed to get myself into an abusive relationship. I think I was just so desperate to be with someone at this time and so desperately reaching out for the emotional support which I was not receiving at the hands of some close family members. This was not the first time I had been in an abusive relationship and sadly would not be the last. I had previously to this been in a relationship where an ex-boyfriend would shout at me to 'shut-up' in public all the time and was sadly not supportive at times when mum and dad had not been well over the years and when perhaps I could have required his support. My close friends would get angry and upset with me for not leaving him. You may wonder, therefore, how I managed to get myself into yet another abusive relationship but it is very easy to be drawn into these men's lives; especially if they appear to be offering you the one thing you feel you are missing - love and support, which of course is the very thing I did not end up receiving from this relationship. Most of these men do not start out this way and are very charming when you fist meet them. I am sure this is not exclusive to men and is probably also true of women who are abusive to men too. I think on some level I was also looking to acquaint a troubled soul in the belief I could save him - I hadn't been able to save Claudia and felt it was very much my duty to now save the world. I should point out however, that with all my ex-boyfriends each and every one of them had endearing qualities; which is of course also what drew me towards them initially and to be fair there were good times to be had with each of them; else the relationships would of course not have lasted even more than a day.

But this time it was not just emotionally abusive; it became physically abusive too. The abuse happened so slowly; over such a long period of time, that I was almost unawares it was even happening until it was too late. The man in question was sadly a very disturbed soul. He was very controlling and most likely suffering from delusional paranoia. He would often wake me up in the middle of the night asking me strange questions and convinced I was running off with many other men, which of course I was not. I was not allowed to leave the room or go to the bathroom without telling him where I was going. He would even go as far as asking me how many sheets of toilet paper I had used and no doors were ever allowed to be locked between us. He told me how to wear my hair, how to dress and even tried to tell me what I could eat. He also told me I was to give up my dreams of being on the stage. I was only allowed to see friends when he told me I could see them and ring family with his permission - with regards to the latter I took no notice. I only wish I could say this were also true of his other demands. In his eyes women were to serve his madness. He was extremely sexually controlling and forced me to carry out sexual acts with him which I felt very uncomfortable about; especially as I had been religious for many years before meeting him. I personally felt abused sexually and emotionally by this man on a daily basis. He was a lost soul and I originally mistook his troubled mind and sadness for tenderness.

I started buying loads of stuff I didn't really need. It was retail therapy but I wasn't buying clothes; I was buying things to build an ideal home. Whilst in actuality my own family life was slowly disintegrating before my very eyes, due to dad's failing health and certain members of my family's unkindness, I was busily trying to recreate the picture I held in my head of what I thought the perfect family home should look like - the picture of perfection - but at the end of the day all I found myself surrounded by was stuff - stuff I didn't need.

I recall at the height of this relationship, at which time it had reached crisis point for my health, being invited to a local rabbi's for dinner one evening. Around this time I had started to experience mini panic-attacks. My nerves were now starting to resemble something akin to a car-wreck. This rabbi, along with two others, was desperately worried about my health. They could literally see me fading away in front of their very eyes. They were both desperately trying everything they could to get me away from this man. I went to the rabbi's house for dinner and suddenly and without warning found myself horizontally recumbent, as I collapsed to the ground from complete exhaustion from my standing position around the table. I was extremely embarrassed but everyone was very understanding and of course concerned.

The relationship with this man had been going on for around two years and was coming to an end as dad's health slowly deteriorated to the point of no recovery. My friends had seen my mental health deteriorate whilst I was in this relationship and continued to beg me to leave him. Before this relationship I could never understand why battered women would not just walk away from an abusive man but now here was I, very much deeply involved in a subservient relationship with an abusive man and unable to walk away. I could not walk away for two reasons; firstly I felt I had no one left to turn to, although this was probably not the case and secondly this man had consumed every inch of who I was, so that without him I would now be lost. In fact I completely lost my identity to this other person and all sense of who I was, including even what made me tick. On the few occasions I tried to walk away I just ended getting lured straight back into his web again.

On some level I felt I deserved this heartache in my life. I felt I was not worthy of more and I had found a man to acknowledge this belief; although on some level all I really wanted him to do was tell me how worthy I really was. Heartache was all I had ever known and I was comfortable with the feeling it carried. Heartache had become my friend. This was not a man whom I could turn to for any kind of support or assistance. As he worked in a legal profession, where persuasive words are the key to success, he was very good at arguing out his side of the story.

Even when his side of the story made no sense at all, his argument was so powerful he always left me feeling I was in the wrong. By the end of the relationship I was convinced black was white and white was indeed black. I ended up requiring the care of a gynaecologist and a small operation due to this relationship and was then referred onto counselling for women whom had been sexually abused. It was now time to make heartache my enemy rather than my friend. I decided I would never allow myself to loose my identity to someone else again; as if we loose ourselves in someone else, then who are we? People can only take your power from you if you let them. When you give your power away to someone or something else, you are actually making that person or thing more important than you. I started to realise the only thing holding me back from being happy was in fact myself. I started to realise my happiness did not need to be defined by someone else's actions. We attract into our life a reflection of all that we are. This is a rudimentary law of being. Only a free man has the power to spot another free man and therefore really remain free himself. The same is also true for happiness; we have the power to make ourselves happy and should not rely on anyone else to do that for us. We all have the power to change our own destiny with a single thought. I have now learnt not to give my power over to someone else. I have learnt that I am a diamond waiting to be unveiled. We all are. So my advice would be to search hard inside yourself for the answer and you shall seek the diamond inside the coal but be careful not to surround yourself with diamond diggers in the process.

I think the reason I kept running back to this man was two-fold. Firstly I allowed myself to believe that perhaps the next time would be different but of course people don't change over night and in any case, they have to want to change first. There is only so many times you can cover old ground before it ends up swallowing you up whole. The other reason I think I kept running back was in the belief this man was the only person who could save me. He was the one who had dished out the heartache so in my warped vision, I believed he must therefore be the only one who had the power to make it all go away again. I had allowed his actions and words over the last few years to leave me feeling inadequate; so I ran back to the very person that had made me feel this way in the belief he was the only person who could now rectify how bad I felt about myself. I kept hoping he would take away my pain by taking back some of his words and actions but really the only person who could take away my pain was me. I was emotionally travelling at 100mph up the wrong side of the highway and I knew I'd better pull over and stop. I knew it was time to park up on the edge of the slow lane else I was going to crash. I began to realise this man's behaviour towards me was really just inward anger at himself and it was time for me to get away from him, it was time to start driving in the opposite direction within the speed limit.

People who say angry words are really only angry with themselves. You've heard the expression 'when someone points a finger at you, they are really just pointing three back at themselves'? Well this is so true. I think this is also true of when any relationship between two people breaks down and hurtful things are said, which perhaps are not really meant. Anger is a loss of control and when people get angry at someone else, they are usually really just angry with themselves they didn't have it in their power to make things work out or to perhaps walk away from the situation sooner before animosity set sail. Eventually I started to look inwardly for my answers in order to be able to piece together my broken heart and shattered soul and only then was I was able to start the healing process on myself again.

When we break-up with someone or come out of any relationship, be it with a friend, a work colleague or of course even a lover, it is so easy to doubt our decisions from fear of the void that now faces us and it becomes all to easy to allow this doubt to prevent us from moving forward to the next stage in our lives. Fear of being alone, fear of being wrong or just fear of fear itself is what stops us moving forward in life. Fear severs growth and creates doubt. It is all too easy to be swayed by that little naughty voice inside your head shouting 'Jump! Jump!' and just when you are about to jump another little voice pops up inside your head and shouts 'Don't do it!' In Judaism we metaphorically refer to these two little inner-dialogues, which continually live inside our head, as the two inclinations; the good inclination and the evil inclination. We actually metaphorically refer to these two inclinations as sitting on either shoulder, both trying to get you to live out their will. The good inclination always has our best interests at heart, whereas the evil inclination is always trying to push us over the edge and of course the two are regularly in a fisti-cuffs battle for survival. The difficulty however is, trying to work out which one is the good sounding board and which one is the evil! I have learnt the key in trusting your decisions is to separate yourself from the doubt. Remember; don't give your power over to someone else. Only when you can start to believe in yourself and believe in the essence of being, can you truly separate yourself from doubt. Then and only then, will you be able to look at your decisions objectively and really trust in your own decision-making. It is true, everyone is a little bit yin and a little bit yang but balance is truly the key. Since I was a child I have always chosen to only see the light in people but this has, on occasion, made me blind to their dark-side. So now I retain a more realistic approach and keep my eyes open for both elements. Whilst I still choose to believe everyone is fundamentally good and I prefer to remain ever the optimist about people rather than the eternal pessimist, this does not mean I am naïve and unawares people have the ability to behave badly and when they do you have to walk away.

Whilst I still chose to believe everyone is born with the inherent potential to do good and most people I have come across in life are intrinsically of good will, I have however over the course of time become more aware of people who are more tuned in to their darker side. Even although I am always up for giving people a chance, I tend now to try and stay away from these people. I refer to these types of people as emotional vampires; as they sap your emotions dry. I listen to my gut more these days and if I sense a warning sign telling me to run, then you can count on it I will sprint as fast as I can in the opposite direction. For these days I try to make my decisions based upon a certain amount of cerebral injection, rather than those based purely and loosely on warm, fluffy candyfloss of the moment emotions.

It was a non-descript day but I felt odd. I was at the time working as an art teacher in a local school. That morning when I awoke I had experienced one of my strange feelings, so I took the day off work. I rested on my bed and fell asleep. When I awoke in the middle of the day I heard dad's name in my head. I immediately knew something was wrong. I rushed to the care home. I started to walk up the back stairs to his room, the very same stairs I had always walked up. A nurse stopped me in my tracks and said sharply: 'Where are you going?' I responded: 'To see Mr Rose.' 'Oh he's dead!' she responded callously. What, how could this be? Had I just heard her correctly? The nurse softened and said: 'I'm sorry, I thought you worked here, I didn't realise you were family'. I rushed into the room where he lay, now motionless and sat beside his bed still in shock. My cell phone rang and in my shock I picked it up. My friend on the other end heard my voice and in her concern asked if I was okay. In a trance like state and without really even speaking into the phone, I replied: 'He's dead.' Only the night before dad had grabbed my hand tightly, in what had proved to be the most heart-warming moment, as he smiled a huge loving smile at me and continued to hold my hand firmly.

What came next was a misunderstanding, which unfortunately led to more upset for all involved. Mrs Drummond entered the room and let her upset be known at finding me on the telephone in front of dad's lifeless body. The thought that crossed my mind at this point was, if my family already knew dad had passed on, then why had no one informed me? Why had I been left in the dark and left to find out in this upsetting manner? Before I was given the chance however to explain myself and explain what had happened, in her upset I was then asked to lean over and check dad's chest to see if he really was dead. This request made me feel completely uncomfortable - a similar request had also been asked of me by the same family member after mum passed on. In Jewish law the living are not meant to have interactions with the dead in this way and aside from this, this was not something I felt particularly comfortable with anyhow - but not wishing to be the cause of any more upset, I dutifully leant over and placed my head onto dad's cold and lifeless chest, to listen for a heart beat. I found none. No sooner had my ear touched dad's chest, then Mr

Drummond walked into the room and shouted at me for the action I was now carrying out. I started to feel there was no way of winning with these family members. I was damned if I do and damned if I don't. I eventually left the room in a complete daze and made my way home.

No sooner had I got home, Mr Drummond arrived at the house and informed me I now had four weeks to move both myself and all my belongings out of the house and that 'the ball was now rolling'. I was asked to remove all of my belongings, else I was informed they would be removed and placed on the dump. I was also informed with regards to my beloved piano, if I did not manage to get this out of the house within the space of the fours weeks then a decision would be made as to whether or not it would be kept by Mr Drummond or thrown out with the rest of my remaining items too. I had always feared in my heart this day would come and that things would turn sour like this. This was a defining moment in my life - an epoch. I knew from here on in, nothing was ever going to be the same for me again. As I knew this day was coming, I had over the last few months been packing my belongings into boxes and placing them into storage preparing for this time. I took what was mine and only what was mine, including my piano and left the house at the start of the second week.

When I went back to the house for the very last time with my cousin Sam, to collect the last remaining boxes of my personal items, I cried my eyes out. It felt as if I were saying goodbye to an old friend. So much had happened in this house. It was filled with so many memories and was one of the only tangible reminders I had left of my life with my parents. It was a very sad and painful moment for me.

If the above was not upset enough to last a lifetime, not one person could have predicted what was to come next - not even me. Mum and dad had always said they wanted to divide their Will between relatives of The Drummond family and myself equally. They felt this was what they wanted to do for two reasons; the main reason being they had said they always wanted me to have the share of their assets that would have been Claudia's and felt was therefore rightfully my bloodline. The second reason was because they always feared that after they were both gone I would have no family to look after me. In fact, in this same vein, after mum's eyesight deteriorated, mum asked a neighbour to type out a note, which she had wanted to be given to members of the family after her passing. The note simply read:

*'Please don't cry for me. I have had a long and mostly happy life and I am grateful for that. Remember me sometimes, I am with you forever in your memory. I only have one wish, that you stay together as a family, look after one another and do not quarrel.'*

Within the space of the same week of this note being written, dad had informed me that after discussion with members of The Drummond family, he had now decided to change the Will, so that the money was no longer to be divided equally and that I was to have a smaller share of both his and mum's assets. I had myself been privy to the tail end of this very same conversation, overhearing part of it as I walked in the front door upon coming home earlier than planned the day it occurred; so this news came as no real shock to me.

Not someone who has ever been of a materialistic nature, what actually upset me about this decision was not that I would not receive the money but the thought that it had possibly materialised through discussion with other family members who perhaps did not have my best interests at heart and I could not help but wonder if this was somehow not really dad's sentiment at all but once again his weak mind speaking; now that mum was no longer here to be the voice of reason and strength that she always was for him. Dad continued with the words 'There is to be no more discussion on the matter young lady' and that was indeed the last time I discussed the matter with him.

Moving back to the present time; dad had just passed away, my family had rejected me and my boyfriend was telling me the relationship was over - although I was at this point in time still spending time with him, feeling at this point in my life I was

214

unable to completely leave him, as I was unable to face yet still more loss in my life. And so the sexually aggressive nature of this relationship continued; until one day I said I could take no more. I recall, as if it were yesterday, him cupping my face in his hand, which seemed to cover my entire face and pushing me backwards onto his bed from my standing position, then turning his back on me and walking out of the room. This to me indicated a hit. I knew it was time to get out. I left his apartment that day for the very last time.

It was now the week of dad's shiva. The family had decided to only hold one day of prayers. Over a hundred of my young friends must have come and gone throughout the day to pay their respects to my wonderful dad. The day was divided into two halves. The first half of the day consisted of the morning prayers, which was to be held at The Drummond family household and then followed by evening prayers later that same day, also at their house. I attended the morning prayers with three good friends. As we left the Drummond house after the morning prayers I asked the elder daughter if I might have a private word with her. I felt the time had come for us to finally put all our differences aside once and for all. I took her aside and told her I loved her dearly. We had experienced our difficulties in the past but I expressed the sentiment I hoped now, especially as both mum and dad had now passed on, we could work out our differences and move forward from this day on. This relative's response was short and simple and sadly her comments were, shall we say, consisting of the use of very colourful and scathing language, which was very offensive to me. I left the house in tears with my friends. Sadly worse was yet to come in the evening during prayers, as there was the exchange of yet more unkind words from certain relatives.

I stepped outside the house with uncle Ivor's other granddaughter; Rachel, who is my cousin and also close friend. I turned to her and said: 'It couldn't get any worse. My dad has died, my family have rejected me and I've just broken up with my boyfriend.' Just as I said that a pigeon decided to land its lunch directly on my head! Rachel told me it was meant to be good luck and we laughed and laughed amidst the tears.

215

As 7:00pm approached we started to head back towards The Drummond household for the evening prayers. Not one person present could ever have predicted what was to occur next. Towards the end of the prayers Mr Drummond suddenly stood up in the middle of the room and announced in his loud booming voice to both myself, all of my friends and my rabbi, we were to leave the house immediately with the words 'You've had your cake, now get out!' Everyone, myself included, was completely stunned. It is customary to wish mourners a long life as you leave the house. As I started to leave the house, not even really sure if I should be wishing other family members a long-life, as I indeed was a mourner too, in a very small and choked voice, once again almost eating my own words, I said 'I wish you long life' then left. I knew certain family members had probably not heard these words, as they did not reply. I exited the house with my friends when suddenly the husband of the younger Drummond daughter stormed out of the house and grabbed me, shouting words to the effect of 'You get back in there and wish your family a long life, else you are never stepping back in that house again!' I tried to reason with him that I had wished them long life but he continued shouting more abuse. It took a few of my male friends to get me free from this man's grip. We all left the house in complete shock and I knew at that moment I never wanted to step foot in that house ever again.

In the weeks that followed Rachel's parents stepped into the forefront of my life. They had always been very kind to me since I was a young girl but had not really been aware until of late of exactly the amount of hardship and anxiety I had been experiencing in my life. My parents, Vera and Sam, were very kind to my auntie Adrianne (the wife of my uncle John; the son of Vera's first cousin) after her parents past away when she was in her early thirties. In turn over the years, Adrianne has shown the very same kindness and affection towards me. When dad past away, at what proved to be a very difficult time in my life, Adrianne and her family helped me come out the other side of this difficult patch. Both Adrianne and John advised and guided me with occurring legalities. They both advised me with my best interests at heart, as did my rabbi at the time, to seek legal action with regards to dad's Will. To be completely honest, I was prepared to let the money go as, although I am normally frugal with my expenditure, as previously mentioned I have never been particularly monetary based or avaricious but it was never about the money. Suddenly I saw this as a perfect opportunity to finally sort things out in my life. I just wanted certain relatives who there were problems with out of my life once and for all and at the time and in my despair this seemed like the only way to let them know how I felt. As it happens, I did not take the legalities all the way to court in the end, feeling I had received enough heartache already at the hands of certain members of my family. If I could go back in time and find another way to have told them how much they had hurt me over the years, then I think I would rather have gone about things differently but at least they were now out of my life forever and I could finally be free to fly.

Adrianne, a counsellor by profession, was also able to offer me words of wisdom over and above her kindness during this traumatic time in my life. Even if at times the advice felt harsh and sometimes it did - as facing ourselves is never an easy thing to do - I knew without a shadow of a doubt her words were coming from a place of kindness and of caring about my well-being and her words were, nevertheless, good advice and the right advice for me at that time. Her advice thankfully helped me get through this very difficult patch in my life and allowed me to focus on areas of my life I needed to change. It is never easy taking a look at yourself but if you don't know your weaknesses, how can you expect to know your strengths? If you don't know what is wrong, how can you begin to fix it? I had to take a look at myself and my short-fallings to be able to fix them and it was painful. Change is always hard and takes great strength and courage to occur but it is also a very important part of life; as without change we fail to grow. The three main steps of change are: one; recognise you need to change, two; want to make the change and three; work hard to make the change happen. Adrianne and her wonderful family have always offered me a support system since this time and an open invite into their home and their family dinner table on a Friday night. They indeed refer to me as one of the immediate family and Adrianne has even commented she views me as an extra daughter,

217

alongside her own children; Rachel, David and Louise. In my hour of loss I had gained so much. I had found family who really cared about me.

Another family member, who also refers to me as an extra daughter, is the wife of my cousin Henry Winkler. Strangely enough her name is also Adrienne and she too is a counsellor. Having been through a lot of trauma in her own life, believe me when I tell you, a book lies in waiting there too, Adrienne and I understand each other only too well and indeed consider ourselves to be soul sisters. In fact Adrienne, like me, also found herself surrounded by people in the world of celebrity growing up. She is a kind and gentle lady, with a soft approach about her but this is not to be mistaken for weakness or for someone foolish. Not only a very beautiful woman (Adrienne used to be a model when she was younger) but also an extremely intelligent person, Adrienne, alongside Henry, has also offered me so much kindness and words of wisdom through difficult patches in my life.

Both Henry and Adrienne also stepped forward closer into my life over recent years when they discovered the heartache I had been receiving at the hands of other family members. As previously mentioned, Henry was my father Martin's cousin and best friend (Henry's mother was first cousins to my grandmother Rose, Martin's mother) and now the age gap had started to close, both Henry and Adrienne in turn became my best friends too. In fact, over the last four years of my life there has not been a single day which has gone by, when I have not had some form of contact with either Henry or Adrienne. Their fondness and caring for me and likewise mine for them, goes over and above the call of duty of a cousin. They to me are parental figures, cousins and most of all best friends, all rolled into one. If a day goes by when they have not heard from me, I will receive some sort of communication from them to check I am okay. Their house is always open to me and has become my second home over the last few years of my life. In fact both Henry and Adrienne and John and Adrianne, have become for me the light at the end of what has been a very dark tunnel.

I consider myself truly prosperous to have so much love in my life. Thank God I am finally able to say this now, even if all these years down the line. That is not however, to dismiss the great love I received at the hands of my two wonderful sets of grandparents and other close family members over the years; but I have now finally found inner-peace within myself and feel so blessed to be surrounded by so many wonderful family members and friends. I may be a poor jobbing actress but above all else, the one thing that remains important to me is I am happy; and that makes me rich.

After dad passed on and when a sense of calmness finally returned to me life, which took quite a while, I started working at a local school as an art and special educational needs teacher. I stayed at this school for an additional two years after completing my NQT. During this time I was asked by one of the English teachers to become involved with some drama and singing workshops some of the students were undertaking. A number of the students started to compliment me on my singing abilities, whilst I was helping them in class and encouraged me to get involved with a performance a number of the teachers were carrying out for an upcoming school concert. I couldn't think of anything I would have least liked to have become involved in if the truth be known, merely from the sheer embarrassment it would bring along in its wake but after a number of students strongly encouraged me to participate, I finally agreed to sing a rendition of Fairground Attraction's song *Perfect*.

The ever popular and trendy music teacher, Phil, accompanied me on guitar. We were an instant hit with the students and shortly after this, the lovely drama teacher Denise, approached me to help her with some of her drama classes. Around the time I was helping some of the final year students in year thirteen apply to various drama schools, when it started to dawn on me I wanted to apply too! It was also around this time my good friend Beverly secretly entered me to audition for *The X Factor*. Once the programme was aired I thought I was going to go back to the school a complete laughing stock. I couldn't have been more wrong! Suddenly I was a super-star with all the students. When word reached the head of the special needs department, my wonderful boss Jo, I could sing and dance and had an affinity with acting too, she generously badgered me over the coming months to start considering applying to acting schools. In fact it was Jo who was responsible for getting the ball rolling and helping me to eventually find the courage to actually make my application to an acting school - so a big thank you goes out to Jo for believing in me during a time when I had stopped believing in myself.

***Don't allow your past to control your future.***
- Emma Fletcher

# 10

# The X-Factor

**Our mental attitude is the x factor that determines our fate. -** Dale Carnegie

*Paul: Emma was now literally moving on in her life. And in this chapter we find out why auditioning for ITV1's The X-Factor was to make her realise that now - more than ever - she needed to pursue her dream of becoming an actress.*

Emma: Immediately after leaving my home in Wembley, I stayed with my cousin Rachel for just under two months in her little studio flat. Both my numerous boxes and I moved into her small space. The rest of my belongings remained in storage for under a year and only the things I would require on a daily basis went with me to Rachel's flat. Over the next nine months I continually visited the storage centre to retrieve things I needed for my teaching and daily life. I would rummage through my many boxes of stored goods feeling like a nomadic hunter on a scavenger hunt into no-mans land. After two months I felt it was time to give Rachel her life back and, although she never complained once, I felt it was time to allow her to be free once again of cardboard boxes but could not thank her enough for her kindness to me during this time. As it happens, numerous friends kindly stepped forward at this difficult time, offering me a place to stay in their home, most of them offering me a roof over my head rent free. At times like this you realise who your good friends are.

I soon moved in with one of my friends but insisted I pay rent. I remained at this flat for the next nine months. During this time I started my search to buy my own property. I had decided on the area I wanted to live in north London and decided one day to drive through the area to see if I could spot any nice flats for sell. I happened to come across a lovely mock Tudor development.

Tudor has always been my favourite style of architecture and it was also the style of the house I grew up in. I spotted a lovely flat at the front of the development, at the top of the block. The only problem was it was clearly lived in, with a light shining from the living room area and a window open. Suddenly I had one of my strange insights come over me and it was almost as if a voice inside my head stopped me in my tracks and said: 'You will live in this flat.' I ignored the feeling and drove home.

Later that week, I purchased a local newspaper to see what flats were currently on the open market. One of the local estate agents was advertising a flat for sale, which was at the back of the development and on the ground floor. I asked her if she knew of any other available flats in the development and she said there were none. I took a look at the flat that was on sale and liked it enough to place an offer on it. My heart was however still longing for the flat at the front and top floor of the development. The next week I bought the local newspaper again to check to see if the flat I had made an offer on had now been taken off the market by the estate agent. The strangest thing occurred. The estate agent had forgotten to take my flat off the market. I rang my estate agent to find out why they hadn't taken my flat off the market now it was under offer and they informed me it was an oversight but that in this oversight a larger offer had now been made directly to the seller and he had taken it. I had been 'gazumped' and there was nothing I could do about it. The next week I commenced my search again for another property. I bought the same local newspaper and what I found quite literally amazed me. I found a different estate agent was now showing the flat at the front and top of the development as being up for grabs. I quickly rang up this estate agent to see if I could make an appointment to view the property up in the gods of the auditorium and an appointment was immediately made for me to go and view it later that same day.

When I first walked into the flat with the estate agent, what confronted me was; a dining room painted with four bright orange walls, the main bedroom was painted with two yellow walls and two green walls, the spare room was a darker shade of purple all over and the hallway a lighter hue of tangerine. Some of the doors on the kitchen cupboards were hanging off and the bath was so bouncy it was like a trampoline. The estate agent looked somewhat embarrassed to be showing me the flat but I looked at it and saw its potential. 'All it needs is a lick of paint!' I exclaimed in sheer delight.

My offer on the flat was accepted on the spot. Both my treasured piano and I moved into the flat within the month. One night during the first week of moving into my new apartment, I noticed a bright light shinning into the darkened room from outside. I suddenly realised my flat overlooked Wembley Stadium; just as my parent's house had before. It was an odd feeling looking back towards Wembley from my new home and I felt as if somehow I was observing my past from a distance; the distance being my future. Finally, I had a safe haven I could call my own. It was not much to look at when I first purchased it, it's true but over the coming months I worked hard on making this new living space my own little private Idaho. During this time I faced a lot of problems with cowboy decorators; including a bath being left in the middle of the dining room for a number of months - don't ask - a leak which spoilt the ceiling of the neighbour's flat below and rather strangely left a stain on her ceiling, which to both of us somewhat resembled the Hebrew word for 'life' and a number of furniture orders going wrong but I got there eventually! I have to say my flat and I went through a lot together in the first few months but became good buddies in the process.

When I bought my flat I immediately went from having dispensable money to being asset rich only. I was immediately thrown into living hand to mouth, 'pay cheque' by 'pay cheque'. I thought of all the times The Drummond family had taunted me for having an ample savings account. I had savings because I had no parents and I would have preferred to have my parents any day over the money but the truth is; true wealth does not derive from money but from the people you choose to surround yourself with and from leading a contented life. It does not derive from wanting more all the time. I firmly hold the asceticism that through the renunciation of worldly material pleasures true wealth can be found. It is only at times when you loose everything you start to realise what is really important to you and thankfully I discovered early in life that what is really important to me is being surrounded by so many wonderful people who love me for who I am and so I do consider myself truly wealthy.

Not long after I first moved into my new flat I went on vacation with a group of girlfriends. At this stage I didn't even have curtains up in some of the rooms, including the spare room. On the night upon my return from my vacation, I went to get some items out of my suitcase in the spare room. It was dark and I was dressed in very little, having just got out of the shower and preparing to go to bed, so I decided to keep the light turned off. I rummaged around in the dark and bent down to get something out of my suitcase. As I stood up and turned around, I managed to almost knock myself out by catching my nose on the edge of the doorframe. My nose hurt so badly I was convinced I must have broken it. A stream of blood started to shower out of my nose like a fountain and it just wasn't letting up. It was now around 3am but despite this I called my poor cousin Rachel and woke her up. Rachel, the superstar that she is, drove round immediately, picked me up in her car and took me to the local hospital. We had to wait in triage for hours. All sorts of interesting and wonderful characters entered the hospital and passed before our very eyes. It seemed as if it would never be our turn to be seen by the doctor. By now I was so tired I could hardly keep me eyes open. In an attempt to keep myself awake I decided to buy a can of Coke from the vending machine. It started to have an impact, so I bought another. A number of cans of Coke later the doctor called my name to be seen. By the time I saw the doctor I was shattered and high on Coke! The doctor asked me what the problem was with my nose and the only words I could muster were 'Too much Coke!' As you can imagine, the doctor was a little taken aback! Eventually I managed to explain to him the real problem and that my lack of eloquence was due to my tiredness. Fortunately my nose was not broken and I managed to convince the doctor I wasn't using any other type of coke either! But this my friends, is the story of how I bonded with my flat very quickly, including getting to nose, sorry know, the side of the door frame rather intimately.

As I started to settle into my new flat, my lovely auntie Sybil was very supportive to me over the months that followed. She always had been. She was a benevolent, warm lady with a 24 carat gold heart, who brought a smile to the face of all who knew her. She was however heartbroken with how the family had become torn apart but she, like mum before her, always knew this heartache was on the horizon. Before mum passed away, aside from the letter she asked a neighbour to type, she had also called to speak to my father's first cousin, my cousin Myrna, who due to the age difference I have always viewed as a caring aunt figure. As previously mentioned, Myrna and her family had over the years always been very kind to me since I was a young child. Shortly before Vera passed on she had made a surprising telephone call to Myrna. She rang Myrna and asked her to 'always remember that Emma is your family too and always watch over her.' Myrna had not really understood the depth of this conversation until after dad's shiva when her son, who had been present at the shiva, explained how bad circumstances had become for me.

One sunny afternoon I called up auntie Sybil, as I did every day and announced if she was in that afternoon I would like to pop over and visit her. I used to visit my auntie Sybil at least three times of every week. I very much enjoyed her company, as she did mine. We were more like best friends than great aunt and niece. I never even noticed the age difference when I was in her company. She was always of such a jolly and bright disposition and my visits to her always brightened both her day and mine. My lovely aunt said she would indeed be at home and was looking forward to seeing me. We ended the conversation with our usual 'I love you' and then auntie Sybil tagged another sentence on the end: 'Always remember; I love you very much.' I told her I felt the same and then hung up the receiver.

An hour later I called one of my cousins for a chat. I announced I was going over to see auntie Sybil so could not speak for too long. Suddenly I heard someone talking in the background and asked

225

my cousin if anyone was with her. She announced she was on her own. 'We must have a crossed-line,' I exclaimed. The voice came again. It was now crystal clear. The words said: 'Always remember; I love you very much.' A chill ran down my spine. The voice sounded like that of my precious auntie Sybil and the words were the very same words she had last spoken to me. 'Excuse me' I said to my cousin, 'but is auntie Sybil there with you now?' 'No dear, why?' she replied. Then I heard more words, from a voice still sounding like my auntie Sybil: 'I'm here, I'm here' the voice said. Panic set in to every bone in my body. In that instance I knew she had passed on. 'Oh no!' I exclaimed. 'Don't ask any questions, I can't explain. Just put the phone down and call auntie Sybil. If you get no response, then head over to her flat immediately.' We both put the telephone down; I grabbed my car keys and left my flat. My cell phone rang en route to auntie Sybil's flat. It was my cousin. She told me she had called to speak to auntie Sybil as soon as she had placed the receiver down on me and a doctor had picked up instead of auntie Sybil. The doctor had informed my cousin auntie Sybil had passed on seconds earlier, whilst we had been on the telephone to one another. It felt as if a part of me had just died too.

After auntie Sybil's funeral, we all went back to her flat to pay our final respects. It was of course a terribly sad occasion but it also became incredibly uncomfortable having to see members of the Drummond family once more. I had not seen them for a couple of years since dad had passed away. A very close friend of mine came with me to offer support, at what she knew would prove to be a very difficult time for me. This friend remembered my lovely auntie with great fondness and was coming to pay her respects to her too. As my friend exited the toilet, the eldest daughter from The Drummond family was waiting to go in. Even at a sad time such as this, she was, in my opinion, still unable to retain her dignity and said to my friend as she came out of the toilet in a very loud voice 'There is suddenly an awful smell in the room!' Apart from this being completely untrue, my poor friend was left feeling humiliated and hurt. This was of course really a dig at me and had absolutely nothing to do with my friend at all. When my friend came over to tell me what had happened, we suddenly both saw the funny side of the situation and it sent us both into inappropriate fits of uncontrollable laughter. I think our laughter was really just a release of emotion at what was otherwise proving to be a very tense and uncomfortable situation. I only wish I had of had the conviction to laugh like this over the years whenever this same family member was rude to me, instead of shedding so many tears. It is true what they say 'laugh and the world laughs with you, cry and you cry alone.'

It took me nine months to pick myself up emotionally from the floor after all this heartache but pick myself up nevertheless I did. Then I met the man of my dreams, or so I thought. Introduced by friends, I laid eyes on the most handsome American dreamboat I had ever seen. The more I got to know him the more I found myself falling for him. No sooner had I fallen for this guy than I discovered he had not long come out of another relationship and was not over his ex, who had hurt him rather badly and he was in fact emotionally unavailable to me. I think due to my past relationship history, spending time with someone unavailable felt safe for me, especially after the abuse I had received at the hands of my previous boyfriend, so I pursued the relationship further. I decided I could be like Florence Nightingale and save him from his broken and troubled heart but sadly, all that occurred is it resulted in dragging me down emotionally again. What was I to do? My solution was to approach a psychic for answers.

Over the next year I started to form a heavy addiction to going to various different psychics. It became like a drug to me. I started going two, sometimes three times a week. One particular psychic was often very accurate at predicting the future, which only made me want to go back to her for another 'fix'. The only problem was, the very thing I was going there to find the answers to, a broken heart, was the one thing she had no answer for and could not fix. In my desperation I continued to keep going back to her. I wanted her to give me a reason to live, something to believe in. All the hard earned cash I was working so hard to attain was ending up in her pocket. I started to realise what it must be like to have a drug addiction. I should point out, this was completely my own choice to keep going back to this psychic so regularly and on many occasions these sessions even served to help, by becoming a type of counselling or sounding board session but the bottom line was still the same, no one else could live my life for me. The future is inevitable; it is going to happen. We can shape it but what will be will be. Once I learnt to accept this, I could allow myself to just live in the present. Finally this 'man of my dreams' announced he was leaving the country to go and live in, you guessed it - America. This was the third time in my life a man I had felt love towards had announced he was leaving to go and live abroad. I started to feel myself falling down again and then it dawned on me; I had one choice, deal with it or go under. I felt I had worked so hard at staying on top my entire life that going under now must not be allowed to be an option. I started to pick up the pieces of my life again, stopped going to the psychic and decided it really was time to do something in life for myself - it was time to follow my dream.

That same summer my friend Beverly, completely without my knowledge, entered me into a well-known singing competition - *The X-Factor.* The invite arrived in the post for me to attend audition and later that week Beverly rang to check I had received it. 'I have,' I said 'But no way am I going!' After a brief conversation she convinced me it would be a fun thing to do. I was not so sure I believed her but after a lot of persuasion I agreed to go to the audition.

I arrived at my afternoon time-slot to find a merry bunch lining the street, waiting to go into audition. We were each given a number to stick on our tops and waited until we were called in one by one, like cattle for the slaughter. It was an extremely hot day and by the time I reached the holding area, many people were suffering from severe heat exhaustion, having already consumed their little bottles of water over an hour beforehand. Very sensibly the production crew had provided water bottles for the waiting hoard and so there was a controlled rush to obtain one. There was actually a great atmosphere in the holding area, kept alive by presenter Kate Thornton. Just as you see on the show, people were excitedly singing and dancing, whilst awaiting their precarious fate.

228

The production assistant was calling people into the final holding area in groups of ten. After a good couple of hours of waiting, my number was finally called. I was taken to another room, where I found myself once again waiting to be auditioned by two producers of the show. I sang my old time favourite *Mocking Bird* and then for the second required number I sang my own-penned song *Let's Talk*. The producers told me on the spot they thought I was great and that I was through to the next round. I was through! I was actually filled with a mixture of feelings about getting through, as I was partly only there for the fun of it and wasn't really sure if I was taking any of it particularly seriously. I was also not entirely convinced I even wanted to continue to the next round to face public humiliation at the hands of the one and only Simon Cowell!

The second invite arrived for the next audition. Once again this was to be held at Wembley Conference Centre. I was told I was to make an exact repeat of my first audition. Once again I found myself being auditioned by yet two more producers of the show. When I had finished my performance I waited with baited breath until one of the producers said 'I think Simon will love you. You're through!' As I left the audition room I was approached by a member of the team and asked to sign a release form, which declared I would be fine with Thames Television using any part of the footage they were to film during the next part of the audition process. The next part of the process was to meet the judging panel. This part of the process was to happen immediately.

I was then taken to a third holding area and told I would soon be auditioning in front of Simon Cowell, Louis Walsh and Sharon Osbourne. After having already successfully completed the first two parts of the audition process, you can understand why by the time many auditionees reach this third level of meeting the judges they actually believe they are in with a good chance of survival. It is a bit cruel really, especially when you consider some of the auditionees have only gone through to the third level based on laugh factor, rather than x factor. I suppose however, if you are entering a show like *The X-Factor*, you should know what you are letting yourself in for. I waited rather nervously this time,

229

wondering whether I really had the wow factor or if perhaps I was one of the people that had been called back on laugh factor alone. I wondered what insults would be thrown at me by Simon Cowell; although I had come prepared!

Upon entering the studio space I handed all of the judges earplugs and advised they wear them! I stood on the spot marked 'X' and opened my mouth to start singing when Simon said: 'Tell me about yourself, Emma.' Tell him about myself? Was he kidding? It was just as much as I could do to stay standing. Now he wanted me to actually speak? I just wanted to sing and run. What was I doing there anyhow? I spoke about the fact I was a teacher and of how over the years I had written a number of my own songs. After a good 20 minutes of banter, Simon finally asked me to sing my first number. I sang my little heart out and then held my breath afterwards, awaiting the insults I was certain were to follow. There were none! Simon spoke first and said he thought I had a great voice. He started by saying: 'We certainly didn't need these,' referring to the earplugs. The rest of the judges agreed. Simon then told me he thought I was more musical theatre based than pop and asked 'Have you ever thought about acting?' Unbeknownst to him, he had just uttered the magic words. I told him I had once upon a time held onto a dream of becoming an actress. Simon recommended I pursue it further. After another 10 minutes of banter, of what I am also convinced was partly due to the producer in Simon's ear trying to get me to say something juicy for the cameras, I politely said my 'thank-yous' and proceeded to leave the room. Simon called me back into the room three times with a few more comments, of which the last one was: 'I like you' accompanied with his famous wink and me responding: 'I like you too. Don't ever let anyone tell you S. Cowell stands for scowl, as I think you're cute and cuddly!' Another raucous laugh from Simon and then I left the room. As I was leaving I heard the judges continue their praises to one other of my character, which of course was music to my ears.

As I came out of the audition I was once again pounced on by a producer and literally pulled into a small booth called a pod, where they wanted to film my reaction to my audition. Once again

230

it was clear to me they wanted to get an un-ladylike reaction from me to my audition, as clearly that hadn't got what they wanted from the audition itself. I was not prepared to buy into this game, so remained extremely polite in my responses to all the questions they posed, watching out for every word I uttered and saying what a great experience the whole process had been.

When my clip was televised, true to the release form I had signed, allowing the producers to use my footage in any shape or form they desired, the production company had rather craftily edited my conversation with Simon to make it appear the first thing I had said as I had walked into the audition room was: 'I like you', rather than it being the last thing I had said in response to Simon's comment. I guess they got the 'quote' they were looking for after all!

Simon's question of asking if I had considered acting opened up a can of worms and put me directly back in touch with my desire to act. I suddenly became aware I was in fact an actress who could sing, rather than a singer who could act! I had been led astray from my real dream, which was to act and had pursued the path of a singing career instead, merely as acting had until now seemed so unobtainable to me. Mum and dad had forbidden me to undertake a degree in acting and had encouraged me to follow a more desirable degree of interior architecture instead, which they felt would lead to a healthy and normal career path. I had originally started to pursue music as an ambition and then a vocation, simply as at the time it was more accessible to me than acting and I desperately needed an artistic outlet to express the array of emotions caught up inside me through my teenage years. Eventually, when music did not continue to fulfil that outlet, I once again transferred my emotions to my artwork via my undergraduate art degree. A part of me had however, always felt as if it were not being fulfilled. I guess in many ways that is exactly why actors are drawn towards acting, as they get to live someone else's life for a short time, instead of their own. Interestingly, I was recently approached by an up and coming singer to feature on his new album, which he was soon to release with a well-known record label. I was asked to sing guest lead vocals on one of the

231

tracks. As my acting schedule was so hectic I had to turn this offer down. It felt strange turning down an offer, which only a handful of years ago I would have given up all my pocket money for but it showed me how much my desire to act was now completely at the forefront of my mind, over and above a singing career.

Nevertheless, just after *The X-Factor* the realisation I was now surely following the wrong career path hit home and hard. The acting bug was still festering inside me and it was time to let it loose! I decided to investigate various acting summer courses and immediately came across a six-week full-time course being offered at London's famous Poor School. Carrying out this course seemed like an excellent idea, as I was sure by the end of it I would have a better idea if firstly I could act and secondly, if I actually enjoyed the sport!

At that time I was also still going through my battle with religion versus the world of showbiz in my mind, when the world-renowned rabbi to the stars, Shmuley Boteach, was introduced to me whilst he was over in the UK. Shmuley had a long chat with me about my confusion and concerns and assured me everything has its place in the world and that there is a place in the world for both the arts and entertainment. The problem of course is making the two marry in a religious environment. More recently I met David Weiss, the writer of Shrek 2, at a dinner party. A religious Jew himself, David informed me, whilst easier for men, it is still possible to be a creative soul as a woman and not feel one has to give up their Jewish heritage in the process.

It is true; it doesn't have to be all or nothing. Of course, 'all' is the ideal in a religious environment but that doesn't mean if one is not capable of doing it all then nothing is the only option left. I don't give to charity every single day of my life but that does not mean I should never give to charity. Once I realised this it made my internal battle somewhat easier and I was able to stop beating myself up over the fact I was probably never going to become a rabbi's wife. I guess it is possible for both my dream and my religious ideologies to exist together, as both these elements define me - and I exist! Although I admit I do still struggle to successfully marry the two at times, this does not mean I will give up the fight. The word Israel literally means 'to struggle' with inner conflict. Life is a learning process. The day we stop learning is surely the day we die?

***You have to move out of your comfort zone in order to grow.*** - Emma Fletcher

# 11

# All the World's a Stage

**The only way to enjoy anything in this life is to earn it first.** - Ginger Rogers

*Paul: Once Emma had made the decision to apply for drama school there was no stopping her. In this chapter, Fletcher reveals the ups and downs she experienced during her time studying in order to attain her ultimate dream of becoming a professional actress.*

Emma: I love going to the cinema. It has to be one of my favourite past times. The buzz you get sitting in front of that large silver screen; hearing Pearl and Dean's famous jingle and waiting for the flick to commence, for me matches only one other experience and that is of performing itself.

One evening I went with my boyfriend and a couple of friends to see the rather intense film *The Crying Game* in a small cinema in Knightsbridge. No sooner had we walked into the foyer when two young boys walked in followed by a number of security guards. The main doors to the cinema were immediately closed and we were told to take our seats straight away. Strange we thought. We entered the theatre and sat down. Present were; my boyfriend, our two friends, myself and the two young men sitting in the row behind us. Then in walked Princess Diana. The boys were of course princes William and Harry. The doors were closed and the film commenced. When the film had finished we were informed we were not allowed to stand-up until Princess Diana and her sons had left the premises. You see, even royalty enjoy the experience of going to the movies!

Now you may have been wondering if, because of my desire to act, before going to drama school had I ever worked as a film and television extra? Well I did but for one day only. I signed to one of the biggest extra agencies in the UK. I sent in a photograph and an accompanying letter to Ray Knight Casting and within a couple of weeks got called in for an interview with Ray Knight himself. I got offered my first job as an extra that same week. The job in question was to play an ex-lover (fully clothed!) of the internationally and much loved British icon Diana Dors; played by both Keeley Hawes and Amanda Redman. I was told I would even be given my own little crying scene for a few seconds. How exciting, I thought. Okay, so still not the 15 minutes of fame Andy Warhol spoke about but close enough!

Although the shoot required a lot of waiting around, it was still a fun shoot to be a part of and the director Robert Bierman was great to work with. He got to know one of the other girls who was also playing the role of ex-lover and myself fairly quickly and did the highly unusual thing of introducing himself to us. Directors never normally speak to the extras unless it's to shout at them to move a bit in either direction; so much respect goes out to Bob Bierman for this!

All the extras got taken into make-up and costume. My hair was teased back into its natural curl and I was given a mourners outfit to wear, in keeping with the period. Once all the extras were dressed, we were escorted to our first location of the day, which was a cemetery. Saffron Burrows and Joanne Whalley (Kilmer) were both already on set prepping and I clearly recall thinking: 'I wish that were me.'

When the morning shoot was over the extras were told to go and wait in their holding area until they were called to the make-shift canteen for lunch. The extras always have to wait until everyone else has got their lunch before they are allowed to get theirs. This film involved a very large crew and a very long wait. We waited for what seemed like hours to be called to the lunch line. Finally, the extras were informed everyone else had eaten and what was left was ours for the taking. I got into line and waited patiently once more to reach the front of the line. The food pile was rapidly decreasing in height. Finally it was my turn. I picked up the salad servers and placed them into a rather large salad bowl, when

235

suddenly a hand reached over and placed itself on top of mine and an accompanying voice said: 'Do you know who I am? Extras go last.' The hand then proceeded to snatch the utensils out of mine. Never one to hold back, I turned to look at a woman who I had never seen before in my life and said: 'No, I must say I don't know who you are and nor do I particularly care to become acquainted!' then I proceeded to re-help myself to both the utensils and the salad. To this day, I have no idea who this uncouth human being was but I decided after that experience that extra work was not for me and left the agency. One thing I did become more aware of however, is how important the role of the extra is in the making of a film and I have always treated extras with the utmost respect on set of any film I have worked on but then again; wouldn't anyone with manners hopefully do the same? So I'm really not expecting a medal for this one guys.

And back to the plot; I eventually announced to family and friends I had decided I was going to study for a Masters in acting. Having seen me say before now out of the blue I was going to study for a Postgraduate degree in teaching and then witness me go and do just that, my friends and family knew I meant business. I've always believed if you are going to talk the talk, then you must at least walk the walk!

After this decision was made I rang up my cousin Warren and asked if I could go over to his house to have a chat with him about something that was on my mind. His response was: 'Of course, darling.' That day I poured my heart out to Warren about my desire to perform on stage. His response was: 'Darling I have been telling you for years to do it. If you really want to become an actress, then get yourself into a good acting school and take it from there.' I listened to his advice and in 2004 auditioned for a summer course at London's famous Poor School. The course lasted a mere two months but it was more than enough for me to gain a taster of my dream.

Shortly after completing the course at the Poor School, a good friend of mine, who was always actively involved in local theatre productions, mentioned the company she was involved with were looking for actors to take part in a staged version of the play *Personals*, a play written by the writers of the American sitcom *Friends*. Being a huge fan of the series I knew *Personals* would be a hit script and felt this was an opportunity I could not let slide. The production was put on by a local group called The Maccabi players and was being held at a little fifty-seater theatre in Ickenham called The Compass. The Compass is a friendly theatre space and the play, which consisted of a number of short comedy sketches, would provide a good starting point for me to place my feet firmly on acting terra firma. Family and friends came to see the show and what's more, they enjoyed it. By the end of the week's run, I had well and truly had my first taster of what it felt like to be on a stage as part of an entourage of actors and guess what? I wanted more.

I started to look into all the top acting schools in London. I liked the look of East 15. I had heard a lot about the Method style of acting and it very much appealed to me. I visited the grounds of the school and liked what I saw. It was all so green and beautiful; although if the truth be told, it was also a little like stepping into a scene from *One Flew Over the Cuckoo's Nest*! There were couples in ballroom attire dancing in the gardens, scantily clad people with bare feet running around outside near the pond and sword fights going on everywhere and what's more - I loved it!

The audition day at East 15 was great fun and I would definitely describe it as a little different as to what I was expecting. I was so nervous when I entered the beautiful grounds. I had not applied to any other acting school, as I had completely fallen in love with the picturesque grounds of East 15, which I had before this point in time only seen in the brochure. Talk about putting all your eggs in one basket! I had in my head my two audition speeches I had been asked to prepare, one of which needed to be a piece by Shakespeare. I had chosen as my Shakespearean piece a segment from *Romeo and Juliet* and for my modern speech a section from Debbie Horsfield's *True, Dare or Kiss*, which was to be spoken with a Liverpudlian accent. When the tutor heard my accent he asked what part of Liverpool I was from! But what did he know? He wasn't even from Britain! But in all seriousness, this was a huge compliment and I must admit, my Scouse ain't bad. So thanks to the ex-boyfriend from Liverpool for that! Tip: only carry out an accent if you know you can speak it like a native. It is also worth living with the accent for a day or two or as much as you can before your audition, to allow it to become second nature to you.

After we had carried out our first audition speeches we were moved into a different room to carry out our Shakespearean pieces. The very talented and loveable Brian Astbury was the tutor who took us for this part of the audition process. Brian, I would later learn throughout my time at East 15, tends to work in a very out of the box style and today would be no exception to that rule. Brian is actually a genius at what he does to help the actor free themself up. Brian asked me to carry out my Shakespearean piece as if I were Juliet in a mental institution. He continued: 'I want you to imagine you are holding two babies in either arm. One is the nurse and the other is Romeo. I would now like you to sing your audition piece to the babies, in a voice so high-pitched it will shatter glass!' What? Did I just hear that correctly? It felt as if I could almost have an out of body experience then and there, as my mouth seemed to start moving without the aid of my brain! I started to rock violently back and forth in perpetual motion, partly as I thought this is what a mentally disturbed patient might do but mostly because I was overcome by sheer panic and complete fear! I rocked back and forth; not getting all of the words out of my mouth and even messing up parts of the speech altogether. I finished and then tentatively looked up at Brian. 'Brilliant!' he announced to the class! Following this, one guy in the group was asked to rap his Shakespeare prose like Eminem and I was invited by Brian to be one of the backing singers. I was informed I had to repeat some of the tail end words of his lines as an echo. The poor guy! As it happens, it actually went really well for him and it turned out to be a real gas and freeing experience for all of us performing this complete insanity.

Next came the dancing and movement part of the audition, which included me having to act like a zebra caught in a thunderstorm; bucking and rearing in the process. I actually managed to put my back out of alignment with this routine and ended up on the

238

osteopath's table the next day, unable to walk - but being a real trooper, I carried on during the audition and may I add, without complaining. The show must go on and all that jazz!

Next came the long wait in the canteen, which had now doubled-up as the holding area, for the head of the school, John Baraldi, to come out and tell each of us in an *X-Factor* style who would be going through to the final stage: the singing round. My name was announced. I almost bounced off my chair. I performed *Maybe This Time* from the musical *Cabaret,* with the highly respected and well-renowned pianist, the lovely Colin Sell accompanying me on piano. (Colin is famous for being the resident house pianist on shows such as *Whose Line is it Anyway?* and *I'm Sorry, I haven't a Clue.*) Just meeting Colin alone made my day! He was so generous and gave me a standing ovation afterwards, as the rest of the room also continued to cheer on my performance. In fact, all the auditionees were very generous towards each other. John Baraldi announced this was the first time he had ever seen Colin stand up for anyone in an audition, so thank you for that Col! Once everyone had sung, John announced on the spot who would be awarded a place at the school. I waited and waited with much anticipation, praying in my head: 'Please God let him say my name' and then, there it was. This epic moment; bigger than Armageddon: 'Emma Fletcher, I am pleased to say; congratulations. You have been awarded a place on the course.'

My first day at acting school was one of the most exciting days of my life. As I stepped foot onto campus, I felt as if I could explode with excitement at any given moment. I was literally boiling over. As I walked through those famous doors to the main entrance, I pictured in my head some of the many famous faces that had previously graduated from the school and wondered if they had felt the same way upon entering the school for the first time as I was feeling now. As I stepped foot inside the doorway of the main entrance, I felt as if I had just stepped foot onto the set of *Fame* the musical. Either that or I had just entered the loony bin! I wasn't quite sure I could work out which felt more appropriate to describe the atmosphere in that one moment but what I do know is, I liked what I saw! To the left there was a

239

room filled with a group of actors in the middle of a dance lesson. On the lawn outside were a group of stage combat fighters at work. In the canteen there was an eclectic bunch of odd-bods sitting and standing on tables; singing and dancing and tapping out a beat on whatever was available. The tables and chairs had become both drums and platforms alike. It was an insane atmosphere and certainly unlike anything I had ever experienced before. Was this the proverbial box I could finally squeeze into?

We had been asked to prepare for our first class two different poems to describe ourselves. One was to be objective and the other subjective, plus a short passage about our life and a couple of drawings of our-self. I have always fancied myself immortalised as a cartoon character, so for the exercise I drew myself as two different cartoons. The first was a female version of the cartoon character Tasmania called 'Em-mania' and the second was a character called 'Hyper Woman.' I had drawn arrows in the picture, pointing to various parts of her body; to explain why she was called Hyper Woman. An arrow to her chest was given the title; 'she can hyper-ventilate', the arrow to her head read; 'she is hyper-stressed', the arrow to her heart said; 'she is hyper-sensitive', to her foot; 'she is hyper-active', to her eyes; 'she has hyper-latent vision', 'is hyper-mobile' and so forth; geddit? Incidentally, my dream of becoming a cartoon character eventually came to fruition, when I was later approached during my acting career by an American company who were interested to use me as a model for a new 3-dimensional CGI character they were creating for a computer game called *Bold*. Watch out Lara Croft, the Fletch is on your tail!

For my two pieces of prose I created one limerick and one poem. The limerick was to represent my objective piece and is based very much upon how I feel people who don't know me very well mistakenly view me and literally 'objectify' me. These people mistake my sometimes-apparent breeziness for not thinking about what has just been said; when in fact it is actually quite the opposite. When I appear this way, it is often because I have so many deep thoughts rushing around in my head about what has just been said, that I find myself entirely caught up in them, rather

240

than what is going on around me in that next moment. The limerick was as follows:

There was a young lady named Emma
Who appeared always to be in a dilemma
Wherever she goes
A whirlwind follows
That dizzy blonde lady named Emma!

Well, if you can't laugh at yourself, what is life all about? The short poem that came next was my subjective piece of prose and is how the people who really know me hopefully view me:

Who am I?

Sensitive - sometimes over sensitive, a heart filled with warmth and kind
Not to be mistaken for a soft touch or an unaware mind

Outgoing and playful, yet sometimes painfully shy
With friends, a tendency to be gregarious - with strangers a tendency to hide

Happy and easy going - don't mistake this as a weakness or for being too carefree
Profound and often deep in thought about life, the universe and galaxy

Only a fool will take my appearance as if it were who I am literally
This is just a cover for those I do not care to trust or have no aspirations to be

The truth that lies behind the disguise is of awareness, understanding and is just
Of honesty, inner depth and intelligence and someone you can trust.

My time at East 15 proved to be an extremely difficult year for me. What I had hoped would turn out to be my dream year, after

241

having longed to study acting for so long, turned out in so many ways sadly to be more of a nightmare than a dream.

East 15 teaches the Method style of acting. Method acting is a style of acting which requires the actor to search deep inside their soul and rediscover traumatic events from their past and relive them; in order to find real emotions to use on stage. The good thing about this style of acting is it allows for a very real performance from the actor. Name a few of your favourite actors and I guarantee you they will have studied the Method style of acting. Dustin Hoffman; Method, Meryl Streep; Method, Daniel Day-Lewis; Method, Method, Method! Whilst my training was improving my art, it was not however, empowering my mental state. The directors at the school encouraged all the students to reach far into their deepest darkest fears and collect all their bad memories in order to allow them to resurface. Even the ones they had buried long ago; were encouraged to be resurfaced and used in their performance. In fact, the deeper you reached into that dark abyss to collect your worst memories, the more you were praised for your bravery as an actor. Great for the performance but not so good for the ego! The problem was, these directors were not counsellors, so although they helped you resurface old emotions you had buried long ago and had, let's face it, probably buried for very good reason, they did not tell you how to place a lid on these resurfaced emotions and memories once the performance was over. In fact, to add insult to injury, I broke up with a guy I had been dating whilst training at East 15 and when in a moment of upset the director took me aside to what I had assumed was going to be a display of sympathy, (his style of teaching Method was very similar to that of Lee Strasberg, the director and founder of The Method; which by its very nature is a very unforgiving practice) what I received instead was a pat on the back and told 'Good stuff, now remember this emotion so you can use it on stage!'

Needless to say, whilst I was on the course I found myself coming face to face with my inner-child again and found I started to become filled with anxiety and terrors of old that I thought I had got rid of long ago. It turned out, just burying these old fears did not mean I had actually dealt with them; so they resurfaced ten-fold and I annoyingly found myself back in that vulnerable childlike state I had worked so hard over the years to overcome. I spent my first term at acting school walking around in a zombie-like trance; unable to remain rooted in the present and found myself well and truly emotionally stuck once again in my past, faced directly with some of my worst fears and bad memories. This started to play havoc on my mind and I seriously started to wonder about whether I should leave the course, as my dream to act was now rapidly turning into my worst nightmare. After much deliberation I decided to give the course one more chance.

Unfortunately there were three girls in my class, who from now on shall be referred to as The Three Stooges, who I can only describe as the class bullies and guess what? They found their perfect victim in zombie-like me. The shame of it is, I bought straight into their game and allowed myself to play the perfect victim. Well, if you're gonna play the victim at least play it perfectly!

As I was often so caught up in dealing with some of the ugly issues I had resurfaced, I was finding it extremely difficult to remain emotionally present at all times during the first three months of the course. I found myself relieving my past experiences once again and as such found I was starting to loose concentration. I was often so caught up in thinking about a previous emotion I had been asked to resurface, that whilst the rest of the class had already moved on to recalling a new emotion, I was still battling to place a lid on the monster I had just unleashed. Finding it hard to stay in the present I started to miss some of the questions being asked or the important points being raised in class; as I was still too busy trying to refocus and organise my thoughts. This led to me once again appearing as if I was not fully concentrating and I became a perfect shooting gallery for The Three Stooges' bullets. In case any of you are wondering, when I finally caught up with myself later on in the course and found my way back to the present, on one occasion, when The Three Stooges tried to embarrass me by shutting me up in class as I was speaking during the end of term crits, (this is a term used for

243

very harsh and unforgiving constructive criticism given at the end of every term in front of the whole class. Oh yes, a marvellous experience for all. Why not bring along the family for a fun day out!) I did give back as good as I got. No, correction, I gave back better and guess what? They left me alone after that. Why? Because bullies are really just lily-livered beings who, when push comes to shove, are completely scared, even of their own shadows.

So how, you may be wondering, did the bullying start? Well firstly East 15 is famous for its 'Living History Project'. This is a project where the students are expected to eat, sleep and breathe in character for a week (I believe this marvellous experience extends to three weeks if you are on the undergraduate course. Oh joy!) The project runs in a three yearly cycle of themes; Auschwitz, The Black Plague and The Spanish Armada. The kind of projects you just can't wait to write home about!

Our year was blessed with the plague. We took a day trip to Eyam, the town our project was based upon and carried out a good month's research during the vacation before the start of the project. I decided I wanted to play the apothecary's wife and was going to approach the guys on the course to see if any of them were interested to play my husband; the apothecary. Unfortunately the guys had also already decided upon the roles they wished to play, so I decided, against the director's better judgement, I would play the apothecary myself. The director of the project warned me against this choice, explaining woman who were apothecaries would at this time have been seen to be a witch. I explained I saw myself as I white witch. The director however told me he wasn't worried about how I saw myself but how the other characters in the project would choose to see me. I didn't listen, thinking I knew best I stuck with my brave choice. Unfortunately, The Three Stooges used the week of The Living History project as a perfect time to start their bullying tyranny. It started by them ostracizing my character from the other characters in the project and making everyone send me to Coventry. At the end of the day, when we had hung up our costumes, I found The Three Stooges were continuing this behaviour towards me. Had they forgotten where to draw the line, or where they just enjoying themselves a little too much? It felt so peculiar being bullied as an adult. I had been bullied before as a child but here I was again as an adult being bullied. It all surmounted to a very unpleasant time. If it weren't for the help of my mentor on the course - the fabulous Colin Sell, who also became a friend - continuing to repeatedly instil great encouragement in me throughout the duration of the year, I surely would have left at the end of the first term.

One of The Three Stooges came up with the idea of bringing a real pig onto campus, placing it in a shed and keeping it in there until they were ready to slaughter it; and all for the sake of the Living History project. Imagine, slaughtering a poor innocent animal, placing it in a shed all by itself until they were ready to take the knife to it, in a totally inexperienced way, all in the name of art. One of the directors working on this project for some unknown reason agreed to this insanity. I kicked up such a fuss. I informed the class I could not allow this idea to take place for so many reasons: 'I'm Jewish' I announced. 'We're not allowed to eat pigs!' 'I'm not allowed to touch them!' 'I'm a vegetarian!' and; 'So what's next? Shall we go out and kill a human being just so we know how to play a murderer?' and my *piece de resistance*, as if the latter were not enough? 'It's cruel and what's more I will be forced to report this to the RSPCA and governors of the school. Let's see who they agree with... me or you!' Although many members of the rest of the class were, believe it or not, annoyed with me for kicking up such a fuss and felt I had ruined their 'fun', thankfully this heartless task was never allowed to go ahead. I would strongly advice anyone who is thinking of killing something for the sake of their art to read Uta Hagen's book, *Respect for Acting*, first. Hagen talks about a process called 'substitution', which she later renamed 'transference.' Substitution is a process where the actor identifies the character they are playing with feelings and circumstances related to their own lives. The actor then literally transfers those experiences and feelings into the character; allowing them to become the character's history and therefore, giving the character subtext and life. Hagen speaks of transferring the original essence, not the original event, into the scene. So, before you decide to go and slaughter some poor innocent pig, please go and read Uta

Hagen's book first and maybe it might also help save some poor pig!

The treatment I received at East 15 did not go unnoticed by the director working on the project and at the end of the term during the 'crits' he announced in front of the whole group to my sheer surprise, he admired me not only for my staying power, during what had quite obviously been a very difficult time for me but also said 'If I were wearing a hat right now, I would take it off to Emma for having grown more than anyone else in her acting ability on the course this term.' He also went on to say 'The eagle has finally landed'. I shall always remember his words. I felt a mixture of complete embarrassment and complete satisfaction all in the same instance. By the way, the song I decided to sing at the end of the term was *Nothing'* from *Cabaret*. I thought the lyrics made quite a large statement. It also made me giggle a little when the music teacher, who incidentally it turned out I was related to via my cousin Warren, asked me what song I had chosen and I replied 'Nothing!'

Unfortunately The Three Stooges did not know when to stop and actually went as far as bullying some of the tutors too! Our main tutor was sadly an alcoholic. The Three Stooges made it their mission to make sure he and two other teachers got the sack and they also aimed their ammunition at one of the students they did not like either, stating he should be thrown off the course as, in their opinion, he couldn't act. They went around the group asking people to sign a petition. I of course politely told them where they could put it. I'm sad to say they didn't actually listen to my advice as to where they should put their pugilistic petition and their mission was successful. They managed to get rid of three of the teachers but interestingly enough not the student. At a later stage, a course tutor who had not been in the firing line of these girls ammunition, admitted to me he felt The Three Stooges were three of the most unpleasant girls he had ever met during his many years at East 15. What a shame these girls were allowed to ruin it for others because of their obvious own insecurities.

Part of East 15's policy to prepare the actor for the professional world of acting is to help them try and understand every part of the industry. In this attempt, a two-week timetable was planned, where students were given the chance to work with professional directors for the week. We were each to take turns at operating the camera, act as director, assistant director and so forth. This was an invaluable experience and a real eye-opener as to how the crew views the actors and also to the petting order of how things work in the industry.

In the first week students were asked to watch themselves back on camera, in order to analyse their own performances. The director of that particular part of the course, the actor Ed Hicks, choose me first and asked 'Emma, tell us, what is the first thing you notice about yourself on camera?' My response? Pure and simple:

## 'Wow! How big does my butt look in this?!'

During this two-week period we were given mock auditions by visiting casting director Sharon Levinson and television director, Tofa Campbell; who has directed soaps such as the successful BBC television series *Doctors* and *Hollyoaks*. The process of both mock auditions involved being given a script to review and then we were told we had exactly 30 minutes to prepare for audition. The auditions were filmed on both days and both Sharon and Tofa announced who they would each give the job to, if this had been a real audition. On both occasions my name was announced as the person who would be given the job for the most memorable audition. Tofa added he would probably have asked me to change a few things about my performance on the day of the shoot but who cared? I got the job! By the way, this did not go down very well with The Three Stooges but again who cared? I got the job!

During the end of the last term at East 15, we were treated to a week of professionals coming into the school, to meet and greet us and talk to us about the industry. East 15 referred to this process as Professionalisation Week. Students were also privileged to receive a talk from the fabulous Josie Lawrence, who humbly

247

spoke of her rise to fame, starting from the day she graduated from acting school. Josie spoke of her time on the hit programme *Whose Line is it Anyway?* and how to master the skill of improvisation. We were also visited by top casting directors Sarah Bird and Gemma Hancock, agent Howard Roberts, from top British actor's agency Sandra Griffin and television director Martyn Friend. Various actors were also part of the week's panel who generously gave up some of their time to come and talk to us about being a new actor in the industry. Amongst the visiting actors were Paul Higgins, who offered advice about the work ethics of working with different directors and Susan Wooldridge, who spoke about how to survive your first day on set! Very useful knowledge!

The wonderful Marina Caldorone, author of *Actions: The Actor's Thesaurus* also came in to carry out a voiceover workshop with us. I have to say, her book should be renamed 'the actors' life-saver!' This book has saved my life on so many occasions; helping me break-up any speech I am learning into a variety of emotional outputs. During the latter part of the week, we also received a talk by one of East 15's in-house speakers Simon Dunmore, the editor of *The Actor's Yearbook*, who gave us some useful advice about how an actor's resumé should look visually. Theatre producers David Pugh and Dayfdd Rogers were the last speakers and their topic was 'working with actors'. It did make me laugh when the person they chose to speak about to illustrate their ideas was my cousin Warren. We had a giggle about it after. Being the businessperson I am, I not only found this week very helpful but I managed to use it as a networking tool; successfully attaining many contact numbers for myself! You gotta be in it to win it!

Always an avid writer, I jumped at the chance of writing a one-act play for my final showcase, as part of my MA award. I decided to write about the topic of schizophrenia; being that it was so close to home. I carried out three months of research and wrote a two-hander play, which I called *Poetic Nemesis*. Drawing influences from the stylised narrative found in Film Noir, *Poetic Nemesis* was based around two women who were the exact opposite of one another. I set the play in modern times and in the confines of what the audience is initially lead to believe is Holloway prison. It later becomes apparent towards the end of the play; the setting is actually a mental institution. The play introduces the audience to two inmates: Bridget Lasky and Madeleine Shaw. Bridget Lasky is a weak woman with a nervous disposition and has been sent to jail she believes, for a crime of the heart; for murdering the killer of her twin sister. She is left alone in a room with her cellmate, the self-assured and overtly confident Madeleine Shaw. The play takes the audience through an interesting journey, as we see how the weak and vulnerable Bridget is slowly drawn into the dark and unsavoury world of her counter-part Madeleine. As the play progresses we see the character Bridget become more like her protagonist Madeleine, until eventually, it is revealed they are actually the same person. As Bridget starts to realise she is entering a dark void of her own mind, we see a battle of wits ensue; where a fight for survival between the two characters is the only way out. Drawing upon the style of narrative found in Film Noir movies allowed me to advance the storyline quickly and succinctly and get more information across to the audience in a limited space of time.

The play starts with a fight scene; which results in Bridget placing Madeleine into a stranglehold, after which the lights go down and the audience is then taken back in time to a number of months earlier when the pair first met. The play ends as it starts; with the same fight scene, only this time as the lights come up again, the audience now finds Bridget alone on stage strangling thin air. This is of course when it becomes apparent to the audience Bridget is indeed both characters and the audience is immediately brought to the realisation Madeleine was a figment of her imagination. The entire length of the play is built upon the suspense of learning what leads these two women into this fit of rage with one another. Whilst I have always taken an avid interest in writing scripts and have in the past developed various ideas for television, the experience of writing and developing a play for the stage and becoming my own 'third eye', proved to be a very challenging and rewarding learning curve. The project served to increase my knowledge of the process of blocking and staging and after many long nights of re-writes, gave me an even greater appreciation for the value of every single word an author writes. I am proud to say I received great acclaim from the university and from the audience for this work and it has given me the encouragement and conviction when the time is right, to one day go back to writing a play again.

The Three Stooges took pleasure in telling me throughout the run of the course they were better actors than me; as they already had their undergraduate degrees in drama and I of course had not studied drama before. My response? 'Well at least I have an excuse for being here. What's yours?' I never really could understand why, if they were as good as they said they were, why then were they spending so much money and time undertaking yet another course instead of getting out there into the real world of acting and actually getting on with collecting some green minted paper with the Queen's head on? I should point out, however, the majority of people in my year at East 15 were kind and decent human beings. It is, nevertheless, such a shame these three girls couldn't leave me alone to get on with what I was there to do, which was to learn.

When it was time to prepare for the end of year showcase, a lot of hot air was let loose. Nearly everyone was concerned they get the best piece to read on the night, they get more time on stage than everyone else, they get the agent to notice them. Basically it was a lot of 'me, me, me' and 'okay, I've spent a lot of time talking about me, now what do you think about me?' Everyone was told they had to leave 20 headshots out on the front stands for agents to pick up after the show. The next day we were told to go to the office at East 15 to collect the remainder of our photographs; the ones that had not been picked up. It took me over a week to build up the courage to make the obligatory call to pick up the remainder of my photographs. I was certain I was going to be handed all 20 photographs back. One sunny afternoon I sheepishly knocked on the door of the office. One of the ladies working in the office greeted me with 'Ah Emma, we've been waiting for you to collect your photographs. You're the last one left to collect them.' She then held out the photographs for me to take. I looked down at my feet. 'What's wrong?' she asked. I

250

informed her I had waited this long to collect my photographs, as I was worried about discovering none of them had actually been taken. 'You're so funny!' she replied. 'I am?' I questioned. 'Yes. You had more photographs taken than anyone else in your year!' She then proceeded to hand me the remaining three photographs. I counted them, one, two, three - wow! That means 17 were taken!' (Yeah okay, so I'm showing off a little with my counting skills here, so sue me!)

The same week I graduated from East 15, I received three letters in the post; all from the theatre agent Barrie Stacey, asking me to come into his office to meet with him to discuss the possibility of going onto his books as an artist. Later in the week I met up with Barrie and was immediately taken on to his books. I was also taken on to the books of three other agents, as at the time none of them were expecting exclusivity but I was soon required to make a decision on who I would like to have as my soul agent. I decided to stay with Barrie.

The week before Barrie took me onto his books I had my first ever audition. I had only just stepped out of the doors of East 15 and suddenly I found myself face to face with my first real audition. We had practiced audition skills at East 15 but nothing can really prepare you for that first audition and both the sheer excitement and extreme terror you face all at once. I can only describe it as being a feeling similar to the feeling you get just before the start of a sheer drop ride at the amusement park, which goes hand in hand with the unknown territory you are about to encounter. The directors at East 15 said to us during Professionalisation Week. 'You will always remember your first audition.' In my case, my first audition was an experience I will never forget.

I received a breakdown for a job from a casting director, on behalf of a director looking for a red haired woman in her late forties, to play the younger wife of Michael Caine and the older lover of Jude Law, in an undisclosed feature. The only other specifications were she had to be a size 10. I read the breakdown and thought 'Okay, so I'm not a red-head, I'm not in my forties but wait... I am a size

10!' Okay, so I plead insanity here for applying to this job but all I saw were these six little words in my head 'Michael Caine and Jude Law's lover!' So sue me again, I applied! Actually, just before I sent off my resumé to the casting director I received another breakdown for the same job, stating the director was now happy to also receive resumés from women who were in their early forties, brunette or happy to dye their hair red. 'Sure, I'll dye my hair red, I'll even cut it off for the chance to work with Caine and Law', I told myself and in any case it sounds to me like the director isn't really sure what he or she is looking for anyhow!' My job was done. I had successfully managed to convince myself I was exactly what the director required. Now all I had to do was convince the director!

I sent my resumé off to the casting director that day expecting, to be honest, to hear no further. Later that evening, whilst I was out with a friend in a pub, enjoying a seriously tall, cold O.J., my cell phone rang. Now, if you've ever found yourself trying to accept a call in a noisy room, you can't help but shout out your telephone greeting in almost a screech, in order to be heard above the inaudible noise level surrounding you. Shouting isn't lady-like and it certainly is not professional. I heard the soft vocal tones belonging to a rather pleasant lady on the other end of the line respond 'Oh, hello. I'm calling to speak to Emma Fletcher please.' She said my surname. She meant business and I had just answered the call in a voice I was certain only dogs would respond to! 'Quick! Think!' I told myself. 'How do I get out of this one?' I screeched back down the line again 'Hold on please, I'll just go and get her for you!' As quick as a flash I dashed outside to a noise-free zone, placed on my acting hat and in my best business-like voice I could muster from my repertoire of different voices swimming around in my head, I calmly responded 'Hello? Emma Fletcher here.' Bingo! The casting director bought it. She proceeded to tell me the director of the film I had applied to wanted to see me early the next morning. I was informed I was required to bring along a swimsuit, an evening dress and a work suit. I would be auditioning for Guy Heeley and be given a screen test. Guy Heeley! My heart started to race. Guy Heeley was the First AD (Assistant Director) on so many hit films, too numerous to mention and I was going to be auditioning for him tomorrow! I immediately made my polite excuses to my friend and hurried home to get my outfits ready.

The next morning I took the train to Twickenham Studios and made the short power-walk from the train station in the pouring rain to the studio entrance; cursing the rain for messing up my tidily positioned hair, which was now completely bearing residence to a new skew-whiff, 'hey look at me, I've just jumped through a hedge backwards', fashion statement. After checking in to front-desk, I was asked to wait in reception until someone came to collect me to take me upstairs to the holding area. Sitting beside me was a stunning six-foot brunette, somewhat resembling Isabella Rossellini, with a bob to her chin and a centre parting cut to extenuate her perfectly formed face and cheek bones, which were so high they were almost popping out of her small frame. Immediately realising the heterogeneity between this creature and myself; twins we were not, I began to panic. Similar casting types? There was certainly no mistaking us for sadly separated at birth! We were more like the Benedict 'twins' played by Arnorld Schwarzenegger and Danny DeVito in the movie of the same name. 'Remember your cool head on calm shoulders' I kept repeating to myself. 'They wouldn't have asked you to come in if they didn't feel you had something to offer. In any case I may be blonde and only 5 foot six but my hair is golden blonde, so at least I've got some red in my hair. Sure, I'm closer to the mark than some six-foot stunner who happens to be an Isabella Rossellini look-a-like, who can't even speak English because she's probably not even from this planet. I'm cool!'

Shortly into my inner self-prepping dialogue, the production assistant came and collected me to take me to the holding area. 'Have you met Ken before?' she asked. Ken? I racked my brain to try and find an answer but I really wasn't sure what she was talking about. I thought I was meeting Guy Heeley. 'No.' I replied casually. 'Okay' she said.

I followed the PA along the corridors, up the stairs, through more corridors and up more stairs again, wondering all the while what

253

famous feet had touched the ground beneath mine, until finally we reached the holding area. Had I just stepped foot onto some alien turf I wondered? In the holding area were three more girls sitting quietly and they were all exact carbon copies of the Isabella Rossellini-wanabee I had just sat beside in reception. 'Oh - my - God!' my inner dialogue had reached illiterate mania and was literally screaming obscenities at me now. 'Run, run, get out while you still can! Save yourself!' it screamed. 'Escape the Rossellini ambush! Adios cool head on calm shoulders. Here's… trouble!'

Suddenly and somewhat rather excitedly, another one of these alien creatures entered the room to collect the remainder of her belongings. 'What an amazing audition!' she beamed. 'You're going to love Ken!' But who was this Ken enigma I kept asking myself?

Just then a man's head popped around the door. It was Guy Heeley. I could hardly contain my excitement. 'Okay' he said, 'who's next?' He pointed at one of the three remaining Rossellini's and said 'Right, you haven't met Ken yet, so you can go and meet Ken and then I'll see one of you ladies first.' He then pointed at the last Rossellini and said 'Sorry Emma, I'll see you after'. 'That's okay' I said 'I forgive you!' just excited Guy Heeley knew my name! Guy smiled and said 'Someone will come and collect you soon to meet Ken first and then you will audition with me after.' Before I even had the chance to ask who Ken was, both Guy and the last alien woman from planet Rossellini were gone, as had the girl who had just come in to collect her belongings and I was sitting on my lonesome in the holding area looking at my rain-drenched hair contemplating 'Who is Ken?'

At least 15 minutes must have past before one of the girls jumped back into the room gleefully exclaiming: 'You're next, they're coming to get you! You're going to meet Ken!' Okay, enough is enough I told myself and out of my mouth finally popped the inevitable words: 'Who is Ken?' 'Kenneth Branagh!' She said. What? Did I just hear her right? My heart started racing laps like Nigel Mansell in the Grand Prix! It was fight or flight. My heart said fight, my head said take flight… 'NOW!' My legs turned to jelly and my mouth to rubber 'Kenneth B, B, Branagh?' I repeated. 'Yup', she replied breezily before picking up her bag and heading off.

The PA collected me and walked me down the short corridor to Mr B, B, Branagh's room. What must have been literally seconds felt like the longest walk in my life! My inner-dialogue was now carrying out it's own five-act play. Then the door swung open. Standing there was a handsome, silver-haired fox, oozing charisma to the wagonload. 'Hi,' he said in his familiar dulcet tone, holding out a hand for me to shake 'I'm Ken'. Trembling, I somehow managed to shake his hand and utter the words 'Hi' and then completely froze due to the extreme shock of the situation. Growing up around celebrities I had never been star-stuck before but this was different. This was my first audition. This wasn't how it was meant to be. I was meant to be auditioning for some no-budget feature made by final year film students, where I could make all the mistakes under the sun. Wasn't I? Not that I'm knocking final year film students, we all have to start somewhere but that was the plan, wasn't it? At least, for a first audition. Right?

Recognising my shear fear, Ken politely walked me to his computer and said 'Are you any good with computers? Only mine's broken and I can't seem to fix it.' He then proceeded to place his computer in my hands as I uttered 'Not really but I know a man who can!' 'I know a man who can?' I uttered to myself. 'I know a man who can?' I felt like Jennifer Grey's character Frances 'Baby' Houseman in *Dirty Dancing* the first time she meets Johnny Castle, played by the wonderful Patrick Swayzee, when she says 'I carried a water melon!'

After I managed to successfully regain my composure, following a hotchpotch of uber-erroneous sound leaving my mouth, I ended up having a half coherent and fairly orderly, logical half-hour chat with Ken. He told me his plans to re-make the film *Sleuth* and informed me Michael Caine, who was in the original film as the character Milo Tindle, would now be assuming the role of Andrew Wyke, originally played by Laurence Olivier and Jude Law would be taking Michael Cain's original title as Tindle. At this stage Ken said he was not sure as to what degree the wife would be in the film (in the end he did not use an actress for the role at all and instead used a photograph on the wall as in the original film; to represent the wife as an enigma) but informed me if he met people he felt he could work with, there would still be the possibility of perhaps working with him sometime in the future. Ken then politely and in a serious voice said 'You may have to act out a bedroom scene with Jude Law. Do you think you will be okay with this?' Was he kidding? I put on the straightest, most professional face I could muster and slowly said 'Yes. I think I would be able to manage that.' I even managed not to smile whilst saying it. I was very proud of myself. I was now a professional actress after all!

Ken thanked me for taking the time to come in and I of course thanked him for taking the time to see me. I was then properly introduced to Guy Heeley for a half-hour screen test. Guy shook my hand and said 'I see you have met Ken.' 'Yes,' I replied confidently 'I have met Ken'.

I followed Guy into a small room in the studios where all the equipment had been set-up and the film crew were waiting. I carried out a screen test, ensuring to hold my stomach in during the swim wear test shots and was given some lines to say. Afterwards I was measured-up for the purpose of costumes and even my ring size was taken. Finally I was greeted to yet another firm handshake from Guy and a friendly thank you for my time, before making my way out of the studios and homeward bound. And that my friends, is the story of my first ever audition!

***Telling myself the job I didn't get wasn't meant for me helps me focus on the next job in a more positive manner.*** - Emma Fletcher

Spending a Friday night at the Troostwyks. I am always made to feel at home. Clockwise: my aunt Adrianne, me, my cousin Louise, uncle John, cousin Rachel and my wonderful great auntie Sybil.

Me with my wonderful cousin Henry and his beautiful wife Adrianne. They are the light at the end of what has been a very dark tunnel.

I still enjoy the company of animals even today.

Publicity shot taken for my singing career.
Photograph  by Karen Hatch.

Publicity shots taken for my singing career.
Photographs by Karen Hatch.

Still from my Wetherspoon commercial.

In one of the costumes for my role as Queen Elizabeth I
for the series the Mystery Files.

In this recent photograph  taken by Pascal Molliere, you can really
see my new found joie de vivre.

Just as in the previous photograph, Pascal Molliere has really captured my joie de vivre, which is so clearly shining through in this 'jump shot'.

My birth parents Claudia and Martin at their engagement party. Claudia had
a mesmerizing beauty about her presence.

Vera on her wedding day. It is clear to see where
Claudia inherited her beauty from.

# 12

# The West End and Beyond

**Only those who dare to fail greatly can ever achieve
greatly.** - Robert F Kennedy

*Paul: Every actress dreams of taking to the West End stage. Emma, as you
will read in this chapter, managed very early on in her acting career to achieve
that ambition and in doing so appear in an incredibly moving play in the
process.*

Emma: Having made it through so many traumatic events in my
life and coming out the other side still smiling, here I was finally
ready to start living my dream. The stars were now in my sight and
I was ready to reach out and grab them. Finally Cinderella was
going to the ball.

In just under a week after he began representing me, my agent,
Barrie Stacey, got me an audition as an understudy in Ian Dickens'
production of *The Decorator*, starring ex-*EastEnders'* star Leslie
Grantham. Ian immediately offered me the role of understudy and
ASM, saying I was the best person for the job. This was the
vanguard for my career and rudimental in placing my foot on the
first rung of the ladder. By the time I had finished the show,
Barrie had decided to split the agency into two. He took on board
the new agent Ben West, who created Blue Star Associates as an
off-shot of the agency. Ben took on all the younger actors, who
were looking to get into television and theatre and Barrie and
Keith Hopkins continued to represent the older actors and also
anyone else who was interested in Pantomime.

The tour of *The Decorator* was scheduled to last six months. I was
assigned the role of understudy to the fabulous Sarah Manners
and the equally fabulous Sabina Frankyln. Leslie Grantham was to
play the role of the Decorator. Ian Dickens, who was also the

director, informed me I needed to be off-script with both Sarah and Sabina's parts by the start of rehearsals. I knew this was going to be a huge challenge for me but one I had to rise to. I dutifully learnt my way through all the lines, which surmounted to two-thirds of the entire play, with the help of my cousin and actor Henry playing all the other parts as and when required in his front living room; albeit with a silly, high-pitched voice when he was required to act out each woman's part! But in all sincerity, he was a great help and a valuable asset in helping me become acquainted with the two parts.

I was informed I would be given the chance to perform Sarah's role every Saturday matinee and for two weeks solidly whilst she was filming a television project. For one reason or another, this did not materialise and whilst I was given rehearsal time with the co-director, my role as ASM (Assistant Stage Manager) started to become my main role. Lots of lonely hours were spent in various darkened theatres before each performance of the play and after three months I felt I had learnt all I could from my role as ASM. Apart from the privilege of having my name on my own dressing room door, this was not enough for me to want to carry on this lonely existence and after many weepy telephone calls to my family from hotel rooms, for good or for ill I decided it was time to give in my notice. Quite understandably Ian did not take this very well, although later I think he started to understand giving my notice in was the right choice for me at this time. This was however a brave choice for me, seeing as this was my first professional job but I knew it was the right decision.

The three months I worked on *The Decorator*, however, proved to be the most invaluable learning curve for me. Watching these three professional actors at their game advanced my own acting ability incredibly and I am deeply thankful to Ian for giving me this opportunity and for showing me the ropes of the world of theatre.

The cast and crew of *The Decorator* were a really great bunch of people to work with. We all got on exceedingly well and, apart from my lonely hours in darkened theatres before any house lights were turned on, we really all were one big happy family. Sarah and Sabina became close companions for me whilst we were on tour and both ladies were very kind to me. Leslie too became a caring sort of father-figure over the course of the three months and was always very concerned I was eating properly, especially when it was the Jewish Passover and I was confined to eating matzah and vegetarian pâté! He also very kindly took time out of his busy schedule to give me advice about the industry. I think one of the reasons Leslie and I got on so well is that Leslie, who is not known for his subtleties, found I was able to give back as good as I got in the sarcasm department; so we kept each other amused and on our toes for many a passing hour. It turns out Leslie's first agent was also Barrie Stacey. Leslie advised me to hang on to Barrie and said he was one of the good guys. He told me I should not listen to anyone who spoke ill of him, which I have to say I never have. Over the last four years of acting as my agent, Barrie has always been brilliant to me. He has been attentive, generous with his time and advice and very fair with money. The perfect gentleman actually! Everyone at Barrie's agency has always treated me well and with the utmost respect and I feel privileged to have been able to call them my agents for this time. I really can't complain.

One fond memory I have of touring with *The Decorator* was during a performance at the Theatre Royal in Windsor. On the get-in one of the tech guys happily informed us it was rumoured there was a ghost that roamed the grounds of the theatre. Not a fun fact to know during those lonely darkened hours! So one night just before the second half of the show was about to commence, I was backstage with the DSM (Deputy Stage Manager) and all the actors were getting ready to hit their marks on stage. The heavy fire curtain had not yet been raised, when suddenly the large lamp in the centre of the stage started to swing quite violently. There was no draft; just a swinging lamp in the middle of the stage. I have to tell you, that night no one wanted to step foot on that stage! But as you already know, the show must go on and so go on it did. The lamp continued to swing throughout the entire second half of the show. I guess the audience must have thought the swinging lamp was part of the performance; we, on the other hand, were all completely spooked!

In the Green Room, after the first performance had ended, which was also the press and opening night, I was approached by two girls asking if I would kindly autograph their programmes for them. This was the first time I had ever been asked to sign my name to anything other than a cheque, so I was a little embarrassed by the request; especially as I was the understudy and not even in the performance that night. 'Oh I think you are looking for Sarah,' I replied. 'No', they said pointing at the picture of me in the programme 'That is you isn't it? You are Emma Fletcher?' Just at that moment Ian came over and pulled me aside and said: 'Sign the programme!' He continued to say I should try and learn to not be modest about this request but recognise I may be bringing a little bit of joy into someone's life by carrying out this request. With that said, I went back and signed the programme.

Upon my return to London and now just a few months after graduating from acting school, I auditioned for my first full-length feature. I was immediately awarded the role of the nurse and was sent both a script and my sides, which although not a lead part, were five full pages of dialogue. I excitedly told all my relatives and friends about the film, which was to be aired in a selection of local cinemas. We filmed at Ealing Studios and once again I got that little tingle upon entering the studio doors, thinking about all the successful films that had been made there over years gone by. When I arrived at the studios, I was greeted with a firm handshake and a warm welcome by the production assistant with the words; 'Greetings and welcome Miss Fletcher'. Wow! Miss Fletcher! I hadn't been called that since teaching art at high school - and I wasn't too sure it sat comfortably with me even then! I was then shown to my own changing room. The novelty of having my own room was great, that was until I had finished changing. I then started to feel a little isolated, all on my lonesome in this rather large and spacious room, which was filled with strange props and clothes for the production. I decided to do a recce of the studio lot and found the holding area where all the extras where waiting.

Not one to be an acting snob, I decided to sit with the extras and happily chatted until my name was called to go on set.

Our scene was a closed scene, due to the nature of its content. The leading lady was lying naked on a hospital bed, covered in nothing but body paint from head to toe. I positioned myself strategically around the bed to face the direction of the camera. The director then asked a couple of extras to come in to fill up the scene. As one of the extras came in, she pushed me farther around the bed, so that she was now facing the camera and my backside was now facing the lens. 'That's okay,' I told myself. 'I have five pages of dialogue with the doctor whilst she has none. The director will be the person to inform this girl she needs to move around the bed to the other side. I will remain a pro and hold counsel.' Unbeknownst to me, the director had decided not only to cut all dialogue from our scene but also make the film an ultra-glossy art house silent film. So my fabulous acting debut, which was to have its first screening in the well-known local Hampstead Everyman movie theatre and which I had gallantly gloated about to all my family and friends, ended up being a glorified view of my backside! Oh well, I told myself; starting literally at my bottom means my career can only go upwards from here!

Shortly after nurturing back to health my somewhat bruised ego, I came back with a fighting stance by attaining my first advert, for Activia yoghurt. Never one to play by the rules, how I got my first television commercial was, however, a bit cheeky. Shortly after finishing *The Decorator* I received an email from a market research company I was subscribed to. They were looking to interview people who ate Activia yoghurt. Sure, I thought, I can go and buy some yoghurt and try it out. So I applied to the market research job. At the interview I met the well-known presenter Debbie King, who was also there to give her view on Activia. We immediately recognised each other as fellow performers and made an allegiance to keep one another's secret!

After a series of questions about both the product in question and myself, I was told I would receive a call if I had successfully made it through to the next round of the interview process. The call came and once again I found myself face to face in the waiting room with Debbie. We both had a giggle about the situation before being called in separately to the next part of the interview process, which this time was filmed. After this there was one more round of interviews before I was informed I had attained the job. They would be using a group of girls for one advert, which was also to include Debbie and just myself for the main advert. Lift-off! I didn't feel too guilty when I signed the release form, which asked if I had ever carried out any acting work before, as at this point, apart from a rear view to camera, officially I hadn't!

The day of the shoot arrived. I was picked up in a black limo and chauffeured to the famous Black Island studios in Park Royal, fairly near to where I grew-up. After wardrobe, make-up and a serious over-dose of yoghurts, I soon found myself on set surrounded by a crew of around 30 people; including the make-up and hair team, second and third ADs, the camera and sound crew, the director and of course the clients for Activia. All this for a 40 second ad!

The lovely Nell McAndrew was the presenter who would be interviewing me about my thoughts towards the product in the commercial. By the time we had finished the rehearsal process, before filming had even commenced, there was a script of sorts I had to learn on the spot, which had been created by the team based upon things I had said earlier about the product during my interviews. The director and wardrobe kept telling me I was a natural and asking if I had ever thought about going into acting. They were on to me. I knew it and they knew I knew it! The director winked at me and continued the shoot.

Nell was so lovely to work with and was such a generous person in her work approach. During the lunch break she came and sat with me and asked if I was an actress. She was obviously on to me too. I told her I was a recent graduate from East 15 and this was my first acting job. She was very understanding and wished me luck for the rest of the shoot. It was a great day and after the commercial came out I found myself swamped by casting directors and directors asking me to audition for their commercials.

After that the work kept flooding in. Over the course of the next year more adverts were given to me. Sometimes I did not even need to audition. I totalled around 30 adverts over the next year alone. My agent started to affectionately call me his 'little commercial queen'. I also started to carry out a lot of good theatre work, working with many named and fabulous actors and continuing to learn so much from them, for which I am extremely grateful to have been given these chances. I worked on a play by a writer named Stephen Hunt called *I Am Not An I*, later renamed *Impossible Steps*. The play, directed by both Stephen and Peter-Frank DeWulf, was a play about a woman with schizophrenia. Once again the subject matter of the play particularly appealed to me due to my family history. I found myself performing as one of the main characters on stage alongside the terrific actors Rosalind Adler and Julian Lamoral-Roberts in the rehearsed reading and the wonderful Hildegarde Neil and Ben Onwukwe during the actual run, with Robert Hartley Wainwright playing my partner in both and Edward D'arcy Hatton playing my confidante. Hildegarde's husband, Brian Blessed, agreed to be patron to the show and came to watch our performance at the The Rosemary 'Rosie' Branch theatre in Islington. Brian kindly gave us all a larger than life glowing report after the show, expressing his sentiment with words such as 'marvellous, marvellous' 'glorious' and 'fabulous', which was of course extremely encouraging to all present. The Rosie is a pleasant Victorian building, run by the lovely stage manager and director Cecilia Darker. Once renowned for its music hall, it is rumoured Charlie Chaplin played there and Marie Lloyd and Little Titch certainly did.

The run of the play went for the most part very smoothly, although I did make my first and hopefully last rather big blunder as an actor. Usually always on the ball and someone who always stays in character throughout the duration of a play, even whilst behind the scenes - remember I am a Method actor - on one particular night Ben passed me his crossword to complete during the interval. I became so engrossed in the crossword I completely

263

forgot to go back on stage! Hildegarde and Ben were both in freeze-frame at this point, so poor actor Robert Hartley Wainright had the onus placed completely upon him during this short hiatus; which must have felt like a lifetime. The director popped his head backstage and said 'Emma, stage, now!' 'Stage?' I questioned, wondering where I was. 'OMG!' Suddenly the realisation dawned on me. I wasn't at home in my front room, snuggled up on my couch with my legs up doing my crossword; I was in fact backstage at The Rosie! As quick as the cartoon character the Flash, I sped back onto stage, calmly entering from stage left, as if nothing were amiss! After the show Harry Landis, the head of Equity at that time, came up to me to introduce himself and congratulate me on what he felt was a 'fine performance.' It turned out he thought the hiatus in the play was genius! So you see; from an accident can derive genius! As it happens, Harry's words actually meant a lot to me; especially in the realisation of how many different plays he must have watched over the years.

Over the course of the year I also joined the cast of an absolutely lovely one-act play, once again working with director and good friend Peter-Frank Dewulf. The play was entitled *The Muddy Pool*. *The Muddy Pool* was written by newcomer Jilly Gardiner and was chosen by renowned author Fay Weldon, as one of three plays out of many hundreds of scripts, to be part of the prestigious Windsor Fringe awards. I was recently privileged enough to rejoin the cast for the Lost Theatre festival in London and of course jumped at the chance of working with such a talented cast and crew once again.

I often get asked by friends and family alike, which has been my favourite acting job so far. I can honestly say I don't have a favourite acting job, as I have enjoyed all the jobs I have carried out in one way or another. I have been very fortunate to of worked with so many wonderful actors, who are generous in both their work ethic and approach to their fellow actors. One of my acting jobs did however see me living out every little girl's dream of becoming a princess for the day when I was asked to play a princess in the pilot television episode of Paul Andrew's show *Could it be Magic?* This was great fun and during a later episode the production even saw me flying through the skies with presenter Danny Buckler. My ambition to be a princess for the day was however more recently superseded when I won the role of Queen Elizabeth I for the television series the *Mystery Files*, which was to be aired both in the UK and the USA. This was such an exciting project to work on and even more exciting was the revelation the two different wigs I would be wearing to portray Queen Bess were indeed the very same wigs worn by Cate Blanchett in her version of the queen with the same name. The shoot was due to commence at 2:00pm on the first day of filming but due to a series of unfortunate mishaps, the costume did not arrive until 7:15pm. Talk about making a grand entrance! I must say however, the costume was every bit worth the wait and probably could have carried the entire part without me inside it! In fact, so taken were the rest of the cast and crew with the costume, that every little thing I did that day was apparently worthy of a photograph. The rest of the team would exclaim; 'Oh look, the Queen's eating!' 'Oh look, now she's blowing her nose!' This continued throughout the entire length of the day! The costume was incredibly heavy however and it was like carrying a house on the back of my shoulders. I soon began to realise what a tortoise must feel like! There was of course absolutely no going to the lavatory once inside this get-up. So I requested not one person be allowed to mention the word 'toilet' or anything associated with it in front of me the entire length of the day! (Oh come on, everyone is allowed one small prima donna moment in their career!) I must however thank director Ben Mole for giving me this amazing opportunity to portray such a legendary and controversial character as this magnificent Tudor monarch and needless to say this role immediately opened up so many more doors for me.

No sooner had the publicity shots got out for the *Mystery Files*, I had producers from both sides of the Atlantic contacting me with the offer of more work. In fact, one of the jobs I immediately got offered after this role was to make a commercial with a very different type of Queen. I was offered the role of working with Britain's fantastic and loveable 'Queen of Clean' Kim Woodburn, to test and comment on a new cleaning product Kim was endorsing called the 'Ecoegg'. The commercial was to be shown both in the UK and in the States. If working with Kim wasn't enough to pull me in, the company kindly offered me over and above my fee enough washing product to last me 20 years! I was sold. I did consider if I could add to the deal asking the lovely Kim to come and clean my home but seeing as I am stringently clean anyhow, I refrained from asking! The day before filming the commercial I came down with a nasty chest infection and a rotten cold. Not wanting to give anyone else on the shoot my infection, I contemplated whether I would have to tell the director I was too sick to attend the shoot. Not wanting to let the rest of the team down, however and as any actor will always tell you; the show must go on, I bravely made my way to the shoot with a box of tissues firmly in hand. Everyone on the shoot was very understanding and kept me dosed up extremely well with hot drinks throughout the length of the day. Kim was also incredibly caring towards me. To lighten the moment I informed Kim if she caught my cold at least my next claim to fame would be I had given Kim Woodburn her cold! We both had a giggle about this. In fact, Kim and I formed a rapport very quickly on set and an affinity was born.

Falling short of not having a favourite project, I have however worked on one particular project, which probably made the most impact on me as a person. Being involved in the play *And Then They Came for Me - Remembering the world of Anne Frank* is not only one of the most rewarding experiences I have ever had but my time spent working on this play was extremely humbling and will stay with me forever.

I was involved in the project for six months in total, which also included a cast change after the first three months. During the first run of the show Anne Frank was played by the vivacious niece of international business tycoon Sir Philip Green, the lovely Georgia Neville and by the very talented actress Catherine Robey during the second half of the run, whilst Anne's love interest was played by actor Daniel Evaristi-Boyd, son of director Michael Boyd and later by actor Andrew Goddard. The rest of the cast were also a class act. The director, Nic Careem, previously a politician for the Labour party, had admirably taken it upon himself to dedicate his time to work on and develop the increasing coverage of this play; to act as a tool to try and stop race hatred throughout the world. Nic is doing a tremendous job and should be praised for his continued attempts to spread the message of this play.

Nic's involvement in the play is made more praise-worthy and predominant in the knowledge he is a Muslim telling the story of race hatred towards Jews during the Second World War. Nic relates the experiences of the astounding Holocaust survivor Doctor Eva Schloss, the posthumous sister of Anne Frank, to modern day race hatred and talks about how it could happen to any one of us, even in today's society. Nazi Germany was not precious. You were sent to the gas chambers for having the wrong skin colour, being the wrong religion, the wrong shape or size, having the wrong sexual preference or values or for being the wrong social class. Nic continues to spread the message of how destructive this type of hatred is for the world we live in and how it must stop before it's too late.

Nic works closely with John Bird, the founder of *The Big Issue* and John's wife and television presenter Parveen Bird, to bring the awareness of his message alive. Nic's friend Suggs, from the band Madness and renowned director Waris Hussain, also supported the play and came to watch the rehearsal process, both offering Nic valuable ideas in relation to the PR. *The Big Issue was* one of the sponsors responsible for helping put the play on its feet. We all got on so well as a team and on the several occasions we went out for dinner after the performance, all our passions for the vision to make hate history were brought alive again and again, as our passions for a better future always became only too apparent in our discussions.

The play is based around Eva and her and her family's endurance in the prison camps Auschwitz and Birkenau for nine months during the war years. I played Eva's mother Mutti, who in her thirties, was with Eva in Birkenau living alongside Anne Frank and both her sister and mother, whilst Eva's father and brother were sent to Birkenau along with Anne's brother and father Otto.

267

After the war ended Otto married Eva's mother. It was in fact Eva who helped collate Anne's notes from her famous diary and aided Otto in his preparation for their publication. Before the rehearsal period I met with Eva and she related her life story to me. I was very humbled and moved by her experiences.

Eva, now in her 80s, is one of the most amazing and inspirational women I have ever had the privilege to meet. She is a strong, robust and - thank God - positive woman, who has survived Nazi Germany through sheer determination and will to live. Eva toured with us around the UK, being filmed by the BBC, performing at London's Scotland Yard as the first ever play to be shown there and ending up at the famous Criterion Theatre in London's West End. She would appear on stage as a surprise at the end of every performance, carrying out a Q&A session with the audience, who would always welcome her on to the stage with a well-deserved standing ovation. This was always such a moving sight.

One of the most memorable moments of working on this project has to be when one evening, standing outside in the cold, I intentionally stopped myself from shivering; as it ran through my mind how Eva and so many thousands of Jews were left to freeze and perish in the bitter cold Polish winter nights, with no clothes, throughout many months of their hellish time spent in Birkenhau. I did not feel I could justify being cold in Eva's presence. 'Are you cold?' Eva questioned. 'I'm fine.' I replied. 'But are you cold?' she responded. 'You are allowed to be cold you know. Let's get you into the warm' she continued. Here was a woman who had fought so hard for so many years to be able to live a normal life again after the traumas that had ravaged her mind from her time spent in the prison camp and the best revenge against the Nazis was not that she was bitter, for bitter she was not. She was not bitter for the shape that her life had taken but instead, the best revenge was that she had survived and was leading a normal life again, teaching others to rid the world of race hatred and what's more, she was happy.

Another strong memory of my involvement in this play was after one performance, when a group of teenagers came up to both the rest of the cast and myself, with pen and paper in outstretched hands and asked for our autographs, whilst Eva was standing directly beside us. I distinctly recall pointing at Eva and saying 'Please, Eva is the real star here.' Eva then said 'Please, give the kids your autograph if that is what they want.' The cast dutifully obliged and signed the pieces of paper we were handed and then were so pleased and relieved when after this, the group of teenagers excitedly turned to Eva and said 'Ms Schloss, can we now have your autograph too please?'

I eventually left the play after six months, partly due to the extremely strong subject matter becoming too much to continue to handle on a daily basis. Nic kindly offered me a rise in my salary to keep me, which was very kind of him as I knew he was already paying the actors over and above what he could afford but as I am a method actor and tend to stay in character the whole time, I found the play was starting to become fairly emotionally draining and so after six months I felt it was time for me to move on.

Immediately after leaving *And Then They Came for Me*, I was approached to become involved in a play of a completely different nature. I was asked to be part of *The Vagina Monologues*, which was being put on at London's Gatehouse theatre, directly in association with The Helen Bamber Foundation, chaired by actress Emma Thompson. Always having felt the cause the foundation supports is of a very worthwhile nature, without hesitation I agreed to become involved in the production. A head representative of the trust came to our first meeting to thank all the performers for being part of such a worthy cause and told us more about what the charity was currently doing to help abused and battered women and of how the trust is continually trying to bring to the attention of the public the reality of human trafficking.

When family and friends asked me what play I was currently involved in, I just couldn't bring myself to say the word vagina, especially if I was asked the question whilst out in public. I was really struggling! 'The monologues' I would say. 'What monologues?' they would question. 'You know, THE monologues!' I would say. 'No!' was their cry 'We don't know!' 'The V Monologues' I would say pointing to my groin. 'The V monologues?' they would quiz, until I was literally shouting out in some fancy restaurant one day at the top of my vocal capacity 'Vagina!' 'Gosh' said a friend, 'If you're having trouble saying that now, imagine what you're going to be like when they ask you to say the 'C' word!' I was tempted of course to say 'What C word?' but I gracefully didn't rise to the challenge! Incidentally, did you know, the 'C word' was originally a word used as a medical term. I find it so interesting how words and their meanings have changed over the years and how a word can go from being used as a medical term to describe a very important part of a woman's body, to becoming one of offence!

The director told us at the end of the first rehearsal she was giving us some homework to carry out. 'I want you to all go home tonight, find a mirror and study your vagina.' I wondered what secret treasure it was the director was expecting us to find. After thinking about the oddity of the request, I decided to go ahead and carry out the task. When I got home I found a little handheld mirror and held it up in front of myself. I did not see skin or flesh. What I saw was a vessel: an opening to hurt and pain. A wound. I saw a raw place The place where I had been de-flowered against my will. I thought of all the battles women had fought for survival; of all the abused and battered women we were fighting to help. What I found was myself. I saw birth, life, my home, my soul. Then I saw love, the universe. Creation. I saw God.

I believe women should have the right to feel like real women, without having to emasculate themselves to prove their worth. Yes I am a strong woman, an 'Alpha' woman even; or whatever the latest jargon may label a strong-willed woman as. I am also a woman who longs for the love of a good man to make me feel in touch with my femininity. Don't get me wrong, I am glad The Suffragettes fought for our vote but I also believe women have lost what it means to be a real woman in the process. We are so busy trying to act like men all the time in order for our voices to be heard; we have forgotten to behave like women in the process. We shouldn't be made to feel we have to behave or become like men in order for our voices to be heard. We are women and we should be proud of being 'woman'. I am proud of being a woman! God made us different to men for a reason. It's time the modern woman embraced being a woman again. Getting back in touch with your femininity and not being afraid that it will stop your voice from being heard is what being a real woman is all about. It is much more empowering and sexy to act like a woman and be a strong woman than it is to be a woman trying to act like a man in order to gain strength. Reach for the handheld mirrors ladies and embrace your vaginas!

Just after finishing up *The Vagina Monologues* I was called in to audition for a major television commercial for Wetherspoon's eatery. The purpose of the commercial was to advertise their new wine tasting events. It was this commercial, which would see me carry out my first ever screen kiss.

When I arrived at the audition both myself and Peter Halpin, the other actor waiting in the holding area, were called into the audition room and introduced to both the director and producer. The director, Stuart McClymont, read to us the breakdown for the script and said 'So, you both okay with the screen kiss?' Well, neither Peter nor I had read the small print and neither of us had up to this point carried out a 'screen kiss.' 'Screen kiss?' we both yelped in synchronised harmony. 'Is that okay guys?' Stuart continued. Peter and I looked each other up and down, looked back at Stuart and both said: 'Yup!' It was such a funny moment. Of course it was just that, a screen kiss but Peter and I have, nevertheless, stayed good friends since and as it happens, the next piece we worked on together actually saw us trying to kill each other - so I guess that kiss wasn't so great for either of us after all!

The two representatives from Wetherspoon came down to view the shoot on the day of filming. I recall one of them throughout the entire day kept exclaiming: 'Loving your work guys, loving your work!' which made both Peter and I giggle quite a lot. After 'kissing' Peter, I was meant to then try the wine, in a manner wine tasters do; look, smell, taste. I was to tilt the glass, give it a little swirl and then allow the wine to gently roll around in my mouth

271

before spitting it out. When the commercial was aired, it went out with a rather cheeky catch phrase, which had been placed on the screen at the end of the commercial after me spitting out the wine. Now, the cast and crew were all just following the Wetherspoon rep's script for the advert but the rep had not confirmed the script or this catch phrase with his CEO at Wetherspoon. Doh! The commercial ended up getting banned, as short of taking the catch phrase off the end and saving the advert, they said wine and sexual interactions of any sort could not been seen together on screen. The commercial of course ended up as a viral on the internet instead!

A funny incident occurred the week after shooting the Wetherspoon commercial. I was on a blind date, set up by a very good friend of mine. The young man in question, who shall be called Jake for the sake of privacy, took me to a lovely quiet bar in a quiet and secluded area in London. Whilst sipping on our cocktails, Jake mentioned our mutual friend had told him I am an actress. 'Should I recognize you?' he asked. 'Obviously not!' I responded cheekily. Just then, a young couple came over to us both and the lady announced 'I know you! You are that girl from that Wetherspoon ad! I can't believe this!' Wanting to impress my date somewhat, I rather stupidly produced a pen from my bag and held it towards her, making the assumption she wanted an autograph. 'What's that for?' she asked. 'My autograph' I said, now completely embarrassed. She started to laugh then continued 'I was the make-up artist on the job!' Opps! Just goes to show, never assume anything because, as they say, when you 'assume' it only makes an 'ass' out of 'u' and 'me'!

On the flip side of the same coin, there are those people who half recognise you. 'I know you! You were in... Now what was it you were in again?' Suddenly you find yourself in the position of being required to list your life's resumé. 'The Wink Bingo ad?' 'No, not that. What else have you been in?' 'Well, I was in an Activia ad,' 'Nope, that's not it. What else have you done?' 'Erm, well I did a commercial for Andrea Bocelli's album' 'Nah, anything else?' 'A Wetherspoon viral?' 'Not seen it.' 'An ad for Sony Vaio, a few films for television?' (Okay, so I'm name-dropping here again - so you know what to do: sue me. I'll give you my lawyer's number! But it's my book and I'm allowed!) 'Nope, nope, nope.' 'I've done a lot of theatre,' 'Never go. Nope, don't know you! Oh I know what it is! You look like that other actress. Now what was her name again?' 'Well, what's she been in...?'

Aside from my first screen-kiss, one of the most memorable moments of my acting career has to be the time I accidentally knocked out a fellow actress! As it happens I had always taken a little too easily to learning stage combat skills at acting school. I was at the time also studying street fighting martial arts outside of school hours. I had been studying martial arts long enough for it to start to become instinctive, which basically meant if someone were to come at me in attack mode, I would go into automatic auto-defence pilot in order to protect myself, adding a block or a touch down where necessary. This caused me a lot of problems whilst learning the skill of stage combat, as whenever any of the students I was paired up with came at me with a punch, whilst there was a part of my brain which knew this was just a dance routine, there was another part of my brain which leapt into action every time screaming 'You're under attack soldier, you're under attack! Move!' My poor stage combat partner would usually end up in a heap, face down on the floor with me apologising profusely and the tutor coming over and saying 'Emma, will you please stop killing the students!' On this occasion however, I was not to blame for the sudden demise of my fight partner.

I was approached to work on a short piece of footage with the very talented award winning director Ian David Diaz. I must point out here this incident was in no way Ian's fault or due to any negligence on his part. Ian is a very talented director who has staged many a successful fight scene in his time, working with actors such as; Jeff Fahey, Michael Ironside, Claire Goose, Donna Air, Nicola Stapleton, Sarah Harding, Anthony Ofoegbu and Dallas Campbell to name but a few, before working with little ole me - who by the way was very pleased of the opportunity to work with him.

273

The piece of footage we were filming was to be sent to America to act as a small insert in a feature film. The footage was to be viewed on a television screen within the film and serve as a catalyst for a potential killer; who upon viewing the fight between the two women is sent over the edge and thrust into his killing zone. Ian choreographed the piece very carefully and both myself and my fellow actress and model, who shall remain nameless to curb embarrassment, rehearsed the piece with Ian a number of times, over and over all day in slow and small, baby bite-sized stages; like a dance routine, before speeding it up for the actual take. When both my fellow actress and I felt confident enough and Ian felt we knew the piece well enough, we went for a take. Ian shouted 'Action'. We were off, like two race horses running towards the finish line. My counterpart sent a staged punch to my chin; I fell to the floor, rolled over backwards and straight back up again into standing position. This led into a dramatic fight with a knife. The knife was slammed down. The other actress threw a staged right hook towards my left cheek, I went with it; swinging round to my right, then with both fists clenched together, swung back towards her with full-force throttle ahead. Now, the interesting thing here is, the other actress was supposed to move out the way. She didn't. She forgot. My punch connected with her nose and sent the poor girl flying across the room and knocked her out, for only a few seconds albeit but I was devastated.

Filming stopped and an icepack was brought to the rescue, along with a chocolate bar for my fellow actress. Apart from being rather bruised and shaken - and that was just my ego, the actress was fine. I think I had more of a shock than she did. Like a trooper, after around thirty minutes she admirably started filming again and even managed to make it to her modelling shoot the next day. Unbelievably we all managed to laugh about it later and I am still looking forward to the next opportunity I get to work with Ian again but perhaps minus my right hook!

With my career now starting its journey on the upwards spiral, I decided it was time to treat myself to a well-earned break - which for me, still meant business! Since I was a young girl I had always had a dream of going to Hollywood as an actress. I would often talk to mum about this dream and, although protective of my chosen career path, she would still always say 'I will miss you if you go but you must follow your dream.' I always knew my parent's time on this earth was short, as they were not getting any younger and I very much wanted to spend every day I could with them while they were here. There was a part of me which innocently hoped they would live forever or at least long lives like Methuselah but I knew of course this could not ever be the case. So the part of my dream, which involved Hollywood, was placed onto the backburner - in any case, my parent's were far more important to me than my career.

I had been to Hollywood before now, on a vacation with an ex-boyfriend. We had stayed with his family in the hills but up until this point I had never explored Hollywood from the viewpoint of an actress. I decided now was the right time to take a trip to the city of angels with actor and friend of mine, Richard Burke. Richard organises the most fabulous actor networking trips to Los Angeles, under the company name 'Industry Hollywood' (my little plug for you Rich!). I have to say the trip was an amazing and invaluable experience.

I packed my not so little suitcase with sheer excitement, with the thought that now; finally, I was going to take a sneak peek at the bright lights of Hollywood. As the day grew closer for the start of my trip to commence, so did my excitement as I became like a small child again desperate to get on the aeroplane. I have to say the week's break was every bit as exciting as I thought it would be. I immediately found myself befriending an actress named Sarah, who we all joked was very regal in her manner but Sarah had the last laugh as she informed us she was indeed of Malaysian royalty! The entire group actually bonded very fast, which was so important for such a pressurised week of meetings. Richard had arranged meetings for the small group of twelve actors with all the top names in the industry, including representatives from top actor's agency William Morris and the heads at Universal.

My three favourite experiences were the acting classes Richard set up for us. We were privileged to receive time to work with the wonderfully talented acting coach to the stars Margie Haber and the equally talented coach to the stars Howard Fine, at their respective studios. Tickets to these guy's classes are like gold dust. Both Margie and Howard have over the years taught an endless list of stars all the way to the top of their profession. Margie's client list includes; Brad Pitt, Heather Locklear, Halle Berry, Kelly Preston, Vince Vaughn, Téa Leoni, Josie Bissett, Vondie Curtis-Hall, Laura Innes and Tom Arnold amongst many others. Whilst Howard's clientele also includes Brad Pitt, Heather Locklear, Lindsay Lohan, Jennifer Connelly, Chris Pine, Amanda Bynes, Justin Timberlake, Gerard Butler, Michelle Williams, Simon Baker, Michael Chiklis, Salma Hayek, Dwayne 'The Rock' Johnson, Bradley Cooper, Morris Chestnut, Christopher Meloni, Adrian Pasdar, 'Stone Cold' Steve Austin, Alexa Vega, Elizabeth Berkley, Val Kilmer, Sela Ward, Billy Campbell, Jon Bon Jovi, Brooke Shields, Daryl Hannah, Rosanna Arquette, Lee Tergesen, Jason Priestley, Garry Shandling, Geri Halliwell, James Belushi, Scott Wolf, Lori Loughlin, Mark Harmon, Pam Dawber, Maura Tierney, Heather Tom, Jared Leto, Danny Nucci, Tori Spelling, Deborah Gibson, E.G. Daily, Jane Seymour and... breathe! This list is by no means the full extent of either of these guys' resumé but I'm finished name-dropping on their behalf but hopefully you now get the picture; these guys are at the top of their profession. I'm certain by now you can also see how fortunate I felt to be in LA acquiring some of their knowledge, which of course they both happily imparted to the students, spending precious individual time working with each of us.

Howard also invited us to his actors' party in Hollywood. For fun, Howard arranged for the press to take pictures of the group outside the entrance to the venue on the red carpet and told them we were a bunch of very famous actors over from the UK - stars of the top British soap 'Hollywood'! During the course of the week we were also privileged to have workshops with producer Todd Slater, theatre directors Peter Foldy and Paul Lynch, casting directors Cathy Henderson, Ferne Cassel, Paul Weber and Tracy Christian from Buckwald's all of whom have cast for numerous big productions throughout their careers.

As if the chance to meet and work with the above was not enough to provide the icing on the proverbial cake, Richard announced during the latter part of the week he had set up yet another surprise for us. We drove in the mini-bus through the Hollywood hills and into a quiet leafy part of LA. We marched out of the mini-bus and up to the entrance of a beautiful house. Richard knocked on the door. It opened slowly to reveal the wonderfully talented, beautiful and graceful actress Dee Wallace-Stone. This really was a special treat. The cherry on top of the icing on top of the proverbial cake! I cannot tell you how many times I had watched *ET* as a kid and wept my little heart out and now, here I was, standing beside Dee in her home. This brought back a flood of very special memories for me.

Dee invited us into her home and showed us around the ground level. She then took us to a quiet room, where we would become privy to her own special method of teaching. This involved getting the actors out of their headspace and getting them to relax via the use of a dowser. As Dee rocked the little gemstone on the chain back and forth in our individual directions, we all looked at each other a little unsure of what was to come next. Miraculously, Dee managed to somehow reach inside each and every one of us accurately, to reveal and then open and unlock, our emotional blocks; before helping us to release them with both spiritual words and then more formal acting coaching. At the end of the class a huge hug was offered to each of us, amidst a flow of an emotional release of tears. What do you want? We're actors!

I had actually attended some introductions to other networking courses in Hollywood before meeting Richard and I have to recommend Richard's course as really offering the best programme. A number of the actors have gone on to work and star in movies in both Hollywood and over here in the UK; including the extremely talented and unique actor Napoleon Ryan, who has gone on to star in movies being made by Ron Howard and also Conor Ryan who has gone on to star in soaps such as Coronation Street in the UK. Incidentally, in order to prepare notes to write this book, I started to look through some old notes of advice given to us by the directors at East 15. Among my many notes I found a few little guidance lines of things I was advised to do upon leaving acting school. They had little stars placed beside them to display the importance of their value. They read as follows;

Read: Margie Haber's book *How to Get the Part Without Falling Apart* and Howard Fine's book *Fine on Acting: A Vision of the Craft*. Visit the Industry Hollywood website.

How amusing I thought. I can tick all those boxes now as done! Following on from my time spent in Hollywood, I have also been privileged to work with some fantastic acting coaches in the UK, including the director Philip Saville, actress Jean Marlow and actor Joseph Millson. In addition to this, I would eventually find myself working with more amazing acting coaches during my time spent on a course at the famous Pinewood Studios.

No matter how much training an actor gets, nothing can stop you from getting bitten by the dreaded laughter bug! I was trained under a very heavy rod and iron about 'corpsing' at East 15. The rule of thumb I was taught is, unless you are Ricky Gervais and supporting your own budget never, ever corpse! We were continually reminded corpsing is wasting both the director's precious time and producer's money. I have to say, I am very house-trained and am not usually a corpser. Having said that, even the best actors have their moments! So, as I wrap-up this chapter, I will leave you with five of my best deaths-by-laughter outtakes, starting at the bottom of the charts and slowly working their way up:

Sitting safely at the bottom of the pile but by no means least on the death by corpsing chart, coming safely in at number five is; the television commercial I filmed for a product called *The Circulation Booster*. The idea of this product is, you place your feet on a mat, which is attached to a series of tiny electrodes, which in turn are stuck to your feet, back of your arms or anywhere else on your body you are holding tension. These electrodes send tiny electric shocks up through the base of your feet, stimulating muscle contraction, to increase blood flow and hence help boost your circulation. Sound painful? It's actually wonderful! See, I'm still selling the product even now! Anyhow, enough technical jargon and back to the script after that short, yet scientific deviation. The director of the commercial asked me to improvise around a few key words. The key words he gave me were: blood, pumping, faster, circulating and great feeling! Just a small amount of imagination required here and I am certain you can work out the havoc these words wreaked! In fact the director was laughing so hard he fell off his chair! No one prepares you at acting school what to do when the director is laughing so hard even he can't concentrate! But like the trooper I am, I carried on.

Thrown into the mix at number four on the corpsing list of fame has to be the time I was asked to improvise a conversation around a sexual problem for a viral for the relationship company Relate. Never ask actors to improvise around the theme of sex! Please give them a script! What came next was a serious case of giggles, as both the actor playing my husband and myself could hardly get the words out for laughing so much. Take, after take, after take; each time we got to the part of the scene where we were expected to talk about our united sexual problem we could not for love nor money hold the laughter back and in fairness, nor could the producer. This 'giggle loop' as it is referred in the industry, is very hard to break once you start. The director Torben Cook was great with us and our inability to keep a straight face couldn't have upset him too much as he praised us both highly for our work that day and has since invited me to work with him again on many more projects.

Sitting comfortably at number three is being asked to spit at another actor on stage. The actor in question is my good friend Robert Hartley Wainwright, who was playing my boyfriend in Stephen Hunt's play *I Am Not An I*. Even friendship does not mean I would spit at someone, so I told Rob I would 'act' at spitting at him. I think Rob was happy with my acting choice. Unfortunately for Rob, I got a bit too into character one night and was so 'in the moment' that poor Rob got a splattering! Whilst Rob managed to hold his grimace extremely well, luckily for me, my character was a bit cheeky, so I was able to get away with laughing in character.

Nearly at the top spot but not quite, the contender for number two is a rather interesting event that occurred during the filming of a 118 118 television commercial. For those of you who have never seen this series of commercials, they evolve around two guys wearing moustaches and characterising two well-known runners, who sing along in a jovial manner to the *Ghostbusters* theme tune; to a variety of bizarre themes. On this occasion, the production company had set up a theme of a sushi restaurant, where actor Colin Michael Carmichael was to travel along the kaiten-sushi, wearing lots of raw sushi about his being, which myself and two other young ladies were meant to pick off with chop-sticks, whilst singing. Easy enough? Kind of! During one particular take, just as filming had stopped for a five minute break, the director turned the monitor towards the set, to allow the actors to have a peek at what had been filmed so far. I was so excited to watch the progress of the footage that I forgot to move my chopsticks, which were now precariously placed in Colin's direction and as the kaiten-sushi made its way back towards me, my chop-sticks made a rather unfortunate venture up poor Colin's backside! Now that's what you call a real bum start!

And last but by no means least, sitting safely at the top spot in the chart, number one in fact is a double whammy. The first was a rather unfortunate moment in which to corpse, as it happened during a very tense moment in the world famous play *And Then They Came for Me - Remembering the World of Anne Frank*. Taking into consideration the fact this play is based around a very sensitive topic, this really is not the play I would ever advise corpsing in at all! My husband in the play, played by the actor Dani Landau, was meant to rush onto stage and come to my aid after I had just been brutally attacked by a group of Nazis. The idea was I was to call out for him and then with outstretched arms Dani was to run onto stage into my arms saying: 'I'm here.' Sounds simple enough? Well, normally it was but on this particular occasion the stage was bearing weight to some slippery substance. Poor Dani ran out and, due to no fault of his own but instead to the aforementioned

280

health hazard, he wasn't able to stop. Instead he slid right past me, arms outstretched in a pose somewhat similar to Superman in flight. Yes, I corpsed. I was however very proud of myself when I successfully managed to turn my laughter into hysterical tears and the audience were none the wiser.

It never rains but it pours. Also sitting jointly at number one was during the next performance of the same show, when something went terribly astray with the sound engineer's equipment. During another very tense moment between poor Dani and his son, played by actor Daniel Evaristi-Boyd, the theme tune to a well-known British children's show *Postman Pat* started to play. The rest of the cast, including myself, were backstage at this point and did not know whether to laugh or cry. We choose laughter but more out of sheer panic than anything else! Of course this had to be the one night when the town's mayor had come to see the play and a television film crew were filming to boot. When else? The highlight occurred after the play, when a lovely elderly gentleman came over to all the actors to shake their hands and express his feelings of contentment at seeing the play and said in a strong Yiddish accent 'but vhat vas zhis musik? I never heard zis before in Germany?' So there you have it, my five deaths by corpsing!

Well, that's a wrap on the corpsing folks but to close this chapter; I must also just share with you the funniest moment I've had whilst acting, which didn't include corpsing but still involved some serious amount of laughter. The time in question is when both the other actor I was working with and I got called in on very short notice to film a short piece of footage. Now the other actor had not learnt his lines. Tut, tut! No names mentioned here to protect the guilty but you know who you are! The scene involved the actor throwing me onto a couch and holding a gun to my head, before saying a short piece of dialogue to camera and pulling the trigger. Having got all the necessary shots of my fear with the gun being held to my head out the way, the director was now focusing his close-up shot on the top of my head and the other actor's face. He required the actor's eye-line to be looking into my eyes for sincerity, whilst filming the close-up. The actor made a professional choice. As he did not know his lines, whilst filming his close-up he placed the script directly over my face in order to read his lines. I could not stop laughing. Luckily the director also had a sense of humour, so was laughing too. I'm not certain how the cameraman managed to keep the camera from shaking whilst filming however, as he too was in stitches. Incidentally, this actor is not alone with this 'style' of acting, as apparently John Hamilton, who was famous for playing Perry White in the original 1950s *Superman* series; *The Adventures of Superman*, was also infamous for leaving his script on the desk in front of him in case he forgot his lines.

**Often from an accident is born genius.** - Emma Fletcher

## 13

## *Seeing Red*

***If you put a small value on yourself, rest assured that
the world will not raise your price.*** - Unknown

*Paul: Now with various acting credits under her belt, Emma decided it was
time to try her hand at presenting. In the process the phrase 'Seeing Red' took
on a whole new meaning, as this chapter reveals.*

Emma: A year after graduating from acting school I saw a
breakdown for a job to become a presenter on a television
channel called Legal TV, which was based in Birmingham. The
advert also said the production company would train the
successful applicant. Always up for a new challenge, I decided I
was ready to put my hand to a spot of presenting. I sent off my
resumé and was most surprised to receive a response from the
head of the channel, Davy Sing Bal, stating he loved my resumé
and asking me to come up to Birmingham to audition the next
week.

I travelled up by car and parked outside the small studio lot. I was
asked to wait in reception and informed Mr Bal would be with me
shortly. I waited for around half an hour, after which time Mr Bal
came and introduced himself. We moved into the office area and
spoke for over an hour when finally Mr Bal got up, shook my
hand and said 'You're perfect for the job Emma. When can you
start?' I ended up staying at the studios for the rest of the day,
being shown the ropes and trying my hand at the autocue.

The next week I was told I would be filming a live slot for their
long-standing, popular programme *People's Court*, which would
then be aired later that week. Talk about being thrown in at the
deep end! I soon discovered the training for the presenter position
involved actually doing the job! The next week I arrived at the

studio very early and was sent straight out with a cameraman, on an extremely cold winter's day in December, to stand outside Birmingham Magistrates court. My job was to ask people who were exiting the court how they felt their case had gone and smile pleasantly at whatever response they gave; occasionally throwing a spanner into the works to jazz things up a little. Apart from not being able to feel my feet, it was actually a really successful day and a number of people exiting the courts were surprisingly very willing to discuss the private details of their case live on air, in the event of getting their face seen on television.

In the months that followed, Legal TV became RED TV (Reality, Entertainment and Drama) and started focusing more on reality television, as the name suggests. Mr Bal asked if I would be interested to be involved in making a new reality show about my life as an up and coming actress but the thought of a camera crew following my every move, for what would have been a year's contract, was too much for me; especially as in so many ways I am actually a very private person. I know this may seem like a paradox for an actor who is writing a book about her life to also be private but you will just have to trust me on this one. I am an incredibly private person. There was also talk of me heading a chat show but starting to get itchy feet to want to concentrate solely on my acting career again, I put forward to Mr Bal the idea of making a mini-series of commercials for the channel instead. My idea for the commercials was to create a set of commercials, which would follow suite of telling a developing story of three characters, almost in the vein of a mini-soap, like so many commercials before. See where I was going with this?

Originally a lawyer, Mr Bal is also the owner of both Balfor Legal Solicitors and Claims Today solicitors and, as it just so happened, was at the time looking to make some new television commercials for the two sister companies. He loved the idea of making a series of commercials based around one family and agreed to give me a basic camera crew to film with. The crew consisted of one handheld camera and cameraman and a sound guy. Not exactly big budget! We were told we had three hours to shoot the commercial. I was to write, direct and keep it very simple; as there

284

would be no time to edit! 'Sure!' I said contemplating the impossibility of the situation. For a start, the only thing I had ever directed before now was my end of year play for East 15 and of course traffic! (if directing a friend into a parking spot counts!) I was however and have always been a competent writer, so that part of the plan did not faze me too much.

I hurriedly got a script out to the actors, put on my teacher's hat in place of a director's hat, which I would imagine are fairly similar looking hats and got on with filming and trying to act in the commercial all at the same time! Knowing we could not edit the footage, the main direction I gave the actors was 'Don't move!' I did however, keep an eye on what everyone was doing from behind the camera lens as much as I could and rather graciously the other actors gave praise to my directorial skills at the end of the day. The commercial did get aired on television and two more commercials were eventually made in the series. I definitely would not call these commercials a work of mastery but I was, nevertheless, proud of myself for rising to the challenge. Directing these adverts also served to give me an even greater respect for the role of the director. I stayed at RED for nine months in total, then having felt I had gained all I could from the experience, adding to the equation I was getting very tired from the long two and a half hours stuck in traffic 'how much longer will this take, what's the hold up this time and why aren't we moving still?' drive to and from London to Birmingham once a week, I left RED to pursue alternative outlets.

Whilst I was presenting for RED TV I hosted the promotional Vox Pops for Big Brother reality star Aisleyne Horgan-Wallace's new reality show *Aisleyne: Celebrity Stars at Work*. Part of the job incorporated interviewing Aisleyne and her manager Richard Skeels before the shoot. The three of us all went for a slap-up meal in London's very plush hotel The Soho Bar. Yeah, I know; it's a tough job but someone's got to do it! The buffet was incredible. A medley of all the finest food one could feast their eyes on was made available to us and what was more, RED was forking out for the bill! Aisleyne and I clicked straight away, in the discovery we had both unfortunately experienced similar

285

heartache in our personal lives. We chatted merrily and soon made our way to the buffet stand, then suddenly became like two naughty schoolgirls, in a race against time to pick our way through the various food supply. Anyone watching us would think we had not eaten for weeks! I think we both managed to have at least a little bit of everything on offer, minus the meat for me!

During the time I was working at RED, I was invited by a mutual friend of Debbie King and myself, to an industry function being put on in aid of cancer. During the course of the evening I was briefly introduced by Debbie to the host of the event; producer extraordinaire and gentleman David King. Later in the evening, as Debbie introduced onto the stage Jonathan Ansell (then her fiancée now her husband), who immediately proceeded to give a beautiful rendition of a number of popular classics, David came over to the table to re-introduce himself properly. We chatted and soon found we shared a lot of common ground. A bond was instantly forged between David and myself. I can honestly say, David has shown me nothing but kindness over these past few years and our friendship continues to blossom and grow with each day. David has given me a great deal of support both emotionally and on a business level. He always jokes one day he will marry me but the truth is, in one another we have both found a life long friend and that is worth a million red roses. The next highlight of the evening, after David himself of course and arranged by David, was the solo performance given by, be still my beating heart, the magnificent Harry Connick Junior.

During the evening I also became acquainted with David's daughter Sophie, who was with her original band members of The Dolly Rockers; Lucy Kay and Brooke Challinor. The girls took it upon themselves to look after me throughout the duration of the evening. I was then also introduced to Sophie's boyfriend, who at the time was in a boy band. Sophie had met her boyfriend during the finals of the popular television show *The X-Factor*, which both bands were involved in. In fact, whilst I was presenting at RED, one of the plans was to regularly interview the two bands and monitor the progression of the girls against the boys over the course of a number of interviews. Unfortunately, as both bands

286

were in the process of changing record labels, the idea never got off the ground.

Shortly after this evening David took me out for a meal with one of his good friends, Jimmy Osmond. Jimmy had just been signed up to a cameo performance in the new stage version of *Grease*. On the way to David's house after the meal, rehearsing in the car, as one does, we all started to sing various numbers from *Grease*. So I graciously thanked Jimmy and informed him I can now say I have officially sung with one of the Osmond boys - but perhaps I won't place this credit on my resumé, as that might be stretching things just a little too far!

Not long after leaving Red TV to pursue my acting again, I came upon a breakdown for a new short film for television being made by Paul Burton Films. As always, I religiously researched the company and upon viewing Paul's vast resumé, very much liked what I saw. I auditioned for Paul's film, which was later released under the title, *Amy*, at Elstree Studios. Paul had structured the day of auditions so he would get the chance to personally meet all the prospective actors and actresses before they auditioned, in order to get to know a little more about each of them first. This proved to be a good way for both the director and the actor to acquire an affinity with one another and is certainly a good way for any director to discover which of the actors he or she feels they would be comfortable working with. The audition process itself incorporated both individual and group auditions and an interview with Paul.

Paul informed all of the actresses who were successful in gaining a role at the end of the group auditions. I had landed one of the lead roles and agreed to be in the film on the spot, sensing it would prove an invaluable experience for me and would also serve as another good credit to have on my thankfully expanding resumé.

Paul had successfully acquired a named actress to play the lead in the film and I was to play a smaller lead role alongside this actress, as her best friend. Shortly before we were set to start filming,

287

unfortunately this actress had to pull out of the project. Despite the knock back and never one to give up, Paul rewrote the screenplay and I soon found myself receiving a telephone call from him informing me he had decided to go ahead with a new version of the film, to which he invited me to play a lead role. Once again I agreed.

The following year, Paul asked me if I would film with him again on his next short film for television, *Resentment*, which stars much-loved actress Vicki Michelle. I didn't even have to think twice about my response, which was of course a resounding: 'Yes, I would love to work with you again, Paul.' Who knew my first meeting with Paul would result in seeing me appear in a total of two of his short films for television and of course, working together on this very book?

Whilst my career was on a continuing upwards spiral, my personal life, however, was sadly not looking so hot. Once again I met a man who made my heart skip a beat. He was talented in the looks department, there was no doubting that but I knew he spelt trouble. If the truth be known, I knew from the bitter start the relationship was ultimately doomed. I knew we probably didn't have enough common ground to last the distance and the relationship was born more from physical attraction rather than from real substance; and we all know any relationship based upon physicality without any real substance can only ever be short lived. So why did I allow myself to fall for this guy? The answer was simple. The reason I allowed myself to fall for this man's allure and charm was because of my past record. I had, previously to meeting this guy, been interested in a man who was not interested in starting up a relationship with me and now, here I was, presented with the possibility of spending time in the company of a man who was interested in me and it felt good. So I foolishly allowed myself to base a decision about my future around the outcome of a past experience. Rather than allowing myself to base my decision upon what was good for me in the present, I allowed my short fallings from my past to dictate the success of my future. It had been far too long since a man had made me feel good about myself in this way, so I lapped it up, even in the face of danger

288

and the danger this time was of course a broken heart again. It was, nevertheless, the short-fallings of this relationship, which allowed me to realise just how much I had grown as an individual, by the manner in which I dealt emotionally with what was to follow.

As expected, the relationship was not long lasting and the man in question soon announced he was planning to leave the country to go back and live in his own country - you guessed, he was going back to America, making this the fourth time a man would leave me for the good old US of A. Unfortunately, this was the first in line of what was to be a string of untruths. When I initially met this man, he had informed me he was not planning to go back home; which was part of the reason I had allowed myself to start to become emotionally receptive towards him. Sadly it turned out he had told me a lot of things about himself, which did not turn out to be entirely true. Now excuse me here for venting for a line or two but personally I've never seen the point in a lie. Apart from being dishonest with others when you tell a lie, you are also in effect only being dishonest with yourself too. Usually all that occurs when you tell a lie is the truth will inevitably catch up with you eventually anyhow and bite you directly on the backside, so quite frankly, what's the point? The truth will always out. Okay, so back down from my moral high ground, sad to say but it turned out this man was also involved emotionally, even if not physically, with another woman and with many a promise made to her too. To me this still spelt out betrayal and was literally hemlock for the heart. He was not being fair to either woman in his behaviour; telling me he was just friends with this other woman and that she was okay with our relationship and for the first three months of our dating it turned out he was telling her we were not an item. I soon started to feel pleased I hadn't gone down the route of purchasing twin-set tattoos! He already had one stamped on his backside; which should have read 'run while you still can!'

When this other woman eventually found out we were dating, instead of looking at this man's poor behaviour and recognising he was at fault, she chose instead to blame me for his betrayal. I think the reason women blame other women for men's bad behaviour instead of focusing the blame where it belongs, directly on these men; consequently leaving these men free from blame, is to justify why they still continue to love these badly behaved men so much. My aim is not to bible-bash men here and I am completely aware this scenario can just as equally occur the other way around with women behaving badly towards men too but I am merely trying to illustrate a point here of how easily people can misplace their trust and consequently reflect their blame in the wrong direction. Once again, my little heart was left shattered into many small pieces. I also felt completely misrepresented by the 'other' woman, who said a variety of deliciously unkind things about me to the guy I was dating. Unfortunately, what made it worse for me, was by the time I discovered he was being emotionally unfaithful, I had already found myself starting to fall head over heels for this guy and had already willingly started to give him several pieces of my once complete heart; whilst throughout this entire time he was continuing to allow this other woman to carry on with her tyranny of bad behaviour towards me - and that was when I realised it was time to get out of the relationship, I had reached damage limitation.

I soon started to realise that guy who had taken me out for the little 'potato skins soirée' a while back was actually a step closer to being fairer than this guy, who was really doing exactly the same thing, only under the guise of a relationship for 'x' number of months. He had been encouraging me to believe there really could be a lasting relationship, when in fact all he was really looking for was a trip down the old Milky Way! Not cool and so No-K! This type of person is really just a love thief, a one arm-love-bandit, a plain old picaroon, a double-dealing-do-badder, Dick Dastardly, double-crosser with bells on that don't even ring; as really all they are doing is stealing your precious time and as soon as I was able to come to this realisation, unlike so many times previously, I was able to pick up the pieces of my broken heart fairly quickly and allow myself to get up from the slippery-sloped, tear-drenched floor and move on speedily in the other direction away from Mr Wrong. This short-lived relationship and the heartache which pursued, was indeed a learning lesson. It informed me that long gone where the days when I would hang around and wait to be emotionally battered some more; I had finally become the strong and levelheaded woman I had always aimed to be. No longer was I prepared to allow my heart to be held to hostage by someone who did not respect me. This time I did not allow myself to go downhill nor buy a one-way ticket to the black abyss. It also made me realise next time I would have to become more careful about who I chose to give my heart to. Next time I would need to wait a bit longer to get to know someone a bit better before I trusted them enough to place my precious heart in their hands. Our hearts are delicate and need to be held with kid gloves. Having long since thrown away my rose-tinted glasses, after just a few weeks I was ready to get on with the rest of my life again, although not before one last defiant gesture went horribly astray. A good friend suggested I flush the ex-boyf's telephone number down the toilet, as a symbolic gesture. So I did. But guess what? The darn thing wouldn't flush and just continued to float precariously on top of the water in the basin - and yes, you guessed it. I had to put my hand down the toilet to retrieve the darn thing! Now that's karma!

As you can see, I have in the past been an excellent judge of character when it comes to men! So why do so many people like myself get themselves involved in bad relations? Speaking for myself, I believe it is because I didn't value myself enough due to my past experiences and my choices were more of a reflection sadly of my own lack of self-worth. For example, I became attracted to a womaniser because I had previously been rejected. I got into a physically abusive relationship because the guy before didn't pay me much attention in the bedroom. I was attracting into my life the wrongs things for me as I was focusing my energy each time on the wrong solutions to my problem. I believed only a troubled soul would be able to understand me and be able to handle some of the things I have been through in my life. For a start, what new date would expect 'meeting the folks' to be a trip to the local cemetery? I apologise if this comment appears crass but I can't begin to tell you how difficult it has been over the years for me to explain to any new date why I can't invite them home to introduce them to my parents.

As time has moved on I have learnt, although my experiences have shaped me they don't have to define me. Being in a relationship makes you take stock of who you are and self reflect. I made a decision I was no longer prepared to take responsibility for the ill behaviour of some of the men I was dating, or be their Florence Nightingale any longer, as all that happens when you take on this role is it results in pulling you down with their sinking ship. And it's usually the one person in the relationship who is trying to save the other who ends up receiving the blame for their bad behaviour. Why? Because we allow it. So now my search remains for a man who is already comfortable in his own skin before letting him anywhere near mine!

I do believe however, no two people enter a relationship willing it to end. Most people enter a relationship hoping it will work out but when two people find things are not going as smoothly as they had planned, instead of trying to work things out in a calm and rational manner, emotions take over and of course people's interactions with one another sadly and far too often, start to become fully-charged. People's anger towards each other is often only inward anger at themselves that things didn't work out. What often occurs next is they usually end up becoming angry with their partner and pass the buck of blame; rather than taking a step back and recognising perhaps they too need to work on themselves first before the relationship can work. If, however, the relationship is starting to look like a no-fly zone, as both parties involved are heading in two very separate directions, then it is also important to be able to recognise when it is time to let go. Additionally, I have learnt it is also important to recognise when something is wrong from the start and to be able to walk away once that recognition occurs, rather than carry on walking straight into trouble in the hope you might be able to save or change someone. Although, turning this notion completely on it's head, it does occur to me, in today's society too many people fail to think about how they might work 'with' their partner to make a relationship work and are far too ready to call time on a relationship before putting any real effort in to make it work. I am not for one-minute suggesting keep tail spinning and stay in a bad relationship but in today's society it seems to me too many people are far less interested to

292

'work things out' and are unfortunately far to interested in saying 'next'. Yup, this phrase isn't just saved for the audition room my friends. This mentality seems to stretch to so many things in today's society.

I have always been raised with a very traditional set of values and morals, which, I would argue, sadly pale into insignificance when compared to the morals of today. Unfortunately, people appear to have forgotten to place a value on things as precious. We live in a throwaway society, where everything is replaceable. If we break something, no problem, we'll just buy another. Remember the lady in the fashion red Lamborghini? And yes, in my opinion this mentality stretches as far as relationships too, which is also why there are still so many single and lonely people in the world today. Part of the problem is, we are faced with too much choice. We are spoilt. In fact microwave $y$ and $z$ generation 'I want it yesterday' surmounts to overkill. For instance, have you ever walked into the supermarket to purchase some lemon Pledge and found it takes you over half an hour to make your choice from the smorgasboard of cleaning products displayed on the gondolas? Okay, so maybe that's just me. I'm a Libra, what can I tell you? We can't help it, making choices isn't one of our selling points but once we've made a decision, at least we stick to it - unless of course it was the wrong decision! Hey, I'm a Libra! So what do we do in modern day society when we can't decide which i-pod, cell phone or latest gadget, thingy-me-bob, with dangly bits hanging off it to purchase or even which guy to date? Easy, we choose them all! Okay, so perhaps I'm exaggerating somewhat again here but the point I am illustrating remains the same; people have lost their sense of value and with it, a sense of purpose.

This throw-away mentality has also led people to literally throwaway their own self-worth and in some extreme cases, even throwaway life; both their own or that of others. It makes me terribly upset to witness how kids are behaving on the streets today and the morally culpable behaviour, which sadly exists towards both one another and towards their elders. Growing up with an elder generation I have always held the greatest respect for my elders and it particularly upsets me dearly how young people

293

today seem to have lost respect for the older generation. We are faced with a real problem today and we can only heal the world if we take responsibility in healing ourselves first. If we all learned to take responsibility and embrace our own actions and their consequences, rather than continually pass blame, the world would be a better place to live in. We need to learn to respect ourselves again. I believe God gives us the right tools for the job that He has placed each and everyone of us here to do. Working out your *raison d'etre* and which job you are meant to be carrying out can sometimes be tricky it's true but if everybody were to become a little less discerning about what everyone else's earnings and lifestyle entail and concentrate a little more on what it is they have been placed here to do, rather than try to continually outwit their neighbour, we would all be living in a less troubled world. People would start to realise they already have all they need for their journey and would stop wanting more. Let's face it, 'I want more' leads to jealousy - and we all know what jealousy is the root of. The key is contentment and in knowing how to enjoy what you have. As Socrates wrote; *'He is richest who is content with the least; for content is the wealth of nature.'*

So what exactly have all my relationships taught me over the years? Not to date an American? Nope. To go and live in the Americas, so they have nowhere to run? Wrong again. My experiences have taught me to be careful what you ask for because you just might get it. Too true! This phrase doesn't just mean be careful what you pray to God for, what it literally means is be careful what you focus your thoughts on. We are all very capable of visualizing what we want and then bringing that visualisation into fruition; even if what we visualize our thoughts on may not be good for us. Okay, let me illustrate by example with this little anecdote; you start to pray to God every night before you go to bed for your dream guy, who just happens to be Mickey-Mouse (or Mini for the guys!). Go with me on this one. So before you know it, our floppy-eared friend with the high-pitched voice rocks up in your life. 'What? How? Why?' I hear you cry. Simple, because when you pray for the same thing over and over, you focus all your energy and thoughts into wanting that thing so much, the thought of it goes from your ideas and dreams and transpires itself directly into your subconscious and daily waking life. Before you know it, soon you find yourself consciously focusing your every effort on attaining that goal. So every time a potential partner introduces himself to you, no matter how much of a catch he or she may be, if they don't have the loveable personality of our little floppy-eared friend, you reject them in your continued pursuit for the mouse. 'So what happens next?' I hear you cry again. Easy. You end up buying a one-way ticket to Disneyland and with Swiss cheese in hand, voila! *Mission fait accompli*; you get exactly what you prayed for!

Okay, back down to the landing pad and away from the Disney metaphors, this has happened to me on so many occasions. Just remind yourself of my track record for a start! It's not by now breaking news in the past I have made the wrong life choices born from previous experiences. Okay, perhaps there are no 'wrong' choices, only different choices and yes, our previous experiences are indeed there to teach us but be careful what you take from each one and be sure you are focusing your energies and thoughts on the right thing before you move onto the next because your thoughts can become a reality. Learn to become a master of your own thoughts, for only then will you truly be free.

I am a great believer in mind over matter and in visualising what you want and in bringing that visualisation to fruition. This is called the law of attraction. Our thoughts are just a bunch of magnetic impulses. One thought has the potential to change your destiny but remember; magnets attract so be careful what it is you wish for, as you may not like what you attract into your life. We have to change our thoughts first before we can change ourselves. Learn to desire what is good for you. So work on yourself and your thoughts before you take off to Disneyland or wherever it is your travels will take you next and make sure you are drawing positive energies into your life because if you don't work on yourself first, then I have news for you; no matter where your travels take you, you will still be carrying the same hand luggage and attracting negative energies into your world.

You might want to take a deep breath and sit down before you read this next line; YOU CAN'T ESCAPE YOURSELF! Absorb the fact: you can't escape yourself. If you don't work on yourself, then you will just end up carrying the same baggage with you wherever you go in life; from one place onto the next and what's more, you will find yourself always coming face to face with the same old issues over and over again; relieving them in different ways. I don't care if the luggage you carry is a top of the range Louis Vuitton satchel or a rucksack from the local trickle down store - news flash; it will still be the same garbage inside and believe me, it will still weigh the same at check in. So lighten your load. Don't just change the label from a high street brand to a Versace. Leave your old baggage behind you, as the less you carry the farther you will go. You must resolve what it is you are trying to escape. So before you run, ask yourself this question first; 'Am I running towards something, or am I just running away from something else?' To deal with your problems, first you must face them square on, then work on resolving them and only then can you about turn and leave them square behind.

Now I am not expecting to find a partner who hasn't any baggage, I mean just look at me, I have a whole suitcase load and in the past it has gotten pretty heavy too but at least I have worked on emptying out some of the contents and left them well and truly where they belong - in the past. So don't do what I have done before now and try to carry everyone else's hand luggage en route, when I had enough problems just trying to lift my own! It will only unbalance you and tip you over and we all know, you can't help other people unless you are standing on solid ground yourself. If you're not happy within yourself, then how can you expect to make anyone else happy? We draw into our lives a reflection of all that we are. If you are living an unhappy existence, all that will occur is you will end up surrounding yourself with other unhappy souls. Surrounding yourself with other unhappy souls allows you to validate your reason for remaining unhappy, giving you the opportunity to have a good old mope and wallow in the mire and of course the chance to stroke one another's forlorn egos in your individual contest to see who can remain the most downtrodden. This pattern of behaviour also allows you to keep alive various negative thoughts and their associated feelings and causes you to become stuck emotionally in the past. It may seem like an inescapable pattern of behaviour once you are in that ever-increasing circle of unhappiness but there is always a way out.

My advice? Well, the opposite of any given scenario is of course also true. So be kind to yourself. Get yourself some big fat happy of your own by doing things in life which you enjoy and what's more spend time in the company of happy people, of people who bring a smile to your face. If you surround yourself with positive people, a funny thing will occur; soon you will find you become one too. Don't give yourself an excuse to be unhappy and don't make someone else's problems your own. Respect yourself enough to realise you do not need to own someone else's issues; you have enough on your plate just trying to take ownership over your own! Why allow people who are living their own nightmare to tell you how to live your dream? If you want advice on how to live a dream, then ask someone who is already living the dream. You wouldn't ask a chef how to cut your hair, you'd ask a hairdresser. Get information from successful people in the field you want to be successful in, whether it is love, finance or just being happy. Oh and by the way, now I am always careful what I pray for because guess what? I just might get it! So now I pray to God to help me find the right person or the right thing for me, rather than pray for things which, in the short term may seem great but in the long run might actually be bad for me; and I now ask God to always help me find the wisdom to recognise the difference between the two.

Speaking of attracting things into your life when you focus on them, around the time of dating Mr Wrong the lovely actress Bettine Le Beau called me up out of the blue to introduce herself to me. I had actually been friendly with her son for years previously but now she was calling to introduce herself to me personally. Although her call was acting related, it just so happens Bettine now practices as a relationship guru. Bettine invited me round to her home for cream cheese bagels and chat. I have to say she fed me well. The age gap didn't seem to bother either of us and we spoke for hours on end, as if we were indeed friends of old who had in fact known one another for years. As Bettine related her fascinating and often harrowing life story to me, there were tears of sorrow as she talked me through her time spent in a Nazi prison camp and then tears of laughter as she showed me early footage of herself acting alongside the marvellous Benny Hill. She also told me what is was like being an ex-Bond girl and finally gave me a special treat of a tour around the house of some of her pride and joys; her private collection of her own hand-crafted magnificent bronze sculptures.

The night Bettine called I was having a p-j night. Come on ladies, we've all had pyjama nights haven't we? Those teary-eyed evenings spent alone, snuggled up to your pillow after we've just broken up with 'the man of our dreams' - or was that nightmares? - and all we want to do is sit in front of the television, watch a Rom Com and cry our eyes out for hours; contemplating how the relationship could possibly have failed, when you'd already checked the sound of their second name against your first a number of times and found it was a great match? Come on ladies, you know we've all been there! Well, I've had several of those nights, sitting on my own in front of the television with a Chinese take-out, contemplating the rocky road ahead - and I'm not just talking about the hard-hitting reality of your new found singledom - I'm talking about the Rocky Road tub of double, double choc-chip fudge ice-cream now perched neatly on your lap. In fact, it actually got to the point when I rang my local Chinese take-out to place my usual order and discovered they knew the number of my order by heart! Well, Bettine saved the day or should that be night and her advice really couldn't have come into my life at a more fitting time, for a start, there's only so much choc-chic fudge a girl can handle! Her advice was informative and sometimes even positively daring but nevertheless Bettine helped me to come through the other side of what could have proved to have become a much more difficult period in my life without her.

Bettine gave me that little nudge I required to help me refocus my thoughts. She helped me think about what it was I was really seeking from a partner by refocusing on who I was first. These little bagel-fuelled chats helped to make me remember how

298

important it is we are with a life partner who not only has our best interests at heart but also brings out the best qualities in us; thus helping us achieve our life ambitions and goals rather than becoming a hindrance to them. Relationships, after all, should not be about the 'give and the take' but all about the giving. What do I mean by this? When you meet a potential life partner, you should not be thinking 'I wonder what he or she can do for me' but instead how you can help to serve each other's growth; by thinking about what it is you both have to offer one another. This is particularly important when you are working in a tough industry such as mine, as you need to surround yourself constantly with supportive and caring people. I must point out, however, giving in a relationship does not mean you should allow yourself to turn into a doormat either. Although you should allow yourself to focus on the giving more than the receiving, you still need to ensure you are in a balanced, healthy relationship. It is the same with anything in life. Balance is always the key and in any case, if two people are always giving to one another, then by its very nature, ultimately you are both receivers anyhow. The most defining element to make a relationship work is respect. Respect your boyfriend or girlfriend. The clue is in the titles you give each other: be a 'friend' to one another.

Age has taught me with complete certainty, you cannot change someone, they have to want to change themselves and you cannot make someone love you or do anything they don't want to do. Time has also taught me, if someone does not want to be with you, there is absolutely no point in trying to force the relationship to work or in trying to change yourself to make it work. I'm afraid this never works and I learnt the hard way on more than one occasion. So change your outlook and your focus or what or who it is you are looking for but don't try and change your partner. If you have to change someone to be with them, then ask yourself; can you really be with the right person? Yes, a relationship is about compromise but if someone has decided they don't want to be with you, then instead of beating yourself up over why they don't want to be with you and why you aren't good enough for them, as I have in the past, try and see that perhaps they are just seeing something about the two of you together that you haven't spotted yet. If a relationship is not right for one person, it cannot ultimately be right for the other person either. So don't change yourself to be with someone. You are wonderful just the way you are. Perhaps they are wonderful too but you are just not wonderful together and you both deserve the best. A friend said to me recently 'You can choose pain or champagne?' Let's face it, given the choice most of us would choose champagne. So if you have already worked out you are walking down a different path to your ex, my advice would be, keep on walking! Stay on your own path and then you will at least give yourself a fighting chance of meeting someone along the way who is hopefully heading in the same direction as you.

So, how do we find the perfect partner? I'm not certain as I'm still looking but I guarantee I will let you know when I find him! One thing I am certain of however is; we need to start by looking within ourselves first. You cannot find 'Mr Right' or even 'Mr Right Now' unless you are sitting comfortably in your own skin. The mistake people often make is thinking they can find someone who will fill a gap in their own lives or make them complete somehow. And how do I know this? Guilty as charged! We need to be comfortable with ourselves first and then when we are we can find someone who compliments that and works in opposite harmony with us. Yes, I did say 'opposite harmony'. 'So what the heck does that mean?' I hear you cry. God made men and women very different for good reason, so we can learn to compliment each other through our differences and therefore help each other grow together as a unit. Two souls complimenting each other is where the idea of becoming 'one' was born. It doesn't mean loose yourself in another person's identity - again guilty as charged; but it does mean find that special someone who brings out the best in you. Their characteristics should work in harmony to compliment yours; thus completing you if you like. If you are with someone that makes you look in the mirror and not like the reflection you see starring back at you (going to have to 'take the fifth' on this), then you know you are with the wrong person. My advice would be, don't try and meet the right person, try and be the right person first.

Okay, so back to reality - and yes it bites! I admit, I haven't always found it easy over the years to accept when a relationship is over but you definitely know it is over when your boyfriend wins an award (for being the biggest jerk) and you say: 'Baby, I prayed for you to win' and he replies 'I don't need your prayers, I would have won it anyway!' Or in the throws of passion you notice a picture of another woman's picture by your dream date's bedside table and innocently ask: 'Who's that?' and he says 'My ex. I've been thinking about getting back with her again!' Or when he turns to you and says: 'What would you say if I told you I'm gay?' Or: 'It's God or me. You can't have us both!' Yes, yes, yes and yes to all the above! Been there, done it, read the book, signed the movie deal, got the t-shirt, matching socks, gloves and a frilly hat with bobbles and badges to boot! No siree; dating has not been an easy ride for me. More like a toreador riding a bull!

So why am I still single? You may well ask! Well I'll tell you. I'm looking for a nice Jewish man. 'So, vhat's zhe problem?' I hear you cry. Well here it is, candy coated: when you look at the Jewish population in the UK it's small. So now I need to look at which of the population are of the male species: the margins are closing in. Next I need to find out which ones are Jewish, male and single: getting tighter. Now I'm looking at Jewish, male, single and in my age bracket: getting into an even finer percentile and finally, I need to find the Jewish, single men of my age bracket who have no issues; getting into dangerously small territory here but then… Bingo! You find him. The man of your dreams! Pop the cork; white wash the ceiling! But does he return your call? Hell no! And that my friends, is why I am still single!

My married friends are always saying to me 'Emma, you're too fussy. Go on a date with him already!' And my response to this? Firstly I inform them they can't really call me an *OFD*; an 'overly fussy dater', as just look at some of the disastrous relationships I've had! No disrespect meant to any of them, I know it takes two to tango and for that matter play tennis, sing a duet and all that jazz but give me a break; I'm just illustrating a point! 'Give him a chance. Go on a second date!' they cry. Why? If you have to force yourself to like someone then surely there is no point in taking things through to round two? Attraction has to be mutual and I'm not necessarily talking about with just one mere glance suddenly you find your knees turn to jelly and your instantly bawled over with double back-flips. Attraction is of course so much more than just the way a person looks. Being attracted to someone or for that matter not, can surmount to their body language or even to a certain smell or air they have about them. Like I said, know what it is you are looking for and if you are not sure what it is you are looking for, then at least have an idea of what it is you don't want! I do believe however, it is always better to focus your energies on what you want rather than what you don't want; as that is a more positive outlook for your energies. My rabbi always says, 'If he doesn't make you want to vomit, then give him a chance!' Okay, okay, so I'm all for giving people a chance but I'm not gonna marry the guy just to have a diamond-enhanced ring-finger! Marriage is, or at least should be, for life. So yes, if that means I am a little fussy in whom I choose to date, then bring it on and no, I'm not expecting fireworks every time I meet a guy but at the very least a few sparklers wouldn't go amiss! Thank God, I had wonderful role models in mum and dad. They loved each other unconditionally and were so kind and supportive to one another, even through all the heartache they suffered over the years. Up until the day mum passed away, dad brought her breakfast in bed every morning. Now that is devotion. I know this type of love is possible and can still exist, so if my *modus operandi* seems somewhat long-winded in my ever continued search to find a life-long partner, it is because I have seen what true love can look like and I think it is worth holding out for that little bit longer.

Sadly, I have so many friends who are divorced and although a few of them are now happily remarried to their true loves, if possible I would like to not add Dolly Parton's d-i-v-o-r-c-e song to my long list of hits. I am in fact trying to avoid the divorce diversion altogether and save myself the heartache of becoming yet another statistic in the search for my life partner. I feel I owe it to myself at the very least to try and avoid that heartache if I can. I would rather be on my own than be unhappy with someone else. So yes, I remain that little bit fussy and cynical in my choices of dating, in the hope that if I hold out just that little bit longer I will still meet Mr Perfect before I go grey! Oh and by the way, I don't believe anyone is perfect and no, I'm not looking for 'The' Mr Perfect, just the Mr Perfect for me. If the shoe fits then wear the darned thing! And yes, even after all my string of unsuccessful dates and horror stories, I do still love men and yes, I am still searching for that kind and loving soul to spend the rest of my life with. Now that I am in a more comfortable headspace I now know what it is I am not looking for and for that matter what it is I am looking for! Remember I told you at the start of this book, if you fall once the next time you will tread more carefully; the next time you will know where not to tread? Well this is true for anything in life. Just watch where you place your footing next time. I know I certainly will. I do still believe in fairy tales and I know my Prince Charming is still out there waiting somewhere. He's probably just busy polishing his shiny, metallic suit, waiting to sweep me off my feet upon my imminent arrival!

During the time I was going out with Mr Wrong, I ended up becoming ill again but this time it wasn't a conscious choice. I hadn't stopped eating and I wasn't spending endless hours in front of the mirror contemplating how ugly I looked. This time it was due to the indiscernible silent killer - stress. It is true; I am a worrier. A wise person once said to me 'What is the point of worrying? It will not change the outcome but will succeed in making you ill.' As Miriam Makeba famously said *'Worry is interest paid on trouble before it is due.'* How right both these parables are. Whilst I have learnt over the years to become more Zen, on this occasion worry crept up on me unawares from behind. Whilst I was busily worrying about how I had once again managed to get myself into a bad relationship, although I felt fine on the outside, my internal organs had other plans.

After a fairly routine check-up at the doctors I discovered I was suffering from high-cholesterol. I was at first quite taken aback as I have a healthy diet, do not eat meat, am of slight build and exercise well. I wondered if perhaps it could be familial but knew there was no way of ever checking. It hadn't occurred to me stress might be the causing factor. Upon visiting my local surgery I found myself in the position of being spoken to by the locum as if

303

I were a naughty schoolgirl back in detention once again and being faced with some serious choices about lifestyle and my consequential health. The following is in fact a short story of will power and sheer determination.

I was informed I had a cholesterol level of seven. Having never had to worry about my cholesterol levels before this time, I had no clue what my levels should be. The locum versed me with the knowledge I should be a five. 'Well, at least I'm only two out!' I said: 'Two out? Two out?' she screeched, 'Even 6.9 is too high young lady!' Point taken. She continued with extreme vigour 'Obviously you are eating too much red meat, smoking too much, don't exercise enough and are over-weight'. Having been accused for the most part of my life as looking painfully under-weight, the last part of her comment made me let out a small but nervous giggle. 'That's not me' I replied. 'I'm a vegetarian, don't smoke, exercise regularly and am definitely not over-weight.' She continued, 'Oh I see, so you think being over-weight is funny do you?' I informed her I did not think being overweight was something to laugh about at all but did find it a little strange she thought I was overweight. Actually I thought her comment was completely irresponsible if the truth be known; to accuse a young woman who is 5 foot six inches in height and at that point in time weighing in at 9 stone as being overweight. 'You are fat!' she retorted, which was quite a statement from a woman who was no stick insect herself. 'Fat?' I replied. 'Have you checked my BMI?' I questioned. 'How tall are you?' she asked. If she had to ask, clearly she had not. Her round of bullets continued to be fired, every shot hitting a little harder each time. And then one of the slugs got under my skin as she finished with 'You need to loose weight' 'Really?' I asked. 'How much weight do I need to loose?' 'A stone' she said. 'A stone? But that would take me down to 8 stone!' I responded. 'Loose a stone, else you will drop down dead within the space of five years' she replied. Wow! That was quite a shocking statement and sent the fear of God rushing through me. 'Cut down your fat intake' she continued. Being a vegetarian and living with a healthy diet anyway, I was not really sure what else I could cut out of my diet so questioned 'How many calories do you advise I am allowed each day?' 'Calories? Calories?' the

304

slightly unhinged woman replied 'I'm a doctor not a gym instructor! I don't do calories! I'm talking about saturated fat!'

Now, not being someone who has ever had to worry about loosing weight, as my concern over the years had always been how to keep weight on me, which believe me can be just as daunting; so forgive me if I sound naïve but I found this all a bit disconcerting. 'You are to start on statins immediately' she said. statins! Now that really scared me. I'd read all the horror stories in the press about the side effects of statins so wanted to learn more. 'Can you tell me, are there any side effects?' I quizzed. 'Yes!' she replied, offering absolutely no more information, 'Could you perhaps expand on that please?' I asked. 'You may have trouble walking.' That didn't help. 'Are there any other side effects?' I continued 'Yes' 'Could you tell me what they are?' I questioned further. 'No, as you may never get them!' she said. As I have never been big on popping pills, I informed the doctor I wanted to try and get my cholesterol levels down naturally over the course of the next six months, without the aid of statins and be monitored accordingly during this time. If I couldn't achieve this goal by then, I would consider taking the statins. 'You will take the statins!' she continued. I continued to express my desire to take the route of nature first. 'Well' she continued 'I can't sit by your bed at night and force them down your throat but you won't succeed in getting your levels down yourself, even to a 6.9'. Having always been a great believer in mind over mater and having witnessed three different close friends get through greater illness than this via a positive mind-set, I felt this was a challenge I could take on and win, pill free. Plus this doctor's attitude was completely unprofessional and to be honest a little scary. Not only did she nearly scare me to death, so I may not have had to worry about the five year count down anyhow but telling me to loose a stone in weight, having not measured my BMI and knowing nothing of my previous eating habits was not selling me her idea of taking the statins.

Her strong words did however, have the desired effect of making me change my diet. I decided I would get my cholesterol down naturally whatever it took, so immediately cut out cheese and cake and cheese cake for that matter but that was easy to do, as I can't bare cheesecake anyhow and can't really understand why anyone would ever consider placing cheese and cake together as a food choice. I actually think God was having a funny five minutes when he placed this suggestion into man's mind! Anyhow I digress. I was very strict and stuck to my new diet rigidly and for good or for ill, lost a stone in weight. I also managed to get my cholesterol levels down to a 5 by sheer will power alone! Bring it on! Don't mess with the Fletch!

Incidentally, after my interactions with this doctor, I spoke to a relative who is also a doctor, yes every Jewish household has a doctor and guess what? He informed me it is a legal requirement for a patient to be monitored naturally for six months before going on to statins anyhow. So there you go. Now I am in no way advocating you don't take a doctor's advice or medication where absolutely essential, that would be irresponsible of me but what I am saying is willpower and sheer determination really can stretch a long way; as does the power of the mind, which I happen to believe is a great healer. The essence of this story is to believe in yourself and your own convictions and of course to stop worrying! Think about what feels right for you in life on a visceral level; whether it's with regard to the person you are dating, the food you are eating or the job you are in. That gut instinct is usually right. You may not be able to control all events in your life but it is certainly within you power to control how you deal with what life confronts you. All experiences in life are just a series of learning lessons, some harder than others but learning lessons nevertheless. The faster we learn, the quicker we grow.

Shortly after this time, I had an experience which was nothing short of groundbreaking and which also helped me shed some of the remaining negative weight I was still carrying on my shoulders of old. This unexpected experience helped me unlock a new door that had been waiting to be opened for a very long time.

Interestingly enough this new experience found me, rather than me going out in search of it. Remember the law of attraction? Sometimes what you need seeks you out but you had better be ready for it; else the moment will pass you by. I was invited by my cousin Henry to a small gathering of actors, in a rather swanky bar in London. Whilst getting to grips with a very tall bitter lemon - believe me when I tell you this drink was angry - BBC producer Peter Kinkead approached me to introduce himself to the girl in battle with the bitter lemon. After a small amount of polite verbal exchange, Peter said he would like to introduce me to his good friend Bernie, whose party it was. I turned to find myself being introduced to Bernard Hiller. Bernard is the acting coach to the stars. Having taught people such as Cameron Diaz and Chace Crawford and worked with many numerous others including; Jeff Goldblum, Billy Crystal, Richard Dreyfuss, Vanessa Hudgens and Jennifer Garner, his classes are highly sought out and have even received a public recommendation from Leonardo DiCaprio. I was soon about to find out why.

After taking an overdose of happy, Bernie was soon to find himself as the receiver of the rather jolly persona and over-sized smile I was adorning that evening. In response, Bernie proceeded to present me with an invite to join his one-week master class. Wrongly believing that as I was a regular jobbing actress I did not require any further training - big mistake! - to my complete embarrassment, I found myself politely declining his offer; stupidly not realising at the time what an amazing opportunity was in fact being made to me. 'Okay, I get it, you're a chicken!' Bernie said. Boy, did this guy really know how to ruffle my feathers! Just like Michael J Fox's character Marty McFly in *Back to the Future*, no one calls Emma Fletcher a chicken! Bernie had fathomed me out and he knew how to get to me! 'I am not a chicken!' I said, ruffling my feathers some more. 'In fact, I'll do the course just to show you I'm not!' Bernie shook my hand and smiled a knowing smile.

When I tell you this class forced me to face my demons, that is an understatement. During the second day of the course one of the most amazing things happened, which I will never forget. Whilst participating in one of the acting exercises, I found myself sitting on the floor and suddenly crying like I had not cried since the day Claudia died and I couldn't stop. The sound that came out of my body was terrific. It was almost as if it were not coming from me.

I was literally wailing. It was a deep rooted visceral sound and it was as if something, which had been buried deep inside of me and festering for a long time, had suddenly been let loose. I came to the realisation on some level I still blamed myself for Claudia's death. All these years I had managed to hide my grief behind a large, false smile: Smile and the world smiles with you. There is plenty to be said for smiling it is true. For one, it releases endorphins, which can help to create a more positive state of mind but when your smile is merely a façade, all you are really doing is covering up the pain. I had not smiled and meant it for years. My smile was indeed just a cover up. Bernie had seen straight through it and now my impenetrable armour had been barricaded and broken in battle by the truth. One by one, the thirty-four other students in the class came up to me and held me tightly; creating one large group hug; a ball, in which I was the nucleus, being held in place firmly by the rest of the group. And then the most amazing thing happened. Each and every one of the people in the ball, one after the other said 'I am here for you.' It was one of the most empowering moments in my life.

This moment was the start of me being able to release the block I had held onto for so many years. I changed my perception. If you recall, I told you earlier towards the start of the book, perception is really just our mind's way of dealing with our circumstances. If you can change your perception of an event, then you can change your entire outlook and how you deal emotionally with that event. The event cannot change but your perception of it can and once this change occurs its circumstances do not need to rule your mind any longer. I started to realise I was able to stop blaming myself for Claudia's death. I felt free. My soul felt cleansed. The students commented on how my face literally changed its appearance and how after this experience I looked at peace. I was finally released from my torment. Once more I was able to look in the mirror again and for the first time, in a very long time, I liked the person starring back at me.

This experience was an awakening and not just for me. Immediately after this a number of the other students in the class approached me and thanked me for my honesty and for opening up. They explained it had given them the chance to open up too. They revealed to me they had also lost a father, a brother, an uncle or a friend to suicide. It was as if someone had turned on a switch. Finally I had woken up and I felt alive once again. It is funny how one single moment can change everything. This moment did that for me. Perhaps it was long overdue and this experience just gave me that little extra nudge I needed but this experience helped me to remember; if you want to be able to allow yourself to love someone again or even to be loved by someone else, the first thing you have to be able to do is love yourself again first. It helped me forgive myself for the pain I have put myself through over the years and remind myself I deserve only the best. People get into abusive relationships all the time, as they don't love themselves. The person they search out and find becomes a reflection of their own negativity and the things they don't like about themselves. They seek out an abusive person in the belief that is all they deserve and are worthy of. Thus the abusive partner gives them affirmation of their beliefs. Bernie's class allowed me to re-find the courage to search deep inside my soul and rediscover the person I was before all my demons took over. I thank both Bernard Hiller and Peter Kinkead for encouraging me to take the course and Bernard for helping me re-discover myself again, as I had been lost for many years. So if you're considering Botox for those worry lines, my advice would be to take Bernard Hiller's course instead! It's an instant solution to getting rid of those nagging doubts and deep-set lines. I looked and felt ten years younger after I had completed the course. I had re-found my real smile again and I liked the feeling enough to tell myself I never want to allow myself to go back to the way I was feeling beforehand.

At the end of the week, Bernie told me he knew I was meant to do the course and he knew what he needed to say to give me the strength to take the plunge. When I argue this man is a miracle worker that is an understatement. His course saved me from myself and to think I nearly missed the opportunity of being part of a life changing experience is shameful. Acting - and for that matter, life - is not a sport; it is a skill, which continually needs fine-tuning. Bernard also helped me realise, in order to be a good actor, one needs to be a whole and rounded person and comfortable with themselves first. This is also true of life. Your acting and your life become one; a sentiment which was also endorsed on the course by the amazing actor Iain Glenn and screenwriter Simon Beaufoy, both who graciously gave up their precious time to come and talk to the actors. It dawned on me, as an actor, any part of your own life you are not comfortable with is soon revealed on the stage for the world to see. This of course is also true in life. So you had better be ready before you reveal yourself to the world and you had better of worked on yourself before that time occurs because no man is an island and not one person can hide behind him or herself forever.

Fun awards were given out on the last day and an even larger smile was placed on my face as I soon found myself being awarded 'the best breakthrough actress' on the course and being presented with a bag of 'Starbursts' to represent me being a star waiting to 'burst' into action. Well I did do a Gwyneth Paltrow and 'burst' into tears when everyone, including Bernie, cheered me on to receive my award! Bernie came up to me on the last day of the course and said 'You have talent. You need to become a star! Imagine how amazing it would be if you became a star after all the upset you have gone through in your life. You have an amazing story to tell the world. Write your book. Write about everything you have been through. You have the chance to give people inspiration. You have been through enough sadness, now it is your time to shine.'

***Learn to become a master of your thoughts, for only then will you truly be free.*** - Emma Fletcher

# 14

# An Actor's Life for Me

**The future belongs to those who believe in the beauty of their dreams.** - Eleanor Roosevelt

*Paul: Having experienced many of the highs and lows of working as a professional actress, Emma feels she is more than able to share some nuggets of advice for any would-be actor who is serious about a career in the profession. In this chapter, Fletcher does just that. Her advice is, nevertheless, capable of lending itself to any profession and useful reading material for career-minded individual.*

Emma: When someone is a right side of the brain user and truly has an artistic flair, it usually means they are in for a hard struggle in life. I'm not talking here about people who are just fame seekers, I'm talking about those of us who are governed by our creative streak and live and breathe this creativity. The world doesn't cater properly in the financial department for the creative minded soul, especially for actors, who came about once upon a time as the court jester. In fact the jester started out life as a Jewish resident in the courts of the Roman Empire. They would entertain the ruling house in an attempt to earn a few coins. Both Eva Schloss, Bettine Le Beau and a number of holocaust survivors have expressed to me how Jews would also gather together with entertaining stories during their times in the prison camps, as this was one of the only methods of retaining a positive state of mind; thus giving people a fighting chance at survival.

Today the actor is seen either as an out of work bum or glorified to such high, almost unreasonable iconic status. If you are an 'A-lister', you may find yourselves completely over paid in comparison to the job you do. At the lower end of the scale, any profession in the arts and those seeking it out, continue to find themselves faced with years of financial battle and heartache lying in the waters ahead. Yet they continue to search out this path heedless of this destiny, be it as a painter, musician, singer, dancer, thespian or any other creative talent that drives them, as without remaining true to this drive they are lost.

A creative streak is not and should not be one that can be ignored if it drives the very essence of who you are and is a desire, which just like any other, needs to be nurtured and fed properly. I am living proof this desire can be met properly and one does not need to starve themself in the process. It goes back to just being a case of focusing your thoughts and energies on the right things to achieve your goals. My advice is to find a way to express your artistic flair with a balanced healthy diet and a happy disposition!

I'm so grateful my parents did encourage me to take the path of an alternative career first, as ironically having other skills under my belt has ultimately been the key to allowing me to eventually follow my passion and make a living from it. So in this following chapter, I would like to give you, the budding actor, some tricks of the trade I have learnt over the last few years and some friendly tips to keep your head above choppy waters, if you are planning to enter the unforgiving world of acting. As it happens, the ideas I would like to impart with you I believe don't necessarily equate just to helping the aspiring actor alone. I feel they are business skills which, when used correctly, can also be transferred to serve up a dish of complimentary success in any job or ambition.

The first thing I would say is 'be a realist' and know you niche. Don't apply for the role of the redhead who is in her late forties, if you are blonde and your playing age is early thirties or under! Know your market, so that when you get to the audition there are no unpleasant surprises for you or the casting director. Remember, the casting director is the nerve centre of the industry, so you really do want to keep them happy! (I would also highly recommend keeping a note for future reference of all the casting directors or employers who have ever shown an interest in your work.) Be canny and think like a casting director or future employer when placing yourself up for a job. Ask yourself 'Would I employ me?' and if not 'Why not?' Of course meeting Kenneth

Branagh was one of those unusually pleasant surprises of not being a realist but normally, aspiring to become a professional tale-telling Baron Munchausen or fibbing Pinocchio is not a wise plan.

So as said, be a realist when applying for jobs, unless you are content with never getting any responses to your applications. In the same manner, just as you must be a realist you also need to take a chance. I am what one could call a calculated risk-taker. This means I take chances but I always try and work out the risk factor in advance and consider all possible outcomes of taking those risks first. I weigh up all the possible pros and cons, so that hopefully there won't be too many nasty surprises waiting for me on the other side but that doesn't mean I have to stop taking a chance. It is a fine balancing act but do nevertheless take a chance, as you never know when it might pay off. So do take a chance but if you're going to jump into the deep end of the pool, you'd better make certain you can swim first! Okay, so don't say you can ride a motor bike if you've never sat on a bike in your life, although I do know an actor who did just this and got the part but I really wouldn't advise it. In fact, usually you might get shouted at by the casting director and struck off their books for wasting their time if you get to the audition and say 'Erm, I don't actually participate in the mastication of meat' when auditioning for one of Maccie D's finest. I have had to let auditions go when food was related because either meet or fish was involved or some type of non-kosher substance. That is a choice I have made. You need to know early into your career what you are and are not prepared to do and what skills you can honestly make claim to. Do however put yourself forward for a part if it is just a case of being slightly unsure if your look fits the bill. Let the casting director be the judge of that. My audition for Sleuth alongside a plethora of Rossellini look-a-likes bears weight to this. You can't be your own judge and juror at all times, plus there is such a thing as hair dye!

After my 'Have you met Ken?' experience, I gained a lot of practice at auditioning. I found the best way to get the job is to eliminate your competition first and no, I'm not talking about reaching for Arnie's Uzi nine millimetres and becoming The

Acting Annihilator or telling the competition to tread carefully down that rather steep flight of stairs on a dark night. I'm talking about the ability to recognise you don't have any competition! That's right, you don't have any competition. Believe you are the best person for the job. Become your own avatar. It's a simple shift in perception again. So instead of reaching for the nine millimetres, think more cloak and dagger. Don't allow yourself to get involved in the idle chit-chat and gossip grenade heading your way from your quidnunc neighbour auditionees, gleefully taking the chance to tell you ever so helpfully at every possible opportunity about all their previous television and theatre appearances and why they are so much better equipped for this role than you; whilst they carefully and surreptitiously usurp your derrière from beneath the very chair on which you sit. Love thy neighbour but also keep your own counsel and stay calm and focused on your goal, which is to complete the audition or interview process to your best potential.

Okay, so perhaps there was one time I stretched the truth a little to get the job but if you're going to stretch the truth, at least make it interesting! I was approached by a producer, who was casting an advertising campaign for a very well known telephone company, to participate as lead in the shoot. 'Fantastic!' I said. 'Of course I would love the job!' 'That's great!' the casting director said 'And could you also bring your boyfriend to appear in the shoot too, as we are looking for a real couple?' Now at this particular point in time I was single. 'I need a man!' I thought. I rang up my good friend and actor Robert Hartley Wainwright, who I had worked with a number of times before now and said 'Rob, how do you fancy being my boyfriend for the day?' 'Lovely!' he said. If only I could tell you it ended there. I informed the casting director my boyfriend had agreed to carry out the job with me. 'That's great!' she said again. 'Now could you send me some natural pictures of you both together before tomorrow, so we can see your on-screen chemistry?' The hours which followed were something akin to the chaos witnessed in a *Carry On* film. As quick as a flash Rob got on the train and met up with me in a local shopping centre, bringing with him a selection of different tops. My poor friend Debbie Chazen was then unwittingly dragged into the plot. 'Right' I informed Debbie 'you are now part of a conspiracy to make a casting director believe Rob and I are really a couple!' Debbie took a couple of photographs of Rob and I after which she strangely had to dash off! Actually, she really did have plans. Rob and I for the next hour ran around the shopping centre, like two headless chickens, going into different restaurants, each time changing our tops beforehand and accosting the waiters to take our picture in different loved-up poses. We made a lovely couple actually and managed to successfully fool the casting director into giving us the job! Did we feel a little guilty about it? Of course not, we're actors! For a start, if the company were that concerned about hiring 'real people' they shouldn't have approached an actor. Am I right, or am I right?

So in order to get that job, keep telling yourself the job is going to be yours. This really is the only place from which to start with anything in life, as even if you don't get the job you are giving yourself the best fighting chance. If you start out with a negative outlook then you are already failing yourself and this will inevitably come through to any future employer in the interview room. For if you don't believe in yourself, then why should anyone else? I once experienced in the audition holding area one of my neighbour auditionees convincing herself she was way too ugly for the job! If you are already on a career suicide mission, then why bother attending the interview? Although I have my own personal issues with the way I look, I don't take those issues into the audition room. I walk in with an air of confidence in the belief I really am the best person for the job. Come on guys, we're actors! Even if you don't really belief in yourself start acting as if you do! The act will soon catch-up with reality and before you can say 'beauty queen' what do you know? You will soon find you've been crowned 'Miss Everything of the Year'! If I am too ugly for the role, let the casting director be the judge of that! I don't have to spoon-feed them the thought and in any case, we all know how you walk and hold yourself can indeed affect the entire image you portray. Attraction is not just about the way someone looks but about his or her body language too. So walk into that audition room or interview room with an air of confidence and literally make yourself attractive to your future employer.

The particular audition in question above however, was for a high-profile music video, being cast by top casting director and television judge, Mark Summers. This same neighbouring auditionee turned to me and said 'Mark can be very open about his feelings towards the way people look'. You may be lucky enough to have witnessed his formidable style of approach on television. Simon Cowell, eat your heart out! This girl continued to give me the heads up that 'If Mark thinks you are ugly, he will tell you on the spot!' Well there's a confidence booster! To make matters worse, the room we were about to carry out our audition in, in London's famous Pineapple Dance studios, was open plan. So each girl waiting to audition was watching everyone else's performance. Okay I admit, my ugly insecurities did indeed start to rear their vicious little heads and I was now highly nervous at the prospect Mark might say to me 'too ugly!' in front of a host of attractive girls. The butterflies in my stomach were already into the second act of their full-blown tango; moving sharply one-way, then with extreme vigour back in the opposite direction. I was however still determined to walk into that audition room with my head held high and an air of confidence about my person. My name was called. I approached Mark with extreme caution. I walked up to him slowly then stopped. Mark gently cupped my face in his hand, turned my head from one side to the other then nodded for me to commence my audition. I took a deep, sharp intake of breath and told myself 'you are beautiful!' in the hope this would come out in my body language. At the end of my audition Mark informed me it was a good audition. I didn't get the job but was grateful to Mark for not reinforcing my 'little uglies'. But wait. Perhaps the credit should really go out to myself for not reinforcing my insecurities or allowing myself to feed them a five-course meal in that audition room. For that moment I allowed myself to believe I truly was that crowned beauty, standing before Mark and whatever the outcome, it felt good to wear that label.

Even although you are an actor who is capable of portraying many different personalities and guises, the director and producer still want to see what you personally have to bring to the role. This is true of any future employer. They are interested in your individuality, not just that of your neighbour and the best way to bring your own individuality to the table is indeed to stay calm and focused. So take some calming reading material into your audition, or the sides to go over, only as long as that doesn't panic you further. Obviously the idea is, by the time you go into the first audition for any part and certainly for those of you graced to get a call back, you should be confident enough to know the frills of your character and script by the audition stage. Unless of course you are carrying out a cold reading but personally I have always approached the director and asked if I can take half an hour out to familiarise myself with the script before my reading anyhow. Usually you will find the director is always very respectful of your professional attitude and will more often than not agree to this request. Don't forget, you are there to give your best performance and the director wants this as much as you do, so if that extra half hour will help you to give that award winning performance, then why would any director in their right mind refuse this request?

This 'time out' is also your chance to impress the director with your ability to 'learn' lines quickly too. I trained via the 'Method' school of acting approach, where we were actually trained not to learn the lines but learn the impulses, which lead to the intention and reason for saying the words. The idea is to act from instinct, in other words, I don't think of the words, just the feelings they evoke. In theory this should mean you will never give exactly the same performance twice, which should result in keeping your performance fresh. On the flip side of the coin, if you get it right, being instinctive in your acting also leads to similarities in each performance too. What this does mean, however, is your emotional interpretation of what is happening on the page and your internalisation of the words should propel you towards your action. So in theory, as long as you know where your body needs to move to next, the words should fall out of your mouth automatically!

At East 15 we were taught to act from impulse initially through the famous 'object exercises'. This activity requires the actor to carry out three very ordinary and mundane routines on stage, in succession, which lead to a finished event. This is not exactly high-stakes theatre. For example, getting ready to go out might

317

include: showering, getting dressed and putting on make-up or brushing hair. During the first week of acting school I decided to volunteer myself as first in line to take the plunge and carry out the very first object exercise. The director informed the class we had to 'prepare' thoroughly for this exercise. I hadn't quite understood the notion of 'prepping' yet, so when I had completed the exercise and the director asked for proof of my preparation, I dutifully produced a folded piece of paper from my bag; which was basically a shopping list of items I had brought into class to help aid the reality of my exercise. 'No!' he yelled. 'Where is your internal preparation?' 'Ah well, why didn't you say!' I thought to myself. 'That's easy! Surely that's inside of me and not something I could physically show anyone else anyhow?' I later learnt the director was looking for a song or scented candle or something that sparked an emotion to put me in a certain frame of mind for the start of the activity.

When we first started to prep for a piece of work it took most of us a whole minute to peak. The director informed us that one day we would all be able to get the internal prep down to a fine art of being able to call upon any emotion in a mere split second. None of us believed this was possible at that time but just as the director had said, I am now able to conjure up any emotion almost within a split second by going into my reserve bank of memories and their attached internal emotions, in order to use them on stage. I am also pleased to say, I am now also able to place a lid on these very same emotions when I have finished using them in my performance, just as quickly as I called upon them. This is so important for any actor to do, in order to remain personally detached from the emotions called upon for their performance, hence keeping themselves separated from these emotions and their associated memories in their own normal daily rhythm. Acting is of course just a study of life and this concept is also a lesson a number of people should learn to embrace as part of their everyday life skills, as so many people in life allow themselves to become continually held back by their past and its attached emotions. If we could all learn to embrace the now and place a lid on fraught emotions of old, there would be many more happy people walking the face of this earth. Just as an actor who is not

318

listening to how his acting partner is saying his lines and reacting accordingly is known as a selfish actor, this of course is also true of life. If you get stuck in one way of feeling about a situation, then you are not really interacting with life and are not reacting accordingly to your surroundings. This is why so many people become depressed. Just as an actor should stay in a scene, we also need to stay present in our daily interactions.

In fact acting should really be called reacting or 'being', as a number of directors in the States now refer to it. When you act you need to listen to what the other person you are acting alongside is saying to you and then allow yourself to be moved naturally in order to react. If you can't move yourself, then how do you expect to move anyone else? Allow yourself to hear and internalise the words as if it were the first time you are hearing them. Absorb what has been said to you and react naturally. A good speaker is a good listener. Remember; stay in the scene. This means when you learn your lines you must not allow yourself to get stuck in only one way of saying them. For example, think about what would be natural to say next from what you have just felt and this should bring you to the lines you need to say. This is what helps an actor to remain fresh in their approach. Start the scene small so you have somewhere to go with it and then build to a climax. It is the actor's job to make each scene exciting. Don't push the drama but instead play every moment with integrity and real emotions and allow the drama to naturally unfold and play itself out. Most importantly, don't create an attitude; let the moment create the attitude. Take this into the audition room with you and onto the stage and screen at all times throughout your career and you can't fail but to remain alive. Take this it into your own life and you will be an amazing person to be in the company of.

So by the end of that half-hour you should be able to walk into that audition room with confidence, throw the script on the floor and give your best performance off-book! I have done this a few times and believe me it always manages to secure you the role on being an impressive and brave move alone. Even if you don't get the words exactly right you are going to give a much better and

319

more believable performance when you are not holding the script in your hand and if nothing else, you will impress the director with your ability to pick things up quickly, so much so, that hopefully he or she just 'must have you in my show darling!' I would advise, however, if the writer is also present at audition, check with them first they do not mind you being slightly out of kilter with some of their words. The worst thing you can do is upset the writer! If the unthinkable instance occurs and you get some of the words wrong, try not to get flummoxed or break out in an Irish *Riverdance* of nerves and never, ever apologise with some sugar coated, wondrous lame excuse such as 'it's a full moon and I'm hormonal' or 'I got out of bed the wrong side this morning, slipped on the cat and hit my head on the floor!' No one is interested in a cocktail of excuses. Just keep going. This is a fundamental rule. Don't stop! It's not good kudos. Speaking of scripts, I would also advice a contingency of always keep a couple of opposing styled monologues stored in the recess of your brain. Don't be hoodwinked into a false security that there will always be a script waiting for you on the day, unless of course you have already safely received the sides in the palm of your hands beforehand. I recently turned up to an audition for a music video believing a script would be made available to me, there wasn't and I was asked to carry out my own monologue on the spot. After a little bit of coaxing my mind and mouth to come to a congenial agreement to move in sync, following my lips desperate attempt at a full-blown revolt against my brain, I successfully managed to pull a speech out of the bag and got the job. Be prepared for this eventuality, it could happen to you! I would also add be brave with your choices of how you read the script. Don't be afraid to be different. Give it a shot, you never know, it might just secure you the job.

If you are given feed-back from the director and asked to try the scene or monologue in a different way, with a different set of emotions, don't suddenly become a backseat driver in the audition room and start arguing with the director 'No, I really think this is how it should be played' as this is akin to literally shaking your own death-rattle. Quite often the director is just testing to see how well you can take direction. In any case, why would they ask you to stay longer if they thought you sucked? So, once you have managed to successfully crawl out from the six-foot grave you have just dug beneath your feet for yourself, listen to the director's advice and allow your performance to be guided by this. If you are however, someone who is easily offended by people and you are not open to change, then you are probably about to enter the wrong profession. To be able to survive in the acting industry, or in fact through life, you have to make this following oxymoron work for you: You need to have a balance of strength and humility. That is to say, you need be strong enough to not be offended by constructive criticism and yet also have the sense to use it wisely to help you develop. Likewise, you also need be humble enough to take the criticism in the first place.

Make sure you chose an audition piece you are familiar and comfortable with. An audition can be a nerve-wrenching experience at the best of times; so don't choose a speech which will add fuel to your nerves. Never apologise for your choice of speech or start with the precursor 'I only learnt it yesterday, so I may be a bit rusty' unless you are planning to cross the Rubicon and check out the other side of the door. Try and colour the speech with layers of depth and shape to keep it inspiring. If you choose a good speech it should help you find the layers naturally. It's your job to impress the director, so prepare yourself properly for the audition, as you only get one chance to make a first impression. Even if you are not right for that particular job, if you make a good impression the director may call upon your services to work with him or her on something else they are working on in the future, this has happened to me.

Back to the idea of having no competition; I am firmly of the belief that what is meant to be yours in life will come to you, so there really is no point in getting depressed if you don't get the role. If something is meant for you, then it will be yours - and that is why I say, you have no competition. This does not mean I am advising you to sit back on your laurels and do nothing to aid your success. Luck is not chance. You make your own luck and subsequently your own success but know when to change direction too. There really is no point in trying to flog a dead horse.

So to recap: when you go to an audition; keep a cool head on calm shoulders. Make a good impression. This should also include making both your introduction and exit positive, complete with a strong handshake. A good entrance and a strong exit leave a lasting impression and give out a sign of confidence in your own ability. Take your time to put yourself in the right moment emotionally and then off you go with your award winning speech. Oh and here's the science bit: only attend an audition or interview in a public space. If you are feeling a little queasy about the location spot for the meeting, don't go! It's as simple as that. If you really must go, however, take along a pal or at least tell a sensible adult where you are going before setting sail on the mother ship. Seriously guys, sorry to preach but I once attended a public audition, which was advertised as a breakdown for a television series in the vein of *Little Britain* and to be aired on CBS in the States but when I got to the audition I found the breakdown wasn't exactly as it said on the tin. In fact, it was a complete rouse and I found I had been lured into a web of porn! As you can imagine the only view of my backside they received was when I exited the room in a rather hasty retreat! It can happen to the best of us. So be wise and stay alive!

It is also worth checking out the production company you are auditioning for in advance; not only for safety's-sake but also to show an interest in the company and impress the producer with your knowledge of their historical output, as well as of course checking to see the company is exactly who they say they are and that they do really exist. I was once offered the lead role in a feature film and informed a very high-profile star would be playing alongside me. Upon my commencement of research into the production company, I happened to be invited that same week to a party with my old pal Albert, being hosted by West End producer Bill Kenwright. The star I was meant to be playing alongside, as fate would have it, happened to be present at the party, so I went up to him and asked about his participation in the film. It turned out he had never even heard of the film in question. Remember what I said about the truth eventually biting you directly on your derrière? This was indeed a fast catch-up with the truth and on this occasion I was glad it is such a small world. Obviously I didn't accept the role.

So what should you wear to your dream audition? My advice would be to wear either casual or smart attire, depending on the role but certainly don't feel the need to go to the audition dressed as Queen Elizabeth I, complete with iron corset and farthingale or some other diaphragm and chest constricting garment worn by the character you are auditioning for. The only time you can get away with dressing in character for an audition is for a commercial. I have a friend who dressed as a French maid, complete with mop attached to her hip, as this is what she explained to me the advert required or at least so she said! I've never done this before myself but my friend did nevertheless get the job. So with adverts I guess it really is whatever floats your boat!

Whether you or your auditioning neighbour are successful at attaining the role or not has, however, almost nothing to do with how many successful television appearances you have attached to your name and sometimes not even to do with 'how marvellous your audition was darling' but everything to do with the director and producer's choice and believe me, sometimes it's even the producer's mum who has the final say! So if the fruits of your labour are not successful and you don't get the role, don't give up. This doesn't mean your acting career is over. It simply means this particular role was not meant for you. It will be some other acting job that will get you that shiny Oscar. There is a role out there to suit everyone. Sometimes not getting the job really does just come down to the fact you have the wrong colour eyes or are too tall or too short to stand beside the leading lady or guy, unless of course that leading lady or guy is in fact you!

Recently I auditioned for the international musical *Girls Night*. I chose a speech from the play *Five Kinds of Silence* by Sheila Shenlagh. If you have ever read this play you will immediately know the intensity of it. The director, Jack Randall, praised me for my brave choice of speech and said he felt I had layered and coloured the piece very well. 'Excellent choices' he said. If you choose a memorable speech you know you are comfortable enough to perform well, then you will be remembered for all the right reasons. In fact so much so, Jack emailed me personally soon after the audition to tell me he was sorry he couldn't give me the job but on this occasion it really had come down to me having the wrong hair colour. He also said I was very welcome to audition for him again in the future. Receiving a personal email directly from the director is usually unheard of and not only did this give me such encouragement in my convictions as an actress but it also reminded me not to give up just because I didn't get one job.

Okay, so it's true when you don't get what you are striving for it can be a disappointment but sometimes the things we want the most are not always the things which will be good for us. When I don't get what I am aiming for I try and remind myself, if I know God gives me all I require to live a happy life, then perhaps the thing I desire which I am not being given is not good for me; or at least not good for me at this point in time, which is ultimately why God is not allowing me to have it. This mentality not only helps me get over disappointment but also helps me refocus my energies with complete clarity on the next new idea or project. Similarly, sometimes when I am held up at a traffic light, I tell myself it is just God's way of pressing the pause button, to adjust my day so that everything will be in sync the way He has planned. So if you don't get the job please don't beat yourself up over it. Keep telling yourself it just wasn't meant for you at this time. Success is not convenient; be prepared to win and equally be prepared to loose. I know people who beat themselves up on a regular basis when they don't get the job and this mentality only prevents them from moving forward in their career. They are so busy beating themselves up over their last pitfall that when they get offered the next audition they are still focusing on the last job they didn't get and taking this energy into their next audition. Don't take bad energy into the audition room. Directors are like pit-balls. They can smell fear! Okay, so I admit, I have in the past been great at beating myself up over failed relationships but when it comes to business I put on my business hat and that's that! I'm business all the way. I remain focused, on task and professional at all times. I believe it is this mentality, which usually lands me the role. A successful audition is not just about how well you can 'read' the lines, it is also about giving across the notion you are a professional and someone the director and crew would find pleasurable and easy-going to work with.

You've got your dream job. Congratulations! Roll the Fletcher theme tune and get out the glass. Now it's time to go and celebrate with a night out on the town! A word of advice: if you're planning to party into the early hours, choosing the night before the shoot is not a good plan. Always make sure you turn up to the job looking awake! It's not professional to look like you are still suffering from the night before (you know who you are!) walking in with a bottle of white-eye in one hand and a strong double, double caffè macchiato in the other. Tardiness does not go down well with directors, so make sure you turn up on time and leave yourself plenty of extra time for traffic or train delays. I'm not suggesting you set anchor and take residency in the theatre space or sound stage the night before, however nice the set might be; but do leave yourself plenty of time to arrive in a relaxed frame of mind and if you are driving to the audition ensure you have filled up the tank the night before. If you are anything like me and find yourself always on the go, sometimes checking the simple things in life like a full tank of gas can escape you. There is a small part of me that expects the car to constantly keep running on its own. Don't trust this to be the case!

Ladies (and gentlemen too, if the shoe fits) don't turn up to the shoot wearing make-up if you have already been advised there will be a make-up team on set. This only wastes time and frustrates the make-up team if they have to remove all your make-up before putting it on you again - and trust me; one person you do not want to get on the wrong side of is the hair or make-up artist! A tip worth a million: exfoliate your face and lips the morning of the shoot and the make-up artist will be your best friend forever.

Do however take reading material to the shoot. This may well be your trusty companion for the day and be your survival kit during those long waits between shots, when the crew are dismantling and setting up again.

Creating a good impression on the day and building a good working relationship with the people you are working with is so important. I have often been approached by directors I have worked with to work with them again on other projects. This is not necessarily because I am the better actress than someone else but because, I believe, they saw in me someone they found reliable and easy to work with. Now there really is only one thing left for you to do - act your little socks off, then give yourself a huge pat on the back for all your hard work!

Now here's a big don't: Don't be a prima donna! (And before you say it, my little toilet request during the *Mystery Files* shoot does not count!) One particular television commercial I worked on, the director had placed two chairs outside on set, one for me and one for my leading man. Whilst my leading man was being filmed I was contentedly sitting on the ground beside my chair (I know my place guys!) One of the crew innocently sat on my chair and before you knew it the director leapt on them shouting: 'That chair is for Emma!' I politely explained to the director I was actually very happy where I was. He responded: 'But that is your chair and has been placed there for you!' Now this was a very new experience to me and it actually made me feel a little uneasy, so I said to the director 'Do you think I am a prima donna?' to which he responded with a resounding 'Of course not!' 'Do you like working with prima donnas?' I continued. His response was yet again another resounding 'Of course not!' 'So why,' I asked 'are you so intent on turning me into one?' The director appreciated what I was saying but it occurred to me his rather large reaction to one of the crew sitting on 'my chair' was probably born from the many times he had been forced to appease a situation because an actress was indeed behaving like a prima donna. He was merely trying to pre-empt what he thought might be the case of yet another prima donna blow-up and probably felt he should dive in to save the day before it reached that point of no return. I have myself been witness to an actress hissy-fit and believe you me, it ain't a pretty sight! So ladies, please behave like ladies, else it gives the rest of us a bad name. We are all replaceable in this industry, whoever you are and no one wants to work with a prima donna twice!

So how do you get the next job? Ideally I would advise get a good agent. If however you do not have the luxury of a good agent or indeed an agent at all, the secret is all in the marketing. How successful you are is all about how well you market yourself. If you market yourself the right way, then hopefully not getting the job won't happen to you too often. It all starts with knowing your own worth as an actor. If you don't know your market value, then how do you expect others to know? You are a business. Market and place a value on yourself as such. For a start, why work for free? If you were hiring an accountant, would you expect them to work for free? Of course you wouldn't! Hiring out an accountant for free is unheard of. So why should you, a professional working actor work for free? You are a professional after all, are you not?

In this industry you really are only as good as your last job, so you'd better make sure your last job was a good one! The key to success in the acting industry, as indeed in most industries, has a great deal to do with representing yourself correctly. When casting directors look at your resumé they want to see each of your credits is attached to either a good production house or a good director, else they will strike any credit that is not from your resumé. So choose the jobs you apply for carefully and if you have an agent or manager, make sure they are also only applying to the jobs, which are the right type of jobs for you. I am very fortunate as my current agent and I, just as my previous agent did too, work as a team on my career. This means my agent allows me to apply for jobs independently and quite often, unless she has had a lot of input in the job once I get it, she won't take commission from me. I do however, always touch base with my agent and let her know of any job I am working on, even if it is one I attained for myself. I would advice however; if you are going to choose your own acting jobs to apply for, make your choices based on projects, which will help advance your career.

Choice is a luxury. With choice comes freedom, so leave yourself time to make the right choices and choose wisely. If you choose to spend your time working on a job, which is not going to advance your career in any shape or form then you are wasting precious time and whilst you are busily tying yourself up to a dead-end acting job, you might be missing out on an opportunity better suited to your capabilities. Again, no other profession would expect you to keep taking jobs which don't advance your career, so why should you as an actor? If you have the luxury of an agent then check out the jobs you apply for with them first if you are concerned. Because we all know, a happy agent is a happy artist! Incidentally, you may recall at the start of the last chapter I told you I originally started out my acting career with four agents. Whilst this seemed like a good idea at first, as I believed this would serve to generate me more work, I soon realised it was not. On a couple of occasions two of the agents both placed me forward for the same job and if this was not bad enough, they both placed me up for different parts. This did not make for a very happy casting director and I don't think either agent was particularly jumping over the moon with joy at the thought of it either. My advice would be, if you want to retain a good working relationship with your agent just stick to having the one because greed can only lead to gluttony!

I have recently reached a cornerstone in my career where directors are approaching either my agent or myself directly to offer me work, based upon my previous experience alone and sometimes skipping the audition process altogether. I now find myself in a position to be choosier about the work I take. This basically means I am able to turn down jobs I feel are not right for me, without fearing I have made a bad choice by turning down work; especially as every actor will tell you, including me, if you are getting any offers of work in this industry you should feel grateful. This shouldn't, however, stop you making choices about the work you take. For example, I was recently offered to be the face of what would have been my second bingo commercial. Oddly enough it didn't seem to bother this company I had carried out the lead in a commercial for one of their competitors. Tip: always read the small print! Upon reading the contract I found a small disclaimer at the bottom, which read that as the face of this company's brand I would not be allowed to undertake any other acting work for a whole year without their approval first. Of course my agent would love that - not - and I can't say it was particularly making me reach for the champagne flutes myself. So I turned the job down. This job was not so hard to turn down but I have had other jobs presented to me, which I have had to turn down as they would have been wrong for me to do for one reason or another but believe me, turning down any work in this industry does not get any easier.

I have worked very hard to get to the point in my career where I feel I am comfortable to be able to turn down jobs which feel wrong for me but the decision to turn down work hasn't happened over night. It has been a hard slog to get to a place where I am starting to feel more at ease with being able to say 'I am a professional actress. I really can do this'. I have no illusions of grandeur and am aware my acting career may not and probably will not last forever and I am grateful for each day that I am able to live my dream. In many ways I am always a little surprised each time I get the next job but I have always said I will only give up acting either when it gives up on me or ceases to become enjoyable. Friends ask me 'Do you enjoy what you do?' and I ask them 'Are you insane? No one in their right mind would be an actor if they didn't enjoy it!' Acting isn't a vocation; it's a hard, unforgiving, precarious career choice. You never know from one day to the next if you will be working and still able to continue to call yourself a 'jobbing' actor or if you will be using the title of a 'resting' actor but when you do get the job, the satisfaction that comes from the performance makes all the hard work and the chase worthwhile. Acting is not the kind of job that comes with an easy life or an instruction manual (although I'm hoping for some of you this chapter might help guide you in the right direction) and yes, in many ways I wish I didn't desire it so much but when you've been bitten by the acting bug there really is no escape. So yes, I do love what I do - and yes, being a little crazy helps too!

I would advice, if you are serious about a career in acting and again I would advice the following for any new venture you are undertaking in life, to have a business plan for you company because as the old saying goes 'if you fail to plan, then you plan to fail.' This saying is so true. Create your own brand. Create a company name and perhaps even a logo. Remember, as an actor you are your own company and your stage name is your company brand. In the last semester at East 15 we were advised to register our stage names with Equity and were also advised to run our ideas for a stage name via the head of the school first. I recall a number of other students rushing to the front of the line with their glorious and exotic ideas for a stage name. I too approached the head of the school with a list of surnames attached to my own first name. Each idea I presented to the head of the school was met with a resounding 'no, that doesn't work', until finally he said 'Emma, what is your second name?' 'Fletcher' I replied 'I like it. Use it' he said. The key for picking a brand or stage name is to choose something you are comfortable with and something that is easy for people to say and to remember but more importantly, it should be a name which, when called you will remember to answer to!

I have worked hard to turn my name into a brand but I have also managed to detach myself from it. When I see myself in a commercial or even the picture on the front of this book, I separate myself from that person. That person is to me that girl named Emma Fletcher, with the styled hair and nice make-up and good lighting. I don't look like that all of the time. Oh don't get me wrong, I do like to take pride in my appearance but to look like these images all the time I would literally have to walk around with a lighting crew and make-up artist attached to my hip! When I see myself on television, or someone tells me they have seen me on television, I always think: 'Ooh, they're talking about her again!' A complete dichotomy and slightly 'schizo' maybe - what can I tell you; it runs in the family - but it keeps me from getting sucked into the image that is brand Fletcher and keeps my feet firmly on terra firma. The Emma Fletcher on television is not the same Emma Fletcher I am confiding with you about in this book. That Emma Fletcher is the brand name I have created for myself, the persona that enters an audition or interview room with me. I believe to remain grounded and on top of your career it really is important to not get sucked into your own image or the fame game.

Get a personal website. This doesn't have to be an expensive venture but it does say 'I am professional at what I do.' Keep it simple. Casting directors are simple folk. They don't like to be made to sift through loads of footage or loads of anything for that matter. They just don't have the time. So don't pull all the video footage you've ever had taken of you and place it on the site. Leave the ones of your family picnic where they belong - at home in the attic. Get a showreel and put this on your website. Your showreel should speak volumes about your capabilities on its own merit, even aside from your résumé. Only place your best work on your showreel. There are mixed opinions in the industry about whether you should include a montage at the start of your showreel or not, so I shall leave this one for you to decide. As a rule of thumb, a montage will only help you with commercial agents. In total, your website should say: 'You need me' not scream out 'I need you!' Even if that is secretly how you feel, keep it a secret! Success is attained by setting your goals higher; so step up to the next rung of the ladder and face the dizzy heights. Embrace your destiny. The artist Salvador Dali rose to fame by gatecrashing elite parties and wearing an eye-catching moustache and exceedingly loud clothes, which yelled: 'Look at me.' Once he felt he had caught everyone's attention, he would announce in a rather exaggerated manner he was leaving the party to attend an even better one! Of course this left everyone asking who he was, immediately incrementing his profile. Clever, eh? Dali knew the key to success is to surround yourself with people who can teach you something and to compare yourself only to the best. Now I'm not suggesting you gatecrash your way to stardom wearing a moustache and comparing yourself to iconic screen legends if you are only at the start of your career, as fun as that may be but I am suggesting you promote yourself in a manner which states you are a professional working actor. Remember; you are the best person for the job and they would be lucky to hire your services.

To stay on top of your game you need to stay healthy. Your body, mind and soul all need to be in tune and they all need fuel to keep them working properly. For me, this fuel and ammunition comes in the form of a healthy balanced diet, relaxation and exercise, which could even come in the form of the occasional shape throwing on the dance floor! Okay, so I admit, I'm a workaholic it's true but I do try and apportion this with a heavy dose of family and friends. I always try to make time for the people who really matter to me and I always will but sometimes, I admit, I forget to make time for myself. I don't recall the last time I took a proper vacation and trips to study at a seminary in Jerusalem or a networking trip to the city of angels don't count as relaxing by the way; so this means I have to find other ways to relax. The last time I can recall having a really relaxing break was a number of years ago. I went to Spain with a group of girlie friends. Dane Bowers was the resident deejay at the hotel we were staying in and as there were not many other young people staying in our remote hotel, we had Mr Bowers as our own personal deejay for the entire holiday. It was great and made for many a fun night of shape throwing on the dance floor, which certainly kept me fit, albeit not the most relaxing break I've ever had.

I must confess, I've never found relaxing comes easily to me. In fact I find relaxing positively hard work! Relaxing is an art. I get so caught up in my job and the constant decision making it involves, I sometimes forget to take the time to sit back and look at just how far I have come and what I have actually achieved. Okay, I may only be on the first rung of the ladder but at least I'm on the ladder! The problem is, I am a perfectionist and I am still learning to delegate in certain areas of my life, so that I can leave myself quality time to just relax. Every second of the day our lives are continually filled with decision making; you're just about to get into that nice warm bath when the telephone rings. Pop quiz: what do you do? Do you answer the telephone or just let it ring? I'm so sure there is a device in my telephone which causes it to ring every time I step foot in the bath! So next time you run the bath, question: do you take the telephone off the hook first, switch to ansa-phone or pick it up? And what about those big-life decisions? Do I break-up with the guy, or marry him? Obviously when your decision involves someone else's feelings you have to be considerate of that before you say 'I do', 'I don't' 'not ever' or even 'let me just sleep on that – alone!' but you also have to remain true to yourself. The point is, no decision can be made, however big or small, if you are so worn out you can't even think straight. Relaxing is not only important for our health but for retaining clarity.

In the hectic generation we live in we can become so accustomed to living with stress that after a fashion we barely recognise it is even there. Stress, however, hasn't forgotten you! Stress can cause doubt and doubt can interfere with you achieving your goals. This is why it is so important to learn to relax. Relaxation is the important ingredient in life, which serves to keep us grounded. So try and work out what factors trigger your stress. If you are someone who always finds themself in the position of reacting to every situation in a stressful manner, then refocus your thoughts to channel your emotions in a more productive way. This will allow you to remain calm before entering into a highly charged dialogue with the ever-ready set of circumstances awaiting your imminent arrival.

Being a perfectionist is not always a good thing, as it means I have been known to work till I drop, sometimes even to the point of forgetting to eat; which believe me does not help your performance in the slightest. One such time was as follows; at the start of this year I was approached to encompass the identity of a nefarious mother in the heavy rock band Sanguine's latest music video, *For Love*. The breakdown for the shoot explained it would be a Burtonesque styled fairytale, horror and placed in a very grand setting. This was a completely fair description. We were filming in the gorgeous surroundings of Thursley, in the stunning grounds of a mansion once belonging to Queen's drummer Roger Taylor and before that to members of the band Pink Floyd. This mansion was also where Freddy Mercury had spent his last year of life, whilst in remission from his illness. In fact, the house was so grand, even the kitchen was worthy of its own postcode!

The day of filming was long and intense but nevertheless fun. Both the actor playing my husband and I went at our roles like troopers and didn't stop all day for love nor money or for that matter for food or water in the burning heat of summer. Big mistake! Halfway through the day, as the director Carl Shanahan shouted 'Action', suddenly the room went dark and I felt my legs turn to jelly. I was going down! I have never fainted before in my life, only coming closest to it when I had my moment of exhaustion around the rabbi's dinner table but never before a complete blackout, this however this was a close call. My fellow actor caught me and gently walked me to the sofa. I felt a bit of an idiot actually but everyone was very understanding, rushing around me with fans, water and food. Talk about your prima donna!

So now I force myself to place time in my busy diary for both food and relaxation! This relaxation period allows me to reenergize and to refocus my goals. I call this period of relaxation 'brain rejuvenation'. I go and treat myself to a body massage or pedicure. In fact one of my favourite things used to be to treat myself to an Indian Head massage at my local hair salon, to relieve the usual tension headaches and migraines I have suffered from over the years. I would then pop into Subway sandwiches, which was next door but one, for my usual veggie sub. I love Subway sandwiches but if I'm honest that wasn't my only reason for my frequent visits. It was also to exchange my regular hello to the cutie behind the counter, who by the way eventually left Subway to become one quarter of the band JLS. See, I told you he was a cutie and this was definitely a fine way to relieve a migraine! Sorry, I digress. So moving swiftly back to where we left off before I decided to take my little scenic diversion, the above is how I recharge my batteries for the next round.

It is so important to learn to just relax. Relaxing not only rejuvenates our mind and our soul but also helps us maintain a healthy mindset, allowing us to stay motivated. I would also highly recommend that as well as placing time in your overcrowded diary every day to relax; you also do three things every day, which make you happy. Invest in a little you time. Getting a good night's kip is another important way to rejuvenate your body. I can't stress enough (see I'm stressing again!) how important it is for an actor or indeed any professional to be rested in order to be able continue their route of success. Just like your car needs a regular service, your body also needs a regular *MOT* too.

So here are the six ingredients, in my little home recipe, to the art of relaxing:

1. Remove all telephones from hook (or place on silent)
2. Draw a bath
3. Poor in bubbles
4. Play relaxing music (candles and wine optional)
5. Sink slowly into the bath (don't forget to undress first!)
6. Switch off your mind and just allow yourself to unwind and relax in a halcyon of bubbles!

Now the next time you need to relax, wherever you are, think of that relaxing bath and what it felt like to be in it and use this memory as a trigger to place your mind back into a mode of immediate relaxation again.

If after all the above you are still thinking of becoming an actor, whilst I would not advise you place too many open castings in your diary, everyone should experience at least one, if nothing else for the sheer insanity of the experience! Advice: take your sleeping bag, as you may be there a while! Whilst open castings may well be very worthwhile for dancers and musical theatre performers, it is a whole different ball game for stage or film acting, which as a rule does not usually involve open castings and for very good reason may I add. Be warned: if you aren't waiting outside the doors the night before the casting, there is a good chance you may not get seen. In fact, I know many people who have waited patiently in line for their turn to get to the front only to be told when they got there 'Sorry we're closing our doors now'. I've actually born witness to a foray of extremely frustrated actors actually beating down a door crying: 'Let me in, I've come from another country to be here!' This is obviously not the best mindset to enter an audition with!

Very early on in my career, in fact probably around the very first few weeks after graduating from acting school, I heard word of an open casting for a Boots commercial. I arrived with an actress friend and we found it was completely empty when we got there. Result! My friend, however, needed to use the bathroom and after I had given her the 'Why didn't you go before we left?' lecture, I started to realise rather quickly the mere mention of the word toilet meant I now needed it too! Both of us left the very small line of actors, knowing this was probably not a good plan. Not even five minutes later, when we re-found our way back to the holding area, we returned to find ourselves face to face with a line of actors stretching to infinity and beyond. We waited hours to be seen amidst the hundreds of faces and only got seen eventually because we both happened to have a last name which started with a letter high up in the alphabet; although if truth be told I was seriously getting ready to change my last name by deed pole there and then to anything starting with the letter 'A!' to hurry up the process. In just under a week after the casting I received a telephone call from casting director Simon Allen's PA. I had out of all the hundreds of girls been whittled down to a recall along with only six others. Okay, so on this occasion I did not get the gig but I knew I was now on Simon's radar. Over a year later, I heard Simon Allen was now holding an open casting for the new 118 118 commercial. Knowing that Simon now knew who I was, I thought I would retry my luck. This time I got there early and made sure I had been to the toilet first! Out of all the hundreds of people that applied for the job, guess who got offered the role? Yours truly! So it just goes to show, sometimes you do have to put that little extra bit of effort in to give yourself a fighting chance.

A year after the Boots casting I was offered a closed casting (invite only) to a Halifax advert. When I got there I found my agent had been given incorrect information and again it was actually an open casting. As I had another audition to attend later that day the other side of London, I decided I could not stay for the Halifax casting. Just as I was about to leave, a lady from the casting company started to walk down the line giving every one a number. As she was approaching me rather rapidly I stayed just to inform her of my decision to leave. Then a funny thing happened. The lady whispered in my ear: 'Don't leave. You are exactly *who* the client is looking for.' Suddenly I got pushed to the front of the line, had my photograph taken and said a few words to camera, then left for my next audition. Later that day I received a call from my agent to say I had got the Halifax job! Now I'm not quite sure why this was the process that occurred for me to get this job but as you can see, it's always worth going to high-profile castings if you think you might be in with a chance of attaining the role.

So what happens when you are offered an excellent acting job but an even better audition at exactly the same time? Most people say: 'Take the money and run!' Right? I agree it is always better to take the job on offer. However, the Fletcher charm and continual persistence does not end there! In these situations it is always worth politely asking the casting director who is casting the audition and sometimes even the director of the shoot, if schedules could be changed. 'What?' I hear you cry. 'Are you crazy?' Oh yes my friends, this is called 'chutzpah!' Let the back of the throat roll on the sound of the 'ch'! It's a guttural sound. This word is always used with an exclamation mark and if it is not, then it should be. It means 'pleasant cheek' and I have plenty of it. If someone likes you enough, believe me they will shift things around to either keep you on the job or see you at audition level. Now I'm not suggesting you turn into the goddess Caligo, creating complete chaos in your wake, expecting heaven and earth to move around your plans, heaven or earth forbid but if you don't ask you don't get. Right? It really is that simple. It's all about putting on your business hat and knowing your self-worth again and about making things work for you. I can't tell you how many times this approach has worked for me and resulted in me getting the two jobs instead of just the one. If you let people know you are already scheduled on a shoot on the time slot they have offered you, you will be amazed how much this just makes people want you even more. They respect you and what's more you become a sought after commodity. This is the Fletcher charm in action! It really does work, only be warned; use the charm wisely and don't over kill because abuse it and loose it!

Chutzpah is also really just another word for ambition. It's good to have ambition but don't be fame hungry. Don't allow the things you are striving for to end up ruling you. I don't strive for fame, what I strive for is to be good at what I do. If recognition follows that is a different matter but if you strive for fame then your striving will become strife! Ambition, like anything else, is a good tool if used the right way. Strive for becoming a better person tomorrow than you were today, strive to help others and strive to master a skill you are good at and use that skill to help people but don't strive for fame. Fame is a falsehood, manifesting itself in the guise of success. So keep yourself in check and make sure your feet are always touching ground zero.

As well as the highlights, I've of course had my fair share of disappointments in my career too but that goes hand in hand with my career choice and perhaps indeed with any career. To succeed you have to have a tough skin and be prepared to take rejection like a man (or indeed a woman!) During the start of the recent economic crisis I was offered three commercials and one film for television, all of which had to be cancelled at the eleventh hour due to the severe economic climate. The film did eventually happen at the end of the year but unfortunately the commercials did not come about. I was also offered a featured role in a music video for the band Lightspeed Champion but sadly had to turn this down due to other acting commitments. The latter was to be filmed by director Saam Farahmand at Partizan Films, who is renowned for shooting videos for Janet Jackson.

One of the commercials I was offered was for All Bran cereal. I was to be flown out to Spain for a couple of days and ride a horse on the beach, playing a character similar in style to Uma Thurman's portrayal of The Bride in *Kill Bill*. The commercial was to be shown on television internationally and would incorporate a mini-plot, which I was told may have launched my career internationally. For this pleasure I was to receive £10,000. Unfortunately, just as with the other cancelled work, my agent received that unenviable call to inform him the job had been cancelled. We both wept into our All Bran for at least a week, then picked ourselves up and moved on.

Around this time a breakdown for the soap *Chalkhill* was sent out by director Steven Surridge. I was invited to audition and told successful applicants would be informed after the weeklong audition process. The next week I received an email with the header '*Chalkhill* soap' and opened it in trepidation. It was an invite to a callback. I excitedly emailed Steven to let him know I would be glad to accept his invitation. I was then sent the biggest amount of sides I had ever seen in my life and an email attached explaining I would be required to learn all of them for the callback, which would be in the style of a workshop in just under a week's time. I travelled the hour-long journey by car to the lovely seaside village of Portsmouth and upon arrival breathed in the wonderfully fresh air, contemplating how amazing it would be to film here on a regular basis. The audition process was fantastic. The day's workshop really gave each actor present the chance to shine and display their individual abilities. Not long after the day of the callback, the assistant director called me to tell me I had successfully acquired the role of one of the leads in the soap. I questioned which character I would be playing and was informed my character was a teacher. How funny I thought to myself and let out a small giggle. The AD asked me what was so funny. I explained to him I used to be a teacher and that this would mean I was now going from once being a teacher to acting being a teacher. In fact, would I even be acting at all? He saw the funny side too. As it happens this was not oddly enough the only time I would be approached to play a teacher in a film and was once again approached to be a teacher in director Obi Emoloyne's feature for television *Mirror Boy*. Art imitating life or life imitating art?

*Chalkhill* was a soap that successfully aired on the BBC Sky network from 2004 to the start of 2008. It had a good-sized fan-base and was to be brought back to television and also aired via the Internet, as a catch-up format. This was a production that could possibly launch my career into the big time. At the start of 2009 the world's economic crisis became more than apparent and many companies started to go under. Film production companies started to take old footage off the shelves to use instead of spending valuable production money on new projects. The world's market was in trouble and the film industry had not escaped the hit. The international players AOL were the company set to sponsor *Chalkhill* but suddenly they found themselves having to pull out their interest in the soap. I received the news filming was to be delayed until October 2009. October soon arrived with fresh new hope and AOL was indeed back on board with the possible promise of rescuing the soap. I, along with the other actors who had also secured lead roles, waited with baited breath to be informed we would now start filming either December or January 2010. This wasn't so bad, I told myself. I was already involved in a number or other productions anyhow, so January would not be too long to wait. When January arrived Steven emailed me the good news things were looking as if they were now moving forward again but sadly, come the end of March 2010 I received the rather upsetting news the project was cancelled once again due to sponsorship from AOL not materialising. However, whilst writing this book I have been informed the good news that Steven is now looking into other alternative ways to sponsor the soap and that he has found some interested buyers. So all hope is not lost and fingers are now well and truly crossed!

As well as the disappointments, I have made mistakes too but I just see mistakes as a way of learning: learning what we will not do again. The biggest mistake I made was not getting a contract signed on one job I undertook, choosing instead to trust the director. As you can imagine my agent said 'Darling, get him to sign a contract!' Perhaps rather naively, I believed the particular director in question to be trustworthy, merely based on the fact we had been in communication via email for nearly an entire year before I worked with him on his production. Including the rehearsed reading, rehearsals and the show itself, I was involved in the project for exactly three months. The initial verbal agreement, which had occurred between the director, myself and my soon to be leading man - after we had both been encouraged to consume a glass of red wine and treated to a delicious meal paid for by the director - was an agreed figure of minimum Equity payment a week and, as the play was profit share, we were also informed any additional amounts of profit received would be shared out between cast and crew over and above this agreed figure.

During the rehearsal period the director commented the play would now be Equity minimum only, with no additional payments made out. This was a disappointment but I decided to stick with the play anyhow, as it had an excellent cast, whom I was very keen to work with and gain experience from. At the end of the rehearsal period I asked one of the cast members if he knew when we would be receiving our first cheque. 'Don't you know? It's profit share only,' my fellow cast member innocently replied; to which both my leading man and myself immediately responded with a resounding 'No, we didn't!' My heart started to race as I thought about all the bills, which would ultimately start pilling up on the doormat waiting to be paid. What should I do? Should I stay in the play or leave? I rang my agent, whose advice was to leave immediately. But the opening night was the next day. How could I do this to the rest of the cast? Surely that would not be professional of me? My agent however rightfully said 'But darling, you are a professional and if someone is not going to treat you as such, then to remain true to your own self-worth you must walk away.' Perhaps I should have listened but instead I chose to stay the duration of the play, as I did not want to let the rest of the cast down. We received not a penny from this show. The director did not even pay our expenses, let alone a thank you for our services. I got behind with paying my bills during this period for the first time in my life. It later also evolved the director did not pay the theatre for the pleasure of its use either. My advice: unless you have willingly agreed to work on a collaborative production, never enter into a production without getting a signed contract in your hand first. If a director or producer does not give you a contract then produce one for them to sign. If they are worth their salt, they will gladly sign your contract or happily produce one of their own. If they refuse to do either, then you know they are someone to stay away from and perhaps this is a not a project you should be entering into. My agent was right, know your worth and don't devalue yourself.

As any actor will tell you, unless you are Angelina Jolie or Brad Pitt, you are going to find yourself with time on your hands between acting jobs in any week of the year. Once I have finished sending off my application to the next acting job that is going to orbit my career into outer-space and place me firmly on the map, chased up my agent for the latest hot updates, returned calls to those all important casting directors who are desperate to use me for the next job they are casting, even if they don't know it themselves yet, or answered work related emails, I still find time on my hands during the week, not much it's true but enough to earn some bread and butter money to sustain a pleasant roof over my head.

Falling short of continuing my pursuit for my shiny new Oscar, on many an occasion I have asked my agent to allow me a week off here and there between acting jobs, to spend a bit of time in the teaching arena. I find teaching keeps me grounded and helps me maintain some sort of semblance of sanity. It also helps me refrain from becoming an over-obsessive actress.

During the first part of this year during one of those 'days off,' I found myself working as a teacher carrying out home tuition, as part of a teaching network attached to the local government. I worked with students who were out of school either for behavioural, emotional or physical learning difficulties. The team of teachers I worked with were a fantastic bunch of talented singers, musicians and writers who, like me, had decided teaching in between their respective creative jobs was far better than waiting on tables in some Hollywood dive, not that I'm knocking waiters, they work very hard and often for very little wage.

I had always successfully managed to organise my diary so I never double-booked an acting job with a teaching post but I was aware the day would come when I would be asked to carry out both on the same day and I always wondered what I would do if it was the acting job which came along after I had planned a day of teaching. I had started teaching a wonderful young man named Oscar Thomas. Oscar has Lowe Syndrome and his mother Lorraine Thomas has worked very hard since the day he was born setting up The Lowe Syndrome Trust, fronted by presenter Jonathon Ross and backed by many celebrities. The foundation's main aim is to raise awareness of this unusual condition and raise money to aid its research. It was always such a pleasure working with Oscar.

342

Oscar is a delightful young man with a happy disposition, who always and without fail, manages to bring a smile to the face of all who know him. There is no room to be unhappy when you are in the presence of such a wonderful and delightful soul such as Oscar.

It was during the month of May, just before the general elections, I was approached by a producer to be part of a prolific political viral, on a day I was already booked to teach Oscar. What was I to do? It was my last week of teaching Oscar. I knew Lorraine would not have minded had I of taken the day off but it would have broken Oscar's heart, as he was expecting to see me every day of that last week. The choice was an easy one to make; I turned down the acting job. As you know by now, I believe everything happens for good reason. Sometimes the reason is not one that is always evidently apparent at the time and sometimes the benefit is not directly meant for us but on this occasion the silver lining around the cloud was all to evident. Just seeing Oscar's beaming smile when I walked into the classroom was award enough for me. On that day it became obvious I didn't need to chase my shiny new Oscar any more, as the real prize, the real Oscar, was right in front of me. Not only did I make this young man's day a little brighter and he mine but my choice helped me keep my dignity and integrity in tact and incidentally, the director of the acting job contacted me shortly after the day of the shoot to tell me he would like to use me in another project he was doing in the future instead. So you see; when you make the right choices for the right reasons, good things will happen.

Of course another way to use your 'resting' period as an actor is to continue training. Don't think that just because you are now a professional your training has to stop. If you recall, this was a mistake I nearly made when I first met Bernard Hiller, until he reminded me how important it is to keep up your training and improve your skills, no matter how far ahead you are in your line of work. Any professional will always tell you it is important to continue to hone and tone your skills and keep up with the times. A career in acting is certainly no different and does not defy this rule.

As it happens, immediately after my course finished at East 15, I had enrolled myself on a ten week Saturday course at Pinewood Studios. Having studied Method for the most part of the course, I now wanted to familiarise myself with a different style of acting. I now also wanted to gain a broader spectrum than just the East 15 way of learning. I was particularly interested to discover more about the Meisner technique. We had touched upon this style of acting at East 15 and it had interested me greatly. I felt by broadening my horizons this would give me more of a fighting chance in the industry, as the more tools you have in any trade, the better equipped you are. Not only did I want to attain a different approach to acting in addition to what I had already learnt but I also wanted to be in a position to answer any director who asked me if I had ever worked with Mesiner before with a confident: 'Yes'. Incidentally, shortly after my training at Pinewood was complete, this is exactly what happened and I felt comfortable enough to be able to answer the director with that resounding 'Yes.'

Entering Pinewood was another of those spine tingling experiences for me. It felt so grand to be visiting a real working studio, especially one that was the home to many great British films. Also enrolled on the course were fellow actress Samantha Smith and television personality Alicia Douvall who, like me, were also looking to hone their acting skills via the Meisner technique. Once again, I found myself in the lucky position at Pinewood of working with some fantastic tutors and visiting lecturers including; director Nic Phillips, the fabulous actress and voice coach Valerie Colgan, casting director Catherine Willis and representatives from the renowned Hubbard casting.

Meisner, as well as Method, trains the actor to break up the play into different sections (also referred to as units) and these sections into different beats or phrases. For example; a number of different sentences said in any one passage by the same character might all be aimed at achieving one objective. Let me illustrate; there are many different ways to get someone to stay. The character might ask them outright 'Please, don't leave!' or they might indicate it with words such as 'Why don't you sit down?' Both sentences hold the same motive; of getting the other person to stay a while longer. This would become the actor's intention or 'objective' for that section of the play.

Although both Method and Meisner use similar ways of breaking up speech, Meisner looks more closely at what happens to an actor emotionally when they use repetition and sense memory. It studies what happens to the actors both physically and verbally when they repeat the same word or sentence in many different ways and looks closely at the different ways of 'actioning' the same phrase. For example; there are many ways to say the same sentence. Depending on the emotion you convey when saying the words, you can action the sentence in different ways. This means you can have a different impact on the person you are talking to by changing the intention behind what you are saying. For example, when you say the words: 'Come here!' are you trying to seduce, belittle or alert? Here are three very different actions placed on the same sentence. Then of course you can even action the actions in different ways too, as there are different ways to seduce, belittle and alert. So, once I have read any new material sent to me once, I then read it again to break it up into units and then once more to start breaking up my character's speeches into actions and beats. Once I have carried out this process, I completely abandon it in order to allow myself to remain free as an actor and to prevent myself from getting locked into saying a speech one particular way. Going through this process is however, initially a very helpful way to help an actor attain a clearer understanding and insight into both their character and the play. The overall objective (also known as the overall action) is something that needs to be considered after the first-read through of any new script. The overall action/objective needs to cover the character's plan throughout the entire script and through-line of action (the through-line is the entire story in correct continuity or chronological order of events) that is; it must convey the character's overall ulterior motive. The actor must also consider both the prime event that occurs at the start of the play and also what has happened to their character before the play starts.

345

The next thing I do, after having read the script at least three times, is find out more about the character I will be playing. I start to ask myself a series of questions to help me understand my character better and generate my character's biography. The questions I ask myself about my character are: What are her likes and dislikes? What does my character like and dislike about herself? What three things would she never leave the house without? What is her relationship like with all the other characters in the play? What does each character say about her in their dialogue and what does she say about them? What would my character be prepared to tell the other characters about herself and what would she not want them to know? What is the essence of the relationship between my character and the other characters in the play; for example teacher and student? What is her point of sympathy towards the other characters and likewise theirs in relation to her? What drives my character? Finally, the most important element any actor needs to acquire to play a character successfully is, to find a point of empathy with the character they are playing. In other words, you have to find something you like about your character and can connect to on a personal level. Additionally, if I am playing someone with a happy disposition, I try and look for any underlying subtext or find some concern the character is internally battling or trying to overcome, to give the character more colour. Likewise, I will turn this around and look for the exact opposite if I am playing someone unhappy. If I am playing someone inherently evil, I will find the good in them and if I am playing someone good, I will seek out their darker side.

Next, to help shape my character, for example how she will walk, talk and move; I use a series of techniques taken from the Laban quality of movement, to help clarify these decisions. This technique, created by Rudolf Laban, looks at how motion is directly connected with its environment and spatial patterns. Laban qualities ask the actor to consider their character's inner temper. Is it quick, steady or slow? How does this relate to their outer characteristics? For example; a person can operate via a rapid succession of quick-firing thoughts inside their mind but still appear calm on the outside. Laban also asks the actor to think about where their character's imaginary centre is, that is to say;

where do they feel their energy is most focused and from whence is it derived? For example, is the character propelled forward by their gut, legs or even their head? How does this effect the way they talk, walk and move? What feelings govern them, i.e. their heart or intellect?

Having worked out all the above, it is still very important for the actor to colour and shape the character with their own personality. Remember what I said earlier in this chapter? The director wants to see what it is you personally can bring to the table and what could possibly be more unique about your performance than bringing some of your own signature stamp to the role? When I play a role I am really just extending myself into that situation, rather than playing someone else. There is only one you. So if you bring yourself to the role, then your acting cannot fail but to be unique and real.

Studying Meisner at Pinewood did indeed succeed at opening up my vision and horizon further as an actor. I firmly believe as an actor, or indeed as any professional, you should not stop learning your trade just because you are now earning those little green notes and calling yourself a professional. It is important to keep studying your trade, not only to keep up with ever changing trends but fundamentally to keep your skills on form. Remember, gaining success is not just about having the vision but also about putting in the time and working hard to achieve your goal. The only luck in this world is the luck we make for ourselves.

***When you make the right choices for the right reasons, good things will happen.*** - Emma Fletcher

## 15

## *Now and Then*

**It's all right to have butterflies in your stomach. Just get them to fly in formation.** - Dr Rob Gilbert

*Paul: In this chapter Emma reflects on life now and as it was back then. More importantly, she looks forward to what her life and career may bring.*

Emma: After watching the magnificent film *Eternal Sunshine of the Spotless Mind*, it made me question if there were a tablet I could take to forget all the bad experiences in my life, would I? Yes, quite a question. But who would I be without my life experiences I asked myself? Don't get me wrong, I don't love trouble and when it knocks on my door I do my best not to invite it in for a full English tea; but would we not be poor shadows of ourselves without our experiences and surely none the richer nor wiser? To appreciate the highs, we need to have at some point in our life experienced the lows. Not that I would wish my more unfortunate experiences on anyone but they have certainly made me appreciate the finer things in life. So I decided, if there were a tablet I could take to make me forget all the bad parts of my life, I wouldn't take it. You read that correctly. I wouldn't take it. In fact I think it would be a pretty bitter pill to swallow if it were to make me forget all the things I have been though in my life and all that I have learned to get me to where I am standing today, to be the person I am.

I have realised in recent years tragedy can strike at any time and with it comes the power to make or break you. In my case I thank God it has made me strong. God's plan is not always apparent when adversity strikes but you can guarantee it usually is the making of someone, one way or the other. I say choose the upwards spiral if you can! Look at someone like the mother of Sarah Payne, who has worked so tirelessly since her daughter's tragic and untimely death, to create a new law, to help prevent a similar crime occurring again. Her trauma has made her the strong woman she is today, although of course no one would argue it is terrible she had to go through the ordeal of loosing her beloved daughter to find the inner-strength to help others but she has, nevertheless, helped so many people in her continued quest. I am a great believer in will power and sheer determination. I believe these ideologies can help to get you through any upset or tragedy you face in life. I also believe trauma is sent to test us. As the philosopher Friedrich Nietzche wrote, *That which does not kill us makes us stronger'*. The upset I have received at the hands of other people over the years has indeed taught me to believe in my own conviction and has ultimately made me a more resilient and stronger individual.

I have learnt whilst it is okay to reflect upon past experiences, in order to learn from them, it is not okay to indulge in them but I don't want to forget them completely either; as they remind me how far I have come. There are two schools of thought; that which says we should sit down and talk about our past to an impartial counsellor for hours, so we can reflect on where we went wrong in order to not make the same mistakes again and that which says, leave the past completely behind and focus only on the here and now. My little anecdotes and antidotes on these two schools of thoughts are as follows; whilst I feel we can learn something from both these ideals we have to be careful not to adhere to either of them in complete isolation. If we spend too much of our life reflecting on and indulging in our past experiences, we can become very self-absorbed and start to re-live in the past again. I know I have been guilty of this myself many times before now. I call this self-inflicted emotional vandalism. However, if we reflect only on our daily interactions and live only for the moment, forgetting the past completely, then we loose a sense of depth and who we are. Reflecting helps us not to make the same mistakes again in the future - isn't that what the history books tell us? Likewise, indulging causes us to get stuck in the past. So the trick is not to become so engaged in the past that it prevents you from moving forward but to recognise its lessons. Where we have come from is inherently a part of what makes us who we are, although it does not necessarily need to define us. I think there is a happy medium which lies somewhere between the two schools of thought, which allows us to recognise old habits, so as not to repeat them and yet remain in the present, working on ourselves in the here and now. So remember the past, live in the present and look forward to the future. It is a fine balancing act. More little Fletcher theories and therapies to follow...

Rather than have therapy which makes you re-live your past or therapy which tells you to block out your past all together, the solution surely has to be to just acknowledge your problems? So many of us and I include myself in this scenario, are guilty of allowing negativity from our past to literally control our present. As soon as any new negativity confronts us, we suddenly find ourselves connecting it to all the negativity we are still holding from our past and allow all our old demons to rear their ugly heads again. This only results in making the problem bigger than it ought to be. Don't allow your past to control your future. Too many people spend far too much time dwelling on their past and end up missing out on the present altogether. I faced my demons and forgave myself and others who have hurt me in my life. I have now learnt to not dwell on the past and to forgive myself for some of the choices I have made. I have learnt to leave the past where it belongs, which is in the past and to leave tomorrow until tomorrow. This allows me to live where I belong: in the present. This really is the only way to move forward in life. This mentality has also helped me to remind myself, if I want to be able to allow myself to love someone again, the first thing I have to be able to do is love myself first. People get into abusive relationships all the time, as they don't love themselves. The person they search out and find becomes a reflection of their own negativity and the things they don't like about themselves. They seek out an abusive person in the belief that is all they deserve and are worthy of, thus the abusive partner gives them affirmation of this belief. Bernie's class allowed me to re-find the courage to search deep inside my soul and rediscover the person I was before all my demons took over.

So to summarise, you have to face the mistakes you've made in order to work out how not to repeat them again but you don't have to keep relieving them. The expression *'ignore it and it will go away'* in my opinion is a dangerous myth, which surmounts to ignorance and ignorance is not bliss. Burying things does not necessarily make them go away; it just keeps them buried until they resurface in a different guise and usually two-fold. Better to face your fears, so if they do resurface you are ready to take them on with strength. Recognise your mistakes from an objective rather than subjective viewpoint. Old habits are merely an addiction and any addict will tell you in order to change yourself, you must do it one day at a time. As the saying goes, *'Don't leap before you can run.'* This is so true, as you will only fall over. I ran and I fell and it hurt! If you can't manage a day, try an hour; then slowly break your habit by increasing the hour to two and so forth.

For me regret is now also a thing of the past. If I'm upset about how something has turned out, I will either try and change the outcome or if I am unable to change the outcome, then I allow myself to let it go, else you can spend your life worrying about what could have been to the point of digging yourself into an early grave in the process. I've learnt to love the moment, as only in the here and now can real change occur. Regrets are a waste of precious energy. I used to regret everything. My favourite expression was 'what if?' Now the only thing I regret is that I wasted so much time regretting! Don't focus on what is lacking in your life, just on what you want to achieve. The passage of time is relentless and will wait for no man but it can also be a healer. For although time cannot change the past, it can serve to soften the pain. Whilst I was writing this book I learnt the father of the Drummond family had past away. This news conjured up a whole array of emotions inside of me and brought a lot of my past to the forefront of my mind. The knowledge of his passing did bring a tear to my eye. It saddened my heart to think of the relationship we could of had, had things of been different. But we cannot change the past, so we must not allow it to dictate our future. We also have to learn to forgive because if we hold on to anger or resentment or retain ill feeling towards others, all that happens is it

351

ends up eating us up from the inside out and we become embittered. So whilst I can never forget some of the hurt I have experienced at the hands of others, I do forgive.

Although my past no longer defines me, it is, nevertheless, certainly the essence and building block for who I am today. I have asked myself before now if, God forbid, there were a fire in my home, which belongings would I rescue if I had the time? A strange question I hear you cry. Well yes, I admit I do ask myself strange and testing questions it's true, perhaps it's the actress in me carrying out a constant character breakdown of myself or perhaps it's just the fact I tend to over-analyse at times but I think these type of questions force us to take stock of ourselves and discover what truly makes us tick as individuals. They also make us reflect on whom we have touched in our lives and what and who is important to us. They make us question what important selfless acts we have carried out over the years. So, as strange as this question is, you know you want to know the answer! So what items would I save? Would it be my vast collection of DVDs? Perhaps I would grab my jewellery box from my closet or the trophies and certificates from my wall? Actually it would be none of the above. The items I would save are my photo albums; my life in pictures, the scripts and the music I have written and my artwork. In fact, what I have just described to you surmounts to grabbing memories of most of the things that make me who I am. When I am laid to rest, it is not important to me to be judged on how many precious items of jewellery I have collected around my neck but on how many people I have touched, hopefully with kindness. We can't take our diamonds and pearls with us when we are laid to rest. The meaning of life is not about what you take with you but what you leave behind, so choose wisely what type of person you wish to become.

I once had a dream of seeing myself on television and performing on a stage in the West End. From a young age I always knew I wanted to make a dent in the world and leave my mark, a lasting impression if you will. Surrounded by a celebrity dynasty, my dream seemed ever more the reachable and fuelled by the belief mum instilled in me from a young age, that no matter what the odds were against me, I could achieve anything; I could achieve my dreams. I have now indeed achieved those things. I dared to believe in myself and to believe in better; for when you make your desires bigger than your fears you can achieve greatness. All fears are really just questions, questions that require an answer. When you can stare your fears directly in the face and answer them with a resounding 'yes', then they will disappear; for what you want in life is bigger than your fears. The bigger the dream, the better the life. I don't believe in obstacles only in obtaining goals. *Veni, vidi, vici!* Literally translated as; I came, I saw, I conquered. Anything is possible if you believe it is. Don't let anyone ever tell you otherwise. I decided to start living a life of being special. I have worked hard to become the person I am today both emotionally and in my career.

I am aware however, there are still areas of my life I need to work on. We always need to work on ourselves through life. From a young age I've always had mini panic attacks whenever I walk into a room filled with people, even if it is a room of people I know. All I see is a faceless sea of eyes starring back at me. I'm not in my element around crowds at the best of times and can tend to feel a bit suffocated. The butterflies in my stomach start doing a merry little dance and usually not in formation before I walk into a room and sometimes even before I go out of an evening. I call this the butterfly effect, as it starts to manifest itself into worry about whether people will accept me. This fear has on occasion stopped me going out. Although I can be gregarious around people I know well and able to express my inner thoughts to them, I can also be painfully shy and feel alone in a crowd and am not normally someone who likes to draw attention to myself. I have often asked myself how I am, therefore, able to get on a stage and perform or walk into an open audition space with confidence? The answer is two-fold: my acting becomes another form of communication, an extended expression of my soul. As although I am communicating emotions via assuming the identity of someone else when on stage, I am nevertheless, intrinsically still bringing a part of myself into each character I play. Perhaps hiding behind the guise of a character has, in the past, allowed it to become easier for me to communicate a message and channel emotions, which otherwise I would have been to shy to release outwardly. The places actors get to go to emotionally on stage are often places they may never get the chance to go to emotionally in their own lives. I would imagine this could be what drives a lot of actors to act. When I get on the stage or in front of a camera I come alive. Acting makes me feel alive.

It is true I initially became an actress to fulfil a void in my life. I had a strong need to be loved born from rejection of old. I chose the stage for my voice to be heard. Having spent so many years struggling for my voice to be heard amongst members of my own family, when I took to the stage I could become someone else, I could become the person I had always wanted to be. My voice could finally be heard. It was so much easier to live someone else's life rather than my own, although thank God, I now am learning to live my own life and love myself in the process, warts and all! I had spent so many years living up to the expectations other people have placed upon me but now I am just trying to live up to my own expectations, which believe me is hard enough! At some point you have to ask yourself the question: 'Do you own your life, or are you just renting it?' If you have to ask the permission of others all the time, then you are just renting it. This was a question Bernard Hiller posed to the group during one of his classes. Thankfully I am now able to answer this question with a positive response, as I do now own my life. Don't people-please. I did for many years and I lost myself in the process. Now that I have learnt to love myself again, I realise surely it is better to be disliked for who you are, rather than liked for who you are not? You can't please everyone, so start by at least pleasing yourself first. Be true to who you are and take a risk in doing so. Yes, taking risks might make you unpopular for being different but you have to take a chance and be willing to live in uncertainty in order to grow. For without taking risks there can be no possibility of growth. Let life guide you and remember to follow your instincts, as they are usually never wrong.

I struggled for a long time with the question of; am I giving to society when I act in the same way I am able to give to society when I teach or is acting just a self-indulgent existence? I began to realise actors are doctors for the soul. Not only are they able to provide escapism for people but they can serve to raise awareness and bring to the public's attention important and pressing issues, which may otherwise lie dormant or unrecognised. Actors can also convey a message, which may have the ability to help a person who is going through a similar event and may even help to awaken their soul and change their life. I enjoy acting, however, and I realise in life we must do what it is we enjoy and as long as what you enjoy is not hurting anyone else, I began to realise it is not possible to help anyone else in life unless you are comfortable within your own skin first. Having rid myself of my demons, I no longer want to act to live the life of someone else. Now that I am beginning to feel more comfortable in my own skin and have learnt to live in the present, my passion to act derives from the desire to move people emotionally and communicate a message of hope. This is what I have also tried to achieve by writing this book. My acting is no longer a self-indulgent mission and hopefully more of a selfless act than perhaps it was a number of years ago.

So where do I see myself in five years time? I have asked myself this question a couple of times over the years and for the most part I have fulfilled some of the dreams I desired to fulfil but I am still not exactly where I plan to be in every aspect of my life, as life doesn't always work out that way. If we were exactly where we want to be at all times, we would stop learning but we are exactly where we are meant to be most of the time. I do believe however, it is always important to hold onto your dreams and have a vision of where you would like to head in life, as if you don't have a vision, how can you see where you are going? If you can visualise yourself achieving your goals, you will give yourself a far better chance of meeting them face-to-face.

There was a time I would map out every single detail of how I wanted my future to look. I would spend hours in my mind planning out my future but soon discovered God indeed had other plans for me. I started to realise one can never plan for the unexpected eventualities around the corner. They say how do you make God laugh? The answer? Tell him your plans for next year.

In my case it's usually tell him my plans for next week, or sometimes even for tomorrow! I've learnt man can make plans but God will change them. I've discovered the idea when making plans is to not get in the way of them. You can have an idea of where you want to go but you also have to step back and trust in God that the plan will fall into place if it is meant for you. Be proactive in starting to get the plan into action but also know when to step back and allow the plan to take its own course, else you will end up blocking your path if you try and control everything. God wants us to put our plans into action, as often He uses our plans to mould them into what He truly intends for us. Sometimes our plans get turned into a different outcome by God, which may mean the plan you had intended for yourself may result in a different purpose to that which you initially intended but may still be what is best for you. I have an idea of where I would like my life to keep heading but I don't allow myself to get stuck anymore in one way of thinking about the future. I've had to learn to roll with the punches and get to what's real but that is not such a bad thing, as life is forever changing and you have to change with it.

I am now more of a 'come what may' type of girl. This does not equate to me being irresponsible but as one never knows what tomorrow may bring, I've learnt to seize the day; *carpe diem*, as tomorrow you may not be given the chance. I do however like consistency in my life, which is still possible even when the career path you have chosen is a precarious one. My faith gives me consistency. Even although I am still in a battle to tame my wild side, which does at times get the better of me and can still rock my world if I let it, my faith for the most part keeps my feet on solid ground and it is this same faith in God, which keeps me moving forward through life in a healthy and positive manner. It is this mentality which also saves on disappointment but mostly my disappointment is curbed because I have learnt to live in the now. I say embrace the present; it is, after all, in fashion! As William Watson Purkey famously said:

*You've gotta dance like there's nobody watching, love like you'll never be hurt. Sing like there's nobody listening and live like it's heaven on earth; and speak from the heart to be heard.*

So whenever I am feeling a little blue or as if life is confronting me with a challenge I'm finding somewhat difficult to come out the other side of, I try to remind myself not only does God want me to be going through this situation right now for my growth but when I reflect on my life so far, I tell myself I'm still standing. Nothing was ever so bad I couldn't get through it. I always remind myself of this now whenever trouble knocks on my door for that English tea and remind myself the not so good times are just there to help us appreciate the good times even more. It took me years to realise I am not the cause of all the good and bad that happens in my life. How arrogant I was to think I had that much control! No one knows enough to afford to be a pessimist. Let's leave that one for God. It's not about thinking more; it's about thinking less. Get rid of 'I can't'. Stop blocking yourself. I learnt to allow myself to just trust in the moment, as the moment really is all we have and it is perfect. I learnt to let the moment take me forward on stage and in life, for if the here and now is all that really matters, then it can only ever be in the now that real change can occur.

I have always said I will only stop acting when either it gives up on me or when it stops becoming enjoyable. If the day comes when acting gives up on me first, then I won't kick and scream or throw a tantrum. I will gracefully search my heart and soul to discover what the next path in life is I am meant to be walking down. For now my path continues to be acting but shortly along the line, I would very much like to meet my Prince Charming, settle down and have children. I hope there will still be room in my life to continue to develop my passion for acting, should the desire continue but I guess only time will hold the answer to that riddle but one thing I am certain of is, the right person for me will understand and help me nurture my passion for creativity, rather than expel it.

If I am to be blessed with children one day, I have been asked before now, would I allow them to become actors? Well, you can't stop people's dreams. Whilst I would understand any parent's concern if one of their children said they wanted to enter the precarious world of acting, I would not prevent them from following their dreams. I would, however, firstly ensure they received a good education; like my parents gave to me, to serve as a good back-up plan and then I would offer them all the love and support to follow their heart and pursue their ambitions. I would set them free to give them a proper chance to meet their potential, in whatever field of career choice that might be. I believe every one deserves the chance to meet their full potential and you have to give yourself that chance in order to meet it. For how can we ever know what we are truly capable of unless we try?

We all need to learn to harness our potential. To quote Arthur C Clarke; *'The only way to discover the limits of the possible is to go beyond them into the impossible.'*

When you can move past your fears, anything is possible. Remember that ant in the song High Hopes? No one ever thought he'd move that rubber tree plant but he did! So have the courage to see where life can take you and remember, life is a gift, so choose wisely what you do with it.

**Life is too short for regret, so if you have a dream you have to follow it. If the shoe fits, wear it.**
   - Emma Fletcher

*Little is the person who's scornful in his wake*
*But big is he who surely knows honour for honour's*
*sake.*

- Emma Fletcher

# Postscript

Having never kept a diary in my life, when Paul asked me to write a book with him I was unsure how the process would make me feel. As I am a very private person, my initial reaction was I didn't want to write the book. I didn't want to write down my personal experiences and intimate feelings on paper for the world to read, leaving myself open and exposed. My next thought was, as I have been through so much upset in my life, perhaps the memories were best left in the past, where they belonged.

It was nearly a year ago now when Paul originally approached me with his idea to turn my story into a book. My initial reaction was: 'Why would anyone want to read a story about my life?' Paul's response was simply: 'Because your story is inspirational and you have so much to share.' I was aware if I were to tell my story I would have to tell the whole story, as half my story would only reflect half of who I am but I was also concerned the book should not turn into one of name telling or finger pointing. The most important element would be for it to become a book which might inspire and help others to overcome adversity in their own lives and to demonstrate through my story how it is possible to come through the other side of heartache with a smile still on your face and your faith in humanity in tact; and that is exactly what I hope you the reader feel having read my story. If reading this book can indeed inspire you to follow your dreams against the odds, then I have succeeded in my mission and this book was worth writing.

Paul assured me writing the book would be a rewarding and therapeutic experience and one I would be pleased I agreed to. Whilst the journey of writing this book has been a complete roller-coaster of a ride, not to mention the many long days spent slaving at my computer into the small hours of the night typing up my endless thoughts, Paul was right; it has, nevertheless, been cathartic and I would highly recommend the experience of writing an autobiography to everyone! As a thank you for writing this book with him, Paul presented me with the very thoughtful gift of some seeds for a new hybrid rose, created in my name. How apt he should purchase seeds for me. These seeds represent to me new beginnings and as I bring this book to a close, I am all about embracing new beginnings, as with new beginnings change and growth is found. As I close this chapter in my life, I feel a new chapter is daring to begin.

Firstly a big thank you goes out to both Paul Burton and my publisher Tim Hirst, for helping me turn this book into a reality. A huge thank you also goes out to my family and friends, without whose support I would surely not be standing on solid ground today. My close girlfriends in particular are like sisters to me and I am blessed to have so many wonderful sisters in my life who, as testament has shown, have been there for me during my darkest hours. Thankfully there are too many of you to mention but you all know who you are. The following quote by Edna Buchanan expresses my dearest sentiment towards you all: *'Friends are the family we choose for ourselves'*.

Finally, I feel no actor's autobiography would be complete without a 'characterisation' exercise carried out on themself. So I leave you with what I personally consider to be the best and worst parts of me, in the form of a Laban character breakdown. Enjoy!

## *If 'I were', what would I be?*

**An element:** Air (I am a typical Libran. My head may sometimes seem in the clouds whilst I am taking time to balance out the odds but when I make my decision you can be certain it is ascertained from weighing up both sides of the coin and there is usually no swaying me once my mind is made up - well almost!)

**A time of day:** Evening (just before dusk. This is when I am at my most creative. I am a night owl at best.)

**A landscape:** Fields of green (I like nothing better than to run through fields of green bare foot and directly in contact with the elements.)

**A type or profession:** An actress of course! Need you ask?

**A piece of clothing:** A coat of armour (I am highly protective of those I love and will shield them from upset and danger where possible.)

**A dessert:** Rich hot chocolate fudge cake, laced with double, double choc-chip ice-cream. (Okay, you got me! This may not be the dessert which describes my character the best but it is my personal favourite!)

### List your character's likes and dislikes:

**Likes:**

Spending time with loved ones.
Reading: especially spiritual books and books on quantum physics.
Creative writing and painting.
Theatre, movies, music and good food.

**Dislikes:**

Disloyalty and meanness.
Big fat hairy spiders - especially the ones that stare at you as if they are embarking on a mission to make your day hell!

### List your character's inner and outer characteristics:

**Inner/Outer:** Thoughtful and creative/Quick firing statements.

**Inner/Outer:** Loving and caring/Generous and sensitive.

**Inner/Outer:** High morals/Pervicacious.

**Inner/Outer:** In touch with my inner-child/Playful.

**Inner/Outer:** Rational/Sensible.

**What is your character's inner predominant motive?** My heart.

**What is your imaginary centre?** My gut is my nucleus and also my 'third eye'.

**What is your character's super objective (through-line) in life?** To find inner-peace.

**What does your character like about herself?** Empathic and sensitive.

**What does your character dislike about herself?** Over-sensitive.

**Character Biography:**

**First kiss:** I was only nine when I had my first kiss. (It was with a young man who lived up the street named Ben Bud. Ben was three years older than me. He was in foster-care and the local rebel without a cause. Ben stole a first kiss from all the young girls in the neighbourhood, although we were all rather too young to actually like it! Nonetheless, we all thought Ben was the best thing since sliced-bread.)

**Favourite movie:** *Sweet Charity* and of course *Cinderella* (but I am also just as partial to a good sci-fi flick too.)

**Favourite band:** Cold Play (but I am just as content to listen to Mozart.)

**Choice of sport:** Martial arts, yoga and horse riding (especially galloping bare back on the beach – remember; the horse not me!)

**Happiest moment:** The birth of my cousin Sam's beautiful

daughter, Chloe.

**Scariest moment:** When I was 17 a group of drunken teenage boys forced me off the road at high speed, pushing me into a game of chicken with an oncoming vehicle.

**Most surprising moment:** Being held upside down by my legs over the side of a mountain (apparently for fun or at least, so I was informed afterwards!)

**Most freakish moment:** A friend and I seeing what appeared to be a ghostly apparition.

**Most questionable moment:** Seeing an unidentified flying object (note, I wrote 'unidentified'; which means just that. It was a peculiar red glowing ball hovering in the sky, with smoke coming out of it, when suddenly and extremely rapidly it disappeared out of sight. I am more than happy to take suggestions on this one. I'm very willing to accept any rational explanation of what it was. Any takers? Anyone? Perhaps they had come to take me home? Just kidding - no really guys, I'm kidding! But this strange site was also reported over the local radio. Chilling!

**Most embarrassing moment:** Going to sit on the edge of the stage during monitoring an exam, by hoisting myself up, via pushing my feet against the side of the stage behind the stage trim, to find their was no side to push my feet against; thus falling right through the underneath of the stage with a thud and landing on the floor, face down in a pose somewhat similar to a starfish in front of 100 students!)

*You may not be able to choose your destiny but you can choose how you deal with what life confronts you.*
- Emma Fletcher

# Afterword

I'd like to make a few comments on a beautiful, delightfully intelligent and talented young lady, Emma Fletcher.

When she first spoke to me thirteen years ago in that beautiful, softly spoken voice, I was hooked by her.

She is like a butterfly. Always up and changing to suit the times and following her passion in a hot summer wind.

She has enhanced my life with her innocence and laughter through so many difficult times we've shared together.

I wish this wonderful lady nothing but both happiness and love that she so deserves and gives out.

Love, her dearest friend.


*Denis Ingoldsby*

*Music Producer*

# *Emma's Homegrown Quotes*

**It has never been and never will be easy work. But the road that is built in hope is more pleasant to the traveller than the road built in despair, even though they both lead to the same destination.**
- Marion Zimmer Bradley

Emma: I would like to leave you with some of my favourite little homegrown quotes, which have sprouted with glorious fruits from writing this book and have been picked especially for you by my very own hand. As I was not able to place all of the quotes directly in the main content of the book, I would like to leave you with these little thoughts now; in the hope they will serve to brighten your day and help you face any new challenge with a positive outlook and of course with a smile on your face.

So, without any further delay, I present to you in alphabetical order Emma's 'homegrown quotes'.

*Actors are doctors for the soul. An actor can convey a message which may have the ability to help a person who is going through a similar event and may even help to awaken their soul.*

*All fears are really just questions, questions that require an answer. When you can stare your fears directly in the face and answer them with a resounding 'yes', then they will disappear; for what you want in life is bigger than your fears.*

*Arrogance is self-betrayal; as it severs our desire to learn in the belief we know it all already.*

*Balance is the key.*

*'Carpe diem'; seize the day, as tomorrow you may not be given the chance.*

366

*Change your attitude, not your goal. For the outcome will be greater if your attitude is born from wisdom rather than arrogance.*

*Choice is a luxury. With choice comes freedom, so choose wisely.*

*Don't allow the things you are striving for to end up ruling you... if you strive for fame then your striving will become strife! Ambition, like anything else, is a good tool if used the right way. Strive for becoming a better person tomorrow than you were today, strive to help others and strive to master a skill you are good at and use that skill to help people but don't strive for fame.*

*Don't allow your happiness to be defined by someone else's actions… You control your own happiness. Your happiness is not defined by your circumstances but your attitude towards your circumstances… It is within your power to make yourself happy.*

*Don't allow your past to control your future… learn to live in the now.*

*Don't be afraid to fall. We learn from our misguidance.*

*Do not fear that which you do not understand. Embrace the chance of the rewards of new discovery.*

*Don't focus on what is lacking in your life, just on what you want to achieve.*

*Don't give your power over to someone else. You have the power to change your destiny with one single thought.*

*Don't try and carry everyone else's hand luggage when you have enough problems trying to carry your own! It will only unbalance you and tip you over and we all know, you can't help other people unless you are standing on solid ground yourself first.*

*Don't try to meet the right person, try to be the right person.*

*Do three things each day, which make you happy. Learn to invest in a little you time.*

*Embrace the present; it's in fashion!*

*Every person you meet is important; so thank people for being a part of your day.*

*Every problem reveals who you are, by how you deal it. What you are going to do about the problem reveals your personality and how you deal with it makes you impressive or not.*

*Fame is a falsehood, manifesting itself in the guise of success.*

*Follow your instincts, they are usually right. It is usually when we don't follow our instincts we find ourselves in trouble.*

*Give yourself the chance to meet your potential. How can you know what you are truly capable of unless you try?*

*God only gives us what He knows we can handle.*

*Have the courage to see where life can take you.*

*Humans are the best architects of their own downfall. Alternatively, humans can be the architects of their own dreams.*

*I am not expecting to find a partner who hasn't any baggage, look at me I have a whole suitcase load and it's pretty full too but I do want to find someone who has at least worked on lightening their load.*

*I believe the important part is not in the winning but in the taking part. These words aren't just a cheap attempt at becoming a poor metaphor for loosing but from the realisation of how much we can learn so much about ourselves from the taking part. If you don't at least try, then you are only cheating yourself. It is actually the times we loose we learn more about ourselves than the times we win. But nevertheless I always aim to win!*

*If we loose ourselves in someone else, then who are we?*

*If we were exactly where we want to be at all times, we would stop growing and learning but we are exactly where we are meant to be most of the time.*

*If you are afraid of your teacher, then you are not able to learn.*

*If you are not willing to loose, then you are not prepared to win.*

*If you are offended easily, then you are not open to change.*

*If you can change your perception of an event, then you can change your entire outlook and how you deal emotionally with that event. The event cannot change but your perception of it can and once this change occurs its circumstances do not need to rule your mind any longer.*

*If you can't change other people's behaviour towards you, then change your attitude towards their behaviour.*

*If you can't move yourself, then how do you expect to move anyone else?*

*If you don't know your weaknesses, how can you expect to know your strengths? If you don't' know what is wrong, how can you begin to fix it?*

*If you fall, the next time you will know where to tread. If you fall, the next time you will tread carefully.*

*If you want to be able to allow yourself to love someone again or even to be loved by someone else, the first thing you have to be able to do is love yourself again first.*

*I started to realise this God I had hated for so many years perhaps did exist after all. This realisation was my eureka moment.*

*It is always important to hold onto your dreams and have a vision of where you would like to head in life, as if you don't have a vision, how can you see where you are going? If you can visualise yourself achieving your goals, you will give yourself a far better chance of meeting them face-to-face.*

*I've always tried to live a truthful and honest existence. Personally I've never seen the point in a lie as, apart from also being dishonest with yourself, the truth always catches up with you eventually and bites you directly in the butt.*

*I've spent so many years living up to the expectations other people have placed upon me. Now I am just trying to live up to my own expectations, which believe me is hard enough!*

*I would rather be on my own than be unhappy with someone else.*

*Just one thought can change your destiny.*

*Learn to become a master of your thoughts, for only then will you truly be free.*

*Learn to harness your full potential.*

*Life is a gift, so choose wisely what you do with it.*

*Life is too short for regret, so if you have a dream you have to follow it.*

*Love the moment; as only in the here and now can real change occur.*

*Luck is not chance. You make your own luck and subsequently your own success but know when to change direction too. There really is no point in trying to flog a dead horse.*

*Mistakes are just a way of learning what we will not do again.*

*No man is an island and not one person can hide behind his or herself forever.*

*Often from an accident is born genius.*

*One thought can change your destiny.*

*Only a free man has the power to spot another free man.*

*Only when you can start to believe in yourself and believe in the essence of being, can you truly separate yourself from doubt.*

*People can only take your power from you if you let them.*

*Regrets are a waste of precious energy. I used to regret everything. My favourite expression was 'what if'. Now the only thing I regret is that I wasted so much time regretting!*

*Relationships should not be about the 'give and the take' but all about the giving. You should not think when you meet someone 'I wonder what he or she can do for me' but instead how you can help to serve each other's growth... if two people are always giving to one another, then by its very nature, ultimately you are both receivers anyhow.*

*Relaxing is an art. Learn to relax.*

*Remember the past, live in the present and look forward to the future.*

*Remember to praise yourself for your good deeds.*

*Search hard inside yourself and you shall seek the diamond inside the coal but be careful not to surround yourself with diamond diggers in the process.*

*Smile at five people each day.*

*So many of us are guilty of allowing negativity from our past to control our present. As soon as any new negativity confronts us, we suddenly find ourselves connecting it to all the negativity we are still holding from our past and allow all our old demons to rear their ugly heads again. This only results in making the problem bigger than it ought to be.*

*Sometimes when I'm held up at a traffic light I tell myself it's just God's way of pressing the pause button to adjust my day so that everything will be in sync.*

*Strive to be a better person tomorrow than you were today.*

*Success is attained by setting your goals higher; so step up to the next rung of the ladder and face the dizzy heights. Embrace your destiny.*

*Success is not convenient. Be prepared to win and be prepared to loose.*

*Surround yourself with people who can teach you something and compare yourself only to the best.*

*Surround yourself with positive people and you will soon find you become one too.*

*Take a chance but if you're going to jump into the deep end of the pool, you'd better make certain you can swim first.*

*Take responsibility. Embrace your actions and their consequences rather than pass blame.*

*Telling myself the job I didn't get wasn't meant for me helps me focus on the next job in a more positive manner.*

*The meaning of life is not about what you take with you but what you leave behind.*

*The more I learn, the more I realise how little I actually know and how much more there is still to learn.*

*The not so good times are there to help us appreciate the good times more.*

*The only luck in this world is the luck we make for ourselves.*

*The only thing holding you back is you. You attract into your life a reflection of all that you are.*

*The past is what happened but the present is what counts.*

*There are no ordinary moments; every moment is extraordinary.*

*Time is relentless; it waits for no man. Time can also be a healer. It cannot change the past but it can serve to soften the pain.*

*To be able to survive in the acting industry, or in fact through life, you have to make this following oxymoron work for you: You need to have a balance of strength and humility. That is to say, you need be strong enough to not be offended by constructive criticism and yet also have the sense to use it wisely to help you develop. Likewise, you also need be humble enough to take the criticism in the first place.*

*Tragedy can make or break you. In my case I thank God it has made me strong. God's plan is not always apparent when adversity strikes but it is usually the making of someone, one way or the other. I say choose the upwards spiral if you can!*

*You can't escape yourself!*

*You have to move out of your comfort zone in order to grow.*

*You may not be able to control all events in your life but it is within your power to control how you deal with what life confronts you.*

*You must take a chance and try a new path in order to grow.*

*Your happiness is not defined by your circumstances but your attitude towards your circumstances.*

*Your thoughts can become a reality.*

*We have to change our thoughts first before we can change ourselves.*

*Whenever those naughty blues start to creep in, remember life is also filled with greens, yellows, pinks and many other magnificent colours too.*

*When you can move past your fears, anything is possible.*

*When you cry out to God for what you have lost, He shows you what you have found.*

*When you make the right choices for the right reasons, good things will happen.*

*When you make your desires bigger than your fears, you can achieve greatness.*

*Why are you allowing people who are living their own nightmares to tell you how to live your dreams? If you want advice on how to live a dream, then ask someone who is already living the dream. You wouldn't ask a chef how to cut your hair, you'd ask a hairdresser. Get information from successful people in the field you want to be successful in.*

*With choice comes freedom.*

*Without hope all is lost.*

*Without rain we could not appreciate the sunshine. Without the difficult times, we could not appreciate the good.*

*Without risk there can be no growth.*

**And finally…**

***If the shoe fits wear it ~ and then go and buy another one to place on the other foot!***

*Emma Fletcher*

# Anneke Wills : Self Portrait

This is a moving, witty and candid account of a fascinating life among the talents who defined the swinging sixties. Appearing in ground-breaking television from an early age, Anneke Wills was one of the busiest actresses of the 1960s – her role as Polly establishing a template for one of television's most iconic and prized roles – the glamorous Doctor Who girl. This is a beautifully written story of a unique childhood, life at the heart of swinging sixties London, and a turbulent marriage to a leading actor. Anneke's life revolved around the eccentrics, actors, film-makers, painters, designers, poets, satirists and drunks who were changing the world. She counted among her friends the leading lights of the time – from Peter Cook to Sammy Davis Jnr. Illustrated in full colour with previously unseen photographs and Anneke's own drawings and paintings, this is the story of a rich and colourful life, and the growth of a truly remarkable woman.

# Anneke Wills : Naked

Anneke's familiar, intimate style continues her story as she leaves the limelight of television for rural family life. Fully embracing the liberal zeitgeist of the seventies, she lives 'The Good Life' in the idyllic countryside of Norfolk, travels to India and becomes a disciple of the notorious spiritual teacher Bhagwan Shree Rajneesh. In the 1980s, she lives among artists on a small Canadian Island, works as a designer and gardener in California, endures unbearable tragedy and two more unorthodox marriages. She returns to Doctor Who in the nineties, which leads to worldwide travels, emotional reunions and new adventures. This 37 year voyage, filled with tears, laughter and discovery, will leave you breathless. Anneke's story is truly stranger than fiction. To this day, Anneke's life continues to be unpredictable and bizarre. This book – hilarious and heartbreaking in equal measure – brings us up to 2008, laying bare the story of a true renaissance woman. As with the first book, 'Naked' is in full colour and includes rare personal photos and Anneke's own artwork.

# Extract from Self Portrait,
## by Anneke Wills

*This segment takes place in the late 1960s. Please note that Anneke refers to her husband, the actor Michael Gough, as 'Mickgough' throughout both books, the reasons for which are explained in 'Self Portrait'.*

In the kitchen, sometimes the 'phone goes and it's Mickgough's 'ex-wife number one' who I have to make horrible lame excuses to but occasionally he will speak to her and the seething, vicious tone of his voice makes me frightened. I vow I'll never get in that position with him. But this time the 'phone goes and it's Rexy!

'Darling, I'm chartering my yacht in Venice and we will go down the coast to Greece. Would you and Mick like to come?'

'Are you kidding?! Yes!' When Mickgough returns from work, I tell him. We are both thrilled to bits. Virginia lends me a lovely, long, silvery dress, because I don't have any evening wear. Mick packs his espadrilles. We have told all our neighbours,

'Off on a yacht with Rex Harrison, yeah!' When we get on the plane, Mick, in his most theatrical voice, says,

'Put the champagne on ice, darling,' to the stewardess. By the time we get to Venice, we are pissed. We get into the water taxi.

'What's the name of the yacht?' Mickgough asks me.

'I don't know, he didn't tell me. You mean you haven't got it?' *Oh God.* Here we are in the Lido surrounded by hundreds of glamorous ships and we don't know which is Rex's. In drunken, made-up Italian, we get our gondolier to start cruising around; Mick is standing up as we approach some vast yacht.

'Rex Harrison, hellooooo, hellooooo, Rexy!'

'No, no,' shaking faces appear at the top. We try another. Now Mick is doing a Rex imitation,

'*I've grown accustomed to her face*', he sings, all the time wobbling away. Eventually we get an affirmative.

'Si, si, this is his boat, but he's gone to the airport to meet you!' We are shown into our lovely cabin and we unpack. It's all mahogany and white linen and brass taps, very classy. We meet

Elizabeth Harris, who is together with Rexy now, and we are all to go to dinner on another yacht. Dirk Bogarde, Trevor Howard, Vladmir Ashkenazi the famous pianist, and his wife. The conversation and the champagne sparkling and everyone gets unbelievably drunk.

I am sitting between Mickgough and Rexy in my silver dress. Waving his fork, Rexy turns to me and whispers in my ear,

'How would you like it if I stuck this fork up your c***?' I may be drunk, but this completely shocks me. My smile freezes. This bizarre moment passes. The next day our crew is making preparations for our trip, so Mick and I take off to see a bit of Venice. We sit in St. Mark's Square and have a very expensive coffee and he tells me how sad he feels because he and Annie (wife number two) had been such intimate friends with Dirk Bogarde, but now, because of me, he disapproves and Mick misses his friendship. Alec Guinness is also disapproving of me…

We set off. Rex and Elizabeth, her brother and his girlfriend, and Mickgough and me. Trevor Howard will join us later. So six of us and a crew of fifteen! We gather at the back of the yacht. The chilled champagne flows endlessly and the sun loungers are spread about. Elizabeth has her hair wrapped in towels and huge sunglasses and her nose in Agatha Christie for most of the time. Down in their cabin I've seen a whole load of wigs she's bought for the trip. It is our first morning, and we are all relaxing and enjoying.

*

I'm starting a journal, making notes of the changing coastline, doing little drawings with my pencils, and the sun is gentle. At night we dine in the yacht's dining room, with its oval mahogany table crystal glasses, silver, and the waiters bring us roast beef and Yorkshire pudding and chocolate mousse. The yacht has been stocked up with food from Fortnum's! At one point, I go to help myself to some more veggies,

'Wait!' says Rexy, and presses the button by his side. We wait. I'm protesting,

'I can do it!'

'No, no,' says Rexy, 'that's what I pay them for.' The steward comes, and I get my now cold veggies.

As we travel down the coast, arguments begin to happen. Elizabeth wants to stop in very large ports so that she can go to a hotel, 'phone her children and have her hair done'. Rexy and Mick and I want to stop off in all the interesting little fishing ports so we can wander around in the ancient streets and bars. The Captain also only wants to moor in the big ports because it's less hassle. Late one night it's just Rex and me in the salon. I roll him a joint. He gets stoned for the first time. He is sitting on the floor with bare feet. He's happily trying to remember which battery is which for the tape recorder because now he wants music. I do a drawing entitled *Rexy's Toes*.

'Darling,' he says, 'we must get more of that lovely marijuana. I'll tell the crew. Maybe at the next port?'

'Rexy, this is Yugoslavia – they'll get shot!'

We all set off to see some ancient caves. As we are entering deeper and deeper into the dark, dank atmosphere with all the other tourists, Elizabeth has fainted. A terrible fuss, she is carried out, and everyone is most concerned. Rexy says to me dryly,

'It's the ****ing slimming pills, darling, they're driving her crazy.'

One night at our Fortnum's dinner, I have a row with Rex. We are talking about theatre – he is of the old school. I'm telling him about Joan Littlewood and her workshop theatre in the East End. No stars, just a team of actors. He hates it.

'That's not theatre!' he storms. 'And what's more, we won't have any more of this. The subject is closed.' Everyone's gone quiet and embarrassed and I'm miserable. We arrive in Dubrovnik. Elizabeth has gone to have her hair done. I'm leaning over the side of our yacht and moored next to us is a beautiful, small family boat. The family are sitting cross-legged on the deck eating huge salads. The father is playing his guitar, the children are laughing. I feel like a spoilt little rich girl and also I feel homesick. I go to Mick.

'I don't like this. They're all so neurotic. Let's leave. I want to go home to the children.' Mickgough can't face Rexy directly so the next morning at the crack of dawn, we leave a note and we tip-toe out of the boat and along the harbour to a taxi and the airport and home to heavenly Fulham and my beautiful children and ordinary life. If that's what it's like being a star, I don't need it. I've learned a very important lesson.

**Self Portrait
By Anneke Wills
Hirst Publishing**

**ISBN:
978-0-9557149-0-0**

# Extract from 'Naked' by Anneke Wills

*The following segment describes events of the summer of 1983, and is set some years after Anneke last visited the ashram of spiritual leader Bhagwan Shree Rajneesh in India. By now, she has moved to an artists' colony on Hornby Island, near Vancouver, and things have changed in the Bhagwan camp...*

July 1983. We drive down to Oregon for the festival and meet Yogi who is here taking photographs and working on the audio equipment in Buddha Hall. He's a young man now with his own life. It's emotional for me to see him again, after Polly. The mother in me mourns my little white haired boy – got to let go – let go. The ranch is more developed. There is now a town with shops and bars and restaurants. Rashid and his team are turning this desert into an oasis. They have dammed the lake and in the centre is a raft which hundreds of Sannyasins are diving off, while drummers drum. The tent cities spread up into the canyons. Bhagwan is a tiny figure in the distance. Everyday there is a drive-by. He is driving a Rolls Royce along the Sannyasi filled roads, and rose petals are being scattered by an aeroplane – there is now an airport. Bhagwan now has a fleet of 100 Rolls Royces. These cars are notorious. It's pressed everyone's buttons.

'But he's a spiritual leader!'

'He doesn't own them! They've been given to him from some of his wealthy disciples. They're owned by the foundation – He doesn't own anything. He's way beyond all that!'

'But he does love to drive them very fast, around the ranch!'

'But... a hundred Rolls Royces!' This is the way I see it: we are talking about an enlightened Master, and this is his device. What more brilliant way of getting the world's attention than by moving to the most right-wing state of the richest country in the world, and then flaunting a hundred of the most potent symbols of wealth... and, he has the added audacity to have his artist disciples paint them, with clouds and swans and lotus flowers. Well, that's got everyone's attention. He's here to wake up the world, because, as he says, we have to have a revolution of consciousness if we are going to survive what's coming...

Bhagwan is being guarded by Sannyasins carrying machine guns. Machine Guns?! When I see Rashid and Veetasmi I ask them about it but they just accept this state of affairs. Can't they see what's happening here? I sense a kind of elitism going on – us and them – I am never comfortable with that.

All the people are lined up on the road for the 'drive by' and I am alone, wandering off to the lake on the opposite side.

'Anita!' bawls one of the Mas, over a loudspeaker. 'Get in line!'

'No thanks. I'm off to the lake.' All this adulation is too much for me. But on the last day, Veems and I are walking way out on one of the ranch roads, and mounting the hill, comes Bhagwan in his rose-covered Rolls. As he sees us he slows down and the window is lowered. Veems and I are rooted to the spot in Namaste.

'Can you take these roses away?' says Bhagwan. We rush to do his bidding. He smiles and then... brilliant! He does a double-take.

'Hello, Anita!' he beams at me, and away he drives. The glow stays with me all the way to California

*

382

A little mouse climbs into our VW while we are at the ranch, and now he has travelled with us all the way to Mill Valley, which is steep and wooded, and many of the houses are built on stilts. It's an affluent, alternative Californian society. Van Morrison lives here. The main town square is like Hampstead – full of boutiques, health spas, bookshops, and with a large square in the centre, with benches, and people roller-skating and playing guitars under the orange trees. While we look for somewhere to live we stay with my Uncle Hans and his wife Hennie in their trailer-park home. She had wondered if she should hide the kitchen knives in case we were like the Moonies. Hans tells us stories of the Nazi occupation of Holland – how they managed – eating cats. How my grandmother died of starvation.

'Ja dats true,' calls Hennie from the kitchen. But when Hans talks of the earthquakes here in California, how the roads are like waves, she's in total denial. 'No Hans, dat never happened, it didn't.' It amazes me what we human beings are able to endure.

I find us a lovely home to rent, up a quiet canyon. Four bedrooms, all on one level. A large deck, running the length of the house at the back. It has skylights and big sofas. I'm in disguise, dressed in a green trench coat, with high heels and painted nails, playing the part of a posh lady, bullshitting the owner about how financially secure my partner and I are, about how we need the extra space for visiting family.

'And do you have a favourite furniture polish you would like me to use?' That clinches it. I sign the papers, hand over our last few dollars, for first and last and deposit, always such a stretch, and whistle to the mates – there will be six of us sharing. Funny how, it's at these times, when I've got to find work and a car and pay the rent that my back gives out, and I'm flat on the floor, pillows under my knees, in pain and worrying. There are lots of Sannyasins living and working here, so there is dancing, music and meditations. Veems and I love to walk in the redwoods, on Stinson Beach and up Mount Tamalpais. We will save our money so that we can afford to live on the ranch. Veems's favourite day out is in these massive superstores. He's absorbed with all the power tools he's starting to collect. We have to find ourselves amenable fellow Sannyasins to marry, so that we can get our green cards. There is a side to Veems that drives everyone who knows him mad. It's like a cloud descends, and he becomes black, and 'in his head', and vicious with it. I fight with him then, to survive, because he wants to destroy. Many of my women friends will resort to a Zen stick, in the form of a hefty clout over the head to stop him. But I can't hit anyone, ever, for any reason. So I run away, or I stand and fight, or I jump out of the car as it's going along.

'Stop it! Leave me alone!' I can't live with him, but, I can't live without him.

The agony and ecstasy of relationship.


**Naked**
**By Anneke Wills**
**Hirst Publishing**

**ISBN:**
**978-0-9557149-1-7**


Both of Anneke Wills' books are available signed, direct from the publisher:

**www.hirstpublishing.com**